A view of London, ca. 1710–20.

The Theatre in the Haymarket is marked with ★.
(Detail from *A Prospect of the City of London, Westminster and St. James Park*, drawn and engraved by John Kip. London: London Topographical Society, 1903.)

A History of the Oratorio

A History of the Oratorio

VOLUME 2

THE ORATORIO IN THE BAROQUE ERA

Protestant Germany and England

---

by Howard E. Smither

THE UNIVERSITY OF NORTH CAROLINA PRESS   CHAPEL HILL

Illustration on title page: The Sheldonian Theatre, Oxford, where George Frideric Handel's Oratorio *Athalia* (1733) was first performed. (For a view of the interior, see Figure VI-7, p. 206).

Music Examples by Helen Jenner

Copyright © 1977 by
The University of North Carolina Press
All rights reserved
Manufactured in the United States of America
ISBN 0–8078–1294–3
Library of Congress Catalog Card Number 76–43980

Library of Congress Cataloging in Publication Data

Smither, Howard E.
    A history of the oratorio.

    Bibliography: v. 1, p.   ; v. 2, p.
    Includes indexes.
    CONTENTS: v. 1. The oratorio in the baroque era:
Italy, Vienna, Paris.—v. 2. The oratorio in the baroque
era: Protestant Germany and England.
    1. Oratorio—History and criticism. I. Title.
ML3201.S6   782.8'2'09   76–43980
ISBN 0–8078–1274–9 (v. 1)
ISBN 0–8078–1294–3 (v. 2)

To Ann

❦ Contents

❧ Illustrations

❧ Music Examples

Examples covered by copyright are printed with the permission of the publishers cited below and with modifications as indicated:

❧ Preface

This volume is the second of a planned three-volume *History of the Oratorio*, the purpose of which is to report on the present state of knowledge in this field. Volume 1, *The Oratorio in the Baroque Era: Italy, Vienna, Paris*, deals almost entirely with the oratorio in Italy and in centers where the genre was essentially an Italian importation. The first chapter of volume 1, however, introduces in general terms some basic concepts about the oratorio in the Baroque era that are relevant to both volumes 1 and 2. The present volume treats the oratorio in Protestant Germany and England, and volume 3 will discuss the history of the oratorio since the Baroque era.

Although it was not until the early eighteenth century that the oratorio with a German text became a generally recognized genre in Protestant Germany, in this volume I treat a number of the seventeenth-century antecedents of the German oratorio. These are the *historia*, the *actus musicus*, the oratorio Passion, the sacred dramatic dialogue, and Buxtehude's sacred dramatic works performed at the *Abendmusiken* in Lübeck. I include these genres to show their relationships to the oratorio as it was conceived in seventeenth-century Italy, as described in volume 1, and as it came to be conceived in eighteenth-century Germany. Treated quite briefly, because they are less closely related to the oratorio, are the narrative-dramatic poems of Klaj, sacred plays with incidental music, and sacred operas.

As in the first volume, in this one I have synthesized and summarized information in secondary sources and have verified these sources whenever possible by reference to the music or documents treated. Although I have consulted some primary sources in manuscript and printed form, I have found the existing specialized studies and modern editions of music to be far more numerous and more nearly adequate for the writing of this volume than for that of volume 1. For instance, the modern editions and studies of seventeenth-century sacred dialogues and *historiae* of Protestant Germany and the modern editions and studies of Handel's oratorios greatly facilitated my work. Yet many lacunae remain in our knowledge of the Baroque oratorio in the geographic areas treated in this volume. Some research projects that will help to fill these lacunae are now in progress; if this study stimulates others, it will have performed one of its most important functions. The bibliography is not exhaustive but is intended to be full enough to provide a point of departure for further study in a considerable variety of areas related to the oratorio.

The selective approach of volume 1 is continued in this volume for parts 1 and 2, on the Protestant German oratorio and its antecedents. That approach has not been followed, however, for part 3, on the English oratorios of Handel. His oratorios are so significant, both musically and historically, that I have considered it essential to deal with each one individually. It is inevitable that my treatment of Handel's oratorios rely heavily upon the splendid, monumental study of Winton Dean, *Handel's Dramatic Oratorios and Masques* (London, 1959). Yet I have endeavored to include the most significant results of the research of other Handel scholars, to make my own modest contribution, and to treat each oratorio in a succinct manner, which seems appropriate for a general history of the oratorio.

So many persons have helped me during the preparation of this volume—often in ways unknown to themselves—that I could not possibly list them all. Yet there are a few whom I should like to mention for their special contributions. For valued advice and encouragement I am grateful to my former teacher Donald Jay Grout and to my colleagues and friends in the Department of Music at the University of North Carolina at Chapel Hill—particularly to Calvin Bower, William S. Newman, James W. Pruett, Thomas Warburton, and Ann Woodward. Among those who have contributed by sharing the results of their unpublished research or reading portions of the manuscript and offering useful criticism are Adolphe Furth and the late Christa Furth of Vienna, Howard Serwer of the University of Maryland at College Park, and Kerala J. Snyder of Yale University. Henry L. Woodward kindly read all of this volume, as well as volume 1, and offered much useful advice. To Frank Glass, Mary Kolb, and Kay Tuttle, the graduate assistants who helped me during the final stages of the manuscript preparation, I owe a debt of gratitude for their patient work with bibliography and proofreading. To my graduate students of the past several years, particularly to those in my courses in the history of the oratorio and in the music of Handel, I wish to express my thanks for participating in lively discussions on many points in this book and for being responsible for my introducing a number of revisions. And to Helen Jenner, of Chapel Hill, I am indebted for the autography of the music examples. I am grateful to the staff members at the libraries included below in the list of library abbreviations for their help either in person or by correspondence. I especially wish to express my thanks to the staff of the Music Library of the University of North Carolina at Chapel Hill, and particularly to Kathryn Logan and James W. Pruett. I gratefully acknowledge the receipt of two grants, from the University Research Council of the University of North Carolina at Chapel Hill, that contributed to the preparation of this manuscript. A portion of the cost of publication was defrayed by a grant from The Andrew W. Mellon Foundation.

In this volume, as in the first one, spellings of personal names have been standardized. The names of composers usually conform to the usage in *MGG*; an exception is the name George Frideric Handel, which is an English spelling used by the composer. References to biblical passages in this volume correspond to the King James Version. Biblical passages in German that are used as texts of music examples are given literal translations—to facilitate an understanding of relationships between words and music—rather than standard English translations. In the music examples from German sources, the names of personages are translated into English without special comment.

Chapel Hill, N.C.   HOWARD E. SMITHER
September 1976

❧ *Abbreviations*

Libraries

D-brd/	West Germany: Bundesrepublik Deutschland/
F	Frankfurt am Main, Stadt- und Universitätsbibliothek
Hs	Hamburg, Staats- und Universitäts-bibliothek
Kl	Kassel, Murhard'sche Bibliothek der Stadt Kassel und Landesbibliothek
LÜh	Bibliothek der Hansestadt Lübeck (formerly Stadtbibliothek)
D-ddr/	East Germany: Deutsche Demokratische Republik/
Bds	Berlin, Deutsche Staatsbibliothek, Musikabteilung
GOl	Gotha, Methodisches Zentrum für wissen-schaftliche Bibliotheken, Forschungsbiblio-thek (formerly Landesbibliothek)
GB/Lbm	Great Britain/London, British Museum
I/	Italy/
Rli	Rome, Biblioteca dell'Accademia nazionale dei Lincei e Corsiniana
Rsc	Rome, Biblioteca musicale governativa del Conservatorio di Santa cecilia
PL/WRu	Poland/Wroclaw (Breslaw), Biblioteka Uniwersytecka
S/Uu	Sweden/Uppsala, Universitetsbiblioteket

US/	United States/	
	NYp	New York, New York Public Library
	PHf	Philadelphia, Free Library of Philadelphia
	Wc	Washington, D.C., Library of Congress

Other Abbreviations

(For bibliographical abbreviations, see the Bibliography.)

A*	alto, altus
B*	bass, basso, bassus
b. c.	basso continuo
C	cantus
Ecclus.	Ecclesiasticus (Jesus Sirach)
Eph.	Ephesians
Isa.	Isaiah
Matt.	Matthew
m(m)	measure(s)
MS(S)	manuscript(s)
Ms	mezzo soprano
Ps. (Pss.)	Psalm, (Psalms)
S*	soprano
T*	tenor
Tob.	Tobit, Tobias
trans.	translated, translation, translator

Note: With reference to the above designations of voices that are marked by asterisks, when two or more voices sing together, as in an ensemble, this is indicated by an absence of spacing or punctuation. (For example, SS indicates a duet for two sopranos, and SATB could indicate either a quartet or a four-part chorus, depending on context.)

PART I

Protestant Germany:
The Seventeenth-Century
Antecedents and Origins

CHAPTER I ## *The Lutheran* Historia *and Passion*

🔊 *The Lutheran* Historia *before Schütz* [1]

The Latin word *historia,* or the German *Historie*, when first used as a term in the Lutheran church, generally designated a biblical story. By the late sixteenth century the term was also applied to a musical genre that used a biblical story as its text, nearly always in German. The genre itself dates from the earliest decades of the Lutheran Reformation and represents a continuation and further development of Roman Catholic practices of singing the Passion. The text of a musical *historia* consists of a story either quoted from one of the Gospels or compiled from the four Gospels. The latter type of text, called a *Gospel harmony*, is the one most often found. Even when the title of a Passion *historia* states that the text is from one of the Gospels, the work often includes a Gospel harmony near the end in order to present the seven last words of Christ, since no single Gospel includes all seven. The only portions of a *historia* text that are not quoted from the Gospel story are the *exordium* and *conclusio*—that is, the introductory and concluding passages. The story of the Passion is the most common one for *historiae*; that of the Resurrection is next most common. Other

---

1. For surveys of the Lutheran *historia*, see W. Blankenburg, "Historia," in *MGG*, 6:cols. 466–80; Blume, *Kirchenmusik*, pp. 114–20, and Blume, *Kirchenmusik*-Eng., pp. 117–85; Matthäus, "Evangelienhistorie"; and Moser, *Evangelium*, pp. 54–59. For surveys restricted to the Passion, see Kade, *Passionskomposition*; Abraham, "Passion" (I) and "Passion" (II); Ameln, "Passionshistorie"; W. Blankenburg, "Protestantische Passion" in "Passion," *MGG*, 5:cols. 911–33; Braun, *Choralpassion*, pp. 11–26; and Smallman, *Passion*. Miller, "Oratorios," is a survey of the *historia*, Passion, oratorio, and related genres in Protestant Germany, with special attention to performance practice.

stories, such as that of the Nativity or of John the Baptist, are rare. A significant influence on the texts of Passion and Resurrection *historiae* was the "harmonized" version of these stories published by a theologian and colleague of Luther, Johann Bugenhagen, under the title *Die Historia des Lydens und der Auferstehung unsers Herrn Jhesu Christi aus den vier Evangelisten* ("The Story of the Suffering and Resurrection of Our Lord Jesus Christ from the Four Gospels," Wittenberg, 1526). This work was often reprinted and was widely read in Lutheran churches in the sixteenth and early seventeenth centuries.

The musical recitation of the Passion story had been an important feature of the Mass during Holy Week in the pre-Reformation church; the Passion *historia* continued this function in Lutheran church services. *Historiae* on the subject of the Resurrection, and probably those on other subjects except for the Passion, appear to have been performed during vespers.[2]

In their musical settings the *historiae* may be classified as responsorial, through-composed, or a mixture of these two types.[3] The responsorial, derived from the most common type of Passion setting in the Roman Catholic church, is by far the most significant; it was the earliest, remained in practice the longest, and exerted the strongest influence on both the oratorio Passion, which culminated in the Passions of J. S. Bach, and the German oratorio. Less closely related to the oratorio are the through-composed and mixed types, characteristic only of the sixteenth and early seventeenth centuries.

The earliest Lutheran responsorial *historia*, a St. Matthew Passion by Johann Walter (1496–1570), dates from about 1530.[4] As is characteristic of this type, the parts of the individual personages are set to plainsong recitation tones and are sung by three soloists (the Evangelist, T; Jesus, B; all other personages, T), and the parts of the *turbae*—such as the Disciples, the Jews, the High

---

2. Matthäus, "Evangelienhistorie," p. 100.
3. This classification is that of Blume, *Kirchenmusik*, p. 114, and Blume, *Kirchenmusik*-Eng., p. 178, which is similar to that for Italian Passions presented in Fischer, "Passionskomposition," pp. 200–205, and K. Fischer, "Die mehrstimmige und katholische Passion" in "Passion," *MGG*, 10:cols. 898–906. For a different classification, using some of the same terms but with different meanings, see Schmidt, "Passionshistorie."
4. Printed in Ameln, *Kirchenmusik*, vol. 1, pt. 3, pp. 13–32, and pt. 4, pp. 26–30; Kade, *Passionskomposition*, pp. 274–305; Walter, *Werke*, 4:3–22. For a discussion of this work and its sources, see Haas, "Walther," and the foreword by Werner Braun in Walter, *Werke*, 4:xv–xix.

Priests, and the Soldiers—are set for chorus (SATB). These choral sections are in *falsobordone*, an extremely simple note-against-note style with no polyphonic elaboration. This Passion by Walter was a model for numerous other sixteenth- and seventeenth-century works, including an anonymous St. Matthew Passion (attributed to Walter) in a manuscript of 1573 and the St. Matthew Passions by Jakob Meiland (1570), Samuel Besler (1612), and Melchior Vulpius (1613).[5] These works tend to retain Walter's procedures for the soloists but provide more elaborate choral numbers.

Of the responsorial *historiae* on subjects other than the Passion, the earliest is an anonymous setting of the Resurrection story from about 1550.[6] This work is much like Walter's Passion in that the individual personages are sung by soloists to recitation tones (the Evangelist, T; Jesus, B; Mary Magdalene, S; and the Angel and Cleophas, T) and the parts of two or more personages are sung by the chorus in *falsobordone*. Another example of a Resurrection *historia*, using similar material for the soloists but more elaborate choruses, is Nikolaus Rosthius's *Die trostreiche Historia von der fröhlichen Auferstehung unsers Herrn und Heilandes Jesu Christi* ("The Comforting Story of the Joyful Resurrection of Our Lord and Savior Jesus Christ," 1598).[7]

In through-composed *historiae* the entire text is set polyphonically. Such works vary stylistically from *falsobordone* to a contrapuntal motet style, with the individual personages either not distinguished musically from one another or distinguished only by various groupings of voices. Thus the through-composed *historia* is less realistically dramatic than is the responsorial type, and for this reason the former is less closely related to the oratorio. The through-composed type of setting was occasionally used for Roman Catholic Passions in sixteenth-century Italy,[8] but it was much more prominent in Lutheran Germany. Particularly important for its influence on the Lutheran through-composed *historia* is the Latin Passion printed by Georg Rhaw in 1538 under the name of Jakob Obrecht but attributed in earlier Italian manuscripts to

5. All four works printed in Ameln, *Kirchenmusik*, vol. 1, pt. 3, pp. 33–61, and pt. 4, pp. 31–43.
   6. Printed ibid., pt. 3, pp. 111–21, and pt. 4, pp. 95–99.
   7. Printed ibid., pt. 3, pp. 122–32, and pt. 4, pp. 100–109.
   8. Four such works printed in *MD*, vol. 1.

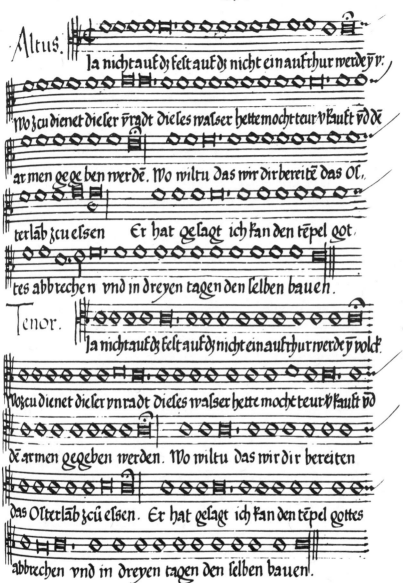

FIGURE I-I. The first four choral sections, in *falsobordone* style, of Johann Walther's St. Matthew Passion, from the choir-book manuscript at Gotha. The manuscript does not include the plainchant parts for the soloists.
(Reproduced by permission of D-ddr/GOl: Chart A 98, fols. 276^v–277^r.)

Antoine de Longueval (or Longaval).[9] This work, still widely performed in Lutheran Germany in 1568,[10] is based chiefly on the Passion according to St. Matthew; it also draws on the other Gospels in order to include the seven last words of Christ. Particularly noteworthy among the through-composed *historiae* of the sixteenth and early seventeenth centuries is Leonhard Lechner's *Historia der Passion und Leidens unsers einigen Erlösers und Seligmachers Jesu Christi* ("Story of the Passion and Suffering of Our One Redeemer and Savior Jesus Christ," 1594).[11] Other through-composed *historiae* are those by Joachim a Burck (1568),[12] Johann Steurlin (1576), Johann Machold (1593), Johannes Herold (1594),[13] and Christoph Demantius (1631).[14]

Historiae that mix the characteristics of the responsorial and through-composed types are those in which the part of the Evangelist is performed by a soloist to a recitation tone, in the manner of the responsorial *historia*, but the parts of individual personages are set polyphonically, as are those of the through-composed *historia*. The earliest-known Lutheran *historiae* of the mixed type are those by Antonio Scandello (1517–80), a musician at the Dresden court beginning in 1549 and one of Schütz's predecessors there as Kapellmeister (1568–80). A similar plan is adopted in both of Scandello's *historiae*, the St. John Passion (1561 or earlier) and the Easter *historia*, the latter entitled *Osterliche freude der siegreichen und triumphierenden Auferstehung unsers Herren und Heilandes Jesu Christi* ("Easter Joy of the Victorious and Triumphant Resurrection of Our Lord and Savior Jesus Christ," 1561? 1568? 1573?).[15] In both works the lines of Jesus are always set *a 4*, the other individual personages *a 2* or *a 3*, and the *turbae a 5*. The text of Scandello's Easter *historia*, "harmonized" from the four Gospels and including an *exordium* and a *conclusio*, was set

9. Two versions, *a 4* and *a 6*, printed in Obrecht, *Werken*, [vol. 9], fasc. 28; the *a 4* version also printed in Kade, *Passionskomposition*, pp. 246–73. For discussions of the work, see Reese, *Renaissance*, pp. 273–74; Moser, *Evangelium*, pp. 12–13; and Smallman, *Passion*, pp. 136–39.

10. Cf. the foreword to Joachim a Burck's *Die deutsche Passion* (Wittenberg, 1568), printed in *PubAPTM*, 22:51.

11. Printed in Ameln, *Kirchenmusik*, vol. 1, pt. 4, pp. 153–84.

12. Printed in *PubAPTM*, 22:49–80.

13. Printed in *MAM*, vol. 4. For a discussion of this work, see Moser, *Österreich*, pp. 66–70.

14. Printed in *Chw*, vol. 27.

15. The Passion printed in Kade, *Passionskomposition*, pp. 306–44; the Easter *historia* printed in Ameln, *Kirchenmusik*, vol. 1, pt. 3, pp. 133–40, and pt. 4, pp. 110–30.

again by Rosthius in 1598 (his responsorial *historia* mentioned above) and by Schütz in 1623. Other noteworthy *historiae* of the mixed type are two closely related works by Rogier Michael (ca. 1554–1619) on the conception and birth of Jesus: *Die Empfängnis unsers Herren Jesu Christi* and *Die Geburt unsers Herren Jesu Christi*, both of 1602.[16] Schütz would certainly have known Michael's works, for the latter was a musician at the Dresden court beginning in 1574 and was Schütz's immediate predecessor there as Kapellmeister (1587–1617). A work unusual for its subject matter is Elias Gerlach's *historia* of the mixed type on the life of John the Baptist, *Historia von dem christlichen Lauf und seligen Ende Johannes des Täufers* ("Story of the Christian Vocation and Blessed End of John the Baptist," 1612).[17]

The Historiae *of Schütz* [18]

Among the most important composers of the Baroque era, Heinrich Schütz (1585–1672) is significant in the history of the German oratorio for his introduction of the stylistic elements of Italian dramatic music into the German *historia*, which brought that genre to the threshold of oratorio. As a young man Schütz left his native Saxony to study in Venice from 1609 to 1612 with Giovanni Gabrieli. From 1617 until the end of his life, he was Kapellmeister for the Elector of Saxony at Dresden. He was absent from the Dresden court in 1628, when he traveled to Monteverdi's Venice to familiarize himself with the most recent developments in Italian music. He was also absent when he served as the director of music at the court in Copenhagen for several years during the disturbed times of the Thirty Years' War. Of Schütz's five works that he called *historiae*, two are settings of the Easter and Christmas stories and three are Passions. Schütz's *historiae* bear various relationships to the German oratorio, and two of them, those for Easter and Christmas, have often been loosely termed oratorios in musicological literature. Schütz's Seven Words of Christ, called

16. Both works printed in Ameln, *Kirchenmusik*, vol. 1, pt. 3, pp. 1–12, and pt. 4, pp. 3–25; and both are discussed in Osthoff, "Michael."

17. Printed in Ameln, *Kirchenmusik*, pt. 3, pp. 141–44, and pt. 4, pp. 131–50.

18. For discussions of Schütz's *historiae*, see Moser, *Schütz*, pp. 317–26, 424–27, 550–80 (also Moser, *Schütz*-Eng., pp. 365–76, 492–97, 649–84), and Matthäus, "Evangelienhistorie," pp. 112–49, 170–91.

FIGURE I-2. Heinrich Schütz (1585–1672), at 85 years of age. An
oil miniature by an anonymous painter, 1670.
(Reproduced by permission of the Bärenreiter Bild-Archiv,
Kassel.)

neither a *historia* nor an oratorio by the composer but occasionally termed an oratorio today, is also treated below.

The Easter Historia[19]

Schütz's *Historia der fröhlichen und siegreichen Aufferstehung unsers einigen Erlösers und Seligmachers Jesu Christi* ("Story of the Joyful and Victorious Resurrection of Our One Redeemer and Savior Jesus Christ," Dresden, 1623) is his earliest work in this genre. According to its title page, it was "to be used for spiritual, Christian edification in princely chapels and chambers at Eastertime." Its text is virtually identical to those of the Easter *historiae* by Scandello and Rosthius. Not only are the texts of these three works "harmonized" from the four Gospels in exactly the same way, but the *exordium* and *conclusio* (the latter of which Schütz calls the *Beschluss*) of all three—the only parts that are not Gospel quotations—are also the same. The three texts differ only in an occasional word choice or spelling. The main body of the *historia* includes three principal "scenes." The first takes place at or near the sepulchre of Jesus; it begins with the visit of the three women (the three Marys) to the sepulchre and closes with their encounter with Jesus. A brief episode follows in which the guards are bribed by the chief priests to spread the word that Jesus' body has been stolen. The second principal "scene" begins with Jesus' encounter with two of his disciples, Cleophas and a companion, on the road to Emmaus, and it closes with their recognition of him as he breaks bread with them. The final "scene" takes place in Jerusalem: the two men who had met Jesus on the road to Emmaus tell the apostles of their experience; Jesus then appears to the apostles and gives them his final instructions. The *exordium* and *Beschluss* are both characteristic of *historiae*. The former consists merely of an announcement of the subject of the *historia*: "The Resurrection of our Lord Jesus Christ as described to us by the four Evangelists." The *Beschluss* is a brief thanksgiving, emphasizing the victory over death: "Thanks be to God, who has given us the victory through Jesus Christ our Lord! Victory!"

The similarity between the Easter *historiae* by Scandello and Schütz does not end with the text. The Evangelist's plainsong recitation tone in Schütz's work is much like that in Scandello's

19. Printed in Schütz, *Neue Ausgabe*, vol. 3; Schütz, *Werke*, 1:1–46.

HISTORIA

Der frölichen vnd Siegreichen,

Aufferstehung vnsers einigen Erlösers vnd
Seligmachers Jesu Christi,

In die Music vbersetzt

Durch

Henrich Schützen/

Churf. S. Capellmeistern.

VOX EVANGELISTÆ.

Dresden/
Bey Gimel Bergen/ Jm Jahr/
1623.

FIGURE I-3. Title page of the Evangelist's partbook of Heinrich
Schütz's Easter *Historia* (Dresden, 1623).
(Courtesy of D-ddr/Bds.)

(and in others of the sixteenth century as well), and the roles of the individual personages in both *historiae* are given polyphonic settings, making both examples of the mixed type of *historia*. The differences between Scandello's and Schütz's works are far more striking than the similarities, however, for the latter's work represents a modernization and affective intensification in the manner of setting the text. In Schütz's *historia* the dialogue among the personages bears a close resemblance to his four-voice Easter dialogue (SSAT), *Dialogo per la Pascua*, beginning "Weib, was weinest du," which dates from around 1624.[20]

According to Schütz's foreword in the publication of his Easter *historia*, the performers are divided into two groups, one for the part of the Evangelist and the other for the personages. The former consists of the soloist for the Evangelist's part, a basso continuo, and four viole da gamba. Schütz intends the Evangelist to be accompanied by either the viole or the basso continuo but not by both. For the continuo realization he suggests an organ, lute, pandora, or another suitable continuo instrument. He prefers that the viole parts be used rather than the continuo, however, and recommends that one of the viole improvise ornamental passages. The viole are used only for the Evangelist's part; the basso continuo accompanies the remainder of the work, the earliest-known *historia* to require a basso continuo.[21] The performing group for the personages consists of Jesus (AT); the Youth, or Angel, in the grave (AA); the Two Men, or Angels, in the grave (TT); Mary Magdalene (SS); the Three Women, or Three Marys (SSS); Cleophas and his Companion (TT); and the High Priests (TTB). Except for one brief solo passage sung by Cleophas, the texts of all the individual personages are set as duets. Schütz states that the duets may be performed as solos, if one wishes, by either playing one of the voice parts on an instrument or by omitting one of them. (These passages are so effectively conceived as vocal duets, however, that it would seem too great a musical sacrifice, despite the more realistic dramatic effect, to perform them as solos.) According to his foreword, Schütz has used the word *chorus* to indicate that the passage may be performed by the full chorus; this

20. Printed in Schütz, *Werke*, 14:60–64; facsimile edition of the autograph: Schütz, *Dialogo*. For a comparison of this dialogue and portions of Schütz's Easter *historia*, see Moser, *Schütz*, pp. 428–30 and Moser, *Schütz*-Eng., pp. 497–500.
21. Moser, "Generalbasspassion," pp. 18–19.

indication occurs three times: in the *exordium* (SSATTB), the *Beschluss* (SATB-SATB, plus the solo voice of the Evangelist), and the chorus of the Apostles (SSATTB). Unusual for a *historia* is the visual element that Schütz recommends for the performance; he prefers a mysterious effect in which the Evangelist is visible to the audience while all other performers remain concealed.

The style of the Evangelist's part is that of a modernized plainsong recitation tone. The *initium* and *tenor* of the tone are often those of sixteenth-century Easter *historiae*, as are some of the cadential formulas. A departure from the tones of earlier *historiae*, however, is the use of more than one *tenor*. Although the mode is Dorian and the pitch of the *tenor* is most often *a* (as in the first and last plainsong sections of Example I–1), other pitches that have the tenor function are *f* and *c′* (as in the second and third

EXAMPLE I-1. *Historia der Auferstehung* (Schütz, *Neue Ausgabe*, 3:10–11).

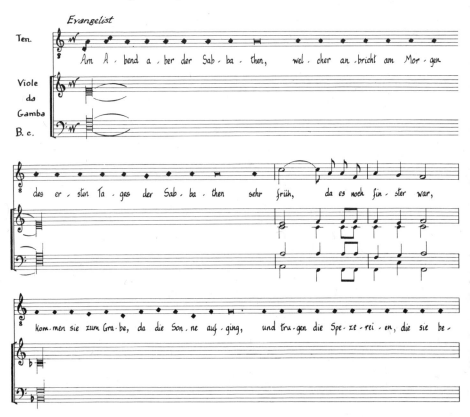

(EXAMPLE I-I, continued)

But in the night of the Sabbath, very early in the morning of the first day of the week, as it was still dark, they came to the tomb as the sun rose, and they brought the spices which they had prepared. And, behold, there was a great earthquake, for the angel of the Lord descended from heaven, and came and rolled back the stone from the door, and sat upon it, and his countenance was like lightening and his rainment white as snow.

plainsong sections of Example I–1) and, exceptionally, *b*-flat and *d'*. The most striking modernizations of the recitation tone are the addition of an accompaniment and the rather frequent inclusion of passages in mensural style. In Example I–1, for instance, the sections using the recitation tone have the rhythmically free plainsong notation and an accompaniment of sustained chords in the viole. In the more prominent cadences, however, as well as in the sections where word painting or text expression are used, the plainsong style and sustained chords are usually abandoned, as they are in Example I–1, in favor of mensural notation, sometimes with a slightly polyphonic accompaniment. Particularly striking for its word painting in this example is the passage beginning "den der Engel," which depicts the descent of the angel and the rolling away of the stone from the door of the grave. Occasionally word painting is introduced even in the plainsong—as near the end of this example, where the words "und setzte sich drauf" are decisively painted with a descending passage terminating in a long note.

In the settings of the texts of individual personages, Schütz makes frequent use of a variety of rhetorical figures, which abound in virtually all his works.[22] A case in point is Example I–2, Mary Magdalene's anxious speech to Simon Peter and the other disciples

EXAMPLE I-2. *Historia der Auferstehung* (Schütz, *Neue Ausgabe*, 3:17).

22. For studies of text treatment including rhetorical figures and musical symbolism in Schütz's works, see Eggebrecht, *Schütz*, and Huber, *Motivsymbolik*.

(EXAMPLE I-2, continued)

They have taken the Lord from the tomb, and we do not know where they have laid him.

when she believes someone has taken Jesus' body away. The first six measures express her anxiety by chromatic progressions (*patho-poeia* in musical-rhetorical terminology) and by sequential repetition at the upper second (*climax*). Measures 9–16 continue the musical-rhetorical *climax* by fashioning a climactic section from a fourfold statement of a motive two measures long, treated in imitation. The duets of the individual personages are particularly effective for their contrast with the sober style of the Evangelist's part, which rarely includes musical-rhetorical figures and never those of repetition.

The most effective and longest of the choruses is the *Beschluss*, for double chorus and tenor soloist, the latter being the singer of the Evangelist's part. Schütz did not reserve the word "victoria" for the end of the chorus, as both Scandello and Rosthius had done, but introduced it in the seventh measure in the solo tenor voice, which repeats it while the chorus sings an antiphonal setting of the text of thanksgiving. The chorus finally joins the soloist in a victorious closing section.

The Seven Words of Christ[23]

Perhaps the best known of Schütz's works treated here is *Die sieben Wortte unsers lieben Erlösers und Seeligmachers Jesu Christi so er am Stamm des Heiligen Creutzes gesprochen* ("The Seven Words of Our Dear Redeemer and Savior Jesus Christ Which He Spoke on the Holy Cross"), which dates from about 1645. Although it does not include the term *historia* in its title, it relates closely to the *historia* tradition. Its text, entirely biblical, is much like that of the final section in the type of Passion *historia* that includes the seven last words of Christ "harmonized" from the four Gospels. The essential difference between this text and that of the final section of such a Passion *historia* lies in the greater length of the Evangelist's part in Schütz's work. The texts of the opening and closing choruses, called the *introitus* and *conclusio*, provide a kind of unifying frame, for they consist of the first and last verses of the Passion chorale "Da Jesus an dem Kreuze stund."

The vocal and instrumental forces required include a chorus (SATTB) for the *introitus* and *conclusio* and five unspecified instruments (SATTB) to play the *symphonia*, which contributes to the framing of the work since it is introduced immediately after the *introitus* and is repeated just before the *conclusio*. The text of the Evangelist's part is distributed among three soloists (S, A, and T) and on a few occasions is given to a chorus (SATB). The purely solo parts are those of the individual personages in the story: Jesus (T), the Robber on his left (T), and the Robber on his right (B). Jesus' solos are accompanied by a "halo" of two unspecified treble instruments and continuo, but all other solos are accompanied only by the continuo, which is used throughout the work. (A special accompaniment for Jesus' voice is used later in the St. Matthew Passions of Johann Meder and J. S. Bach, as mentioned below.)

In its musical style Schütz's Seven Words of Christ is considerably farther away from the *historia* tradition and closer to the Italian oratorio than his Easter *historia*. The austere plainsong recitation tone, normal in *historiae*, has been abandoned in favor of the modern dramatic style of the time, that of recitative in the Italian manner, which is used for all solo passages. A contrast between the simpler recitative style of the Evangelist and the more elaborate style of Jesus is evident throughout. This contrast is

---

23. Printed in Schütz, *Neue Ausgabe*, vol. 2; Schütz, *Werke*, 1:145–58.

clearly established in the first solo passages, as may be seen in Example I–3. Although the Evangelist's recitative is usually somewhat more elaborate and less like plainsong recitation than it is in this example, it rarely includes text repetition and musical-rhetorical figures. In the recitatives of Jesus, on the other hand, the affective quality is heightened by the instrumental accompaniment and an arioso style in which text repetition and musical-rhetorical figures are prominent. The choruses are essentially in imitative

EXAMPLE I-3. *Die sieben Worte* (Schütz, *Neue Ausgabe*, 2:10).

EVANGELIST—And it was the third hour when they crucified Jesus, but he said. JESUS—Father, forgive them, for they know not what they do.

style with some chordal passages, and the *symphonia*, important for the establishment of the mood of the Passion theme, is brief and largely chordal.

The Christmas Historia

Of the few known Christmas *historiae* some either preceded or were contemporaneous with the one by Schütz. Among these are Rogier Michael's Christmas *historia* of 1602, mentioned above; an anonymous *Historia nativitatis Christi*, dating from about 1638–39; Thomas Selle's *Evangelium zum Heiligen Christtage* from the 1640s; and Tobias Zeutzschner's *Historie von der Geburt Christi*, which apparently dates from the mid-century or slightly later.[24] Michael's *historia* is entirely vocal, but the others require a continuo and other instruments. In the anonymous work the Evangelist's part resembles that of Schütz's Easter *historia* in that the plainsong recitation tone is abandoned at cadential passages in favor of mensural style. Exceptional for *historiae* in the first half of the century is the inclusion in the anonymous work of some nonbiblical words: a quodlibet is formed from the Christmas song "Joseph lieber Joseph mein" and the music of the shepherds in the fields. This section, introduced by a *symphonia*, bears the indication "Rocking by the chorus, *piano*," referring to a "rocking" motive in triple meter that foreshadows Schütz's use of a similar motive in his Christmas *historia*. In Selle's *Evangelium* and Zeutzschner's *Historie* recitative is used instead of plainsong. Selle sets some of the narrative passages for duet and one for double chorus. Of special interest in Selle's work are the six sinfonie, one of which is used as an introduction and the others as interpolations; one of them, a "sinfonia lacrimosa," follows and sorrowfully reflects on the text "because there was no room for them in the inn."

In 1664 Schütz published at Dresden the Evangelist's part, together with its accompanying basso continuo, of his *Historia der freuden- und gnadenreichen Geburth Gottes und Marien Sohnes, Jesu Christi, unsers einigen Mitlers, Erlösers und Seeligmachers* ("The Story of the Joyful and Gracious Birth of God and Mary's

24. For descriptions of the anonymous work and the one by Zeutzschner, see Moser, *Schütz*, pp. 619–24; Moser, *Schütz*-Eng., pp. 714–19; Matthäus, "Evangelienhistorie," pp. 192–97. Both authors report the manuscripts of these works as extant in the Breslau Stadtbibliothek (nos. CCLV–M1236 and CCXa, respectively), which collection is today in PL/WRu. For a printed edition of Selle's work, see *Kantate*, no. 155; for a discussion of the work, see Günther, *Selle*, pp. 93–96.

Son Jesus Christ, Our Sole Mediator, Redeemer, and Savior"). The print appeared in three books—one each for the voice (T), organ, and violone. Schütz explains in the foreword of the print that these three books are for one of the two groups required to perform the work. The other group consists of the singers and instrumentalists required in the ten concerted pieces: the choral introduction and *Beschluss* plus eight numbers—all called *intermedia*—for soloists, ensembles, and chorus, which are settings of the texts of individual personages and groups in the story. Regarding the concerted pieces, Schütz says in his foreword,

> The author has hesitated to publish these pieces, because he has observed that outside of well-appointed princely choirs these inventions of his would hardly achieve their proper effect. But he leaves it to the discretion of any who may wish to acquire a copy of them to apply either to the Cantor in Leipzig or else to Alexander Hering, organist of the Creutz-Kirche in Dressden, where they may be had, together with these three printed copies for the Evangelist's group, for a reasonable price. Moreover he leaves those who may wish to use his music for the Evangelist to adapt these ten concerted pieces (of which the texts are included in these printed copies) to their pleasure and the musical forces at their disposal, or even to have them composed by someone else. Finally his excuse is that it is only in order to save laborious and extensive copying that he has had a few copies printed of the music for the Evangelist's group, and if it had not been for this consideration he would have withheld them, too.[25]

The parts for the larger group were never published, although manuscripts of most of its music have been found in Upsala, Sweden, and in Berlin. The manuscripts make possible a nearly complete modern edition of the work.[26]

Schütz's Christmas *historia* begins with a traditional introduction, which is merely an announcement: "The birth of our Lord, Jesus Christ, as it was told to us by the holy evangelists." This is followed by the Christmas narrative in Luke 2:1–21, then by that in Matt. 2:1–23, and finally by Luke 2:40. The *Beschluss* is a mainly nonbiblical text of thanksgiving and praise. The per-

25. Translated in Schütz, *Christmas*, p. vi.
26. For descriptions of the sources of Schütz's Christmas *historia*, together with bibliographies of writings about them and information on performance practice, see the remarks by Arthur Mendel in his edition of the work (Schütz, *Christmas*, pp. iii–xvii) and Friedrich Schöneich in his edition (Schütz, *Neue Ausgabe*, 1:79–82). These editions supersede that in Schütz, *Werke*, 1:161–72.

sonages and performing forces of the work's ten concerted pieces are as follows:

Introduction	(Only the b. c. is extant, but the performing forces intended are those of the *Beschluss*.)
Intermedium	1. Angel (S; 2 violette; b. c.)
Intermedium	2. Chorus of Angels (SSATTB; 2 violins; an optional complement of viole doubling the voices; b. c.)
Intermedium	3. Shepherds (AAA; 2 recorders, bassoon; b. c.)
Intermedium	4. Wise Men (TTT; 2 violins [or two horns?];[27] b. c. with bassoon)
Intermedium	5. High Priests and Scribes (BBB; 2 trombones; b. c.)
Intermedium	6. Herod (B; 2 trumpets [*clarini*] or *cornettini*; b. c.)
Intermedium	7. Angel (S; 2 violette; b. c.)
Intermedium	8. Angel (S; 2 violette; b. c.)
Beschluss	(SATB; 2 violins, viola, 2 trombones [or 1 trombone?],[28] bassoon; b. c.)

The *intermedia* are, of course, linked together by the Evangelist's narration, since the text follows exactly the Gospel passages cited above. With its ten concerted pieces and large complement of voices and instruments, this is the most elaborate *historia* considered thus far.

The Evangelist's part is set in recitative throughout. The recitative style is at times reminiscent of a plainsong recitation tone, as it is in Example I–4a, the Evangelist's opening passage.

EXAMPLE I-4. *Historia der . . . Geburth Gottes* (Schütz, *Neue Ausgabe*, 1:4 and [iv]).

Example a:

27. For the possibility of two horns, see Hofmann, "Schütz" (I).
28. For the possibility of one trombone, see Hofmann, "Schütz" (II).

(EXAMPLE I-4, continued)

aus - ging, dass al-le Welt ge-schät-zet wür - de, und die-se Schät-zung war die er - ste und ge-

schah zu der Zeit, da Cy-re-ni-us Land-pfle-ger in Sy-ri-en war, und je-der-man ging, dass er sich schät-zen

lie - sse, ein jeg-lich-er in sei - ne Stadt.

Example b:

Es be - gab sich a - ber zu der-sel - bi - gen Zeit, dass ein Ge-bot von dem Kai-ser Au-gus-to *etc.*

Now it came to pass at the same time, that a decree went forth from Caesar Augustus, that all the world should be enrolled. And this enrollment was the first, and took place at the time that Cyrenius was governor of Syria. And everyone was going to be enrolled, each to his own town.

In that example the pitch functioning as the *tenor* in measures 1–3 is *a*; beginning with measure 4, however, the style becomes more flexible, with repeated notes conveying the impression that other pitches (especially *b*-flat and later *g*) have momentarily assumed the function of the *tenor*. That the relationship between plainsong recitation style and the recitative of this work was consciously conceived may be inferred from Schütz's remarks in his foreword on the alternatives for performing the Evangelist's part:

The intelligent director will choose for the Evangelist's part a good, bright tenor voice, to sing the words solely in the meter and tempo [*Mensur*] of intelligible speech (without any time-beating with the hand). And the composer is content to let intelligent musicians judge to what extent he has been successful or unsuccessful in the melodic and rhythmic setting, in the *Stylo Recitativo*, which is new and has hitherto, so far as he knows, not appeared in print in Germany. In this connection he wishes only to observe that if anyone prefers to employ the old speaking [i.e., chanting] style of plainsong (in which the Evangelist's accounts of the Passion and other sacred stories have hitherto been sung in our churches, without organ), he hopes the present setting will not fall far short of the mark if it be sung from the beginning to end in the manner begun in the following example: [see Example I–4b].[29]

Thus, aware of the novelty of recitative style in Germany and conscious that it might be unacceptable in some churches, Schütz suggests the alternative of a plainsong performance; he no doubt had that alternative in mind while composing it. Yet when performed as written, the part is sufficiently varied in its patterns of rhythm and pitch that one is scarcely conscious of the occasional plainsong influence. Rhetorical figures are not prominent in the Evangelist's part, although they appear occasionally. For instance, in Example I–5 a chromatic passage in triple meter is used to express Rachel's weeping for her children; this passage is particularly striking for its contrast with the preceding and following diatonic recitative.

EXAMPLE I-5. *Historia der . . . Geburth Gottes* (Schütz, *Neue Ausgabe*, 1:50–51).

29. Translated in Schütz, *Christmas*, pp. v–vi.

(EXAMPLE I-5, continued)

... then was fulfilled what was spoken through Jeremiah the prophet, who then said: cries were heard in the mountains, much lamentation, weeping, and crying. Rachel weeping for her children.

Somewhat like the numbers of an opera or oratorio of the time, the *intermedia* are pieces distinctly separated from what precedes and follows them. They function musically, but not textually, much as do the numbers in operas and oratorios, for they are all clearly metrical and thus provide a marked stylistic contrast with the freer recitative of the Evangelist's part. The solo *intermedia* of the Angel have in common the occasional use of a two-note basso ostinato in triple meter, as seen in Example I–6, the beginning of the first *intermedium*. This motive contributes to general structural unity, for it occurs in the first and in the last two *intermedia*, and it is of further interest as a musical description of cradle rocking: in Schütz's heading for each of the Angel's *intermedia*, he describes the number as a soprano solo "under which the Christ Child's cradle is occasionally introduced."

Do not be afraid! Behold, I bring you great joy.

Among the most attractive features of the Christmas *historia* are the variety and appropriateness of the vocal and instrumental combinations in the *intermedia*. As may be seen in the above outline of the work, Schütz treats the instruments as elements of dramatic characterization. In the first and last pair of *intermedia*, he combines the Angels with high strings (the soloist with two violette, or discant viole da gamba, and the chorus of Angels with two violins). In the four central *intermedia* (nos. 3–6), those of male personages in various social positions, he emphasizes winds; thus he combines King Herod (B) with the traditionally regal trumpets in their *clarino* register (the *cornettini* would seem to be barely adequate substitutes), and the trio of Shepherds (AAA) with the folklike sounds of recorders and bassoon. The High Priests and Scribes are portrayed as figures of utmost gravity and seriousness by the extremely unusual ensemble of a quartet of bass voices combined with two trombones. The Wise Men are represented by a trio of tenors, a bassoon, and, strangely, two violins (which were also used with the Angels); there is reason to believe, however, that the original instrumentation for the Wise Men might have been a more dramatically appropriate one, consisting of two horns in *clarino* register (as indicated in brackets in the above outline of the work) rather than two violins.

In this *historia* Schütz came closer to the Italian oratorio of his time than in any of his other works. The recitative in the narrative portions and the distinctly separated pieces for the personages contribute to the oratoriolike impression. Yet the text, which quotes the Gospel throughout, is clearly that of a *historia*, not an oratorio. Important as this work is among the antecedents of the German oratorio, to call it a Christmas oratorio, as is often done, is to misname it from the standpoint of Schütz's time.

The Three Passion Historiae[30]

Schütz applied the term *historia* to all three of his Passions: *Historia des Leidens und Sterbens unsers Herrn und Heilandes Jesu Christi nach dem Evangelisten St. Lukas* (also, . . . *St. Johannes* and . . . *St. Matthäus*). Dating from 1665–66, all are late and must be counted among his greatest works; yet they differ strikingly from his previous *historiae* because of their conservatism. Schütz uses neither the recitative style, which had been a significant feature of his Seven Words of Christ and his Christmas *historia*, nor the accompanied plainsong recitation tone of the Easter *historia* but rather unaccompanied plainsong—in fact, no instruments are called for in any of the Passions. These works include a variety of plainsong styles, ranging from that of a simple recitation tone to a more elaborate and dramatic style for the most affective moments, such as that of Jesus' "Ely lama sabacthani" in the St. Matthew Passion. All three Passions are responsorial: thus the plainsong is used for the Evangelist and for all the personages of the story

30. Printed in Schütz, *Neue Ausgabe*, vol. 2; Schütz, *Werke*, 1:49–144.

except the *turbae*, which are set polyphonically. Schütz's highly conservative Passions have only a distant relationship to the oratorio, a relationship similar to that of the sixteenth-century *historia* to the oratorio.

The Actus Musicus *and the Later* Historia

In the mid-seventeenth century some composers, particularly in the areas of Saxony and Thuringia, began to use the term *actus musicus* ("musical [dramatic] action") for works with some of the same characteristics as those called *historia*.[31] The new term was analogous to *actus oratorius* ("oratorical action"), a term already in use for festive spoken dramas with musical numbers given in schools, partially to provide exercise for the students in the skills of oratory. In the second half of the seventeenth century, the *actus musicus* and *historia* were similar in function and general structure. Both were to be performed during a Lutheran church service, both characteristically quoted narrative and dialogue passages drawn from a biblical story, and both could include nonbiblical interpolations—either stanzas of chorales or freely composed poetry or prose. The *actus musicus* differed from the *historia*, however, in its greater use of nonbiblical interpolations and greater emphasis on dramatic elements, such as musical characterization and quasi-theatrical performance practice, as in Andreas Fromm's work described below. Although the *historia* tended to remain close to the liturgy, as a musical and dramatic elaboration of a scriptural reading, the *actus musicus* was less liturgical and was at times quite close to the oratorio.

Aside from the Passion, to be discussed below, the most frequently used subject of *historiae* and *actus musici* in the second half of the seventeenth century was the Resurrection. Extant works on this subject are Thomas Selle's *Die Auferstehung nach den vier Evangelisten* (ca. 1660),[32] Friedrich Funcke's *Trostvolle Geschichte der sig- und freudenreichen Auferstehung Jesu Christi* ("The Comforting Story of the Victorious and Joyous Resurrection of Jesus Christ," 1665),[33] Andreas Schulze's *Historia resurrec-*

31. B. Baselt, "Actus musicus," in *MGG*, supp. 1:cols. 25–27; Baselt, "Actus" (short version), pp. 231–32.
32. Described in Moser, "Generalbasspassion," pp. 29–30.
33. M. Runke, "Funcke," in *MGG*, 4:col. 1146.

tionis Domini nostri Jesu Christi secundum quatuour Evangelistas
("Story of the Resurrection of Our Lord Jesus Christ, according to
the Four Evangelists," 1686),[34] and Abraham Petzold's *Actus
paschalis* (ca. 1690–1702). Only two Christmas works are known
to be extant. One is an anonymous *Historia von der Geburt
Christi* (performed at Grimma in 1686 but probably of earlier
origin), and the other is Johann Schelle's *Actus musicus auf Weih-
Nachten* (1683).[35] Two works on the subject of Pentecost are
Philipp Heinrich Erlebach's *Actus pentecostalis* (1690) and F. W.
Zachow's *Actus pentecostalis* (ca. 1690–1702). Based on other
subjects are Andreas Fromm's *Actus musicus de Divite et Lazaro*
(Stettin, 1649),[36] Georg Calmbach's *Actus musicus de filio perdito* (1675),[37] Johann Kuhnau's *Actus Stephanicus* (ca. 1690–
1702), and Abraham Petzold's *Actus [in Festo Michaelis]* (ca.
1690–1702). Lost are the ten *historiae* by Johann Philipp Krieger
—five each for Christmas and Easter—that were performed at
Weissenfels between 1684 and 1720.[38]

Fromm's Actus Musicus

The earliest work known to have been called an *actus musicus*,
Andreas Fromm's *Actus musicus de Divite et Lazaro* ("Musical
Action of the Rich Man and Lazarus"), deserves special attention
because it is unusual for its time and because it has been termed
"the first German oratorio."[39] Fromm (1621–83) became the
cantor at Stettin in 1649, the same year in which his *Actus* was
published there.[40] He was also a theologian, and beginning in the
1650s, he became more active in theology than in music: he
published several theological writings, held positions in various

34. This work and all the others named in the remainder of this paragraph are either
listed or described in Baselt, "Actus" (short version), pp. 232–33. A lost work by Nicolaus
Adam Strungk, performed at Dresden in 1686 and 1690, may have been a *historia*, but it is
called "ein Oratorium, die Auferstehung Jesu," in a Dresden MS chronicle of the time; this
is a remarkably early use of the term *Oratorium* for a Protestant German work. (Steude,
"Markuspassion," pp. 102–3.)

35. Printed in Schelle, *Himmel*.

36. Printed in *DMP*, vol. 5. For a description of a printed libretto (1664) of a work by
Thomas Strutius on the same subject and of another by him on the Christmas story, see
Rausching, *Danzig*, pp. 266–68. Strutius's works were not labeled *actus musicus*, but they
are much like those so labeled.

37. Described in Noack, "Erfurt," pp. 100–103.

38. Listed in *DDT*, 53–54: xxxv; W. Blankenburg, "Historia," in *MGG*, 6:col. 482.

39. Schwartz, "Oratorium."

40. For Fromm's biography see H. Engel, "Fromm," in *MGG*, 4: cols. 1007–8.

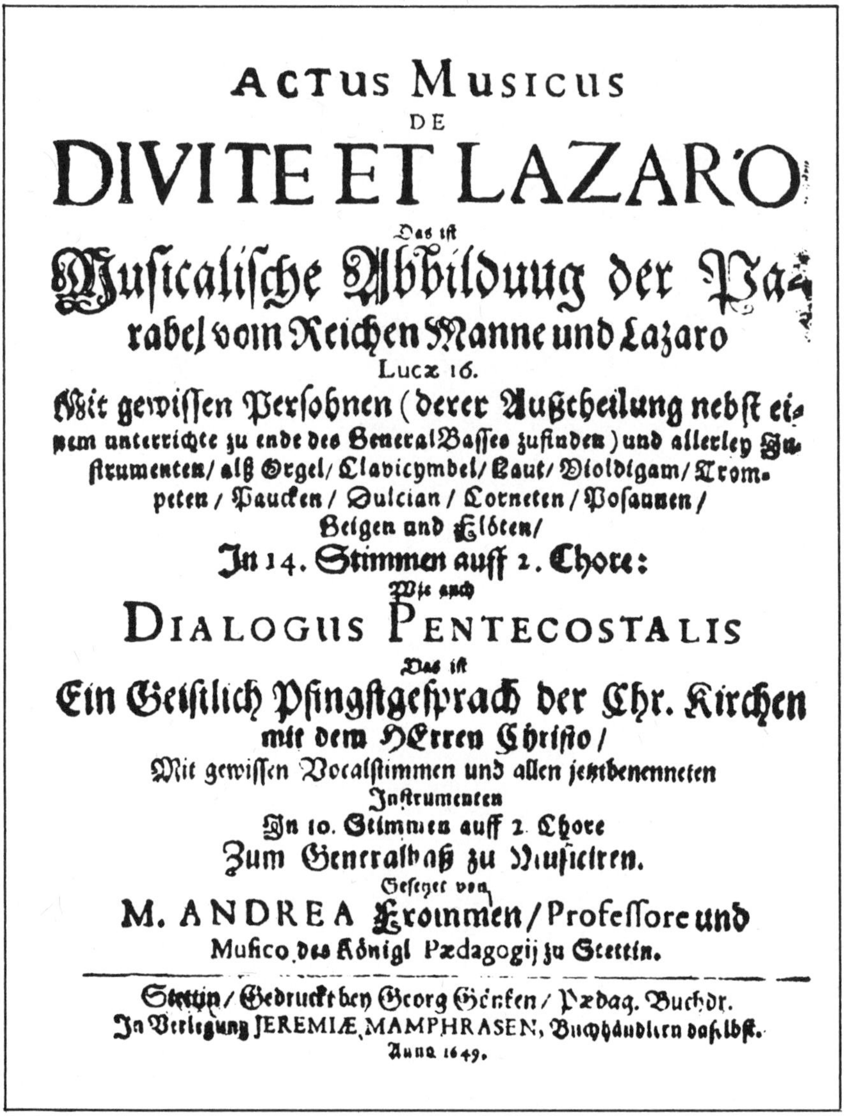

ACTUS MUSICUS
DE
DIVITE ET LAZARO:
Das ist
Musicalische Abbilduug der Parabel vom Reichen Manne und Lazaro
Luc. 16.
Mit gewissen Persohnen (derer Außtheilung nebst einem unterrichte zu ende des General Basses zufinden) und allerley Instrumenten/ alß Orgel/ Clavicymbel/ Laut/ Violdigam/ Trompeten/ Paucken/ Dulcian/ Corneten/ Posaunen/
Geigen und Flöten/
In 14. Stimmen auff 2. Chore:
Wie auch
DIALOGUS PENTECOSTALIS
Das ist
Ein Geistlich Pfingstgesprach der Chr. Kirchen
mit dem HErren Christo/
Mit gewissen Vocalstimmen und allen jetztbenenneten Instrumenten
In 10. Stimmen auff 2 Chore
Zum Generalbaß zu Musicirn.
Gesetzet von
M. ANDREA Frommen/ Professore und
Musico des Königl Pædagogij zu Stettin.

Stettin/ Gedruckt bey Georg Gencken/ Pædag. Buchdr.
In Verlegung JEREMIÆ MAMPHRASEN, Buchhandlern daselbst.
Anno 1649.

FIGURE I-4. Title page of Andreas Fromm's *Actus musicus de Divite et Lazaro* (Stettin, 1649).
(Courtesy of PL/WRu.)

cities as a pastor and a teacher, and eventually went to Prague, where he became a Roman Catholic convert and deacon. His *Actus* is one of his two known musical compositions. He seems to have been clearly aware of the novelty of the designation *actus musicus* and of the relationship of the term to *actus oratorius*. As if to support his use of the new term, he discusses in the foreword to the *Actus*[41] the close relationship between the oratorical art (*ars oratoria*) and that of the musician.

Fromm's *Actus* is divided structurally into fifteen numbers, as follows:

1. *Symphonia* (2 vlns., b. c.)
2. Evangelist: Prologue, "Es war ein reicher Mann" (Luke 16:19–21; T solo, b. c.)
3. Lazarus: "Herzlich tut mich verlangen" (chorale text and tune; A solo, viola da gamba obbligato, b. c.)
4. *Symphonia* (2 vlns., b. c.)
5. Lazarus: "Mit Fried und Freud ich fahr dahin" (chorale text and tune; A solo, viola da gamba obbligato, b. c.)
6. *Symphonia* (2 recorders [Flöten], b. c.)
7. Sacred chorus: "Ecce quomodo moritur" (by Jacob Handl [Gallus], scored for SATB, 2 vlns. [*Dulcian Geigen*], bass viol [*Bassgeige*], b. c.)
8. Angel: "Die Seelen der Gerechten" (S solo; b. c.)
9. Secular chorus: drinking song of the Rich Man and his Brothers, "Wohl her, lasset uns wohl leben" (ATTTB, b. c.)
10. *Symphonia* (2 cornetts, b. c.)
11. The Rich Man and God: dialogue, "O Tod, wie bitter bist du mir" (TB soli, b. c.)
12. The Rich Man and God: *symphonia* and dialogue, "Vater Abraham" (Luke 16:24–25; TB soli, 2 vlns., b. c.)
13. Full chorus: "Wie bin ich doch so herzlich froh" (text and melody from the chorale "Wie schön leuchtet der Morgenstern"; SATTB, 2 tpts., cornett, recorder, tbn., b. c.)
14. S solo: "Ach, es hat kein Auge gesehen" (b. c.)
    Lazarus: "Zwingt die Saiten in Kithara" (text and melody from "Wie schön leuchtet der Morgenstern"; T solo, viola da gamba obbligato, b. c.)
15. Full chorus: "Singet, springet, jubilieret" (SSATTB, 2 cornetts alternating with 2 tpts., 4 tbns. doubling lower voices, b. c.)

41. Printed in *DMP*, 5:5.

The text of this work is based on the parable of the rich man and Lazarus in Luke 16:19–31. As may be seen in the above structural outline, however, the only Gospel quotations that Fromm uses are Luke 16:19–21 (in number 2) and 24–25 (in number 12). After its brief opening *symphonia* the text commences with the prologue (which Fromm labels *Prologus vel Evangelista*), which is the following narration from the Gospel: "There was a rich man who used to clothe himself in purple and fine linen, and who lived every day magnificently and in pleasure. But there was a poor man, named Lazarus, who lay at his door, covered with sores and longing to be filled with crumbs that fell from the rich man's table; even the dogs would come and lick his sores." Rather than continue the narration, however, Fromm replaces the next Gospel verse with two chorales sung by Lazarus: number 3—"Herzlich tut mich verlangen," expressing Lazarus's longing for heaven— and number 5—"Mit Fried und Freud ich fahr dahin," symbolizing his death and entrance into heaven. Each chorale is followed by a brief *symphonia*. There follows the motet by Jacob Handl (Gallus), "Ecce quomodo moritur," which functions as a choral commentary on Lazarus's death: "Behold, how the just man dies, and no one takes it to heart . . . His abode is in peace, and his dwelling is in Zion." (This text from matins of Holy Saturday, in Handl's setting, was often interpolated in Lutheran Passions of the Baroque era.) An Angel then reflects on the bliss of Lazarus in heaven. Although the texts from the beginning through number 8 relate mostly to Lazarus, those from numbers 9 through 12 relate to the Rich Man. Number 9, a drinking song, reflects the Rich Man's life on earth; in number 11 he laments the bitterness of his death, and God condemns him to hell's fire; and in number 12, which uses the words of the Gospel, the Rich Man calls out from hell: "Father Abraham, have pity on me, and send Lazarus to dip the tip of his finger in water and cool my tongue, for I am tormented in this flame." Nevertheless, God (Abraham in the parable) rejects his plea: "Son, remember that thou in thy lifetime hast received good things, and Lazarus, however, evil things; but now he is comforted whereas thou art tormented." At this point, between numbers 12 and 13, there was probably a sermon or a moment of silent prayer.[42] The final three numbers are expressions

42. Schwartz, "Oratorium," p. 63; Schering, *Oratorium*, p. 154, n. 2.

of rejoicing for Lazarus's happiness in heaven, with numbers 13 and 14 based primarily on the chorale "Wie schön leuchtet der Morgenstern."

This libretto is a remarkably imaginative combination of Gospel quotations with borrowed and free elements; in its preponderance of text extraneous to the Gospel, it resembles the libretto of an Italian oratorio. The narrative Gospel quotation at the beginning is like that of a normal *historia* or *actus musicus*; but unlike the majority of the works bearing those designations, this one returns to Gospel quotation only once, at about the midpoint. Rather than a quoted Gospel story with interpolations, as are most *historiae* and *actus musici*, this text is essentially a free treatment of a Gospel theme. It is true, of course, that Fromm's work was created within the tradition of the Lutheran *historia* and *actus musicus*, and not within that of the oratorio, a genre that in the mid-century was just beginning to be recognized in Italy; nevertheless, because of the free and dramatic nature of its text, this work would seem to be to sacred music of Lutheran Germany in its time what the oratorio was to sacred music of Italy in the same period. Therefore the term *oratorio*, used analogically, would seem appropriate for it; in fact, Rudolf Schwartz appears to be justified in calling it "the first German oratorio," since no earlier work of this type with a German text is known.[43]

From the standpoint of the work's music, too, the term *oratorio* would seem to be appropriate, since the music includes arioso style, aria style, chorale tunes (which become important in the later, fully developed German oratorio), choruses, and instrumental *symphoniae*. Further, its total duration, more than thirty minutes, makes it comparable in length to a number of mid-century works of Italy that were called oratorios by their composers. Although Fromm is by no means among the better composers of his time, his music shows competence; he was clearly equal to the tasks of a cantor in the relatively small city of Stettin. Example I–7 well represents the solo style of numbers 2 (from which it is taken), 11, and 12. All three of these numbers are in arioso style

---

43. Schwartz, "Oratorium." Schwartz boldly titles this article "Das erste deutsche Oratorium"; Hans Engel, on the title page and in the foreword of his edition of the work (*DMP*, vol. 5), also calls it "das erste deutsche Oratorium," but in his article "Fromm," in *MGG*, 4:col. 1008, he revises his opinion and states that the work was erroneously called the first German oratorio, for it is "an oratorio dialogue," similar to many others. Engel's revised opinion, however, seems less accurate than his original one, based on Schwartz.

EXAMPLE I-7. *Actus musicus de Divite et Lazaro*—Fromm (DMP, 5:9–10).

There was a rich man who used to clothe himself in purple and fine linen and who lived every day magnificently and in pleasure. . . . [Lazarus] longed to be filled with the crumbs that fell from the rich man's table . . .

with generally consonant relationships between the basso continuo and the vocal line. Rhetorical figures of repetition that are found in this example ("ein reicher Mann," "lebet . . . Freuden," "herrlich," "von den Brosamen") are commonly used, and chromaticism is occasionally used to express pathos, as in measures 22–23. (The parallel octaves in measures 3 and 6 are not characteristic.) Several passages in the text of the *Actus* would lend themselves to special treatment—as may be seen in Example I–8, with its emphasis on

EXAMPLE I-8. *Actus musicus de Divite et Lazaro*—Fromm (*DMP*, 5:21).

O death, how bitter you are to me, . . .

the "O" of "O Tod"—but Fromm never ventures to write affective, unprepared dissonances at such places, as many of his contemporaries might have done. With the exception of a few brief chromatic passages, his settings are harmonically and melodically simple and conservative. Example I–9 illustrates the style of numbers 3 (from which it is taken), 5, and 14, for in all three of these numbers the vocal line sung by Lazarus is a clear statement of a chorale tune while the viola da gamba plays a more quickly

EXAMPLE I-9. *Actus musicus de Divite et Lazaro*—Fromm (*DMP*, 5:11).

(EXAMPLE I-9, continued)

Heartily do I long for a blessed end . . .

moving obbligato. The only solo section not yet mentioned is that of the Angel, number 8, which is in aria style; it is quite simple, much like a choral tune. The choruses emphasize chordal writing, and the *symphoniae*, all quite brief, tend to reflect the mood of the moment.

A dramatic element of Fromm's *Actus* that is particularly unusual is the quasi-theatrical placement of the performers, as specified in the foreword.[44] Fromm divides the choral forces into two groups, a secular chorus (*chorus profanus*) that is to be located in the lower part of the church near the congregation, and a sacred chorus (*chorus sacer*) located in a choir loft not far from the organ. The members of the secular chorus are the Rich Man and his Brothers, and those of the sacred chorus are God, Lazarus, the Angel, the Evangelist, and the chorus that sings the Handl motet (number 7). There are two exceptions to these instructions: the part of Lazarus before he goes to heaven is to be sung from the lower location, and the part of the Evangelist, the prologue, is to be sung from a location some distance from the organ so that the congregation may hear every word. Both the secular and sacred choruses join in singing numbers 13 and 15.

Other Actus Musici

Much like Fromm's *Actus*, and perhaps modeled on it, is Georg Calmbach's *Actus musicus de filio perdito* ("Musical Action of the Lost Son"), which was performed in Erfurt in 1675, 1677, 1680,

44. Printed in *DMP*, 5:6.

and later.[45] Its text, based on the parable of the prodigal son, consists of biblical words plus chorales and freely composed songs. Like Fromm's work this one includes a drinking song. Noack describes Calmbach's *Actus* as longer than Fromm's and more interesting for its variety of musical styles.[46] In at least one respect Calmbach's *Actus* is closely related to the liturgy, for at times the Evangelist's narration is set to a liturgical recitation tone.

More characteristic of the late seventeenth-century *historia* with interpolations is Johann Schelle's *Actus musicus auf Weih-Nachten* ("Musical Action for Christmas," 1683), a work about thirty minutes long. The text quotes the Christmas story as given in Luke 2:1–20 and inserts stanzas of the chorale "Von Himmel Hoch" at appropriate places,[47] as follows (chorale stanzas are in brackets): Luke 2:17 [19–11], 8–11 [1–4], 12 [5], 13–15 [6], 16–18 [7–8], 19 [13], 20 [14–15]. Such a text is like those of the *historiae* of the late sixteenth and early seventeenth centuries except for the chorale interpolations, but it is far more literally biblical than that of an oratorio. The Evangelist's part (T) is set throughout in recitative or arioso style, sometimes accompanied by the strings. The only other solo parts are those of an Angel (S), who sings once in aria style and once in recitative, and another soprano, who sings one chorale stanza. The chorus is used for singing the other chorale stanzas, which are set to elaborations of the chorale tune, and for the verses of the Gospel story spoken by the Angels, the Heavenly Host, and the Shepherds. The work is divided into three structural parts, each of which is introduced by an orchestral "sonata"; an additional instrumental number, a "sonata pastorella" based on the chorale tune "In dulci jubilo," is interpolated in the first part.

The Oratorio Passion

The most important *historia* subject in the second half of the seventeenth century continued to be the Passion, and the responsorial type of Passion *historia* continued to be cultivated, not only

45. Noack, "Erfurt," p. 101.
46. Ibid., p. 100.
47. The modern edition (Schelle, *Himmel*) uses *Von Himmel hoch* as the main title, evidently to emphasize the importance of the chorale in the work, and *Actus musicus auf Weih-Nachten* as the subtitle.

in this period but in the eighteenth century as well. In the mid-seventeenth century, however, a modification of the responsorial type, today termed the oratorio Passion,[48] began to appear; it is of special interest as an antecedent of the German oratorio. In fact, in the early eighteenth century the oratorio Passion began to be classified in Germany as a type of oratorio. Like the responsorial type the oratorio Passion uses as its basic text the Passion story, either quoted from a single Gospel or "harmonized" from the four Gospels; soloists sing the roles of the Evangelist and the individual personages, and choruses sing the parts of the *turbae*. The distinguishing features of the oratorio Passion are the interruption of the Passion story by reflective interpolations and the use of modern recitative and concertato styles, as opposed to the plainsong and a cappella styles common in the responsorial *historiae*. The interpolations in the earliest oratorio Passions have texts from books of the Bible other than the Gospels or from chorales; in the late seventeenth and early eighteenth centuries, however, the interpolations are increasingly made up of freely composed spiritual poetry comparable to that found in Italian oratorios. The musical settings of the interpolations vary from the simplest choral and song styles to elaborate imitative and antiphonal choruses and Italianate arias.

The earliest-known oratorio Passion is Thomas Selle's *Passio secundum Johanneum cum intermediis* (1643).[49] The first and second of the three *intermedia* in this work are interpolations consisting of texts from Isaiah and the Psalms, respectively, that were set for chorus, a vocal trio, and an ensemble of instruments. The third *intermedium* functions as the conclusion of the Passion and is an antiphonal setting of the chorale "O Lamm Gottes unschuldig" for the same complement of voices and instruments as was used in the other *intermedia*. An oratorio Passion composed about twenty years later is Johann Sebastiani's *Das Leyden und Sterben unsers Herrn und Heylandes Jesu Christi nach dem heiligen Matthaeo* (1663; printed in Königsberg, 1672).[50] This work includes twelve interpolations, all chorale tunes notated in the so-

---

48. For surveys of the oratorio Passion, see W. Blankenburg, "Protestantische Passion" in "Passion," *MGG*, 5:col. 918; Blume, *Kirchenmusik*, pp. 148–49; and Blume, *Kirchenmusik*-Eng., pp. 220–22. Dissertations in progress on this subject are Malinowski, "Oratorio Passion," and Haberlen, "Oratorio Passion."

49. Printed in *Chw*, vol. 26.

50. Printed in *DDT*, 17:1–103. For a description of the printed libretto of another oratorio Passion, by Thomas Strutius, from about the same time (1664), see Rauschning, *Danzig*, pp. 262–64.

FIGURE I-5. Thomas Selle (1599–1663), after an engraving by D.
Dircksen, Hamburg, 1653.

FIGURE 1-6. Title page of Johann Sebastiani's St. Matthew Passion
(Königsberg, 1672).
(Reprinted from *DDT*, 17:ix.)

prano clef (four marked "solo") and accompanied by four viole and basso continuo. A slightly later oratorio Passion is Johann Theile's *Passio Domini Nostri Jesu Christi secundum Evangelium Matthaeum* (Lübeck, 1673),[51] the four interpolations of which are strophic arias, each with a ritornello for four viole and basso continuo. Of particular interest for its blend of conservative and progressive elements is an anonymous *Matthäuspassion*, dating from between 1667 and 1683, that has been attributed to Friedrich Funcke.[52] Its conservative element is found in the use of plainsong (unaccompanied in an earlier version, accompanied in a later one) for the roles of the Evangelist and all the individual personages; progressive is the use of interpolations at twenty places within the work. Eleven of the interpolations are for solo voice and an instrumental ensemble, eight are instrumental sinfonie, and one is a complex made up of parts 1 and 2 of a motet, "Ecce quomodo moritur." The two parts of this motet are separated by a sinfonia, and the second part is followed by a vocal solo with instrumental accompaniment. An oratorio Passion from around the turn of the century, Johann Georg Kühnhausen's *Passio Christi secundum Matthaeum*,[53] includes eight interpolations (five choruses, two duets, and one solo), all but one of which use chorale tunes and/or texts. A work of considerable importance from around 1700 is Johann Meder's St. Matthew Passion,[54] which includes twenty reflective interpolations—arias, duets, chorales, and instrumental *symphoniae*. The *turbae* are represented by a five-part chorus (SATTB). The texts of the Evangelist and the minor characters are set in simple recitative, and that of Jesus, in arioso style with accompanying strings. Such a stylistic distinction for the role of Jesus, used previously in Schütz's Seven Words of Christ, is later used in J. S. Bach's St. Matthew Passion. Numerous other oratorio Passions of the late seventeenth and early eighteenth centuries are extant,[55] with the Passions of J. S. Bach forming the culmination of the development.

51. Printed in *DDT*, 17:105–99. Regarding numerous errors in this edition, see Maxton, "Denkmäler."

52. Printed in *Chw*, vols. 78–79. For the attribution, the dating, and a description of this work, see Bircke, "Matthäuspassion," and Smallman, *Passion*, pp. 143–47.

53. Printed in *Chw*, vol. 50. For a discussion of this work, see Adrio, "Kühnhausen."

54. For a description of this work, see Smallman, *Passion*, pp. 147–54; Smallman, "Forgotten."

55. For a list of oratorio Passions of the seventeenth and eighteenth centuries, see W. Blankenburg, "Protestantische Passion" in "Passion," *MGG*, 5:col. 920–23.

CHAPTER II

The Sacred Dramatic Dialogue and Other Genres

§❧ The sacred dramatic dialogues composed in Lutheran Germany are much more numerous than the *historiae* and differ from the latter primarily in their brevity, freer treatment of biblical passages, occasional use of a nonbiblical text throughout, and exclusion of plainchant style. The earliest dialogues with dramatic texts, which date from the sixteenth century, are found in Lutheran books for congregational singing and in collections of motets. After the advent of concertato style in the seventeenth century, the dialogues, usually found in collections of sacred concertos, tend to become more realistically dramatic and thus foreshadow the German oratorio.

The Early Dialogue

Dialogues in Lutheran Song Books

In some respects the development of the sacred dramatic dialogue in Germany parallels that in Italy. Like the sixteenth-century *lauda* books the Lutheran songbooks in the same period include pieces with narrative and dramatic elements in their texts. Unlike the *lauda* books, however, most of the Lutheran books with such texts include only monophonic music. Some dialogue texts in Lutheran books are versified versions of Gospel stories. Examples are the texts by Nicolaus Herman published in his *Die Sontags Evangelia und von den fürnembsten Festen über das gantze Jar in Gesenge gefasset* ("The Sunday Gospels and [the Gospels] of the Principal

Feasts During the Entire Year Expressed in Songs," Wittenberg, 1560).[1] Others are freely composed dialogues or contrafacta. Hans Sachs's poem "O Gott Vater, du hast Gewalt,"[2] for instance, is a dialogue between a sinner and Christ, which is a contrafactum of "Ach Jupiter hetst duss Gewalt"; the former appeared in Sachs's *Etliche geystliche, in der Schrift gegrünte, Lieder für die Layen zu singen* ("Some Spiritual Songs, Based on the Scripture, For the Laity to Sing," 1525), in Philip Ulhart's *Gesangbüchlein* (Augsburg, 1557), and in later songbooks. Part of this dialogue is set polyphonically in two versions, one by Thomas Stolzer and the other anonymous, in Georg Rhaw's *Newe deutsche geistliche Gesenge* ("New German Spiritual Songs," Wittenberg, 1544).[3] Polyphonic settings of similar texts appeared occasionally in the seventeenth century as well; for instance, Johann Staden's *Hauss-Musik*, part 2 (Nuremberg, 1628), includes a dialogue between the Flesh and the Spirit, with six strophes set in chordal texture.[4]

The Gospel Motet

In Lutheran Germany, as in Italy and other Roman Catholic areas, motets with narrative and dramatic elements in their texts grew increasingly prominent in the course of the sixteenth century. These are usually Gospel motets. Since they were intended for the Lutheran service, their language could be either Latin or German, although the latter had become the most common for Gospel settings by the last quarter of the century. A number of composers in Lutheran Germany in the late sixteenth and early seventeenth centuries composed complete cycles of motets based on the Gospel readings for all Sundays and feast days of the church year. The texts of these motets normally consist of one or more passages from the Gospel reading for the day, and occasionally they paraphrase the reading. The Gospel readings are narratives, many of which include dialogue, and the motets sometimes are settings of the dialogue passages only, a practice that grew increasingly prominent and led to the seventeenth-century proliferation of the dramatic concertato dialogue in Germany.

1. Texts printed in Wackernagel, *Kirchenlied*, 3:1162–86.
2. Text printed ibid., pp. 60–61; also partially printed in *DTB*, 13:lxi–lxiii.
3. Printed in *DDT*, 34:152–57.
4. Printed in *DTB*, 7/1:100–101.

Among late sixteenth- and early seventeenth-century Lutheran publications that consist of motets based on the Gospels of the church year are Leonhard Päminger's *Primus [Secundus, Tertius, Quartus] tomus ecclesiasticarum cantionum* ("First [Second, Third, Fourth] Volume of Ecclesiastical Songs," Nuremberg, 1573–80),[5] Johann Wanning's *Sententiae insigniores ex evangeliis dominicalibus excerptae* ("Notable Thoughts Excerpted from the Sunday Gospels," Dresden, 1584),[6] Andreas Raselius's *Teutscher Sprüche auss den sontäglichen Evangeliis durchs gantze Jar* ("German Passages from the Sunday Gospels throughout the Entire Year," Nuremburg, 1594) and his *Teutscher Sprüche auff die fürnemsten järlichen Fest- und Aposteltäge auss den gewöhnlichen Evangeliis gezogen* ("German Passages for the Principal Annual Feast and Apostle Days Drawn from the Usual Gospels," Nuremberg, 1595),[7] Christoph Demantius's *Corona harmonica, auserlesene Sprüche aus den Evangelien auf all Sontage und Feste durch das ganze Jahr* ("Harmonic Crown, Selected Passages from the Gospels for All the Sundays and Feasts throughout the Entire Year," Freiburg, 1610), Thomas Elsbeth's *Erster [Ander] Theil sontäglicher Evangelien fürnembsten Texte durchs gantze Jahr* ("First [Second] Part of the Principal Sunday Gospel Texts through the Entire Year," Liegnitz, 1616–21), Melchior Vulpius's *Evangelische Sprüche* ("Gospel Passages," pt. 1: Jena, 1612; pt. 2: Jena, 1614),[8] and Melchior Franck's *Gemmulae evangeliorum musicae* ("Little Gems of the Gospels," Coburg, 1623).[9] Although the last four of these publications appeared in the seventeenth century, none of them includes a basso continuo part; thus the roles of the personages in the dialogue texts are set polyphonically, as practiced in the sixteenth century. Polyphonic settings of dramatic dialogue texts continued to be composed occasionally throughout the seventeenth century, even after the solo setting of roles of individual personages had become common. Schütz, for example, set polyphonically several dramatic dialogues—among them his Easter dialogue (John 20:15–17), "Weib, was weinest du,"[10] and his dialogue based on

5. For a discussion, with music examples, of the music in this and the following motet books cited, see Moser, *Evangelium*, pp. 26–37.
6. Excerpts printed in *UONNM*, vol. 8.
7. Excerpts printed in *DTB*, vol. 29.
8. Printed in Vulpius, *Evangeliensprüche*.
9. Printed in Franck, *Evangeliensprüche*.
10. Cf. above, chapter 1, n. 20.

several verses in the Song of Songs, "Ich beschwöre euch, ihr Tochter zu Jerusalem."[11]

The Concertato Dialogue[12]

Dialogues in the new concertato style began to be composed in Lutheran Germany in the 1620s—more than a decade later than in Italy. In these works the role of each individual personage is usually set for solo voice accompanied by basso continuo and at times by other instruments as well. Such dialogues are designated in their sources by a variety of terms—including *dialogo, dialogus, Dialoge, geistliches Konzert, geistliches Gespräch*, and *Evangelium*. Among the numerous seventeenth-century composers of concertato dialogues are Heinrich Schütz, Johann Hermann Schein (1586–1630), Samuel Scheidt (1587–1654), Andreas Hammerschmidt (1611 or 1612–75), Kaspar Förster, Jr. (1616–73), Johann Erasmus Kindermann (1616–55), Johann Rosenmüller (ca. 1619–84), Johann Rudolf Ahle (1625–73), Wolfgang Carl Briegel (1626–1712), Augustin Pfleger (d. after 1686), Matthias Weckmann (1621–74) Christoph Bernhard (1627–92), and Dietrich Buxtehude (ca. 1637–1707). Dialogues by most of these composers are available in modern editions, cited below in the treatment of dialogue texts and music.

Social Contexts

The principal context in which dialogues in the concertato style were performed in seventeenth-century Germany was that of the Lutheran church service. Although motets in sixteenth-century style continued to have a place in Lutheran services, works in the new style became increasingly prominent in the course of the century. Most of the German dramatic dialogues in concertato style are found in books of spiritual concertos for church use. Some dialogues were intended for performance on specific Sundays

11. Printed in Schütz, *Werke*, 14:65–78. Another polyphonic dialogue, attributed to Schütz by Moser but considered of doubtful authenticity by Bittinger, is that on the story of Jesus and the Canaanite woman (Matt. 15:21–28), "Ach Herr, du Sohn Davids." (Printed in Moser, "Unbekannte," pp. 335–38; cf. Bittinger, *SWV*, p. 153.)

12. For surveys of the sacred German dialogue in the seventeenth century, see E. Noack, "Dialog," in *MGG*, 3:cols. 391–403; Hudemann, *Dialogkomposition*; Kliewer, "Dialogues."

and feast days. Examples are the dialogues found in books consisting of cycles of concertos based on the Gospel readings for the entire church year, such as Pfleger's *Evangelienjahrgang* and Briegel's *Evangelischen Gespräch* and *Evangelischer Blumengarten*.

A clear testimony to the growing interest in concertato style and in dialogues at one Lutheran church is a document drawn up by the mayor and city council of Wittenberg in 1644 that specifies the duties of their organist, Johann Lange.[13] As the organist in Wittenberg since 1628, Lange had clearly impressed the Wittenbergers with his skill in the composition and performance of church music in the concertato style, called "die *Concert Music*" in the document. According to this new agreement of 1644, the organist was to be responsible for all church music in concertato style, since the organ is required for such music, and the cantor was to remain in charge of music in the older motet style.[14] The organist was assured the full cooperation of the various instrumentalists and singers whom he would need. The organist and cantor were to alternate—one Sunday the former presenting *Concert Music*, the next Sunday the latter performing "alte volstimmige *Moteten Music*." Even in the motet weeks, however, the organist was encouraged to perform "perhaps a beautiful spiritual concerto [*concert*] such as one based on the *Gospel* or something else well suited (as this piece of the Rich Man and Poor Lazarus composed and set by the organist) and the like."[15] It is of interest for the history of sacred dramatic music that the only work singled out by the mayor and city council in this document as their example of a beautiful concerto is one based on a narrative-dramatic Gospel passage, Luke 16:19–31, normally set in the seventeenth century as a dramatic dialogue. (See below for a discussion of Schütz's setting of this text; and see chapter 1 for a discussion of Fromm's *Actus musicus* on the same story.) The tendencies in the church music of Wittenberg would seem to represent those elsewhere in Germany: by the 1640s concertato style, including the kinds of dialogues under consideration here, had achieved a favored position, and in some cities the organist had begun to rival or even

13. The document printed in Werner, "Dokument."
14. Ibid., p. 311.
15. Translated, ibid., p. 312.

surpass the cantor in significance as the concertato style grew in popularity.[16]

A new context for the performance of sacred music was the public concert presented in a church but not as part of a church service. Such concerts became increasingly prominent in the course of the seventeenth century. The earliest of these in northern Europe appear to have been concerts of organ music. In the Reformed church in the Netherlands—where adherence to the religious thought of Calvin and Zwingli had resulted in the banishment of the organ from church services—organ concerts, usually supported financially by sources other than the church, were given before or after the services or at other times suitable for attracting audiences.[17] In Leiden, for example, such organ concerts, supported by the city council, began as early as 1593. In Amsterdam Jan Pieterszoon Sweelinck (1562–1621) played the organ before and after the church services in the Old Church; it is not known, however, whether he gave concerts apart from these performances as did his son, Dirk, during his tenure as organist at the same church (1621–52).[18] Other areas appear to have followed the lead of the Netherlands in presenting such concerts. In Copenhagen, for instance, Johan Lorentz, who was the organist at the church of St. Nicholas from about 1634 until his death in 1689 and who was probably the teacher of Dietrich Buxtehude, was well known for his organ concerts given three times each week.[19] Although in none of these instances were either voices or instruments other than the organ normally used, that was not the case in the concerts at the Marienkirche in Lübeck, where in 1641 the organist Franz Tunder began to present afternoon concerts. These were originally organ concerts like those of the Reformed churches of the Netherlands and were probably modeled after them, but eventually they came to include a few other instruments and some solo voices as well. Tunder's concerts are the predecessors of the series known as the Lübeck

16. The importance of the position of organist surpassed that of cantor also in Halle (Serauky, *Halle*, 2:100), Zittau, and Sangerhausen (Krickeberg, *Kantorat*, pp. 135–39). The increased importance of the organist's position was not universal, however, for in Berlin, Leipzig, Lüneburg, and Hamburg his position remained secondary to that of the cantor. (Sachs, *Berlin*, pp. 114–17; Schering, *Leipzig*, p. 5; Walter, *Lüneburg*, p. 121; and Krüger, *Hamburg*, p. 126.)

17. Blume, *Kirchenmusik*, pp. 385–86; Blume, *Kirchenmusik*-Eng., pp. 570–73.

18. Scheuerleer, *Amsterdam*, p. 19; Münnich, Review, p. 388; and Söhngen, "Abendmusiken," p. 188.

19. Lundgren, "Lorentz," pp. 183–84.

Abendmusiken directed by his successor, Dietrich Buxtehude. The *Abendmusiken*, of special importance for the history of the German oratorio, are treated in chapter 3 in connection with Buxtehude's larger sacred dramatic works.

Another type of concert series that afforded a context for the performance of sacred dramatic music was Hamburg's Collegium musicum[20]—which flourished from 1660 until the death of its leading figure, Matthias Weckmann, in 1674. The earliest-known reference to this Collegium musicum is in a Hamburg chronicle of 1668 written by Conrad von Hövelen, who states that "on the high feast days one hears an almost angelic music in the churches, and it is highly laudable that in the cathedral on Thursdays a *Collegium Musicale* is held which is public, for both foreign and native music lovers."[21] Johann Mattheson's description of the Collegium musicum in his *Ehren-Pforte* is somewhat more informative: "Two distinguished music lovers established with him [Weckmann] a large *Collegium musicum* in the refectory of the cathedral. They brought together 50 persons who all contributed to it. The best things from Venice, Rome, Vienna, Munich, Dresden, etc. were programmed; indeed, this *Collegium* received such honor that the greatest composers sought to associate their names with it."[22] Thus the Collegium was founded by Weckmann and two other persons, and it was held in the refectory of what had earlier been a monastery at the cathedral.[23] The association of fifty persons evidently made financial contributions to defray the costs for these concerts, which were open and free to the public. From the cities named in Mattheson's description, it is clear that Italian styles were favored in the Collegium's performances; not only are two of Italy's leading musical centers mentioned, but the courts of Vienna, Munich, and Dresden were all strongly oriented toward Italian music. The Italianate tendency of the Collegium reflects Weckmann's training and interest, for he had studied at Dresden with Heinrich Schütz, a champion of Italian music. In fact, the purpose of the Collegium seems to have been to perform music that one could not normally hear in public at Hamburg: most public performances were those within church services, for which

20. For information about the Hamburg Collegium musicum, see Seiffert, "Weckmann," pp. 110–23; Krüger, *Hamburg*, pp. 97–104.
21. Translated from Seiffert, "Weckmann," pp. 110–11.
22. Translated from Mattheson, *Ehren-Pforte*, pp. 397–98.
23. Seiffert, "Weckmann," p. 112.

much Italian sacred music would be inappropriate. An important composer who took an active interest in the Collegium was Christoph Bernhard, a friend of Weckmann; like the latter, Bernhard had studied and had worked under Schütz. Bernhard held the post of cantor for the city of Hamburg from 1663 until 1674. Having traveled in Italy, where he met Carissimi,[24] Bernhard, like Weckmann, was much interested in Italian music. Although there are no lists of works performed in the Collegium, it may be fairly assumed that the most recent developments in Italy were represented and that oratorios, or parts of oratorios, might well have been included. Italianate music by German composers was no doubt included as well. The dramatic dialogues by Schütz and his students Weckmann and Bernhard, plus similar works by Rosenmüller and Förster, were probably heard there.[25] Both of the last-named composers, who lived for a time in Italy, were known for their Italianate music. Förster, a student of Carissimi and a composer of Latin oratorios (see p. 59), was in Hamburg during part of the period in which the Collegium flourished. In 1667 one of his Latin works is known to have been performed at Bernhard's house while Förster was visiting the city;[26] the same work, or others by him, might well have been performed in the Collegium.

The above are the principal contexts in which sacred dramatic dialogues in concertato style were performed publicly in seventeenth-century Germany. Little is known about private performances, such as that just mentioned in Bernhard's house and those that would no doubt have been given in other private homes and in the courts of the nobility.

Dialogue Texts

The general classification of texts used in volume 1, chapter 3, of this study for the dialogue in Italy may be applied to that in Germany as well. Thus the dialogue texts may be classified by language, by the presence or absence of a preexisting source, and by style. The language is nearly always German but is occasionally

24. Mattheson, *Ehren-Pforte*, p. 18.
25. For references to composers whose works were or might have been performed in the Collegium musicum concerts, see Seiffert, "Weckmann," pp. 115–23; Ilgner, *Weckmann*, pp. 50–51. Although Rosenmüller is assumed to have spent some time in Hamburg (Seiffert, "Weckmann," p. 115), his presence there has not been documented. (M. Geck, "Rosenmüller," *MGG*, 11:col. 913.)
26. Mattheson, *Ehren-Pforte*, p. 21.

Latin. The texts are normally biblical, freely invented, or a combination of the two. Usually the combination will be that of an essentially biblical text with free insertions and/or a free conclusion. Exceptionally the source for part of a dialogue is a chorale text, quoted or paraphrased. The styles include a variety of combinations of prose, poetry, narration, dramatic dialogue, and reflection.

A large majority of the German dialogues are biblical, but they treat the biblical texts with varying degrees of strictness and freedom. Among those adhering most strictly to their biblical sources are the majority of the twenty-two compositions in Andreas Hammerschmidt's *Dialogi oder Gespräch zwischen Gott und einer gläubigen Seelen auss den biblischen Texten zusammen gezogen ... erster Theil* ("Dialogues or Conversations between God and a Believing Soul, Drawn Together from the Biblical Texts ... First Part," Dresden, 1645).[27] Although about three-fourths of the works in that book are dialogues with clearly implied personages—usually God and a faithful soul, as indicated on the title page—most are reflective dialogues and thus involve little or no dramatic or plot development. One of that book's more clearly dramatic dialogues, "Maria gegrüsset seist du,"[28] based on the Annunciation story (Luke 1:28–38), is similar in its text to other Annunciation dialogues of the period—including those by Schein (1626),[29] Schütz (1639),[30] and Weckmann.[31] All four of these dialogues delete the narrative introduction and connecting passages of the biblical source—thus only the words of the Angel Gabriel and the Virgin Mary are used—and all include an "alleluja" finale sung either by a chorus or by the soloists who sing the two roles. Other compositions using biblical words are Scheidt's dialogue on the story of the Last Judgment (Matt. 25:34–46), "Kommt her, ihr Gesegneten" (1634),[32] and two dialogues on the parable of the Pharisee and the publican (Luke 18:9–14)—Schütz's "Es gingen zweene Menschen hinauf" (ca. 1630),[33] and J. R.

27. Printed in *DTÖ*, vol. 16; for the sources of the texts of all the works in that volume, see ibid., pp. 163–64.
28. Printed ibid., pp. 123–30.
29. Printed in Schein, *Werke*, 6:80–90.
30. Printed in Schütz, *Werke*, 6:184–90.
31. Printed in *DDT*, 6:22–28.
32. Printed in Scheidt, *Werke*, 9:20–24.
33. Printed in Schütz, *Werke*, 14:55–59.

FIGURE II-I. Andreas Hammerschmidt (1611 or 1612–75), after an
engraving by Samuel Weishun, 1646.
(Reproduced by permission of Bärenreiter Bild-Archiv, Kassel.)

FIGURE II-2. Title page of the basso continuo book for Andreas Hammerschmidt's *Dialogi oder Gespräch zwischen Gott und einer gläubigen Seelen . . . erster Theil* (Dresden, 1645). (Reprinted from *DTÖ*, 16:1.)

Ahle's "Ich danke dir, Gott" (1648).[34] Of these three works those by Scheidt and Ahle both omit the narrative passages of the biblical story, but that by Schütz retains the narrative. Neither Ahle nor Schütz follows the biblical order of the material; instead, the words are rearranged, repeated, and overlapped polyphonically to create convincing musical dialogues. A different type of modification of a biblical text may be seen in Schütz's dialogue on the finding of Jesus in the temple (Luke 2:48–49), "Mein Sohn, warum hast du uns das gethan" (1650),[35] and Rosenmüller's dialogue on the parable of the prodigal son (Luke 15:11–32), "Vater, ich habe gesündiget."[36] In both works not only is the narrative deleted, but a few new words are added to increase dramatic interest. Schütz adds a part for Joseph, who does not speak in the biblical account, and Rosenmüller adds a simple, repeated question ("Was ist das?") to the part of the Elder Son as a substitute for a deleted narrative passage (Luke 15:25–26).

Some dialogues with essentially biblical texts include nonbiblical interpolations, more often in poetry than in prose. An example is Hammerschmidt's Easter dialogue, "Wer wälzet uns den Stein," from his *Vierter Theil musikalischer Andachten* ("Fourth Part of the Musical Devotions," Freiburg, 1646).[37] The text is essentially a compilation of verses from Mark, Luke, and John, but it includes the interpolation of a choral setting of the chorale text "Surrexit Christus hodie," which is repeated as the finale. Longer and more numerous interpolations are used in two works by Bernhard: an Easter dialogue (John 20:13–17), "Sie haben meinen Herrn hinweggenommen," and a dialogue on the parable of the seeds (Luke 8:10–17), "Euch ist's gegeben zu wissen" (1665).[38] The Easter composition includes a long, interpolated nonbiblical dialogue in prose sung by Mary Magdalene and Jesus; the dialogue on the parable of the seeds is a narrative reflective work in which Jesus' narration of the parable is interrupted three times, and then concluded, by strophes of a reflective poem. Two essentially reflective dialogues with texts made up of Bible verses

34. Printed in *DDT*, 5:9–12.
35. Printed in Schütz, *Werke*, 10:42–53.
36. Modern edition in Viles, "Rosenmüller," 2:45–64.
37. Printed in *GK*, no. 80; another Hammerschmidt dialogue (1655) with the same text incipit but a substantially different text and totally different music is printed in *GK*, no. 74.
38. Printed in *EDM*, 65:115–29 and 172–85, respectively.

FIGURE II-3. Title page of the first part book (principally the *Cantus primi chori*) of Andreas Hammerschmidt's *Vierter Theil musikalischer Andachten* (Freiburg, 1646). (Courtesy of D-brd/Kl.)

alternating with spiritual poetry are Kindermann's *Des Erlösers Christi und sündigen Menschens heylsames Gespräch* ("Salutary Conversation of the Redeemer Christ and Sinful Man," 1643)[39] and Buxtehude's "Wo soll ich fliehen hin."[40] In both dialogues Christ's part is made up of quotations from various books of the Old Testament and the Sinner's part is composed of spiritual poetry; Buxtehude draws some of the poetry from chorale texts. The dialogues in Pfleger's *Evangelienjahrgang* (ca. 1665–73)[41] are characteristically composed of fragments from various books of the Bible that are skillfully woven together to create smooth and unified prose texts; in addition, these dialogues sometimes include longer poetic interpolations. Pfleger largely based his dialogue about Jesus' calming the storm, "Und er trat in das Schiff,"[42] on Matt. 8:23–27 but included psalm verses woven into the Gospel story; his dialogue "Heut freu' dich, Christenheit"[43] on the scene of the Last Judgment begins with two poetic strophes, then combines fragments from numerous places in the New Testament, continues with four more strophes of poetry, and closes with a verse from Revelation and a brief "amen" chorus. Textual constructions approximating those in Pfleger's works are also found in the dialogues of Briegel's *Evangelischer Gespräch* ("Gospel Conversation," pts. 1–2: Mühlhausen, 1660–62; pt. 3: Darmstadt, 1681) and *Evangelischer Blumengarten* ("Gospel Flower Garden," pts. 1–4; Gotha, 1666–68).[44]

Of the relatively small number of dialogues that do not quote the Bible, the majority are free poetic paraphrases of the Song of Solomon and thus are essentially reflective. Among these are Kindermann's brief "Mein Hertze" (1642),[45] the text of which is by Martin Opitz, and Buxtehude's *Dialogus inter Christum et fidelem animam* ("Dialogue between Christ and a Faithful Soul"), beginning "Wo ist doch mein Freund geblieben."[46] Although texts that reflect the pietist movement in the Lutheran church are rare in dialogues, this last-named poem, a rather long and ardent one,

39. Printed in *DTB*, 13:155–73.
40. Printed in *DDT*, 14:85–106.
41. For a discussion of the *Evangelienjahrgang*, see Nausch, *Pfleger*, pp. 56–93.
42. Printed in *EDM*, 64:41–56.
43. Printed ibid., 50:16–33.
44. For a discussion of the music in these books, see Noack, *Briegel*, pp. 32–43.
45. Printed in *DTB*, 13:184–91.
46. Printed in Buxtehude, *Werke*, 3:93–100. The text is printed in Geck, *Buxtehude*, pp. 214–15.

Deß Erlösers Christi/ vnd

sündigen Menschens heylsames Gespräch:
Auß der H. Schrifft zusammen gezogen

von

Johann Michael Dilherrn/ꝛc.

Vnd vff besondere Musicalische Wei-

se/ mit 7. Stimmen/ sampt dem General Bass, componirt/
vnd zum Gottesdienst zu S. Egidien / wie auch zu vnser Lieben
Frawen Kirchen/ am Tag deß Apostels MATTHÆI,
musicirt vnd gebraucht worden.

von

Johann-Erasino Kindermann/ Norimberg:
zu S. Egidien Organisten.

Nürmberg/

In Verlegung Wolffgang Endters/ Buchhändlers:

ANNO CHRISTI M DC XLIII.

Deß Erlösers Christi vnd sündigen Menschen heylsames Gespräch.

TEXTUS.

CHRISTVS.

Matth.
11.28.

Ompt her zu mir alle / die jhr müheseelig vnd beladen seyt : Ich will euch erquicken.

Sünder.

Ach / liebster HErr der Sünde mein /
so viel vnd mannichfaltig seyn :
daß mein Gewissen saget mir /
es sey zu der Genaden Thür.

CHRISTVS.

Joh.6.37
El.1.18.

Wer zu mir kömpt / den will ich nicht hinauß stossen. Wenn ewer Sünde gleich Blutroth ist / soll sie doch schneeweiß werden : Vnd wenn sie gleich ist wie Rosinfarb / soll sie doch wie Wolle werden.

Sünder.

O HErr / Ich komme auff dein Wort /
Vnd gehe ein zur Gnaden Pfort :
Nimb meine Sünde hin zu Dir /
Vnd giebe dein Bezahlung mir /
Daß ich sie deinem Vatter bring /
Vnd mich auß allem Jammer schwing.

CHRISTVS.

El.53.5.

Ich bin vmb ewer Missethat willen verwundet / vnd vmb ewer Sünde willen zerschlagen. Die Straffe liegt auff mir / auff daß jhr Friede hättet / vnd durch meine Wunden seyt jhr geheilet.

Sün-

FIGURE II-4. Title page and beginning of the text of Erasmus Kindermann's dialogue *Des Erlösers Christi und sündigen Menschens heylsames Gespräch* (Nuremberg, 1643). (Reprinted from *DTB*, 13:151, 153.)

FIGURE II-5. Johann Erasmus Kindermann (1616–55), engraving by Johann
Friedrich Fleischberger after a portrait by Daniel Preisler.
(Reproduced by permission of Bärenreiter Bild-Archiv, Kassel.)

clearly exemplifies the mystical-erotic" element of pietistic poetry.[47] Other nonbiblical dialogues are Kindermann's *Dialogus: Mosis Plag, Sünders Klag, Christi Abtrag* ("Dialogue: Moses' Misery, a Sinner's Lament, Christ's Suffering," 1642),[48] entirely in prose, and Hammerschmidt's "Was mein Gott will" (1645),[49] which combines two chorale texts, one in the tenor and the other in the soprano, to create a dialogue between two personages.

Works with Latin texts comprise a small percentage of the dialogues composed in Lutheran Germany of the seventeenth century. For this reason they are generally of little significance for the history of the oratorio in this area. Of special interest as examples of the Carissimi style imported into Lutheran Germany, however, are six Latin dialogues by Kaspar Förster, Jr., that date, at the latest, from the 1660s.[50] Förster studied in Warsaw with Marco Scacchi (a student of the Roman composer of dialogues and oratorios G. F. Anerio) and then for three years at the German College in Rome with Carissimi (1633–36).[51] In both their texts and their music Förster's dialogues reflect not only Italian influence in general but that of Carissimi in particular. One of the six dialogues— "Ah! Peccatores graves," which is a Christmas work—has a freely composed text, but the other five use biblical quotations and paraphrases, either entirely or in part. Three of the five are based on Gospel stories: "Et cum ingressus,"[52] on the story of Jesus calming the storm (Matt. 8:23–27); "Quid faciam misera," on Jesus and the Canaanite woman (Matt. 15:22–28); and "Vanitas vanitatum," on the rich man and Lazarus (Luke 16:19–31). The texts of these three are dramatic dialogues composed primarily of Gospel quotations and paraphrases, although "Quid faciam misera" includes some poetic material. These seem to be exceptional in Lutheran Germany for the freedom with which they paraphrase

47. For a survey of pietistic thought and poetry, see Geck, *Buxtehude*, pp. 77–115; regarding pietism and "the mystical Eros," see ibid., pp. 91–107.
48. Text printed in *DTB*, 13:lxvi. The parts for cantus 1 and violin 1 are lost, and thus the work has not appeared in a modern edition. For a music example, see Mitjana, *Upsala*, 1:cols. 195–98.
49. Printed in *DTÖ*, 16:60–64.
50. For a study of the sacred Latin works of Förster that includes these dialogues, see Baab, "Förster." Manuscripts of all the dialogues are in the Gustav Düben collection of S/Uu; they all appear to have entered that collection in the 1660s. (Baab, "Förster," p. 13 and app. 1.)
51. Culley, *German*, p. 208.
52. The complete text is quoted and compared with its biblical source in Baab, "Förster," pp. 99–100.

the Gospel stories. As indicated above, German dialogues often delete and rearrange the words of the Bible, and they interpolate nonbiblical passages, but seldom do they proceed by freely paraphrasing a biblical story. Free paraphrase is more characteristic of dramatic dialogues in Italy than in Germany, and it is especially characteristic of Carissimi's Latin oratorios. The influence of Carissimi is revealed particularly in Förster's two longest dialogues, *Dialogi Davidis cum Philisteo* ("Congregantes Philistei agmina sua")[53] and *Dialogo de Holoferne* ("Viri Israelite audite").[54] In the styles of their texts and musical settings, these works, each nearly half an hour long, closely resemble the longest of Carissimi's Latin oratorios. Thus Förster may be said to have brought the Carissimi type of Latin oratorio to Germany, as Charpentier did to France about a decade later. Yet Förster was much less prolific in the creation of Latin oratorios than his French counterpart; and if Charpentier had few successors in the composition of Latin oratorios, Förster appears to have had none.

Dialogue Music[55]

The vocal and instrumental requirements of German dialogues are similar to those of German spiritual concertos of the same period. Although a small percentage of the dialogues require only two solo voices and a basso continuo—as do J. R. Ahle's Easter dialogue, "Sie haben meinen Herrn weggnommen," and his dialogue on the story of Thomas's doubts, "Es sei denn" (1648)[56] —the majority require two or more soloists, a chorus, and an ensemble of instruments. The basso continuo instrument is usually specified as organ. The other instrumental specifications show an emphasis on strings, although winds are sometimes included with or instead of strings and in some works the instrumental parts are unspecified. The instruments are used primarily to play sinfonie and ritornelli but at times to accompany or double the voices in choruses and occasionally even to accompany the solo voices. Most of the choruses are for four voices, but exceptionally, as in

53. For an outline of the text, a description of the style, and some music examples from this work, see ibid., pp. 112–15, 142–46, and 271–74; and Rauschning, *Danzig*, pp. 201–3.
54. For music examples, see Baab, "Förster," pp. 149–51 and 275–89.
55. Unless indicated, the original dates and modern editions of all works mentioned in this section are cited in the preceding section.
56. Printed in *DDT*, 5:6–9.

Schütz's "Mein Sohn, warum hast du uns das gethan," they are for double choruses of seven or eight voices. Choruses are characteristically found at the ends of dialogues but occasionally elsewhere as well.

In general structure the dialogues are of two basic types, continuous and sectional. In the continuous works the personages alternate and overlap with considerable frequency: one voice sings only a phrase or two before another enters. Such dialogues—exemplified by J. R. Ahle's "Sie haben meinen Herrn weggenommen," "Es sei denn," and "Ich danke dir, Gott"—are structurally the closest to the motet and the furthest from the oratorio. Pfleger's "Und er trat in das Schiff" and Schütz's "Es gingen zweene Menschen hinauf" are continuous throughout the main body of the dialogue, but each has a break before the final chorus. Schein's Annunciation dialogue falls between the continuous and sectional types, in a sense, since it includes an introductory sinfonia and two internal ones that seem to divide the work; yet except for that preceding the final chorus, there is no complete break, no pause, from the beginning to the end. Schütz's Annunciation dialogue is related to the continuous type, but the work as a whole is in four distinct sections: (1) *symphonia,* (2) dialogue between the Angel Gabriel and the Virgin Mary, (3) repetition of the *symphonia,* and (4) final chorus.

A sectional dialogue is composed of a series of independent numbers—each concluded with a strong cadence, a double bar, and an assumed brief pause; the numbers may be solos, ensembles, choruses, or instrumental pieces. Dialogue among personages takes place within the numbers themselves, from one number to the next, or both; sectional dialogues exhibit much variety in the application of these two possibilities. In Scheidt's work, "Kommt her, ihr Gesegneten," based on the Last Judgment, the first section is a dialogue between Christ and the Blessed Souls; the second is a dialogue between Christ and the Damned Souls; and the third is the final chorus. Hammerschmidt's dialogue on the Easter story "Wer wälzet uns den Stein," is in five sections, the second and fourth of which are themselves dialogues, as follows: (1) *Symphonia*; (2) dialogue among the Three Women at the sepulchre of Jesus and the Two Men who inform them of the Resurrection; (3) chorus, "Resurrexit Christus hodie"; (4) dialogue between Mary Magdalene and Jesus; (5) repeat of section 3 as finale. Rosenmüller's "Vater, ich habe gesündiget," in six sections, uses dialogue from one section to the next as well as within two of the sections: (1) instrumental introduction; (2) the Prodigal Son; (3) the Father then the Elder Son; (4) the Servant; (5) the Elder Son then the Father; (6) the final chorus. Weckmann's Annunciation dialogue exhibits the simple alternation of personages from one section to the next: (1) Angel, (2) Mary, (3) Angel, (4) Mary, (5) closing "alleluja" for both voices. Although the majority of the sectional dialogues comprise three to eight sections, some have more. For instance, Schütz's "Vater Abraham," treated below, has eleven sections.

The dialogues discussed in the section on texts exhibit a considerable range of musical styles, since they span a period of about seventy-five years and include numerous composers. In general, the styles are comparable to those found in the seventeenth-century German spiritual concertos, *historiae* (except for chantlike sections), and *actus musici*. Recitative predominates in the dialogues, and the types of recitative range from a simple style with numerous repeated notes (as illustrated on p. 19, Example I–3, mm. 1–8, and on p. 66, Example II–2a) to a more elaborate, expressive style (see pp. 34–35, Examples I–7 and I–8, and p. 69, Example II–4). The rare coloratura passages are used principally for word painting (see p. 67, Example II–3). Aria style is virtually absent from the dialogues before the middle of the century and appears only rarely in those of the second half of the century. Sections in aria style are usually solos but are occasionally duets, and they are virtually always in triple meter. Among the dialogues including sections in aria style are Christoph Bernhard's "Euch ist's gegeben," "Sie haben meinen Herrn hinweggenommen," and "Wahrlich, ich sage euch"; Johann Rosenmüller's "Vater, ich habe gesündiget"; and Augustin Pfleger's "Heut freu' dich, Christenheit." The last-named work is particularly interesting for its structural use of an aria, part of which precedes and the remainder of which follows the dialogue proper: (1) stanzas 1 and 2, to melody a repeated; (2) a long dialogue in recitative and arioso styles; (3) stanzas 3–6, to melodies b, c, b, and a; (4) final ensemble.

Examples of Dramatic Dialogues

The two works described below are characteristic of sacred dramatic dialogues of the period. Both are settings of biblical texts, but they modify some of the biblical passages and delete others for dramatic and musical purposes. Both are sectional, but they represent different treatments of the sectional procedure: in the first the dialogue takes place only from one section to the next, but in the second there is also dialogue within the sections. Both have been called oratorios in modern musicological literature,[57] but their texts, quoted from the Bible, make them quite different from works called oratorios in their time. They are among the finest examples of the sacred dramatic dialogue in seventeenth-century Germany.

Schütz, "Vater Abraham, erbarme dich mein"[58]

This dialogue, which dates from the 1620s,[59] represents a relatively early stage in the development of the concertato dialogue in Germany. The text is based on the story of the rich man and Lazarus (Luke 16:19–31). Like the texts of many dramatic dialogues of the period, this one deletes all narrative portions of the Gospel story and leaves only three alternations between the Rich Man (B) and Abraham (T). The Rich Man, burning in hell, cries out to Abraham to permit the beggar Lazarus (to whom he had been uncharitable and who is in heaven) to help him, but his petition is refused (sections 2 and 3 in the outline on p. 64). The Rich Man then twice begs that Lazarus be sent to his brothers on earth to warn them of the suffering that might await them (sections 4 and 6), but Abraham refuses these petitions too, for "they have Moses and the Prophets; let them hearken to them" (section 5); and further, "If they do not hearken to Moses and the Prophets, they will not believe even if someone rises from the dead" (section 7). Schütz repeats these last two speeches of Abraham by ensembles (sections 9 and 11) that include four personages: two Angels (SS),

57. For instance, Max Seiffert calls Schütz's "Vater Abraham, erbarme dich mein" the "first German oratorio" in Seiffert, "Schütziana," p. 217; and André Pirro calls Weckmann's *Dialog von Tobias und Raguel* (which he attributes to J. Rosenmüller) a "small oratorio" in Pirro, *Buxtehude*, p. 113.

58. Printed in Schütz, *Werke*, supp. 2:37–50.

59. Bittinger, *SWV*, p. 127.

who are not in the biblical story; Lazarus (A), who does not speak in the biblical story; and Abraham.

Some of the work's eleven sections are related by similar or identical material. As he was to do later in his Christmas *historia*, Schütz uses instrumentation to assist in characterization. The following outline indicates the sections, personages, incipits, instrumentation, and some of the musical correspondences among the sections:

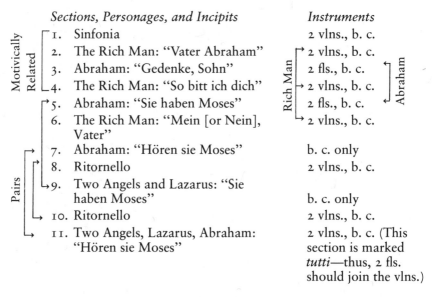

	Sections, Personages, and Incipits	Instruments
1.	Sinfonia	2 vlns., b. c.
2.	The Rich Man: "Vater Abraham"	2 vlns., b. c.
3.	Abraham: "Gedenke, Sohn"	2 fls., b. c.
4.	The Rich Man: "So bitt ich dich"	2 vlns., b. c.
5.	Abraham: "Sie haben Moses"	2 fls., b. c.
6.	The Rich Man: "Mein [or Nein], Vater"	2 vlns., b. c.
7.	Abraham: "Hören sie Moses"	b. c. only
8.	Ritornello	2 vlns., b. c.
9.	Two Angels and Lazarus: "Sie haben Moses"	b. c. only
10.	Ritornello	2 vlns., b. c.
11.	Two Angels, Lazarus, Abraham: "Hören sie Moses"	2 vlns., b. c. (This section is marked *tutti*—thus, 2 fls. should join the vlns.)

From this outline it may be seen that all three of the Rich Man's sections (2, 4, and 6) are accompanied by two violins and the first two of Abraham's sections (3 and 5) by two flutes. Sections 1–4 are motivically related: the final cadential measures of the sinfonia, shown in Example II–1a, furnish the initial motives for sections 2, 3, and 4 of the dialogue, as illustrated in Examples II–1b, c, and

EXAMPLE II-1. "Vater Abraham" (Schütz, *Werke*, supp. 2:37, 40, 41).

Example a:

(EXAMPLE II-I, continued)

Example b:

Example c:

Example d:

d; this unifies the first part of the work by motivic repetition.[60]
Numbers 5–11 include three pairs of related sections: section 5, a
solo by Abraham, is used as the basis for section 9, as illustrated in

60. Regarding similar unification in G. F. Anerio's Italian dialogues of only a slightly
earlier date, see the discussion of Anerio's *Teatro* in the present study, volume 1, chapter 3.

Examples II–2a and b; in like manner section 7, another solo by Abraham, provides the material of section 11; and the two ritornellos, sections 8 and 10, are identical.

EXAMPLE II-2. "Vater Abraham" (Schütz, *Werke*, supp. 2:43, 45).

Example a:

Example b:

You have Moses and the prophets . . .

The vocal solo passages of this dialogue are mostly in an expressive recitative style with frequent, often repetitive, rhetorical figures. Exceptional and noteworthy are the virtuosic runs expressing the flames of hell in the vocal line of section 2; one of them is illustrated in Example II–3. Comparable lines are also used in the violin parts of section 4, again to call forth the image of the flames of hell.

EXAMPLE II-3. "Vater Abraham" (Schütz, *Werke*, supp. 2:39).

... in this flame ...

Weckmann, Dialog von Tobias und Raguel[61]

It seems likely that this dialogue dates from the early 1660s; it was probably among the works performed at Weckmann's Collegium musicum in Hamburg.[62] Like the work just treated, this one is based on a biblical story that, stripped of its narrative lines, contains only the dialogue among personages. The biblical text is occasionally manipulated by the repetition, modification, and addition of words. The dialogue is based on the brief episode of the marriage of Tobias and Sarah, which is recounted in the apocryphal Book of Tobias, chapters 6 and 7. The structure of the work is represented in the outline (p. 68). At the beginning of the dialogue (section 2, based on Tob. 6:10–13), the Angel Raphael (A) counsels Tobias (T) to marry Sarah, the daughter of his kinsman Raguel (B). Tobias and the Angel go to Raguel (section 4, Tob. 7:3–7), who is moved to tears of joy upon hearing that Tobias is his brother's son. Tobias then asks Raguel for the hand of his daughter (section 6, Tob. 7:10–14); after reassurance by the Angel, Raguel

61. Anonymous in its manuscript source, this work was attributed to Johann Rosenmüller by August Horneffer in 1899 (Horneffer, "Rosenmüller," p. 60) and by André Pirro in 1913 (Pirro, *Buxtehude*, p. 113). In 1930 Max Seiffert published a modern edition of it under Rosenmüller's name (*Org*, vol. 21). In an article of 1961, however, Friedhelm Krummacher treated the attribution of the work extensively and advanced convincing arguments for attributing it to Matthias Weckmann (Krummacher, "Weckmann," pp. 196–200).

62. Krummacher, "Weckmann," p. 198.

consents, for he is convinced that his prayers have been heard and thus Tobias has been sent by God to become Sarah's husband. In his final arioso Raguel blesses the union (section 8, Tob. 7:15); this blessing is repeated in the final ensemble (section 9). Omitted from the text is the information provided in the biblical story that Sarah had already been given seven husbands—all of whom had died, allegedly at the hands of a devil; thus Tobias is understandably hesitant to marry her and agrees to do so only because of his faith in the Angel's counsel. It is because of the history of Sarah's marriages that Raguel needs the reassurance of the Angel in section 6 of the dialogue before he gives his daughter to Tobias, and it is for the same reason that Raguel speaks of his tearful prayers to God.

As may be seen in the following structural outline, the nine sections of the work are alternately instrumental and vocal until the final ensemble:

Sections, Personages, and Incipits	Instruments
1. Sinfonia	2 vlns., bsn., b. c.
2. Tobias, Angel: "Wo wollen wir einkehren"	b. c.
3. Ritornello	2 vlns., bsn., b. c.
4. Raguel, Angel, Tobias: "Von wannen seid ihr"	b. c.; in 2d pt., 2 vlns. and bsn. for Raguel only
5. Ritornello (same as no. 3)	2 vlns., bsn., b. c.
6. Tobias, Angel, Raguel: "Ich will heute"	b. c.; in 2d pt., 2 vlns. and bsn. for Raguel only
7. Ritornello (same as no. 3)	2 vlns., bsn., b. c.
8. Raguel: "Der Gott Abrahams"	b. c.
9. ATB ensemble: "Der Gott Abrahams"	2 vlns., bsn., b. c.

Structural unity is provided by the threefold statement of a ritornello (sections 3, 5, and 7) and certain similarities between sections 4 and 6. All the even-numbered sections are accompanied either by basso continuo alone (sections 2 and 8) or by basso continuo initially, with the violins added in the second part of the section (sections 4 and 6). The violin accompaniment of a solo voice is restricted to two of Raguel's solos.

This work is extremely attractive for the variety of its recitative and the skillful manner in which the composer has molded the vocal lines to both the sound and the meaning of the words. The recitative style is illustrated by Example II–4, which begins with

EXAMPLE II-4. *Dialog von Tobias und Raguel*—Weckmann (*Org*, 21:4).

TOBIAS—Where will we lodge? ANGEL—There is a man here named Raguel, your kinsman, of your tribe, who has only one daughter, whose name is Sarah, and no other child . . .

considerable melodic activity in both the vocal line and the basso continuo but continues at the entrance of the Angel with a less active continuo and more repeated notes in the vocal line. The rhetorical repetitions in the first six and last five measures of the example are characteristic of the work, as is the setting of the accented syllables of words to longer or higher notes than the unaccented ones. Of special interest is the composer's emphasis on the point that Raguel has only *one* daughter by the leap to a dissonance on the first syllable of "eine" in measure 15 and by the repetition of the final phrase, "und sonst kein Kind."

Examples II–5 and II–6 illustrate the two principal climaxes of the work, which are similar in several respects. Both climaxes are settings of highly emotional texts sung by Raguel and introduced by the Angel; the violins enter in both examples at the Angel's final note in preparation for Raguel's solo; the violins' initial descending passages are virtually identical; the bassoon enters at the same point with respect to the violins in both examples; and the same principles of textual setting are evident in the two examples: textual repetition together with melodic repetition at the upper second (*climax* in musical-rhetorical terminology) and chromaticism to express the pathos of Raguel's words. The similarities of these portions of sections 4 and 6, together with the threefold statement of the ritornello (sections 3, 5, and 7) that surrounds and separates these two sections, combine to create a highly integrated and entirely convincing central core for this dialogue.

EXAMPLE II-5. *Dialog von Tobias und Raguel*—Weckmann (*Org*, 21:7–8).

The Oratorio in the Baroque Era: Protestant Germany and England

(EXAMPLE II-5, continued)

ANGEL—The Tobias about whom you ask is this youth's father.
RAGUEL—O my dear son, a blessing be upon you, . . .

EXAMPLE II-6. *Dialog von Tobias und Raguel*—Weckmann (Org, 21:9).

(EXAMPLE II-6, continued)

ich zweif - le nicht, dass Gott mei-ne hei - ßen Trä - nen

und Ge - bet er - hö - ret ha - be,

ANGEL— . . . because he [Tobias] fears God. RAGUEL—I doubt not that God has regarded my burning tears and prayers, . . .

Other Sacred Dramatic Genres

Klaj's Narrative-Dramatic Poems

Of considerable interest for their structural similarity to the oratorio libretto are the narrative-dramatic poems of Johann Klaj (1616–56).[63] Having first studied at the University of Leipzig, Klaj moved in 1643 to Nuremberg, where he studied theology under Johann Michael Dilherr, wrote poetry, and taught school. He was among those who made Nuremberg one of the leading centers of German literature in the mid-century. In 1644 he and the poet Georg Philipp Harsdörffer were the founders of a distinguished literary society.[64] Klaj left Nuremberg in 1650 for Kitzingen, where he spent the rest of his life as a minister and teacher.

63. A thorough study devoted exclusively to these works, which includes much bibliography, is Wiedemann, *Klaj*. For a study of Klaj's life and works, see Franz, *Klaj*.
64. The society was variously called "Loblicher Hirten- und Blumenorden an der Pegnitz," "Pegnesischer Blumenorden," "Pegnitzer Hirtengesellschaft," and "Gesellschaft der Blumenschäfer," according to J. Hendrick, "Nürnberger Dichterschule," in *RDLg*, 2:705.

The works of Klaj that relate to the oratorio libretto are freely derived from biblical stories: *Auferstehung Jesu Christi* (Nuremberg, 1644), from the story of the Resurrection; *Höllen- und Himmelfahrt Jesu Christi* (Nuremberg, 1644),[65] from the stories of Christ's descent into hell and ascension into heaven, the former of which is nonbiblical but is a belief expressed in the Apostles' Creed; *Herodes der Kindermörder* (Nuremberg, 1645), from the story of Herod's massacre of the children; *Der leidende Christus* (Nuremberg, 1645), from the Passion story; *Engel- und Drachenstreit* (Nuremberg, ca. 1649—probably written in 1646), from the story of the archangel Michael and the dragon in the book of Revelation; and *Freudengedichte der seligmachenden Geburt Jesu Christi* (Nuremberg, 1650),[66] from the Christmas story. Klaj recited these poems before what he described as "highly eminent" and "German-loving" audiences in Nuremberg's Sebalduskirche after the service on appropriate feast days.[67] It was apparently Dilherr, a strong influence on Klaj and an admirer of his work, who arranged for the poet to recite his works at the Sebalduskirche. For these poetry readings Dilherr also wrote invitations, poems in both Latin and German versions, that were presented to Nuremberg's chief citizens and numerous connoisseurs of literature. The invitations are included with the printed versions of Klaj's poems.

All of these poems by Klaj include narrative passages for the personage designated as the Poet (also called the Evangelist in the *Auferstehung*), and they include dialogues among the other personages and relatively long monologues. The first three works listed above are in rhymed verse throughout, but the others use prose for the narrative passages, which are relatively brief. All but two of the poems (*Auferstehung* and *Herodes*) are divided into acts, called *Handlungen*; *Höllen- und Himmelfahrt* includes only two, but each of the other three works includes four *Handlungen*. Choruses, set to music and performed by an ensemble of voices and instruments, normally conclude the *Handlungen*. In content and style these poems are extremely erudite and reveal the poet's extensive humanistic background. They allude to a wide range of writings from antiquity up to Klaj's own time, and he documents

65. Printed in Schöne, *Barock*, pp. 303–16.
66. Printed in Flemming, *Oratorium*, pp. 27–61; and Keller, *Weihnachtsdichtung*, pp. 65–208; the latter edition includes extensive commentary.
67. For the circumstances surrounding the performances of some of these works, see Franz, *Klaj*, pp. 15–17; and Wiedemann, *Klaj*, pp. 10–12.

the sources of these allusions in the "Anmerkungen" appended to each poem in its printed version. The literary style is highly rhetorical, with special emphasis given to the sonorous quality of the words.

Klaj's narrative-dramatic poems, which are based on typical oratorio subjects, include most of the literary elements characteristic of oratorios. In fact, they are so close to the oratorio libretto that some literary scholars, while recognizing that they were not intended to be set to music throughout, consider the term *oratorio* appropriate for them. Willi Flemming has coined the term *deklamatorisches Oratorium* ("declamatory oratorio" for this genre, and Conrad Wiedemann terms the works *Redeoratorien* ("spoken oratorios").[68] Nevertheless, they differ from most oratorio librettos in several respects—including their erudition, their long monologues, and the greater length of most of them (they range from 577 lines for *Auferstehung* to 1,049 lines for *Freudengedichte*).[69]

All the music for Klaj's narrative-dramatic poems is thought to have been composed by Sigismund Theophil Staden (1607–55),[70] although his name is mentioned in only one of the prints, that of *Der leidende Christus*.[71] Although there is no extant music for the poems, some indication of the nature of the music may be derived from Klaj's remarks about it in the "Anmerkungen." He states that music was used at the beginning and ending of each act of *Höllen- und Himmelfahrt*, as well as at dividing points within the acts, and he mentions that stringed and wind instruments were used. In *Der leidende Christus* he praises Staden's choruses and mentions that three of them (a chorus "of those eating the Easter lamb" and two choruses of Jewish women) were set for three voices (AAA) and three alto violas; the chorus of Roman soldiers used two voices (TB) and three bass shawms (*Bomharden*). In the *Engel- und Drachenstreit* two of the choruses, "Ein feste Burg ist unser Gott" and "Allein Gott in der Höh sei Ehr," were sung to chorale tunes. The *Freudengedichte* includes the greatest number of musical references, with vocal and instrumental ensembles rang-

68. Flemming, *Oratorium*, p. 15; and Wiedemann, *Klaj*. In the latter the term *Redeoratorium* is used in the title and throughout the study. Other writings in which the works under consideration are classified as oratorios are Schöne, *Barock*, p. 303; and Szyrocki, *Barock*, p. 103.

69. Oratorio librettos of the period range from about 350 to 450 lines.

70. H. Samuel, "Staden," in *MGG*, 12:cols. 1116–17.

71. Staden's name appears in Klaj, *Der leidende Christus* (Nuremberg, 1645), "Anmerkungen," p. 40.

ing from a solo voice and a few instruments to an eight-part chorus. The instruments mentioned are viols, lute, bassoon, bass shawm, flutes, and cromornes. Four of the choruses—"In dulci jubilo," "Vom Himmel hoch," "Der Tag der ist so freudenreich," and "Wachet auf ruft uns die Stimme"—were sung to chorale tunes. One of the musical numbers is a dialogue between two shepherds, who respectively sing the praises of Mary and Jesus.

Sacred Drama and Opera

Related to the oratorio in their dramatic treatment of sacred stories are the numerous plays of Protestant Germany that are based on subjects taken either from the Bible or from church history. The majority of such works are school dramas, intended not only to entertain but to provide exercise for students in the skills of oratory and to instruct them and the audience in morality.[72] In purpose and often in subject matter as well, these school dramas are like those of the Jesuits in Roman Catholic areas and appear to have been influenced by them. Although some of the Protestant works are in Latin, as are most of the Jesuit ones, the German language seems to have been predominant. Music usually played a subsidiary role in the Protestant school plays: on the whole it appears to have been less elaborate and less extensively used than in Jesuit plays. The music is normally restricted to choruses at the ends of acts and an occasional number within an act.

Such plays based on oratoriolike subjects, mostly by little-known dramatists, were performed in Protestant Germany throughout the seventeenth century and well into the eighteenth. Examples are Johannes Berthesius's *Der Schalcksz Knecht* (Leipzig, 1606),[73] described on the title page as based on the Gospel for the twenty-second Sunday after Trinity, which is Matt. 18:21–35, the parable of the unmerciful servant; Martin Böhme's three plays published in his *Drey schöne geistliche Comoedien* (Wittenberg, 1618)[74] and

---

72. Little research has been done, from either the literary or the musical standpoints, on the Protestant school drama of the seventeenth century. For some brief general comments and bibliography, see Kaiser, *Mitternacht*, pp. 9–10. For a survey of the school drama in Zittau from the late sixteenth century to the late seventeenth, see Eggert, *Weise*, pp. 22–46.

73. Listed in Faber du Faur, *Literature*, 1:15.

74. Ibid.

based on the stories of Judith,[75] Tobias, and the prodigal son; and several biblical plays, which Johann Sebastian Mitternacht included in a 1646 list of his works, on the subjects of Judith, the Nativity, the birth of Isaac, the Circumcision, Tobias, and Herod's murder of the children.[76] In the late seventeenth and early eighteenth centuries Christian Weise, today the best-known author of such works, wrote numerous school plays for the *Gymnasium* of which he was the rector at Zittau. Many of these plays are based on biblical stories—including those of Jephthah (1679), the sacrifice of Isaac (1680), Jacob's double marriage (1682), David (1683), Nebuchadnezzar (1684), Naboth and Jezabel (1685), Solomon (1685), Absalom (1686), Athalia (1687), Job (1687), Esau and Jacob (1693), the twelve-year-old Jesus (1696), Jacob and Joseph (1699), Cain and Abel (1704), and Dina and Sichem (1705).[77]

Musically more important than the ordinary school dramas are the dramatic presentations for special occasions—which were given a variety of terms including *Festspiel, actus, Festakt,* and *Staatsakt*.[78] Among the occasions for performances of such works are the major feasts in the church year, birthdays and other celebrations honoring princes and other distinguished persons, and important occasions of state, such as the establishment of peace. Often based on mythological subjects, these plays at times utilized themes from church history or the Bible, and thus they bore a relationship to the oratorio libretto. An example is an anonymous work entitled *Von dem erlöseten Jerusalem* ("On the Freeing of Jerusalem"), performed at the *Gymnasium* in Coburg in 1630 in honor of the birthday of Johann Casimir, duke of Saxony. This play, of which the music and a contemporary description are extant,[79] was designated an *actus oratorius*—that is, a dramatic work involving the skills of oratory. It was based on an episode of church history—the events of the first crusade and particularly the

75. The story of Judith was particularly popular in German Baroque literature; for lists of literary works based on this story, including a number of plays, see Baltzer, *Judith*, pp. 59–61, and Purdie, *Judith*, pp. 8–14.

76. Mitternacht's list is reproduced in Kaiser, *Mitternacht*, p. 17.

77. The dates given are those of the first performance or the first publication, whichever is earliest. For full bibliographical information see the list of Weise's dramas in Eggert, *Weise*, pp. 6–18.

78. For a discussion of the *Festspiel* in general, see Flemming, *Oratorium*, pp. 117–40. For the *Festspiele* of Weise, see Eggert, *Weise*, pp. 303–8.

79. The description is quoted and paraphrased and most of the music is printed in Reissmann, *Geschichte*, 2:172–84, and in the "Noten-Beilagen" of that volume, pp. 73–91.

role of one of the leaders of that crusade, Godfrey of Bouillon. The play itself was in Latin and was almost entirely spoken, but a considerable amount of music, by Melchior Franck, was included in the spectacular *interscenia* or *Aufzüge*—these were dramatic entertainments, comparable to the *intermedi* of Italy, performed before the play began and between the acts. Much closer to the oratorio is an anonymous Christmas play performed at the *Gymnasium* in Görlitz in 1668.[80] It was probably written by Christian Gabriel Funcke; the name Abe Lichtenberger, probably the composer, appears at the end of the manuscript of the play's music.[81] The work is in four acts, the first consisting of several episodes from the Old Testament in which the coming of Christ is prophesied; the second, the Annunciation; the third, the Nativity and the stories of the shepherds, the wise men, and Herod; and the fourth, the flight into Egypt, Herod's murder of the children, and his death. The various episodes of the work are introduced and related to one another by a narrator, a personage named Assaph. Because of its inclusion of a narrator and its extensive music, this work is more closely related to oratorio than are most sacred plays of the time. The play is in German and is largely spoken, but there are fifteen musical numbers—including arias, ensembles, and choruses—used at the high points of scenes or dramatic episodes. Two of the numbers are borrowings—one of which is from Hammerschmidt's Annunciation dialogue, "Maria gegrüsset seist du," mentioned above in the treatment of dialogues. The three arias are sung by Assaph, and two of these are based on the chorale tunes "Jesu meines Lebens Leben" and "Herr Jesu Christ dich zu uns wend." The only instruments specified are the spinet, violins, and violas.

Related both to sacred drama and to German oratorio are German operas on sacred subjects. The earliest extant German opera, *Seelewig*,[82] originated in Nuremberg in the same environment as did the poems of Klaj. Its text is by Klaj's friend Harsdörffer and its music by S. T. Staden, the composer of the musical numbers in Klaj's literary "oratorios." Both the text and the music of *Seelewig* were published in the fourth volume of Harsdörffer's

80. For a description of this play and an edition of its music, see Mersmann, "Weihnachtsspiel."
81. Ibid., p. 250.
82. Printed in Staden, "Seelewig."

chief work, the highly erudite but entertaining series in eight volumes called *Frauenzimmer Gesprächspiele*.[83] The opera is a moral, pastoral allegory. The chief personage is the nymph Seelewig, who represents the eternal Soul ("die ewige Seele"), according to an explanatory dialogue that precedes the opera.[84] In the action of the opera, the Soul is tempted by Sensuality (represented by a nymph, Sinnigunda) to submit to the enticements of false Science, Honor, and Wealth (three shepherds—Künsteling, Ehrelob, and Reichimut, respectively), who are the servants of the evil spirit of the forest, the satyr Trügewalt. The attempts of these sinister forces to place the Soul in the power of Trügewalt are foiled, however, by the intervention of Conscience (the matron Gwissulda) and Intellect (the nymph Herzigilda). The text of *Seelewig* is in the same moralistic, allegorical tradition as that of Cavalieri's *Rappresentatione di Anima et di Corpo* (Rome, 1600), a tradition that continued to live throughout the Baroque era in oratorio and occasionally appeared in school drama and opera as well. *Seelewig* is set to music throughout—"in the Italian manner" ("auf Italianische Art"), according to its title page. Nevertheless, the musical style is by no means that of contemporary Italian opera. Most of the music of *Seelewig* consists of simple solo songs, usually strophic, and of passages in conservative recitative and arioso styles.

More characteristic of German sacred opera in the seventeenth century than *Seelewig* are operas based on biblical stories. Many of the operas mentioned below appear to have included spoken dialogue instead of recitative, but they emphasized music more than the school dramas. The music of most of these works either is lost or survives in only fragmentary form. Among the extant librettos are an anonymous *Jakobs des Patriarchen Heyrath oder die Geschicht des dienenden Schäffers Jakobs* ("The Wedding of the Patriarch Jacob, or the Story of the Serving Shepherd of Jacob," Wolfenbüttel, 1662)[85] and Duke Anton Ulrich von Braunschweig's *Der Hoffmann Daniel: Wie er bey dem Könige Dario gedienet* ("The Courtier Daniel: How He Served with King Darius," Wolfenbüttel, 1663).[86] The composer and poet Constantine

83. For a facsimile edition see Harsdörffer, *Frauenzimmer*, 4:85–209 (text only) and 533–622 (musical setting).
84. Staden, "Seelewig," pp. 61–64; Harsdörffer, *Frauenzimmer*, 4:74–83.
85. Wolff, *Hamburg*, 1:24.
86. Printed in Flemming, *Oper*, pp. 125–79. Although this opera deals with a biblical figure, Daniel, the story was taken from the writings of Josephus, rather than from the Bible. (Ibid., p. 126.)

Christian Dedekind's librettos in his *Neue geistliche Schauspiele bekwemet zur Musik* ("New Spiritual Plays Suitable for Music," Dresden, 1670) include two librettos on the birth of Christ and one each on Herod's murder of the children, the Passion, and the Resurrection.[87] Two sacred operas on anonymous librettos performed in Halle are *Die verwechselte Braut oder Jacobs Hochzeit in Haran* ("The Exchanged Bride, or Jacob's Wedding in Haran," 1675) and *Der untreue Getreue oder Der Feindseelige Staatsdiener Haman* ("The Disloyal Loyal One, or the Hostile Civil Servant, Haman," 1677).[88] In 1675 Nuremberg saw the performance of two works with librettos by Johann Ludwig Faber, *Herodes der Kindermörder* ("Herod the Murderer of Children") and *Abraham der Gläubige und Isaak der Gehorsame* ("Abraham the Believer and Isaak the Obedient One"). The material of the latter work was also that of an opera, *Abraham der Wundergläubige und Isaak der Wundergehorsame*, with a libretto by Christoph Adam Negelein; this five-act work included twenty-one arias and nine instrumental numbers.[89]

Of primary importance for the history of German opera is the development at Hamburg that began in 1678 with a sacred opera, *Der erschaffene, gefallene und aufgerichtete Mensch* ("Man Created, Fallen, and Redeemed"); based on the story of Adam and Eve, its text is by Christian Richter and its music by Johann Theile.[90] During the earliest period of operatic activity in Hamburg, sacred operas, along with those based on historical and mythological subjects, were performed with some frequency. From 1678 to 1695, nearly one-fourth of the forty-six operas performed there were based on sacred subjects.[91] Among these, in addition to the one just mentioned on the story of Adam and Eve, there were operas on the subjects of the mother of the Maccabees, David, Esther, the birth of Christ, St. Eugenia, the martyr Polyeucte, Cain and Abel, and the conquering of the temple in Jerusalem and of Mt. Sion.[92] Fewer sacred operas were performed in Hamburg after about 1695; and in the early eighteenth century sacred subjects were left largely to spoken drama, sometimes with musical num-

87. For the titles of these works, see *DLL*, 3:cols. 16–18.
88. Serauky, *Halle*, 2/1: 242–44.
89. Sandberger, "Nürnberg," p. 85.
90. For a full discussion of the libretto of this work, see Wolff, *Hamburg*, 1:24–29.
91. Schmidt, *Schürmann*, 2:67.
92. For the titles, poets, composers, and dates of these works, see ibid., n. 115.

bers, and to oratorio.[93] In Friedrich Chrysander's view, the chief significance of the Hamburg biblical operas lies in their role as antecedents of the German oratorio.[94] He may well have underestimated their intrinsic signficance as musical and dramatic works and their importance as expressions of their time, as Hellmuth Christian Wolff believes;[95] nevertheless, Chrysander did touch upon an important relationship, that between Hamburg's sacred opera and German oratorio. The latter first became a significant genre in the early eighteenth century, and Hamburg was the most important center of its cultivation.

93. Ibid., 2:77.
94. Chrysander, "Oper," col. 327.
95. Wolff, *Hamburg*, 1:37.

CHAPTER III

Buxtehude and
the Lübeck Abendmusiken

§❧ *The Origin and Social*
Context of the Abendmusiken[1]

Of primary importance for the history of the German oratorio are the concerts known as the *Abendmusiken* conducted by Dietrich Buxtehude (ca. 1637–1707) at the Marienkirche in Lübeck. The antecedents of the *Abendmusiken* are the concerts presented by Franz Tunder, Buxtehude's predecessor as organist at the Marienkirche, from 1641 until his death in 1667.[2] Tunder's concerts, which he called *Abendspielen*,[3] appear to have been modeled after the organ concerts in the Reformed churches of the Netherlands, as pointed out on pp. 47–48. Like those concerts, Tunder's were economically independent of the church and were originally restricted to organ music. Tunder referred to the remuneration that he received for the *Abendspielen* as *accidentia*, which he could not depend on as regular income.[4] These *accidentia* were probably gifts from Lübeck's leading merchants and the commercial guilds who had requested the concerts.[5] Few details are known of Tunder's concerts: they apparently took place on Thursdays, and they

---

1. For information on the *Abendmusiken*, see Edelhoff, "Abendmusiken"; Karstädt, *Abendmusiken*; Karstädt, "Buxtehude-Forschung"; Söhngen, "Abendmusiken"; W. Stahl, "Abendmusiken," in *MGG*, 1:cols. 32–35; Stahl, "Abendmusiken"; Stahl, "Tunder-Buxtehude," pp. 8–9, 23–24, 55–67.
2. Regarding the year 1641 as the first year of Tunder's concerts, see Stahl, "Tunder-Buxtehude," p. 8.
3. Ibid.
4. Ibid.
5. Ibid., pp. 23–24.

FIGURE III-1. The Marienkirche at Lübeck (before World War II),
where Buxtehude's *Abendmusiken* took place.
(Reproduced by permission of Wilhelm Castelli, Lübeck.)

eventually included music for a few solo voices and instruments in addition to the organ.[6]

Buxtehude succeeded Tunder as organist at the Marienkirche in 1668; there is evidence, however, that the concerts were suspended at about that time.[7] The earliest documentation for Buxtehude's *Abendmusiken* dates from 1673,[8] but these concerts may have begun earlier than that. With Buxtehude, as apparently with Tunder, the concerts were free to the public and were supported by contributions from individual merchants and the commercial guilds of Lübeck.[9] In several respects Buxtehude's concerts represent a new beginning, however, rather than merely a continuation of what his predecessor had done. Soon after his installation as organist, he was clearly looking forward to more elaborate concerts, for in 1669 he requested that two new galleries be constructed on each side of the church near the principal organ. One gallery on each side already existed near the organ; those plus the new ones could accommodate approximately forty singers and instrumentalists, the maximum number that Buxtehude used for the ordinary *Abendmusiken*.[10] Another change was in the day and season of the concerts. Rather than continuing to give them on Thursdays throughout the year, Buxtehude moved them to Sundays and grouped them in the period before Christmas. Thus there were concerts on the last two Sundays after Trinity and the second, third, and fourth Sundays of Advent. The concerts began at four o'clock in the afternoon, immediately following the afternoon service in the church, and lasted for one to two hours.[11]

Buxtehude would appear to have presented *Abendmusiken* annually from 1673, or perhaps a few years earlier, until his death. Since at least 1677, printed librettos of the texts, most of which are now lost,[12] were made available to the audience for some, and perhaps for all, of the concerts. Our only certain knowledge of the

6. Ibid.
7. Ibid., p. 56.
8. The documentation is quoted in Stiehl, *Organisten*, p. 13.
9. For details see Stahl, "Tunder-Buxtehude," pp. 60–62.
10. Ibid., pp. 56–58.
11. The printed libretto of *Die Hochzeit des Lammes*, discussed below, states that the time was from four to five o'clock, but a contemporary report of the *Abendmusiken* by Hermann Lebermann—quoted in Karstädt, *Abendmusiken*, p. 21—indicates that the concerts lasted from four to six o'clock.
12. For bibliography regarding the sources of information about the lost librettos, see Geck, "Authentizität," p. 410.

FIGURE III-2. Interior of the Marienkirche at Lübeck (before World War II), showing the large organ and the balconies constructed for Buxtehude's *Abendmusiken*.

(Reproduced by permission of Wilhelm Castelli, Lübeck.)

music performed at Buxtehude's concerts is regrettably limited to the conclusions that may be drawn from four printed librettos and one subject of a work known to have been performed at an *Abendmusik*. The four librettos are *Die Hochzeit des Lammes* (1678),[13] *Abdruck der Texte, welche . . . bey den gewöhnlichen Abend-Musicen . . . praesentiret werden* (1700),[14] *Castum doloris* (1705), and *Templum honoris* (1705).[15] The first of these works is analogous to an Italian oratorio, and the word *oratorio* seems to be appropriate for it, even though that term was not yet used for German works; the last two are not analogous to the oratorio, but they have some elements in common with it. All three are discussed below. Of the three, only *Die Hochzeit des Lammes* was performed within a normal series of *Abendmusiken*. *Castrum doloris* and *Templum honoris* were performed at a pair of concerts that the composer himself termed an "extraordinaire Abend-Music"[16] for a special occasion. The second-named libretto, *Abdruck der Texte*, provided the texts for all five of the *Abendmusiken* in 1700, and it showed that each of these concerts consisted of a mixture of sacred vocal works, none of which relates to the oratorio. The composition for an *Abendmusik* that is known only by its subject was mentioned in a letter by Buxtehude as his "Abend Music vom Verlohrnen Sohn," presented in 1688.[17] Based on the story of the prodigal son, this work might well have been analogous to an Italian oratorio, but nothing more is known of it. Two titles that appear to designate extended oratoriolike works by Buxtehude, each in five structural parts for the five *Abendmusiken* of a season, are *Das allererschröcklichste und allererfreulichste nemlich Ende der Zeit und Anfang der Ewigkeit* and *Himmlische Seelenlust auf Erden über die Menschwerdung und Geburt des Heylandes Jesu Christi*. Both titles are listed in booksellers' catalogues of 1684 as *futuri*—that is, books (perhaps librettos) to be available in the future.[18] There is some doubt, however, concerning whether these publications actually did appear and whether the catalogue entries

13. Printed in Pirro, *Buxtehude*, pp. 173–84.
14. This libretto was apparently lost in World War II (cf. Karstädt, *Bux WV*, no. 133). The content of the libretto is summarized in Stahl, "Abendmusiken," pp. 18–20, and in Karstädt, *Abendmusiken*, pp. 37–38.
15. Facsimiles of both 1705 librettos are appended to Karstädt, *Abendmusiken*. The libretto of *Templum honoris* is discussed in Karstädt, "Textbuch."
16. Stahl, "Tunder-Buxtehude," p. 67.
17. Ibid., p. 64.
18. Göhler, "Messkataloge," p. 329.

constitute evidence of the existence of such works by Buxtehude.[19] An anonymous and untitled composition in manuscript has been attributed to Buxtehude by Willy Maxton and has been identified by him as music for the *Abendmusiken*.[20] Maxton has published an edition of the work as Buxtehude's *Das Jüngste Gericht: Abendmusik in fünf Vorstellungen*;[21] he considers the composition to be identical to the one previously known only by title as *Das allererschröcklichste . . .*, mentioned above. The attribution of *Das Jüngste Gericht* to Buxtehude is open to question, however, and the work is only tentatively grouped with Buxtehude's compositions in the following discussions.[22]

The term *Abendmusik* has been used in musicological literature not only to refer to Buxtehude's evening concerts but also, in the sense of a genre, to apply to his compositions that were, or might have been, performed in those concerts.[23] The composer's use of the term, however, was virtually always in reference to the evening concerts rather than to the compositions. The title pages of the four librettos printed for the *Abendmusiken*, cited above, all include the phrase "at the usual time of the *Abendmusiken*," or a variant of it, but the works themselves are not called *Abendmusiken*. Furthermore, the libretto printed in 1700 showed that an *Abendmusik* could consist of a concert made up of a variety of compositions, and in such an instance the term could not refer to a genre. An exception to Buxtehude's normal use of the term, however, is found in the letter mentioned above, in which he identifies his composition "Abend Music vom Verlohrnen Sohn" by this term. This exception anticipates a use of the term that became common in the eighteenth century. In fact, the definition of *Abendmusik* published in 1752 by Kaspar Ruetz, the cantor of St. Catherine's school in Lübeck, is virtually the same as that of *oratorio*.[24] Thus one may see a parallel between the development

19. Geck, "Authentizität," pp. 409–11.
20. The source is in the Düben collection at S/Uu: Vok. mus. i hdskr. 71. The attribution first appears in Maxton, "Abendmusik."
21. Buxtehude[?], *Jüngste*.
22. For a critique of Maxton's attribution, see Geck, "Authentizität," pp. 408–15. For Maxton's reply to Geck, see Maxton, "Authentizität"; and for Geck's counterreply, see Geck, "Nochmals."
23. The term is applied to musical compositions, for instance, in Maxton, "Abendmusik"; on the title page of Buxtehude[?], *Jüngste*; and in Max Seiffert's edition of two of Buxtehude's compositions, alleged to be *Abendmusiken* because they use Advent texts, printed in *DDT*, 14:15–38, 107–38.
24. The definition is quoted in Stahl, "Ruetz," pp. 336–37.

of the terms *oratorio* and *Abendmusik*, for both developed from the designation of an occasion for musical performance (*oratorio*, in Italy, as a spiritual exercise with music; *Abendmusik* as a concert) to the designation of a sacred dramatic genre.

Some Works for the Abendmusiken

Die Hochzeit des Lammes

Like most Italian oratorios of its period, this work is in two large structural parts. Unlike its Italian counterparts, however, it was intended to be performed over a period of two concerts, according to its title page: the first part from four to five o'clock on the second Sunday of Advent, 1678, and the second at the same time on the following Sunday.[25] Buxtehude's name is the only one on the title page; he is said to have been a poet of some skill, and it has been conjectured that he might have been the author of the libretto.[26] The ample title page of the libretto summarizes much of the work's content: "The Wedding of the Lamb and the Joyful Bringing of the Bride to the Same in the 5 Wise [Virgins] and the Exclusion of the Godless from the Same in the 5 Foolish Virgins, As Given by the Spiritual Bridegroom Christ Himself in Matthew 25. Also, According to the Instruction of Other Places in the Holy Scripture, the Pious [Ones] Heartily Longing for the Future with Their Spiritual Bridegroom [and] for Inner Spiritual Consolation and Sweetest Joy, but the Godless in Fear, Both to God's Honor."[27] Thus the text, based primarily on the parable of the five wise and the five foolish virgins, also draws on other biblical passages. Not mentioned on the title page, however, is the presence of chorale texts and newly composed poetry used from time to time throughout the work. The libretto does not include a narrator but proceeds in dialogue among personages. The dialogue procedure is, of course, that of a drama, and indeed, the work has a plot in

25. The two dates on the title page evidently do not refer to two complete performances of the entire work, for it would seem to have been much too long for a complete performance in one hour; furthermore, the word "vorgestellet" on the title page in the phrase "am 2. und 3. Advents-Sonntage in der Haupt-Kirchen St. Mariae von 4 biss 5 Uhr soll vorgestellet werden" would seem to imply a distribution of the work over the two Sundays. Regarding this use of the verb *vorstellen*, see Geck, "Nochmals," p. 178. Regarding a possible performance in 1680, see Geck, "Authentizität," p. 413, n. 71.

26. Pirro, *Buxtehude*, p. 174.

27. See Figure III-3, p. 88.

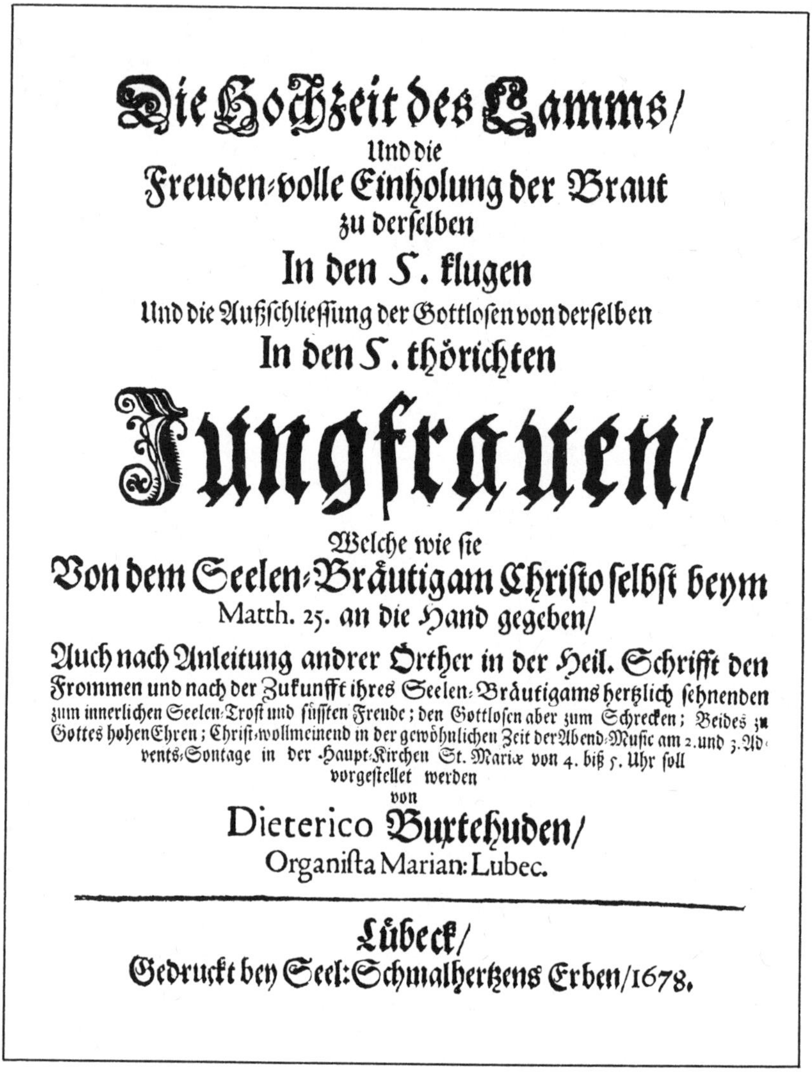

Die Hochzeit des Lamms/
Und die
Freuden-volle Einholung der Braut
zu derselben
In den 5. klugen
Und die Außschliessung der Gottlosen von derselben
In den 5. thörichten
Jungfrauen/
Welche wie sie
Von dem Seelen-Bräutigam Christo selbst beym
Matth. 25. an die Hand gegeben/
Auch nach Anleitung andrer Orther in der Heil. Schrifft den
Frommen und nach der Zukunfft ihres Seelen-Bräutigams hertzlich sehnenden
zum innerlichen Seelen-Trost und süssten Freude; den Gottlosen aber zum Schrecken; Beides zu
Gottes hohen Ehren; Christ-wollmeinend in der gewöhnlichen Zeit der Abend-Music am 2. und 3. Ad-
vents-Sontage in der Haupt-Kirchen St. Mariæ von 4. biß 5. Uhr soll
vorgestellet werden
von
Dieterico Buxtehuden/
Organista Marian: Lubec.

Lübeck/
Gedruckt bey Seel: Schmalhertzens Erben/ 1678.

FIGURE III-3. Title page of the printed libretto of Buxtehude's *Die Hochzeit des Lammes*, performed at the Lübeck *Abendmusiken* on the second and third Sundays of Advent, 1678.
(Courtesy of S/Uu.)

which dramatic conflict arises between the wise and godly personages on the one hand and the foolish and godless ones on the other. Nevertheless the content of most of the libretto is reflective, with much of it—particularly the love lyrics of the bridegroom, Jesus, and his bride, the church—revealing the influence of early pietism.[28] The personages of the libretto are the Angels (SS, S, three unspecified voices, and A), Jesus Christ (B), the Church (chorus, A, S), the Heavenly Chorus, the Foolish Virgins (AA), the Wise Virgins (SS), and a chorus of the Blessed.

Part 1 of the libretto begins with a duet of rejoicing by the Angels; this is followed by Jesus' announcement of his betrothal, quoted from Hos. 2:19–20, "I will betroth thee unto me for ever." (All biblical quotations are identified in the libretto.) The Church then rejoices, and there follows a dialogue between Jesus and the Church, in which the latter is represented first by the chorus, then by alto and soprano soloists. As a part of this dialogue, the Church sings verses of the chorale "Wachet auf, ruft uns die Stimme." After further rejoicing by the Angels and the Heavenly Chorus, the Foolish Virgins express their doubt about the coming of Jesus by quoting from 2 Pet. 3:4, "Where is the promise of his coming?" The Wise Virgins counter with expressions of hope and joy that include quotations from the chorale "Jesu meine Freude"; the Foolish Virgins decide to sleep awhile longer, but the Wise Virgins sing, "I sleep, but my heart watches" (Song of Sol. 5:2). The remainder of part 1 consists of reflections by an Angel, including a long aria of five strophes, and reflections by the Wise Virgins, who sing more verses of the chorale "Wachet auf." The final number is sung by the Angels and the chorus of the Blessed.

Whereas part 1 treats mainly the anticipation of the coming of Christ the bridegroom, part 2 treats his arrival. At the opening of part 2, the Foolish Virgins ask the Wise Virgins for oil for their lamps, but the Wise Virgins refuse. The Angels announce the arrival of Christ, and the latter sings a quotation, with deletions, from Song of Sol. 2:10–14—"Rise up, my love, my fair one, and come, for, lo, the winter is past, the rain is over and gone, the flowers have come forth in the land." The Heavenly Chorus and the Angels respond joyously. There follows a long dialogue between Christ and the Virgins, with interpolations by the Heavenly

28. Regarding early pietism in this work, see Geck, "Authentizität," p. 412.

Chorus, that include verses of the chorales "Wie schön leuchtet der Morgenstern" and "Wachet auf" plus various scriptural quotations. In this dialogue Christ accepts the Wise, but not the Foolish, Virgins; the latter must suffer the flames of hell. After a reflection on the fate of the godless who were rejected by Christ, the work closes with an episode of rejoicing by the Blessed, which includes two choruses followed by a finale-complex consisting of a soprano aria and a chorus. Of structural interest in part 2 are two passages treated as refrains. One of these—a joyful stanza beginning "Wonne, Wonne über Wonne, Gottes Lamm ist unser Sonne," which is sung four times by the chorus at rather widely spaced intervals—provides a general unifying effect; the other is Jesus' response "Ich kenne euch nicht" (Matt. 25:12)—which he sings eight times, once after each of the petitions of the Foolish Virgins as they plead with him for acceptance.

Several musical conclusions may be drawn from this libretto. The composition would seem to have been one of considerable variety, with an attractive mixture of solo, duet, trio, and choral sections. Although only two solo passages in part 1 and one in part 2 are labeled *aria*, numerous others were probably set in aria style: considering the normal procedures of text setting of the time, it would seem safe to assume that the metrical stanzas for soloists were set in aria style and that the prose quotations from the Bible were set in recitative. The chorus enters three times in part 1 and seven times in part 2—it is far more prominent than it characteristically is in the Italian oratorio of the same period. If the chorale texts used in this work were set to chorale melodies, in either simple or elaborated form, the repetition of those melodies, and particularly of the frequently used "Wachet auf," would function as a significant element of unification. Instrumental music plays an important role in this work: part 1 opens and closes with a "sonata" and includes seven ritornellos punctuating the major structural divisions, one "symphonia viole de gambe" for the same purpose, and five ritornellos within the Angel's five-stanza aria. Part 2 opens with a "sonata," includes six ritornellos at major structural divisions (one of them labeled "Ritornello. Tromboni"), and one ritornello within the finale-complex. The libretto also occasionally indicates the number and/or type of instruments that are to accompany the voices—"Soprano con 3 viole"; "3 voci, 7 Instrum."; "2 Sopr. e 5 Violini"; "3 voci & 5 Stromenti"; "2

Soprani & 2 Trombetti"; Basso con 5 violi"; "Soprano con 11 Violinis"; and "3 voci, 5 viole." Thus one could easily imagine an orchestra of twenty to twenty-five members, including those for the basso continuo. If one assume a maximum of about forty performers in all, then the vocal forces would have totaled about fifteen to twenty persons.

Castrum Doloris *and* Templum Honoris

On 5 May 1705 the Hapsburg emperor Leopold I died in Vienna; he was succeeded by his son, Joseph I. The free imperial city of Lübeck paid its respects to the deceased emperor in a religious service with funeral music on 19 July in the Marienkirche. A report on this event written by Buxtehude refers to the deceased emperor as "a great lover of noble music and in that no less than in all other sciences and virtues most highly qualified"; the composer further considers it fitting that an additional musical tribute be paid to the emperor and his successor in the form of an "*extraordinaire* Abend-*Music*" on Thursday and Friday, 2 and 3 December 1705.[29] The works he composed for those occasions and performed on those dates are the *Castrum doloris, dero in Gott ruhenden Römis. Käyserl. auch Königl. Majestäten Leopold dem Ersten* . . . ("Catafalque of His Roman Imperial, also Royal, Majesty Leopold the First, Resting in God . . . ") and the *Templum honoris, dero regierenden Römis. Käyserl. auch Königl. Majestät Joseph dem Ersten* . . . " ("Temple of Honor of His Reigning Roman Imperial, also Royal Majesty, Joseph the First . . . "). It is of interest for the general history of music that the young Johann Sebastian Bach was visiting Lübeck during that season to hear the *Abendmusiken*, and he was undoubtedly present at these performances.

Elaborate preparations were required for these extraordinary concerts, as special scenery was installed in the church for each work. The scenery is described in some detail in the unusually large, folio-sized librettos printed for the occasion. For the *Castrum doloris* the scenery was located near the "newly repaired and completely gilded large organ," according to the description in the libretto—thus in the west end of the church. Four large palm trees supported a beautifully ornamented heaven hung with imperial, royal, and various provincial coats of arms. Numerous angels with

29. Stahl, "Tunder-Buxtehude," p. 67.

CASTRUM DOLORIS,
Dero in GOtt Ruhenden
Römiſ. Käyſerl. auch Königl.
Majeſtäten
LEOPOLD
Dem Erſten/
Zum Glorwürdigſten Andencken/
In der Käyſerl. Freyen Reichs-Stadt
Lübecks
Haupt-Kirchen zu St. Marien/
Zur Zeit gewöhnlicher Abend-Muſic/
Aus Aller-Unterthänigſter Pflicht
Muſicaliſch vorgeſtellet
Von
Diterico Buxtehuden/
Organiſten daſelbſt.

LUBECK/
Gedruckt und zu bekommen bey Seel. Schmalhertzens Wittwe/
Anno 1705.

TEMPLUMHONORIS,

Dero Regierenden

Römiſ. Käyſerl. auch Königl.

Majeſtät

JOSEPH

Dem Erſten/

Zu Unſterblichen Ehren/

In der Käyſerl. Freyen Reichs-Stadt

Lübecks

Haupt-Kirchen zu St. Marien/

Im Jahr Chriſti 1705.

Zu beliebter Zeit bey der gewöhnlichen Abend-Muſic/

Aus Aller-Unterthänigſter Pflicht

Glückwünſchend gewidmet

Von

Diterico Buxtehuden/

Organiſten daſelbſt.

LÜBECK/

Gedruckt und zu bekommen bey Sehl. Schmalhertzens Wittwe.

FIGURE III-4. Title pages of the printed librettos of Buxtehude's two
works, *Castrum doloris* and *Templum honoris*, that
were performed at extraordinary *Abendmusiken* in
1705.
(Reproduced by permission of D-brd/LÜh.)

lanterns were keeping watch over the imperial remains, which were lying in state in a coffin on a catafalque at the center of the scene. The imperial crown was also at the center of the scene, with the royal Hungarian crown on one side and the Bohemian crown on the other and with various additional crowns also displayed. The two musicians' galleries nearest the organ were draped in black. The scenery for the *Templum honoris*, performed on the following day, was constructed at the east end of the church, evidently in front of the altar. According to the libretto, a beautifully ornamented and illuminated temple of honor was surrounded by a strong guard of brave heroes. The virtues and sciences were placed on both sides of the approach to the temple. The doors of the temple were open and inside on the altar was a bust of the new emperor. In the square in front of the temple were Pleasure and Joy with their children, who were carrying various kinds of trophies, garlands and flowers, and palm and laurel branches.

Castrum doloris and *Templum honoris* form the parts of what may be called a large diptych which, if not an oratorio, is closely related to that genre. Like an oratorio this is a large two-part structure with a religious orientation, and it proceeds by recitatives, arias, and choruses, mostly sung by identified personages. It is unlike an oratorio, however, in its reflective character. There is neither plot nor dramatic development but only a very general theme that might be reflected in the English expression "the king is dead, long live the king" or, as it is stated at the end of *Castrum doloris*, "after Leopold, Joseph yet remains . . . after the setting of the sun, no night!" The personages of *Castrum doloris* are mostly allegorical: Report (das Gerüchte), Piety, Justice, Grace, and Sciences are all soloists; the designated choruses are those of Music and of Mourning Women. Some of the solos and choruses do not carry personage identifications. Only one of the personages of *Castrum doloris*, Report, appears again in *Templum honoris*. The latter also includes the personages Germany, Honor, Wisdom, Bravery, and Bliss. In *Templum honoris* personage designations are lacking for all of the choruses and for some of the arias.

The text of *Castrum doloris* begins with a lamentation by the chorus, Music. Report then sings a recitative calling upon Europe to weep for the death of Leopold. The remainder of the work consists of lamentations and eulogies in recitatives, arias, and choruses. Each of the personages Piety, Justice, Grace, and Sciences praises the virtue he represents as reflected in Leopold; Sciences closes his praise with a reference to Leopold's musical excellence. An element of unification in the work is provided by the four choral statements of the chorale "Ach wie nichtig! Ach wie flüchtig." Separated from one another by recitatives and arias, these four choral statements all begin with the same line but continue differently. Another repetition contributing to the work's unity is the twofold statement of a Latin text by the chorus of Mourning Women, the only Latin passages of the libretto. *Castrum doloris* concludes with a chorale, "Nun lasst uns den Leib begraben," performed by "all organs and choruses" and by the audience.

The libretto of *Templum honoris*, like the previous one, begins with a chorus followed by a recitative sung by Report. This time, however, the attitude is one of rejoicing that Joseph has ascended the throne, and this time Report follows his recitative with a two-strophe aria. Texts of rejoicing and praise for the new emperor continue throughout the work, and each of the personages —Germany, Honor, Wisdom, Bravery, and Bliss—contributes his own point of view. *Templum honoris* is less religiously oriented than *Castrum doloris*, and unlike the latter it includes no chorales. The only repetition for structural unity is a choral acclamation in Latin for the emperor (the only Latin of the libretto) that occurs four times; each time it uses the same beginning but a different continuation.

Musical conclusions based on these librettos are similar in many respects to those based on the libretto of *Die Hochzeit des Lammes*. The variety is comparable in the mixture of recitatives, arias, and choruses, except that the chorus is emphasized even more in this pair of works. *Castrum doloris* includes five arias (all strophic), one quartet, eight entrances of the chorus, and two instrumental numbers. Instruments alone play an opening "lamento" and another "lamento" following Sciences' reference to Leopold's musical ability. The latter piece, labeled "Lamento chiaconetta," includes a part for the *campanella*, or glockenspiel. A note at the beginning of the libretto indicates that the trombones, trumpets, and other instruments are muted. *Templum honoris* includes six arias (again, all strophic), nine entrances of the chorus (double choruses at times), and two instrumental numbers plus numerous ritornellos between the strophes of arias. The instrumental numbers are an opening *Intrada* "with two choruses of kettledrums and trumpets" and a concluding passacaglia "with various instruments."

Das Jüngste Gericht

As mentioned on page 86, the only source of the work known as Buxtehude's *Das Jüngste Gericht* is anonymous and untitled, and the attribution and title, both by Willy Maxton, have been questioned by Martin Geck. The latter argues that there is, thus far, insufficient evidence to warrant the assumption that the work is by Buxtehude and was intended for the *Abendmusiken*; Geck also considers Maxton's title to overemphasize the theme of the Last Judgment. Although some elements of Geck's arguments are persuasive, the late Friedrich Blume remained convinced of Buxtehude's authorship, as does Friedhelm Krummacher.[30] The work in question is grouped here with those of Buxtehude because he must still be regarded as one who might have written it and because it relates more closely to the works intended for the Lübeck *Abendmusiken* discussed above than it does to the *historiae, actus musici*, and dialogues of the period. Regardless of who the composer might be, what title one might prefer, or what the function might have been, the work is of primary importance for the history of the German oratorio. In both its libretto and its music it is clearly analogous to the contemporary Italian oratorio, and the term *oratorio* seems to be perfectly appropriate for it. The total duration of the work, about two and one-half hours,[31] makes it by far the longest extant German oratorio of the seventeenth century.

The general theme of the libretto is the conflict between the forces of good and evil and the consequences that await those who treasure worldly rather than spiritual values. The theme of the Last Judgment is secondary. Of the sixty-two vocal numbers in Maxton's edition,[32] the texts of thirty-four are in rhymed verse

30. For the bibliography of the Geck-Maxton controversy, see above, n. 22. For other arguments supporting Buxtehude's authorship, see Krummacher, *Choralbearbeitungen*, pp. 123–25; and Blume, *Syntagma*, p. 894.
31. The estimated duration of the work is based on the actual duration of a partial recording of it, performed by the Heidelberger Kammerorchester and the Mannheimer Bachchor conducted by H. M. Göttsche (Da Camera SM 94006 a–b, recorded in 1965), and on an estimate of the time required to perform the sections omitted in the recording.
32. The present discussion of the work is based on Maxton's edition (Buxtehude [?], *Jüngste*), taking into account his prefatory remarks regarding his omission and reordering

that is "free" (i.e., apparently not based on the Bible, a chorale, or any other preexistent source); twenty-one are biblical quotations or paraphrases; and seven are chorale texts. Both biblical and free texts are set for soloists, ensembles, and choruses, but all the chorale texts are set for choruses.

In its source the work is divided into three acts, each called *actus*.[33] The first act, which functions as a prologue and is about half as long as each of the other two, introduces three allegorical personages—Avarice (der Geitz, S), Frivolity (die Leichtfertigkeit, S), and Pride (die Hoffarth, S)—plus the Divine Voice (die göttliche Stimm, B). The allegorical personages reveal themselves as forces who wish to separate man from God. At first they dispute with one another about which is the most powerful, but soon they join in a trio in which they resolve to unite their arts in order to divide Germany so that nothing good will remain in her. ("Lasst uns unsere Kunst verbrüdern und das teutsche Reich durchgliedern, dass nichts Gutes an ihr bleib.") They continue to emphasize their determination, individually and in trios, for the remainder of the act. The Divine Voice enters three times in the first act; each time he sings a scriptural text, as he characteristically does throughout the oratorio. In his first entrance the Divine Voice counters Frivolity by quoting Eph. 5:6–7, "Let no one lead you astray with empty words"; he then counters Pride in a quotation from Amos 6:8, "I detest the pride of Jacob"; and finally he quotes Isa. 3:16–17, which is a rejection of the haughtiness of the Daughters of Zion. The chorus (SSATB) enters at the beginning and end of the act and once within it. The first chorus is an exhortation for sinful man to fight against the three rebel forces; the second is an exhortation for Germany to awaken, since God's punishment approaches; and the final chorus—the eighth strophe of the chorale "Gott hat das Evangelium gegeben, dass wir werden fromm"—concerns the signs of godlessness presaging the Last Judgment.

---

of some numbers and his addition of some instrumental pieces not in the original. The discussion also takes into account the critical comments regarding Maxton's edition found in Geck, "Authentizität," pp. 408–15, and Geck, "Nochmals." A new scholarly edition of this historically important work is much needed.

33. Maxton discusses the work in terms of its three acts in Maxton, "Abendmusik," but he divides the work into five parts, or *Vorstellungen*, in his edition. For Geck's criticism of the five-part division, see Geck, "Authentizität," pp. 408–9; Geck, "Nochmals," pp. 176–78. For Maxton's defense of the five-part division, see Maxton, "Authentizität," pp. 383–85. For purposes of the present discussion, the three-act division is accepted, since it seems to be closer to the intention conveyed by the source. Act 1 is the same as Maxton's *Vorstellung* 1; act 2 comprises *Vorstellungen* 2 and 3; and act 3 comprises *Vorstellungen* 4 and 5.

The second and third acts are those in which the main dramatic action takes place. The allegorical personages of the first act do not return, but the influence of the vices that they represent is clearly present. The personages of act 1 are an Evil Soul (S), a Good Soul (S), and the Divine Voice.[34] The texts of the Good Soul and the Divine Voice, like those of the choruses, emphasize spiritual values and godliness. The majority of the texts in the second and third acts are of this type, and they serve as a foil to those of the protagonist, the Evil Soul, as he submits to the temptations of avarice, frivolity, and pride in his progress toward his tragic end. At the beginning of the second act, the chorus and the Divine Voice affirm the value of spiritual wealth, after which the Evil Soul—in the aria "Geld! Geld! Sonst ist nichtes in der Welt"— extolls money as the only thing of value. After more expressions of godliness by the Good Soul, the Divine Voice, and the chorus, the Evil Soul enters a second time. He is now materially wealthy and tired from his efforts yet still unsatisfied and driven by his greed to continue his feverish pursuit of money. After contrasting expressions of spiritual joy by the Good Soul and the chorus, the Evil Soul enters again, this time with a quotation from the parable of a rich man, Luke 12:19: "Soul, thou hast many good things laid up for many years; take thy ease, eat, drink, be merry." To this the Divine Voice replies with the very next verse, Luke 12:20: "Thou fool this night do they demand thy soul of thee." The thought of death evokes an anguished lament from the Evil Soul—"O weh, O Wort das eh tödtet als der Todt"—and a comment from the chorus—"O Todt, wie bitter bistu"; the latter is from the apocryphal Ecclus. (Jesus Sirach) 41:1. The second act ends happily, with the Good Soul singing an aria of joyful contemplation of heaven and the final chorus singing a chorale—"Hertzlich Lieb hab ich dich, o Herr."

The third act brings the work to its dramatic climax. The act opens with a chorus contrasting the world of Satan's slaves with that of God's children; the chorus is followed by two solos with scriptural texts sung by the Divine Voice (Isa. 55:1–2) and the Good Soul (Ps. 73:28). The Evil Soul then enters with a drinking

34. The personage labeled in the source as the Divine Voice in act 1 is not so labeled in acts 2 and 3, but its labelling throughout Maxton's edition seems reasonable. The designations "Good Soul" and "Evil Soul" are added by Maxton to the solo parts of the first and second sopranos, respectively. These personages are not labeled in the source, but Maxton's labels seem appropriate and are accepted here.

song—"O frölige Zeit, wenn Krüge und Gläser zum Trinken uns winken"—demonstrating his capitulation to the temptations of frivolity. The Divine Voice counters with a quotation from Amos 6:3–7 about the evils of wantnoness and luxury, but the Evil Soul sings another aria—"Ich kann nicht mehr, gantz voll und toll"—in which he is shown to be completely drunk. The Good Soul and the Divine Voice comment on drunkenness, and finally the chorus sings two stanzas from "Wie schön leuchtet der Morgenstern" to close what would appear to be a subdivision of the third act.[35] In the next and final section of the act, the Evil Soul tries to dispel thoughts of death in a dance song—"Weg Sterben, weg traurige Todesgedanken"—but this song is suddenly interrupted by the Divine Voice, saying, "Now, you whoremonger, now shall you perish" ("Jetzo, ihr Huhrer, itzt sollt ihr vergehn!"). The chorus, this time for three bass parts, addresses the Evil Soul and announces that the horrible abyss now demands him. The Evil Soul's last two numbers are laments, "O schreckliches Schrecken" and "O der grossen Bangigkeit," both of which are followed by solo and choral commentaries that increase the emotional intensity of the situation and emphasize the moral point, the drastic consequences of an evil life. The remainder of the act consists of a choral-solo complex stressing the consequences of a good life; it begins with the seventh strophe of the chorale "Wie schön leuchtet der Morgenstern"; the complex continues with a brief solo by the Divine Voice (John 14:3), a choral commentary nearly as brief, and a closing chorale, "Mit Fried und Freud ich fahr dahin."

The musical settings of the biblical texts are always in recitative or arioso style. Since virtually all the texts of the Divine Voice are biblical, that personage sings almost entirely in those styles; the Good and Evil Souls sing in recitative or arioso style only in the very few numbers in which their texts are biblical. All the arias are settings of original texts in rhymed verse, and the majority of the arias are strophic. The arias are normally accompanied by basso continuo alone, with a ritornello for violins entering at the end of each strophe, but a few are accompanied throughout by violins. Of special interest among the arias are those in the third act that reveal the final stages in the progress of the Evil Soul. His

35. This chorale concludes what Maxton calls the fourth *Vorstellung*. Geck considers the third act to be in two sections, with a brief pause possibly intended after this chorale. (Geck, "Nochmals," pp. 177–78.)

progress from drinking to drunkenness is clearly depicted in two arias, illustrated in Examples III–1a and b; the former is a gay, dancelike song characteristic of its genre, and the latter has a faltering rhythmic style and a minimum of sustained notes in the

EXAMPLE III-1. *Das Jüngste Gericht* (Buxtehude [?], *Jüngste*, pp. 118, 122–23).

Example a:

O happy time, when jugs and glasses beckon us to drink . . .

Example b:

I'm all in, dead drunk . . .

vocal line to depict the instability of the toper, who is indeed "gantz voll und toll." The last two numbers of the Evil Soul, the laments illustrated in Examples III–2a and b, show the last stage in his development. The first is a lyrical expression in minor of the Evil Soul's horror at witnessing the disappearance of his worldly

EXAMPLE III-2. *Das Jüngste Gericht* (Buxtehude [?], *Jüngste*, pp. 153, 163).

Example a:

Oh, horrible horror! Oh, woe! Now all worldly pleasure vanishes like snow, . . .

Example b:

Oh, the great dread, my heart breaks into a thousand pieces . . .

pleasures, and the second, also in minor, is the deeper lamentation of the two; it begins with gasping rests and closes with a rhythmic-melodic expression of his breaking heart (the rhetorical repetition of "zerbricht" and the increased rhythmic activity on "in tausend Stücken). Nearly all the choruses in the oratorio are for five voices (SSATB), although some are for three (ATB, BBB, TBB). The choruses tend to be in simple chordal texture with some polyphonic elaboration, usually toward the end. The last chorus is the only one that is polyphonically elaborate throughout. Several of the choruses are based on chorale tunes, but the only chorale that is repeated is "Wie schön leuchtet der Morgenstern," which appears three times. In addition to the continuo, the principal stringed instruments specified are two violins. In the course of the work, these play several "sonatas" plus brief interludes, ritornellos, and accompaniments for some of the vocal numbers. Two violas are also added for the large choruses; the only wind instruments specified are trombones, associated with the notion of hell at the end of the chorus of three basses.

PART II

Protestant Germany:
The Early Eighteenth-Century
Oratorio

CHAPTER IV

Terminology, Social Contexts, Composers, Poets

ʃ◍*Terminology*

It was in the first decade of the eighteenth century that the term *oratorio*, or *Oratorium*, began to be used in print in Protestant Germany to refer to German works.[1] In 1704 the poet Christian Friedrich Hunold (pseudonym, Menantes, 1681–1721) used the term on the title page of the printed libretto of his Passion oratorio, which was set to music by Reinhard Keiser (1674–1739): *Der blutige und sterbende Jesus, wie selbiger in einem Oratorio musikalisch gesetzet, und in der stillen Woche, Montags und Mittwochs, zur Vesperzeit aufgefüret worden durch Reinhard Keiser* ("The Bloody and Dying Jesus, As the Same [Is] Set Musically in an Oratorio, and Performed in Holy Week on Monday and Wednesday at Vesper Time, by Reinhard Keiser"). Two years later, when Hunold published his oratorio text in a collection of his poems, he made clear the Italian influence by describing the work as being "in verses throughout, and without the Evangelist, just like the Italian so-called *Oratorien*."[2] By the 1720s the term *Oratorium* had become a common designation of the genre in Germany, and by the 1730s it had begun to be defined in German writings about music. Johann Adolph Scheibe (1708–76), in his manuscript trea-

---

1. In Germany the Italian form, *oratorio*, was less often used than the Latin, *Oratorium*. The plural of the latter was formed either by using the Latin *Oratoria* or by adding a German plural ending, resulting in the form *Oratorien*. The forms *Oratorium* and *Oratorien* are retained in modern German. For an earlier MS reference to a German Protestant work as an *Oratorium*, see chapter 1, n. 34.

2. Translated from Hunold's *Theatralische, galante und geistliche Gedichte* (Hamburg, 1706), p. 6, as quoted in E. Reimer, "Oratorium," in *HMT*, p. 3.

tise *Compendium musices theoretico-practicum* (probably written between 1728 and 1736), states that oratorios are "all long pieces of which the poetic organization is *dramatic,* to which Passion Music does not belong."[3] In *Der vollkommene Capellmeister* (Hamburg, 1739), by Johann Mattheson (1681–1764), the author states that "an *Oratorium* is thus none other than a sung poem [*Sing-Gedicht*] which presents a certain action or virtuous event in a dramatic manner" and that "an *Oratorium* is almost a spiritual opera."[4] Mattheson briefly mentions his own oratorios in his *Grundlage einer Ehren-Pforte* (Hamburg, 1740), and in doing so he cautions his reader not to think of an oratorio as "a usual church piece"; rather, it is "dramatically composed and of considerable length, like a complete *Actus.* Scores [comprise] 20, 30, and more sheets of paper."[5] Thus in Germany, as in Italy, the oratorio was generally considered to be a sacred dramatic work of considerable length with a poetic text. Most German works of the first half of the eighteenth century that bear the genre designation *Oratorium* fit that description.

A conception of the oratorio that differed from the one just described and was less widely held is the one that includes works with texts combining prose and poetry, such as oratorio Passions or any other *historiae* with poetic interpolations. Such works had been cultivated in Germany since the mid-seventeenth century, as pointed out above, but they had not been previously called oratorios. In the passage from Scheibe's *Compendium* quoted above, the author excludes the Passion from the category of the oratorio, but in his periodical, *Der critische Musicus,* he reverses his position; in the issue of 26 November 1737, he states that an oratorio is "either poetic only, or prosaic and poetic at the same time."[6] Yet he insists that the essential aspect of the oratorio is its dramatic nature. In prosaic-poetic works, such as those based on the stories

3. Translated from Scheibe, *Compendium,* p. 79. According to P. Benary—the editor of Scheibe, *Compendium*—Scheibe's own manuscript reads "wozu die Passions *Music* nicht gehöret," and the copy made by Graupner in 1736 reads "wozu die Passions *Music* mit gehört." (Scheibe, *Compendium,* p. 79, n. 60.) E. Reimer, "Oratorium," in *HMT,* p. 3, prefers Graupner's version and evidently considers Scheibe's manuscript to be in error; I accept Scheibe's version as it stands in his manuscript, for I assume it to reflect an opinion that Scheibe later revised.

4. Translated from Mattheson, *Capellmeister,* p. 220–21; see also Mattheson, "*Capellmeister*"-Eng., p. 709, 711.

5. Translated from Mattheson, *Ehren-Pforte,* p. 204.

6. Translated from Scheibe, *Critische,* 1:157.

of the Passion or the Resurrection, he says, the narration of the Evangelist does not make the work an epic, for the Evangelist is one of the dramatis personae: "in connecting the action, [he] is a special personage."[7] By supporting the view that an oratorio is always an essentially dramatic work, Scheibe rejects the notion of "a certain great critic," evidently Erdmann Neumeister (1671–1756), who applies the term *Oratorium* to nondramatic works with prosaic-poetic texts composed of biblical quotations, arias, and chorales.[8] Scheibe's rejection of Neumeister's use of the term is easily understood, for Neumeister was virtually alone in his usage.

Of further terminological interest is Mattheson's use of the term *secular oratorio*, apparently for the first time in the history of music. In *Der vollkommene Capellmeister* he states that "there are many sorts of secular oratorios which belong more to the chamber style than to the dramatic style of writing and utilize in composition those rules which have been given above on the cantatas."[9] Mattheson appears to be the only writer of the time who mentions the secular oratorio. He is evidently stating a purely theoretical possibility of extending of the term *oratorio* to the secular sphere, for no secular works from the Baroque period are known to have been designated by their composers as oratorios.

In the following treatment of the German oratorio, primary emphasis is placed on the composition with a purely poetic text, the type most commonly called an oratorio at the time and the type to which the term *oratorio* refers unless otherwise indicated. Less emphasis is placed on the prosaic-poetic "oratorio," of which the main type is the oratorio Passion.

Social Contexts, Composers, Poets

Hamburg

It is not surprising that in the early eighteenth century the most important center for the cultivation of the German oratorio was Hamburg. This city had already established itself as a center of

7. Translated, ibid., 1:159.
8. Ibid., 1:157. For Neumeister's definition of the term *oratorio*, see [Neumeister-Hunold], *Allerneueste*, p. 275.
9. Translated from Mattheson, *Capellmeister*, p. 221; see also Mattheson, "*Capellmeister*"-Eng., p. 711.

German opera and had developed a taste for sacred dramatic music, as shown by the emphasis on biblical opera. Although oratoriolike works were no doubt performed occasionally in the seventeenth century at concerts of Hamburg's Collegium musicum, the continuous history of the German oratorio in this city begins in 1704 with the performance of Hunold and Keiser's Passion oratorio, *Der blutige und sterbende Jesus*, mentioned above. In the first phase of that history, the Passion oratorio with a purely poetic text met with considerable opposition from the clergy and the city fathers; this was not the case, however, with the oratorio Passions (with biblical prose texts and interpolated poetry), which were regularly performed in Hamburg's churches during Holy Week.[10] The Hunold-Keiser Passion oratorio was performed in the Hamburg cathedral on Monday and Wednesday of Holy Week at vesper time, but it was severely criticized by the pastor for being too theatrical and particularly for having omitted all the Evangelist's narrative passages.[11] The work was repeated in the same year at a public performance that evoked further criticism, as indicated in a handwritten note on a copy of the printed libretto in the Hamburg city archive: "This writing [the libretto] has been deposited here [in the archive] because it is something new that such an elaborate performance be held in a poorhouse, and indeed on a stage prepared for it; wherefore many have expressed their unhappiness and even were scandalized. To enter one had to have a ticket (for which one paid 5 *Schilling*) or one had to pay 5 *Schilling*; the libretto also cost 5 *Schilling*."[12] Thus, certain of the Hamburg citizenry appear to have been scandalized by a combination of circumstances: the innovation of an elaborate performance of a devotional work, to which admission was charged, on a stage erected in a poorhouse. (In this connection it is noteworthy that as as late as 1728 Mattheson questioned the practice of performing sacred music in public to make money.)[13] When the Hunold-Keiser Passion oratorio was performed again in 1705, legal action was requested to prevent further attempts to perform such music,

10. For a list of the Passions performed in Hamburg up to 1721, see Hörner, *Telemann*, p. 37.

11. Winterfeld, *Kirchengesang*, 3:62.

12. Translated from Hörner, *Telemann*, p. 27.

13. Mattheson, *Patriot*, p. 128. Frederichs argues that this performance in the poorhouse was staged in an operatic manner (Frederichs, *Brockespassionen*, pp. 73–74); its staging would be even further reason for the scandal.

as may be seen in the following quotation from the official complaint:

The Honorable Magistrate, through the Lord Deputies, is hereby petitioned: Since a so-called *Oratorium* was recently presented in the penitentiary in which the author not only uses offensive expressions (as when he presumes, in the preface, to represent the suffering of Christ more emphatically than the Holy Evangelist, [and] subsequently compares the tears of Peter to baptismal water), but also he engenders hope for similar pageants, unusual with us, on high feast days. On the contrary, however, our church regulation as well as the printed city ordinance, articles 35 and 72, do not acknowledge such unsanctioned change in the church service. [It is petitioned] that the Honorable Senate should emphatically prevent such attempts in which, because of many circumstances, both listeners and viewers are more annoyed than edified.[14]

Here the objections are clearly set forth: the presumption of the poet, the unorthodox simile, the threat of unsanctioned change in church services on high feast days, and the general effect of irritation rather than edification. Despite these objections, however, the same libretto was reprinted five years later, in 1710, for another performance, which was held in the refectory of the cathedral,[15] the same hall that had been used in the seventeenth century for the Collegium musicum.

Of particular interest regarding the attitude of the Hamburg city fathers toward the Passion oratorio is their adverse reaction to a work composed by the organist Georg Bronner (1667–1720) intended for performance in church in 1710. Bronner's work was entitled *Geistliches Oratorium oder Der gottliebenden Seelen Wallfahrt zum Kreuz und Grabe Christi* ("Spiritual Oratorio, or the Pilgrimage of the God-Loving Soul to the Cross and Grave of Christ").[16] Only three days before the scheduled performance, after the libretto had been printed and the work was undoubtedly in rehearsal, the Hamburg senate heard of it and decided not to permit the performance. The senate's objections, recorded in a document dated 14 April 1710, constitute an interesting mixture of aesthetic and religious arguments and shed additional light on the official point of view with regard to the Passion oratorio. The

14. Translated from Hörner, *Telemann*, p. 27.
15. Ibid., pp. 27–28.
16. Ibid., p. 32.

following is a quotation from the introduction, most of the third and fourth numbered paragraphs, and the conclusion of the document:

The organist at the local affiliated and secondary church of the Holy Spirit, George Bronner, dares without authorization to advertise to the public a so-called *Oratorium* and wishes to perform the same in this Holy Week, on the next April 17, Maundy Thursday, here in the church of the Holy Spirit.

. . . .

3. The work itself is so constituted, that it has flowed much more from the spirit of opera than from God's Word, for the Holy Spirit does not know such a method, and we find it nowhere in the revealed divine words that one should treat the sacred story in such a theatrical manner. Paul says that he came not to his listeners with lofty words and lofty wisdom to preach the divine sermon; he did not teach with words which can teach human wisdom but with words which the Holy Spirit teaches. . . .

4. No edification is to be hoped therefrom except that the ears be somewhat titillated by the music. Insofar as, except for the few known versicles from our usual chorales, the rest is very sterile and in superfluous inventions outside, indeed against, God's Word. Useless lamentations, weak exclamations, diffuse conceptions without spirit and power, as continue almost throughout, fail, for the most part, [to achieve] the right purpose of the holy reflection on the Passion. In the same manner, our blessed Lüthers, when he discusses the edifying contemplation of the suffering of Jesus, emphatically indicates that the right and proper goal of the reflection on the Passion must be aimed at the awakening of true penitence, of the holy power of faith, and of the encouragement of a life pleasing to God. The other things, such as violent invectives and exclamations against Pilate, Judas, the Jews (especially when entire sections are filled with them) can by no means be tolerated. . . .

The College [of clergy] will emphatically reprimand the aforesaid organist at the church of the Holy Spirit for his indiscretion and with deserving penalty have him sternly ordered to abandon his announced purpose to perform an *Oratorium*.[17]

Thus judging the oratorio not to fulfill the traditional religious function of Passion music, the senate reacted against the theatricality of Bronner's oratorio and what it considered the work's weak text.

Despite official opposition to Passion oratorios, they continued

17. Translated, ibid., pp. 32–33.

to be performed occasionally and to grow in popularity. A work entitled *Tränen unter dem Kreuze Jesu* ("Tears Under the Cross of Jesus"), with a libretto by Johann Ulrich von König (1688–1744) and music by Reinhard Keiser, was performed on Monday, Tuesday, and Wednesday at vesper time during Holy Week of 1711 in the refectory of the cathedral.[18] Not long thereafter one of Hamburg's most distinguished citizens, Barthold Heinrich Brockes (1680–1747), completed his text for what was to be the most popular Passion oratorio of its time, *Der für die Sünde der Welt gemarterte und sterbende Jesus aus den vier Evangelisten . . . in gebundener Rede vorgestellt* ("Jesus, Martyred and Dying for the Sins of the World, Presented in Verse According to the Four Evangelists"). The text was set to music by Reinhard Keiser and was first performed in 1712 in Brockes's home. The poet describes the event in his autobiography: "After I finished the Passion oratorio, I had it very solemnly performed in my house; as [the performance] was something unusual, not only did the entire foreign nobility gather there, all the ministers and residents with their ladies, but also the major part of the most eminent citizens of Hamburg, so that over 500 persons were present, which gave me no little pleasure, especially since all, praise God! went off in the best order, without any confusion and to the pleasure of all listeners."[19] Considering the opposition to Passion oratorios in the past, no doubt by some of the same distinguished persons who were present at Brockes's house, it is easy to understand his relief that the event "went off in the best order." The performance of this work with a text by one of Hamburg's leading citizens in his own home no doubt did much to promote the acceptability of the Passion oratorio. The Brockes Passion in Keiser's setting was performed again in 1713,[20] and within a few years the text was set to music by three more leading composers—Georg Philipp Telemann (1681–1767) in 1716, Handel in either 1715 or 1716, and Mattheson in 1718.[21] During the fourteen years that separated the

18. Ibid., p. 28.

19. Translated from Chrysander, *Händel*, 1:430–31.

20. Ibid., p. 431.

21. Frederichs, *Brockespassionen* is a study of the Brockes libretto and of these four settings; Frederichs discusses the possible dates of Handel's setting on p. 43. Other composers who set Brockes's Passion text are Johann Friedrich Fasch (1723), Gottfried Heinrich Stölzel (1725), Paul Steiniger, Johann Balthasar, Christian Freislich (ca. 1750), and Jacob Schubach (ca. 1750). J. S. Bach set parts of the text in his Passion according to St. John.

FIGURE IV-1. Barthold Heinrich Brockes (1680–1747). After an anonymous engraving.
(Reproduced by permission of Bärenreiter Bild-Archiv, Kassel.)

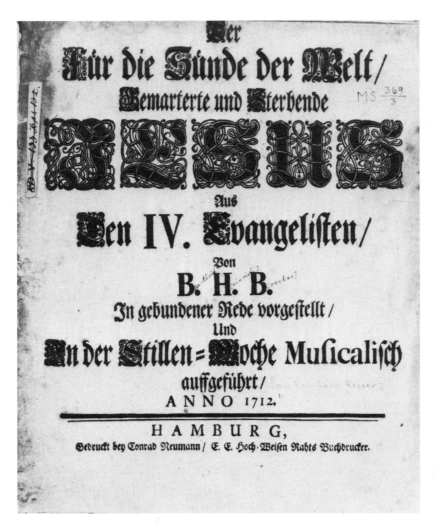

FIGURE IV-2. Title page of the printed libretto used for the first perfor-
mance of the Brockes Passion in a setting by Reinhard
Keiser.
(Reproduced by permission of D-brd/Hs: MS 369/3.)

Hunold-Keiser and the Brockes-Mattheson Passions, the official
attitude toward the Passion oratorio in Hamburg changed remarkably, for Mattheson states in his autobiography that on Palm
Sunday of 1718 he performed his Brockes Passion in the cathedral

"with the approval of many thousands of listeners."[22] In the following year he performed at least three, and possibly all four, of the aforementioned settings of the Brockes Passion.[23] Despite the greater degree of acceptance of the Passion oratorio and its occasional performance in church, it more often formed a part of a public concert; the oratorio Passion retained its position in the church as the principal type of Passion music for Holy Week.

Little is known of oratorios on subjects other than the Passion in Hamburg until 1715, and they seem not to have been performed in churches before then. An early performance of what appears to have been two oratoriolike works on other subjects is that of Keiser's *Der Dialogus von der Geburt Christi* and *Der sterbende Saul* ("The Dialogue of the Birth of Christ" and "The Dying Saul"), which took place on 29 December 1707 at a hall in the Niedere Baum-Haus,[24] a guest house, popular with foreign travelers, that was located at the harbor. The year 1715 marks a significant change in the history of the oratorio in Hamburg, for in that year Mattheson began to direct the music in the cathedral and to introduce oratorios there. His influence was of particular importance, for in the thirteen years that he directed the cathedral's music (1715–28) he composed for performance there at least twenty-five large-scale works that could be termed oratorios, either with prosaic-poetic or entirely poetic texts but mostly of the latter type.[25] Only three of the oratorios were based on the Passion story; most of the remaining ones were based on the themes of the other principal feast days of the church year or on other biblical stories. Mattheson wrote some of his own oratorio texts, but the poets of the majority of the texts that he set are unknown. Those who are known are Brockes and König, Gustav Willhelm Hero,

22. Translated from Mattheson, *Ehren-Pforte*, p. 204.

23. According to the preface of the printed libretto of 1719 (the preface printed in Deutsch, *Handel*, pp. 88–89), that printing appears to have been prepared for a performance only of Handel's and Telemann's settings; Mattheson's setting had been performed twice earlier that year, according to the same preface. Although the preface mentions all four settings, it is not clear whether Keiser's setting was performed in 1719, as assumed in Chrysander, *Händel*, 1:449. H. Becker found newspaper announcements of 1719 only for performances of the Mattheson, Handel, and Telemann settings. (Becker, "Tagespresse," p. 36.)

24. Krüger, *Hamburg*, pp. 260–61.

25. In Cannon, *Mattheson*, p. 60, Mattheson is said to have composed thirty-two oratorios in these thirteen years. From Cannon's descriptions, pp. 161–88, however, it would appear that only about twenty-five could be termed oratorios without qualification. The manuscripts of all of these works were destroyed in World War II.

FIGURE IV-3. The Baum-Haus in Hamburg, a guest house that was the location of concerts, including performances of oratorios by Reinhard Keiser and Georg Philipp Telemann, in the early eighteenth century. After an oil painting by G. V. Ruths.
(Reproduced by permission of the Hamburger Kunsthalle and Ralph Kleinhempel.)

FIGURE IV-4. Johann Mattheson (1681–1764). Aquatint by
Johann Jacob Haid, after a painting by Johann
Solomon Wahl.
(Reprinted from Brucker, *Bilder-sal*, vol. 1, pt. 5, by per-
mission of the Rare Book Department, US/PHf.)

H. D. Hoesst, Erdmann Neumeister, Christian Heinrich Postel (1658–1705), Tobias Heinrich Schubert, Christian Friedrich Weichmann (d. 1769), Christoph Gottlieb Wend (d. 1745), and a poet who signed himself only as Glauche.[26] Postel is the author of the text of Mattheson's oratorio, *Das Lied des Lammes* (1723), which is an oratorio Passion and is the same text that Handel is said to have set in 1704 as his St. John Passion.[27]

Mattheson was successful not only in introducing oratorios into the cathedral's music but also in strikingly modifying one aspect of performance practice there. Never before had women been permitted to sing either as choir members or soloists in Hamburg's churches, but for Mattheson's Christmas composition of 1715, his first large work for the cathedral, he employed as soloists three women who were singers at the Hamburg opera.[28] In the following year, for his oratorio *Chera, oder Die leidtragende und getröstete Wittwe zu Nain* ("Chera, or The Suffering and Confident Widow of Nain"), Mattheson again employed the opera singers, among whom was the leading soprano of the Hamburg opera and the wife of Reinhard Keiser.[29] Many years later, commenting in *Der vollkommene Capellmeister* on the clerical opposition to the introduction of women into the formal music of the cathedral, Mattheson stated that "at first it was demanded that I place them bodily so that no one would get to see them; eventually, however, they could not hear and see enough."[30] Mattheson apparently continued to employ opera singers of both sexes for the solo roles of his oratorios performed at the cathedral.[31]

An essentially secular context in which oratorios were performed was that of the annual festivities of the *Bürgerkapitäne*, attended by the officers of Hamburg's city militia and their invited guests.[32] These events took place in the Drillhaus, a large building

26. For information regarding which oratorios they wrote and for brief biographical notes about some of them, see Cannon, *Mattheson*, pp. 161–88 passim.

27. The MS of Mattheson's work is extant only in a photocopy; the work has been edited by B. Cannon in *ColM*, ser. 2, vol. 3. The setting attributed to Handel is printed in Handel, *Ausgabe*, ser. 1, vol. 2. For a survey of the literature about the authenticity of this attribution, see Braun, "Echtheit," pp. 61–63; Harald Kümmerling attributes the work to Georg Böhm (cf. Walter, *Lüneburg*, p. 159, n. 530).

28. Cannon, *Mattheson*, p. 50.

29. Ibid., pp. 50, 163.

30. Translated from Mattheson, *Capellmeister*, p. 482; see also Mattheson, "*Capellmeister*"-Eng., p. 1443.

31. Cannon, *Mattheson*, p. 51.

32. For information on these festivities, see Sittard, *Hamburg*, pp. 61–63; Menke, *Telemann*, pp. 110–12; and Maertens, "Kapitänsmusiken."

constructed in the seventeenth century for the drills and exercises of the militia. The earliest such festivity at which an oratorio is known to have been performed took place in 1719 at the celebration of the one hundredth anniversary of the *Bürgerkapitäne*. An extant engraving of this event shows that the interior of the Drillhaus was elaborately decorated and that on a balcony in one corner were seated about forty musicians. According to a contemporary account,[33] the music was directed by Matthäus Christoph Wideburg (formerly the Kapellmeister at Gera), and the text of the oratorio was written by Michael Richey, a professor at the Hamburg Gymnasium. The singers included women and castrati. At a passage in the oratorio when "the Ambrosian hymn" was heard, nine cannon were fired. After the oratorio (and presumably after a banquet)[34] a serenata was performed, and it was introduced by the firing of nine more cannon. Richey was also the author of the text of the serenata, entitled *Mars und Irene*. Soon after Telemann entered the service of the city of Hamburg (1721), he became the composer of the annual *Kapitänsmusik*, which always consisted of one sacred and one secular work, an oratorio and a serenata. Telemann is known to have composed forty *Kapitänsmusiken* in the period 1723–63.[35] Among the librettists of his *Kapitänsmusiken* are Richey; two other professors at Hamburg's educational institutions, Heinrich Gottlieb Schellhaffer and Johann Hübner (1668–1731); three other Hamburg poets—Johann Georg Hamann (1697–1733), Johann Matthias Dreyer (1717–68), and Wilhelm Adolf Paulli (1719–72); and Telemann himself.[36]

During the period in which Telemann dominated the musical scene in Hamburg, from 1721 until his death in 1767, public concerts became a regular feature of the city's musical life, and oratorios formed a significant part of the concert repertory.[37] Shortly after arriving in Hamburg, Telemann began to direct public concerts, to which admission was charged, in the Drillhaus. This was to remain his principal concert hall until 1761, when a new one, the Concertsaal auf dem Kamp, was opened. Telemann

---

33. Quoted and paraphrased in Sittard, *Hamburg*, pp. 61–62. For a reprint of the engraving of the festivity, see *MGG*, vol. 5, pl. 59.

34. Hörner, *Telemann*, p. 39, n. 64.

35. Maertens, "Kapitänsmusiken," pp. 336–37.

36. Ibid., p. 339.

37. For information on Hamburg's concert life in this period, see Sittard, *Hamburg*, pp. 60–81; Menke, *Telemann*, Anhang A, "Hamburger Konzertchronik von 1721 bis 1767"; and Becker, "Tagespresse."

GEORGIVS PHILIPPVS TELEMANN.

FIGURE IV-5. Georg Philipp Telemann (1681–1767). Mezzotint by Valentin Daniel Preissler, after a painting by Ludwig Michael Schneider.

(Reproduced by permission of D-ddr/Bds.)

also formed a Collegium musicum, which offered a subscription-paid concert series held in his home.[38] By 1724, when the Collegium musicum concerts had evidently outgrown the available space in his home, he moved the series to the Drillhaus.[39] Concerts were given on various days of the week, except Sunday, usually at four or five o'clock in the afternoon. Oratorios were performed in public concerts a number of times each year: a Passion oratorio, often one of the Brockes Passions, was normally given several performances during Holy Week, and oratorios were programmed as a matter of course at other times as well. Oratorios and other large works that were first performed for select audiences on special occasions were usually repeated in public concerts. These occasional works included the annual *Kapitäns-musiken* and compositions for funeral and memorial services, weddings, special state events, dedications of buildings, ceremonies at the Gymnasium, and special events in the poorhouse and the penitentiary. After 1728, when Mattheson resigned his directorship of music in the cathedral, oratorios seem to have been infrequently performed in churches. An important exception, however, is Telemann's extremely popular Passion oratorio *Das selige Erwägen des Leidens und Sterbens Jesu Christi* ("The Blessed Contemplation of the Suffering and Dying of Jesus Christ"), which was performed annually at the Michaeliskirche.[40] Among Telemann's librettists for his Hamburg oratorios, other than the librettists listed above for the *Kapitänsmusiken*, are Christian Wilhelm Alers (1737–1806), Karl Wilhelm Ramler (1725–98), and Friedrich Wilhelm Zachariä (1726–77).

Other Centers

At Lübeck the concert series at the Marienkirche known as the *Abendmusiken* continued to thrive in the eighteenth century.[41] After Buxtehude's death in 1707, he was succeeded as the Marienkirche organist by Johann Christian Schieferdecker (or Schiefferdecker, 1679–1732), who in turn was succeeded in 1732 by Johann Paul Kunzen (or Kuntzen, 1696–1757). Both Schieferdecker

38. Menke, *Telemann*, Anhang A, p. 5.
39. Ibid., p. 6.
40. Ibid., p. 42.
41. For information about the Lübeck *Abendmusiken* in the eighteenth century, see Stahl, "Abendmusiken," pp. 22–64.

and Kunzen composed new music virtually every year for the famous *Abendmusiken* series, which was presented on the same five Sundays before Christmas as it had been under Buxtehude; both men consistently set oratorio texts, which were so designated (by the term *oratorio* or *Oratorium*) on the title pages of the printed librettos; and the oratorios of both were always in five structural parts, with one part performed at each of the five concerts. The librettists' names are not usually given in *Abendmusiken* librettos, but four whose names are either on the title pages or at the conclusions of the forewords are Andreas Lange, Johann Friedrich von Holten, Michael Christoph Brandenburg, and Christian August Förtsch.[42] The *Abendmusiken*, financially supported primarily by contributions from Lübeck's leading citizens, continued to be free to the public. An additional source of income was added in 1752, when Kunzen began to charge admission to the dress rehearsals, which took place at four o'clock on the Friday afternoons preceding the Sunday performances.[43] At first the dress rehearsals were held in a rehearsal room provided by the Marienkirche for its organist, but this room could accommodate only a small audience. In 1755 Kunzen received permission to hold the dress rehearsals in the Börse, the large stock exchange hall near the Marienkirche, and he instituted a system of advance ticket sales. Thus, in effect, he established an informal Friday-afternoon concert series. It was informal, not only because the performance was a dress rehearsal, but also because the hall lacked chairs: whoever did not wish to stand either brought a chair or arranged in advance for one to be brought for him.

The earliest oratorio heard in Frankfurt was Telemann's Brockes Passion, performed on 2 and 3 April 1716 in the city's principal church, the Barfüsserkirche, where Telemann was the Kapellmeister.[44] The performance had originally been scheduled to be given in the poorhouse, with the proceeds used to assist the poor. The place of performance was changed, however, according to the records of the mayor, "since the poorhouse does not offer enough space, and the landgrave of Hesse-Darmstadt will appear at the performance"; the same records also mention that "an

42. For brief biographical information about each of these librettists, see ibid., pp. 45–47.
43. Ibid., pp. 30–31.
44. Valentin, *Frankfurt*, p. 231. Telemann's Brockes Passion printed in Telemann, *Passionsoratorium*.

armchair hung with black velvet" was to be provided for the landgrave.[45] Other dignitaries who attended were the princes of Nassau-Idstein, of Usingen, and of Löwenstein.[46] The work was performed by the instrumentalists and singers of the Darmstadt court—excellent musicians who often performed in Frankfurt;[47] it was directed by the accomplished musical amateur Heinrich Remigius Barthels, a Frankfurt banker and patron of music.[48] Telemann describes the event in his autobiography written years later: "[The Passion] was performed on several extraordinary days of the week in the principal church, elaborately and excellently decorated, in the presence of various great gentlemen and an immense crowd of listeners, for the benefit of the orphanage. It is hereby noted, as something curious, that the church doors were manned by guards who let no one in who did not appear with a printed copy of the Passion (a good device which serves to sell the books, particularly for a pious cause), and that the highest members of the Reverend Ministry were seated at the altar in their pontifical vestments."[49] Thus the clergy and aristocracy of Frankfurt, in striking contrast to those of Hamburg, immediately accepted and strongly supported the Passion oratorio.

Soon after Telemann had assumed the duties of the director of music for the city of Frankfurt in 1712, he also became secretary of the city's Frauenstein Society. Telemann revived the society's defunct Collegium musicum, which had originated in the seventeenth century,[50] and he introduced weekly concerts for the society, in which musicians from Darmstadt often performed.[51] These concerts were important forerunners of Frankfurt's public concert life. It was for this Collegium musicum that Telemann composed his five "David" oratorios, as the title page of the printed libretto (1718) indicates: *Der königliche Prophete David, als ein Fürbild unseres Heylandes Jesu, in fünff verschiedenen Oratorien, durchgehends vorgestellet und verfertiget von König, in dem grossen*

45. Valentin, *Frankfurt*, p. 232.
46. Ibid.
47. Noack, *Darmstadt*, p. 191.
48. Israël, *Frankfurt*, pp. 17–18.
49. Translated from Mattheson, *Ehren-Pforte*, p. 365. The parenthetical expression is a footnote in the *Ehren-Pforte*. Telemann remembers here that the performance was for the benefit of the orphanage (*Waisenhaus*), rather than the poorhouse (*Armenhaus*) as stated in the mayor's record, quoted above.
50. Valentin, *Frankfurt*, p. 197.
51. Noack, *Darmstadt*, p. 191.

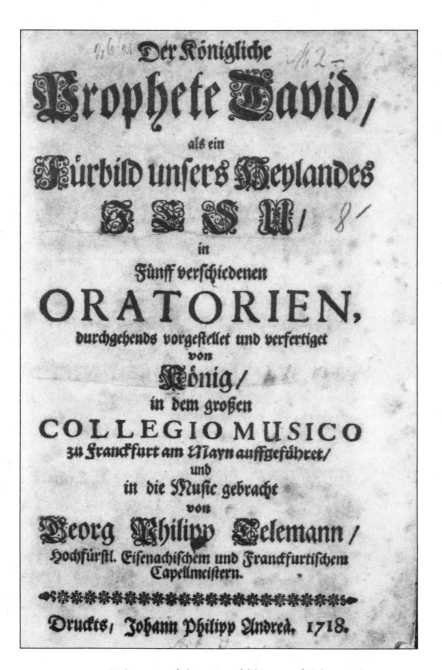

FIGURE IV-6. Title page of the printed libretto of Telemann's "David" oratorios, first performed in Frankfurt. (Courtesy of D-brd/F.)

Collegio Musico zu Franckfurt am Mayn aufgeführet, und in die Music gebracht von Georg Philipp Telemann ("The Kingly Prophet David, As a Prefiguration of Our Savior Jesus, in Five Different Oratorios, Completely Presented and Prepared by [Johann Ulrich von] König, Performed in the Large Collegium Musicum at Frankfort on the Main, and Set to Music by Georg Philipp Telemann").[52] The printed libretto of the David oratorios includes an extended foreword, written by the Reverend Johann Georg Pritius,[53] who strongly approved of oratorios in general and of the David oratorios in particular. Pritius refers to the ancient origins of religious drama, comments on the effectiveness of the oratorios of the Italians, and speaks of the fame of the Brockes Passion; he mentions that this Passion was performed several times in Frankfurt, both in church and in the chamber of a particular music lover. Only the first of the five David oratorios was performed in 1718.[54] Telemann's only other oratorio composed in Frankfurt is *Das selige Erwägen*, for which he wrote both the poetry and the music in 1719; there is no report of its having been performed in Frankfurt, but it became an extremely popular work in Hamburg, as mentioned above. As Frankfurt's public concert life developed during the first half of the eighteenth century, oratorios, especially Passion oratorios, continued to be performed there occasionally.[55]

The cities discussed above appear to have been the most active centers in Protestant Germany for the cultivation of the oratorio, but occasional performances, primarily of Passion oratorios, can also be documented in other cities and smaller towns. At Berlin, for instance, a Passion oratorio was performed in 1708. The work is identified on the title page of its printed libretto as *Christian Reuters Passions-Gedancken über die Historie von dem bittern Leiden und Sterben unsers Herrn und Heylandes Jesu Christi, nach denen Text-Worten der heiligen vier Evangelisten aufs kürtzeste in Reime verfasset und in die Music übersetzet von Johann Theilen* ("Christian Reuter's Passion-Thoughts on the Story of the Bitter Suffering and Death of Our Lord and Savior Jesus Christ, According to the Texts of the Four Holy Evangelists, Written as Briefly as Possible in Rhyme, and Set to Music by

---

52. A copy of the libretto is in D-brd/F: Art. Ff. 836.
53. The entire foreword is printed in Israël, *Frankfurt*, pp. 14–16.
54. Ibid., p. 20.
55. For a compilation of newspaper references to concerts, including oratorios, presented in Frankfurt from 1723 to 1780, see ibid., pp. 23–74.

Johann Theile").[56] A Passion oratorio performed in 1714 at Gotha, with a text by Johann Georg Seebach, is entitled *Der leidende und sterbende Jesus, der getödtete Fürst des Lebens und der gecreutzigte Herr der Herrlichkeit* ("The Suffering and Dying Jesus, the Killed Prince of Life and the Crucified Lord of Glory").[57] Another Passion oratorio performed at Gotha, on Good Friday of 1719 in the chapel of the Friedenstein palace, is *Der blutige und sterbende Jesus zu Erweck- und Erhaltung gottgefälliger Andacht an dem hl. Sterbens- und Begräbnis-Tage dieses unsers Hochgel. Herrn und Heilands* ("The Bloody and Dying Jesus, for the Arousing and Maintaining of Devotion pleasing to God, on the Day of the Holy Death and Burial of This Our Blessed Lord and Savior").[58] The Brockes Passion by Telemann was performed in 1722 at Darmstadt;[59] and the one by Handel, the following year at Lüneburg.[60] A number of oratorios may have been performed at Minden between 1726 and 1735.[61] The oratorio was not generally fostered at Leipzig in the first half of the eighteenth century, although Johann Sebastian Bach used the term *Oratorium* for three of his works—for Christmas, Easter, and Ascension—all of which are treated in the following chapter.

56. For a modern edition of the libretto, see Flemming, *Oratorium*, pp. 65–91.
57. Lott, "Passionskomposition," p. 305.
58. Blankenburg, "Gotha," p. 52.
59. Noack, *Darmstadt*, p. 195.
60. Mattheson, *Critica*, 1:288.
61. Konstantin Bellermann is said to have written the texts of eight oratorios between these dates (D. Sasse, "Bellermann," in *MGG*, 1:cols. 1606–10), but it is not clear that they were in fact oratorios; they are assumed to be "oratorische Schulakte" in Schering, *Oratorium*, p. 351.

CHAPTER V

The Libretto and the Music

§●*The Libretto*

A useful framework for understanding the oratorio libretto of this period in Protestant Germany is Johann Adolph Scheibe's treatment of the subject in *Der critische Musicus*.[1] Although his article is didactic and reflects his rationalistic and highly critical bent, it also imparts knowledge about contemporary oratorio practice. After first defining the oratorio as a spiritual dramatic work, Scheibe indicates that oratorio texts consist of "biblical passages, arias, cavatas, recitatives, and chorales or short verses from psalms and songs of praise."[2] He then classifies oratorios into two types according to their texts: the type that is entirely poetic and the one that mixes poetry and prose. Treating first the poetic type, he says that the subject matter is based on the Holy Scripture, church history, or a noteworthy Christian virtue. Scheibe does not mention, however, that oratorios on biblical stories were far more numerous than those on other subjects and that the Passion oratorio was the most prominent type. Other biblical subjects used were those relating to the major feast days of the church year (especially Christmas, Easter, and Pentecost) and, in fact, most of the same subjects from the Old and New Testaments that had long formed the basis of oratorios in Italy. Among the oratorios based on church history are those for Reformation Sunday. The works presenting Christian virtues in a purely allegorical manner appear to have been less numerous than the other types.

Regarding the personages of a libretto, Scheibe points out

1. Scheibe, *Critische*, 1:156–60.
2. Translated, ibid., p. 157.

that either all of them may be derived from the story on which the oratorio is based or some of them may be fictitious. He recommends the use of fictitious personages but cautions that they must be introduced "in such an ingenious manner that through them the certainty or the plausibility of the action is strengthened even more."[3] A particularly important type of fictitious personage in the German Protestant oratorio is the allegorical type; thus Scheibe states that "one can also go even further in increasing the devotion by personification (*prosopopoeia*), and thus introduce countries, cities, rivers, fruits, seasons, but best of all virtues, vices, and passions, also the faithful or the singing Christian church."[4] Examples of allegorical personages abound in oratorios of the period. For instance, Hunold introduces the Daughter of Zion in his Passion oratorio; Brockes's Passion oratorio includes the Daughter of Zion and some Believing souls; Mattheson's oratorios frequently included allegorical personages—such as the Bride of Christ, Devotion, and Reflection, all of which are found in his Christmas oratorio, *Das gröste Kind* ("The Greatest Child," 1720);[5] and throughout the first half of the eighteenth century, the oratorios performed at the *Abendsmusiken* in Lübeck characteristically included such personages as Believing Soul, Fear of God, and Truth.[6] In Scheibe's treatment of personages, he cautions that one must take care not to introduce such personages as "a chorus of devils, of drunkards, and such dissolute and lascivious personages, for one must always most scrupulously see to the [purpose of] devotion and improvement in godliness."[7] That Scheibe disapproves of such personages in oratorios is not to say that they were not used; indeed, he adversely criticized certain parts of M. C. Brandenburg's libretto of an *Abendmusik* oratorio entitled *Belsazer* (1739), because they include what he considers to be lascivious drinking songs and love songs that are totally inappropriate for an oratorio.[8]

Like Zeno and Metastasio in Vienna, Scheibe insists upon the importance of the three unities in an oratorio libretto: "In addition to all of these things there is the plausibility of the subject and the situations, and further the unity of action, time, and place.

3. Translated, ibid., p. 158.
4. Translated, ibid.
5. Cannon, *Mattheson*, p. 174.
6. Stahl, "Abendmusiken," p. 54.
7. Translated from Scheibe, *Critische*, 1:158.
8. Ibid., 2:fols. [18ʳ–19ʳ].

These qualities must never be lacking in such a spiritual oratorio; otherwise it will be against nature and reason, and consequently will by no means completely convince and move."[9] Scheibe's emphasis on the necessity of a work's conforming to nature and reason in order for it to be convincing and moving is frequently encountered in *Der critische Musicus*. This emphasis reflects the thought of the enlightenment—and particularly of Scheibe's teacher in literature and philosophy, Johann Christoph Gottsched, whom he frequently mentions in the periodical. Scheibe makes clear that many contemporary oratorio librettists do not share his rationalistic views, however, for he immediately adds: "Daily experience teaches how severely and how often these points are violated; and we find an abundance of such poetic pieces in which these qualities are absent throughout, and in which one has drawn together diverse stories which do not accord with one another or which took place at different times, or in which one has introduced various contradictory characterizations of personages which take away the plausibility of the subject and the situations."[10] Recognizing that some biblical stories on which one might wish to base an oratorio are so long and diffuse that they exceed the limitations of the unities, Scheibe suggests that these stories be separated into sections and that each section be made to conform to the unities: "The Passion story, the Resurrection, the sending of the Holy Spirit, as also some other stories, will generally require this organization, if they are to be poetically worked out with the greatest emphasis and advantage."[11] This is Scheibe's only mention of the larger structural divisions of oratorios. Although the Germans seem to have been less consistent than the Italians with respect to structural divisions, many German oratorios, like those of Italy, are divided into two parts, allowing for the preaching of a sermon between them. Many oratorios are in one part, however, and as pointed out above, those for the Lübeck *Abendmusiken* are in five parts.

Scheibe's treatment of the so-called prosaic-poetic oratorio is quite brief.[12] He emphasizes its essentially dramatic nature, despite the presence of the Evangelist's narrative. He states that the

9. Translated, ibid., 1:158.
10. Translated, ibid.
11. Translated, ibid., pp. 158–59.
12. Ibid., pp. 159–60.

principal stories on which such works are based are the Passion and the Resurrection and that the unities of time and place do not apply, since one must follow the words of the Gospel story. In this type of oratorio, he says, the personages are primarily those in the Gospel story, but at certain places one inserts arias, chorales, and other devotional reflections, which are sung by fictitious personages. Scheibe's statements regarding this type of oratorio seem to reflect the general practice of his time. For instance, of Telemann's forty-six oratorio Passions written for Hamburg, all but four include reflective portions sung by fictitious personages, most of whom are allegorical.[13]

The Music

Scheibe's remarks in *Der critische Musicus* about the music of the oratorio,[14] like those about the libretto, are intended to be didactic; yet they also contain information concerning oratorio practice. He makes a distinction of musical style between the type of oratorio with a purely poetic text and that with a prosaic-poetic text. The reason for this distinction, he says, is that the former type is intended for performance for various occasions, both in church and outside of church, but the prosaic-poetic type is performed only in church.

Since the poetic type of oratorio is the one closest to theatrical music, its arias have, according to Scheibe, "a free, lively, expressive nature; with them one observes various rules of the theatrical style. One can fill the melody of the vocal line with more ornaments, extravagances, and running passages; one can give the singer generally more opportunity to elaborate and to make himself heard, and consequently one can also compose the instrumental parts in a far freer and more flowing manner, so that the attributes of the characters of the singing [personages] and the principal actions become all the more exact, lively, and expressive."[15] The arias of the prosaic-poetic type, however, must have a fuller texture and be more cautious in expression "so that one

13. For a tabulation of this and other data about Telemann's oratorio Passions, see the "Katalog der Passionen" in Hörner, *Telemann*, pp. 145–57.

14. Scheibe, *Critische*, 1:169–74.

15. Translated, ibid., p. 170.

achieves all the more consistently and certainly the seriousness of the subject matter and of the place."[16] For this type Scheibe recommends that one observe, in general, the style of church music, rather than that of theatrical music. He considers the same style of recitative to be appropriate for both types of oratorio, and "it is different from theatrical recitative only in that it bears more harmonic extravagances and consequently one can digress more to strange and unusual intervals, keys, and passages, which, however, may almost never be introduced in theatrical style."[17] Another difference between the two types, according to Scheibe, lies in the nature of their choruses. In the oratorios with exclusively poetic texts, the choruses are seldom contrapuntal or fugal, but they are frequently so in the prosaic-poetic oratorio. Thus, for the choruses of the latter type, one observes the style appropriate for such church works as masses and motets.

At the conclusion of his discussion of the oratorio, Scheibe mentions the Italian oratorios, "for these pieces are now heard at many courts with no little enjoyment."[18] The chief distinction that he cites between the Italian and the German oratorio is that the Italian works are composed for the most part in theatrical style, and "choruses such as appear in our oratorios, they [the Italians] do not use at all, because they likewise compose the choruses completely according to the theatrical manner."[19] Indeed, here Scheibe has touched upon one of the most notable differences between the Italian and the German oratorio, for the frequent entrance of the chorus and the use of the chorale are among the chief distinguishing features of the German oratorio.

Some Examples

Handel's Brockes Passion[20]

The date of Handel's Brockes Passion is uncertain, but it appears to be between 1715 and 1717. Handel had been a permanent

16. Translated, ibid.
17. Translated, ibid.
18. Translated, ibid., p. 173.
19. Translated, ibid., p. 174.
20. Printed in Handel, *Ausgabe*, ser. 1, vol. 7; Handel, *Werke*, vol. 15. Frederichs, *Brockespassionen*, includes a study of the libretto and a comparison of the relationship between text and music in the Brockes Passions by Keiser, Handel, Telemann, and Mattheson.

resident of London since 1712, but during the summer of 1716 he traveled to Germany. Whether it was in Germany that he became acquainted with the Brockes text or whether he had previously known it is uncertain. Handel evidently composed the work in England, because his friend Mattheson, in his *Ehren-Pforte*, mentions the Brockes Passion "which [Handel] also composed in England, and had sent here [to Mattheson in Hamburg] by mail in an unusually closely written score."[21] There is no known occasion for which Handel composed the work, but he probably either assumed or had definite word that his friend Mattheson would see to its performance in Hamburg. In fact, he may have composed it at Mattheson's suggestion.[22] Mattheson performed it on Monday of Holy Week, 1719, and on the following day he performed Telemann's setting of the same text. Between 1719 and 1724 Handel's Brockes Passion was performed at least six times in Hamburg,[23] and in 1723 it was performed in Lüneburg, as mentioned above. No evidence has come to light of a London performance.

Barthold Heinrich Brockes is a poet of considerable significance for the history of German literature. A well-educated and widely traveled person, he spent a number of years touring and studying in various parts of Europe before returning to Hamburg in 1704. In 1715 he and the poets J. U. von König and M. Richey (both oratorio librettists) founded a literary society, the Teutsch-übende Gesellschaft, which was replaced in 1724 by the Patriotische Gesellschaft. Among Hamburg's leading citizens, Brockes was appointed in 1720 to the Hamburg senate. He is a figure of importance for the literature of the enlightenment and is particularly significant for his vivid descriptions of nature. It is important for the understanding of his Passion libretto, however, to recognize that he was also an admirer of the early seventeenth-century Italian G. B. Marino, whose *Strage degli innocenti* ("Massacre of the Innocents") and other poems Brockes translated into German. The Passion reflects Brockes's interest in the turgid style that the Italians called *marinismo*, with its extravagant images used for their sensational, shocking effect.

21. Translated from Mattheson, *Ehren-Pforte*, p. 96. For a discussion of the possible dates for Handel's composition of this work, see Frederichs, *Brockespassionen*, p. 43.
22. Becker, "Brockes," p. 5.
23. Becker, "Tagespresse," p. 36.

The libretto of Brockes's Passion, *Der für die Sünde der Welt gemarterte und sterbende Jesus*,[24] is like an oratorio Passion based on a Gospel "harmony," except that all passages that would be in biblical prose in an oratorio Passion are freely paraphrased in poetry in this Passion oratorio. Thus the general format of the work is traditional: the Evangelist (T, in Handel's setting) narrates in a style intended to be set in recitative, although his part is considerably abbreviated; the individual personages of the Gospel story carry out their dialogue in recitative; the chorus (SATB) sings the *turba* parts; and reflective texts (including chorales), which are interpolated, are intended to be set as recitatives, arias, ariosos, ensembles, and choruses. The reflective texts constitute almost two-thirds of the poetic lines of the libretto; some of them are given to participants in the drama (Jesus, B; Peter, T; and Judas, A), but the majority are given to fictitious observers. The latter are the Daughter of Zion (S), the Believing Souls (S, A, T, and B), and a chorus of Believing Souls (SATB). The chorales are always designated "Chorale of the Christian Church" (SATB). A personage added to this Passion who does not have a speaking part in the Gospel stories of the Passion is Mary (S); she sings a reflective recitative and joins Jesus in a reflective duet. The oratorio, in one structural part, is divided into four large sections by chorales that conclude important events in the story: the first is sung at the end of the scene of the Last Supper; the second, after Peter's denial of Jesus; the third, following the Crucifixion of Jesus; and the fourth, in the finale complex in which two chorale stanzas are sung, one before and one after an aria of the Daughter of Zion. An interesting feature of Brockes's text is the appearance, nine times, of the term *soliloquium* to identify a complex, comparable to a brief solo cantata, consisting of one or more recitatives and one or more arias or ariosos (in one instance a duet). This term is not in either of the modern editions of Handel's Brockes Passion, and it evidently does not appear in any of the manuscript sources of that work. Brockes gives a single *soliloquium* each to Jesus, Judas, and a Believing Soul (S); Peter has two such complexes; the Daughter of Zion has three; and Mary has one that is concluded by the duet that she sings with Jesus.

The oratorio text is at times, but not exclusively, in the

24. For a modern edition of the libretto as printed in 1712, see Flemming, *Oratorium*, pp. 92–114.

extravagant and sensational style mentioned above. Indeed, Russell Martineau, who wrote the English translation for the Händel Gesellschaft edition of the Passion that appeared in 1863, considered some of the passages of the text unacceptable for the English taste of his time; he stated that the translator had allowed himself "to diverge from the sense of the original wherever the image presented appeared to him certain to shock or disgust the finer susceptibilities of the present age, as was the case in some of the arias having reference to the scourging, the spitting, and the crown of thorns. In these cases a strict adherence to the sense of the original would have rendered the work incapable of performance, and thus have nullified the very use the translation was intended to serve."[25] An example of the style to which Martineau refers is the aria "Die Rosen krönen," which reflects on Jesus' wearing the crown of thorns and interprets the bloodiness of the scene. In Brockes's text for this aria, the Daughter of Zion speaks of Jesus as a rose, the "Rose of Sharon," and she compares the blood that he sweats to the pearls that Aurora weeps on roses; the Daughter of Zion addresses these drops of blood as "indeed pitiful rubies, which from the flowing blood remain on Jesus' brow! I know, you will serve me as jewelry for my soul, and yet I cannot look at you without terror." Another example in the aria "Schäumest du," a rage aria calculated for a shocking effect, in which the Daughter of Zion, infuriated by those who spit on Jesus, begins with the words "Froth, you scum of the world, spit out your basilisk vengeance, you brood of the dragon." Most commentators on Handel's Brockes Passion, from the nineteenth century to the present, have lamented what they considered the poor taste of the Brockes text. As an author writing for his own time and place, however, Brockes was eminently successful: in late Baroque Germany his Passion was widely accepted with enthusiasm and high praise.

Handel did not set Brockes's text exactly as it appears in the first printed libretto of 1712. The version that he set is modified in several respects. Some of the Evangelists' recitative passages are shortened; numerous words and phrases within recitatives and arias are changed; and two new arias are inserted: the Daughter of Zion's "Lass doch diese herbe Schmerzen" and the Believing Soul's

25. Handel, *Werke*, vol. 15, [p. v].

"Dem Himmel gleicht sein buntgefärbter Rükken."[26] In general, the passages in the 1712 libretto that are marked as arias, ariosos, choruses, ensembles, and accompanied recitatives and those that are unmarked but clearly intended to be set as simple recitatives, (i.e., accompanied by continuo only) are set accordingly in Handel's score.

Of the solo numbers, twenty-seven are arias (nine da capo or dal segno and two strophic), six ariosos, and three accompanied recitatives. The Daughter of Zion has eleven arias, the largest number of any personage. She is followed by Peter with four; the Believing Souls with three (S), three (T), and one (B); Jesus with two; and Judas with one. Of the two arias by Jesus, particularly noteworthy for its characterization is the one in his *soliloquium*—the prayer on the Mount of Olives, "Mein Vater! Schau, wie ich mich quäle." In this aria Jesus expresses both his agony and his heroic resignation in the face of the impending Crucifixion. The aria consists of two strophes, separated by a simple recitative that is also sung by Jesus. Example V–1 illustrates the beginning of the first strophe. In D minor, adagio, this aria is particularly effective for its chromatic passages (for example, see mm. 7–8) and for the contrast between Jesus' lyrical vocal line and the persistent rhythmic pattern, performed staccato by the strings. Of Peter's numbers

EXAMPLE V-I. Brockes Passion (Handel, *Ausgabe*, ser. 1, vol. 7, p. 26).

26. Both arias are also found in the extant settings by Keiser, Telemann, and Mattheson (cf. Frederichs, *Brockespassionen*, pp. 118–19). For a detailed treatment of the libretto's versions, see Frederichs, *Brockespassionen*, pp. 19–29.

(EXAMPLE V-I, continued)

My father! See how I suffer, have mercy . . .

noteworthy is his *soliloquium* following his denial of Jesus, which consists of two arias, "Heul, du Fluch" (Example V–2) and "Schau, ich fall'" (Example V–3), each of which is preceded and prepared by a simple recitative, also sung by Peter. This *soliloquium* is important for the musical characterization of Peter, showing a different side of his personality than does his previous rage aria, "Gift und Glut," which expresses the anger that prompted him to use his sword against Jesus' captors. The first aria of the *soliloquium* expresses Peter's remorse; and the second, his resolution to

EXAMPLE V-2. Brockes Passion (Handel, *Ausgabe*, ser. 1, vol. 7, p. 62).

(EXAMPLE V-2, continued)

Cry out, you curse of mankind! Tremble, wild servant of sin.

EXAMPLE V-3. Brockes Passion (Handel, *Ausgabe*, ser. 1, vol. 7, p. 64).

See, I fall at thy feet, a penitent in strict repentance.

fall at Jesus' feet, confess his betrayal, and ask forgiveness. Both arias are marked *largo e staccato* (the latter applies to their accompaniments), both are in minor keys (the first in A minor; the second, E minor), and both are relatively brief, non–da capo arias. The first, with sarabande rhythm, is starkly accompanied by basso continuo, oboe solo, and unison violins, and the second is more elaborately accompanied by all the strings in a four-part texture. Judas's *soliloquium*, also important for characterization, consists of his only aria, "Lasst diese Tat" (Example V–4), together with the preceding and following simple recitatives. In this impassioned vengeance aria, marked *ardito* and permeated with vigorous dotted

EXAMPLE V-4. Brockes Passion (Handel, *Ausgabe*, ser. 1, vol. 7, p. 80).

Let this deed be not unavenged, rend my flesh, crush my bones, you spectres of that cavern of torture.

patterns, Judas begs the specters of hell to avenge his crimes. The Daughter of Zion does not have a clearly defined character, but her arias are musically important. Particularly noteworthy are her "Sünder, schaut mit Furcht," a brief, contrapuntal trio for solo oboe, soprano voice, and continuo; "Was Bärentatzen, Löwenklauen," a fierce expression of the ravage of which mankind is capable; "Die ihr Gottes Gnad," a serious reflection on the consequences of rejecting God's Grace, set in slow triple meter with some sarabande rhythms and accompanied by the strings, bassoons, and a solo oboe; "Die Rosen krönen," a simple and lovely *siciliano* expressing the floral image, rather than the bloodiness, of the scene; and "Jesu, dich mit unsern Seelen," a dancelike number in triple meter that reflects on Jesus' love.

The chorus sings eighteen times in the work, but most of the choruses are brief *turba* passages that tend to be musically perfunctory. None of the choruses is particularly elaborate, although the opening one, with its contrast between chorus and soli, is quite effective. The four chorales that divide the work structurally are all set in a relatively simple manner.

The opening sinfonia, the only instrumental number of the work, is borrowed largely from Handel's third keyboard fugue, and some of the vocal numbers, too, are said to have been borrowed from his own works.[27] Certain musical correspondences among the settings of the Brockes Passion by Keiser, Telemann, Handel, and Mattheson indicate that the later settings were partially dependent on the earlier ones.[28] Several numbers of Handel's work were used again in his earliest English oratorios—*Esther*, *Deborah*, and *Athalia*.[29]

Keiser's Der siegende David ("The Victorious David")[30]

Born in 1674 at Teuchtern, near Weissenfels, Reinhard Keiser was sent in 1685 to become a student at the St. Thomas school in Leipzig, where Johann Schelle was responsible for most of his early musical training.[31] By about 1692 he was in Brunswick; in 1694 he was named the Brunswick court's Cammer-Componist, which included the duties of Kapellmeister. Best known today as one of Germany's leading opera composers of the late Baroque, Keiser began his operatic career at Brunswick, where his first opera, *Basilius in Arcadien*, was performed in about 1693. The year 1696 marks the first of an extremely large number of perfor-

27. In Chrysander, *Händel*, 1:445, the borrowings are not specified, but they are said to be from Handel's previous odes, Te Deum, cantatas, and operas.

28. These musical correspondences are indicated in Frederichs, *Brockespassionen*, pp. 88–195.

29. For specifics regarding the borrowings from the Brockes Passion in those works, see Dean, *Oratorios*, pp. 641–43.

30. The only known source of this work is a MS, said on the title page to be an autograph, in D-ddr/Bds: MS 11473. A modern edition of the work is lacking, but my edition is in progress. For a discussion of the oratorio together with several music examples, see Winterfeld, *Kirchengesang*, 3:149–58. For my study of this oratorio, I gratefully acknowledge the assistance of Dr. and Mrs. Adolph Furth of Vienna, who painstakingly transcribed the words for me from the often nearly illegible German script of the MS source.

31. For Keiser's biography see H. Becker, "Keiser," in *MGG*, 7:cols. 784–801.

mances of Keiser's operas in Hamburg, where in 1703 he became the director of the opera theater, a post that he held for three years. Keiser lived in Hamburg for the remainder of his life—except for relatively brief sojourns at Weissenfels (1706), Stuttgart (1718?–20), and Copenhagen (1721–23, with trips back to Hamburg). He was active in Hamburg, not only as a composer of operas, but also as a composer and director of music for public concerts and as the cantor of the cathedral, a post he assumed after Mattheson's resignation in 1728. In the field of oratorio composition for Hamburg, Keiser has been mentioned above as the composer of the Passion oratorio *Der blutige und sterbende Jesus* (1704), the earliest extant Protestant German work known to have been designated by the term *oratorio*. Other oratorios by Keiser, most of which were mentioned above, are *Der Dialogus von der Geburt Christi* and *Der sterbende Saul* (both performed in 1707), *Tränen unter dem Kreuze Jesu* (1711), the Brockes Passion (1712), *Der zum Tode verurteilte und gecreuzigte Jesus* (1715), *Die über den Triumph ihres Heylandes Jesu jubilirende gläubige Seele* (1717), and the work to be discussed here, *Der siegende David* (1721).

According to the Hamburg newspaper *Relations-Courir*, Keiser's *Der siegende David* was performed on 9 August 1721 in the Drillhaus, Hamburg's principal concert hall. The work's full title is *Die durch Grossmuth und Glauben triumphierende Unschuld oder Der siegende David* ("Innocence Triumphing through Magnanimity and Faith, or the Victorious David").[32]

The libretto is drawn almost entirely from the "David" oratorios written by Johann Ulrich von König, published at Frankfurt in 1718, and set to music by Telemann (see above, p. 122). It utilizes nearly all of the first of König's five "David" librettos, a large part of the second, and selected passages from the third and fifth librettos. The story is found in 1 Samuel 17–18. Although the libretto frequently departs from the biblical version and omits much of it, certain sections, such as that of the description of Goliath's appearance, follow the biblical text quite closely. The work is in one large structural part, but it may be divided into five sections according to the dramatic action. In the first section the Philistines (SATB–SATB) and Goliath (B) threaten the Israelites

32. Ibid., cols. 791, 796.

FIGURE V-1. Title page of Reinhard Keiser's oratorio *Der siegende David*, from the manuscript in D-ddr/Bds: MS 11, 473. (Reproduced by permission of D-ddr/Bds.)

FIGURE V-2. Beginning of the aria "Frohlockt ihr Philister"
(cf. Example V-5, p. 144) in Keiser's *Der siegende David*,
from the same manuscript as Figure V-1.

(SSATB), who are fearful and about to flee. The situation is described and clarified in an exchange of descriptive comments between Eliab (T), who is David's brother and a soldier in Saul's army, and Abner (B), the captain of Saul's army. The powerful Goliath proposes that the Israelites find one man who will do hand-to-hand combat with him and that they let this combat decide which nation will be the servant of the other. In the second section David hears of the plight of the Israelites and of the rewards of riches and marriage with Saul's daughter for the man who conquers Goliath. David volunteers to fight Goliath, and although a mere shepherd boy, he convinces Saul by his courage that he will win. In the third section David and Goliath meet. The latter, shocked that he is to do combat with a boy, ridicules David, who has decided to come armed only with a sling and some stones but who is nevertheless confident of his forthcoming victory. In his commentary on the combat scene, Abner describes in gory terms the effects of David's single, accurate shot as well as David's subsequent act of seizing the giant's sword and sawing off his head. The fourth section deals primarily with the deep and lasting friendship between David and Jonathan (S), Saul's son. The fifth and final section is that of Saul's jealousy and madness. The Israelite Women (SSSATB) greet the army upon its return from battle; the women praise Saul for having slain one thousand of the enemy but David for having slain ten thousand. Saul grows jealous of David and begins to feel threatened, for he is convinced that David wants to gain the throne. Finally it is clear that Saul is mad—he thinks he sees Goliath approaching and prepares to do battle with him. David tries to calm Saul's fury by singing to him, in a section marked "Cantata con istromenti" in the manuscript. David's cantata consists of two arias separated by a recitative: the text of the first aria is based on Ps. 13:2–3; that of the following recitative, on other verses from the Psalms; and the final aria, on Ps. 46:2–3. David's attempt to help Saul is vain, however, and immediately following David's cantata, Saul hurls a spear at him in an unsuccessful attempt on his life. Saul's attempted murder closes the dramatic action of the oratorio.

In addition to the dramatic action, based on Jewish history, the libretto includes a number of Christian interpolations, all but one of which are used also in the König-Telemann oratorios. In these interpolations certain aspects of the story are either interpreted figuratively in a Christian sense or are used as points of departure for Christian reflections. The reflections are sung by allegorical characters: a Believing Soul (Gläubige Seele, S), two God-loving Souls (Gottliebende Seelen, S and T), a Pious Soul (Andächtige Seele, S), and the chorus of the Christian Communion (Christliche Gemeine, SATB). These personages sing a total of eleven numbers (counting two repetitions), comparable in both context and content to the reflective numbers characteristically interpolated in oratorio Passions of the time. The solo numbers are nearly always preceded by passages of recitative. Characteristic of the context and content of these Christian numbers is the first one, an aria sung by the Believing Soul. Saul has just agreed that David may do combat with Goliath and has expressed his confidence in David, whom he has told to arm himself and to prepare to enter the battlefield. The Believing Soul interrupts the dramatic action at this point with a recitative that begins, "I too, my God, wish likewise to be armed by you," and when the recitative of eight poetic lines is finished, the Believing Soul sings the aria "Es rüste sich wider," in which he says he will arm himself against the devil and the world and will go courageously with Jesus into the battle-field. The longest and most elaborate Christian interpolation is the only section in the oratorio called a *soliloquio*, beginning "Ihr Seelen, erweitert die Thore der Hertzen," sung by a God-loving Soul (S). This *soliloquio*, which was used in a totally different context in the König-Telemann oratorios, is placed at a crucial point in the dramatic action: it separates the chorus of the Israelite Women, who praise David above Saul, from the passage in which Saul reacts to the chorus by revealing his jealousy and madness. In this context the *soliloquio* uses the welcome given to David upon his victorious return from battle as a point of departure for an exhortation for Christian souls to open the gates of their hearts and welcome the victorious Son of David. This thought is elabo-rated throughout the *soliloquio*, which is comparable to a brief solo cantata in seven units: da capo aria, simple recitative, arioso with instruments, simple recitative, repetition of the arioso with instruments, simple recitative, and da capo aria. The two reflective choruses of the Christian Communion use as texts the third and sixth stanzas, respectively, of the chorale "Wie schön leuchtet der Morgenstern." The first of these, "Geuss sehr tieff in mein Hertz hinein," a reflection on Christian love, closes the section that emphasizes the friendship of David and Jonathan; the repetition of the chorale with the sixth stanza, "Zwingt die Saiten," is the final chorus of the oratorio.

Of the fifteen arias in the oratorio, David sings four, the largest number sung by any personage. He is followed by the God-loving Soul (S) with three, and by Goliath and the Believing Soul with two each; the other personages sing one aria each—except for Abner, who sings only in recitative. All but one of the arias are in da capo form, and three have motto beginnings. Other than arias the only numbers for solo voices are one accompanied recitative, in which Saul reveals his madness, and two brief arioso sections with instrumental accompaniment (one sung by Saul and the other by a God-loving Soul), both of which are repeated after intervening simple recitatives to provide emphasis and structural unity.

About one-third of the arias have texts expressing belligerent, bellicose, or pugnacious affections. Characteristic of these numbers is the first aria, Goliath's "Frohlockt ihr Philister." In this number triadic, fanfare-styled melodic lines and long melismas express Goliath's boasting about the military advantage that his strength gives the Philistines (Example V–5a, the beginning of the aria) and about his worthiness to be deified (Example V–5b, the ending of

EXAMPLE V-5. *Der siegende David*—Keiser (D-ddr/Bds: MS 11473, pp. 25, 29).

Example a:

(EXAMPLE V-5, continued)

Rejoice, Philistines, on account of Goliath's strength.

Example b:

Are these not works worthy of deification?

the B section, just before the da capo). Example V–6 is taken from Goliath's aria "Kan auch ein Maulwurff," in which the giant ridicules the shepherd boy who dares to stand up to him. This aria, again pugnacious in affection, is a kind of patter song with triadic

EXAMPLE V–6. *Der siegende David*—Keiser (D-ddr/Bds: MS 11473, p. 95).

Can a mole tame lions, can a sheep take the booty from a wolf, is a hunter put to death by a deer?

lines in melodic sequence and with all the strings doubling the basso continuo most of the time and reinforcing the vocal line occasionally, as they do in this example.

The aria "Poche, schnarche," in which David replies to Goliath, is less serious than Goliath's arias but expresses the boy's courage, and indeed his sense of humor, in the face of the giant's threats and ridicule. The beginning of Example V–7, which starts just after the aria's initial orchestral passage, illustrates David's lighthearted rejection of Goliath's furious raving. Among the humorous touches are the melismatic emphases placed on the unaccented syllables of the first four words—"Poche, schnarche, rase, wüte"; the triadic figures on the word "Drohen" (mm. 31–34),

EXAMPLE V-7. *Der siegende David*—Keiser (D-ddr/Bds: MS 11473, p. 100).

(EXAMPLE V-7, continued)

Boast, snort, rave, rage! My calm spirit mocks your threats.

reminiscent of and perhaps intended to parody Goliath's ridicule of David, illustrated above in Example V–5; and the exaggerated melismatic emphasis of the word "Schertz" (mm. 41–44).

One of the numbers expressing gentle affections is Eliab's only aria, "Ein Schäfferstock kan wenig nützen," the beginning of which is illustrated in Example V–8. Here Eliab tells David to go tend his sheep, for his shepherd's staff will be of little use in battle. Of primary importance in the expression of the pastoral mood is the orchestration, retained throughout the aria, consisting of a transverse flute accompanied by pizzicato strings and muted oboes.

A shepherd's staff can be of little use, . . .

Also pastoral in mood is the aria "Mein Hirt Imanuel" (Example V–9), sung by a God-loving Soul. The text treats Jesus as parallel to David—Jesus the good shepherd and the hero of Israel. The aria is in *siciliano* style, with a solo violin and light accompaniment throughout. In the A section of the da capo structure, the basso continuo plays only at important cadences, and the viola assumes the role of the bass, as seen in Example V–9. Of special interest for

(EXAMPLE V-9, continued)

My shepherd Emmanuel, the hero in Israel, has triumphed.

its orchestration is another number of gentle affection, "Wie lange Herr," the brief ABA' aria beginning the cantata that David sings to calm Saul's rage. As seen in Example V–10, the instruments consist of two chalumeaux, a carillon (in the manuscript called a *spinetto di campanelle*), a lute, and an undesignated basso con-

EXAMPLE V-10. *Der siegende David*—Keiser (D-ddr/Bds: MS 11473, pp. [178–80]).

How long, Lord, will you conceal yourself from me?

tinuo. The chalumeaux, scored usually in parallel thirds, play only at the beginning and ending and between vocal phrases. The carillon and lute accompany the voice and occasionally combine with the chalumeaux.

The chorus receives considerable emphasis in this oratorio: it is used eleven times. Six choruses are allotted to the Israelites alone, two to a combination of Philistines and Israelites, two to the Christian Communion, and one to the Philistines alone. All the choruses except those of the Christian Communion have a dramatic function. The oratorio's opening number is a chorus of Philistines (SATB-SATB), "Zum Kriegen, zum Streiten," in which their eagerness for battle and their pride in Goliath are expressed by fanfare-styled melodic lines in both vocal and instrumental parts (the latter including three trumpets and timpani) and by quick-note running passages and antiphonal style. This is one of the longest choruses of the work and one of the two that are in da capo form. After some recitative passages by Eliab and Abner, a brief, chordal, and declamatory chorus of the Israelites (SSATB), "Flieht, flieht," expresses their fear and readiness to flee. For further emphasis of the Israelites' fear, the opening ritornello and the last part of this chorus are repeated after Goliath's aria "Frohlockt ihr Philister." Two of the oratorio's choruses include solo passages sung by personages in the drama. In the first of these, "Ein schwacher Jüngling," some Israelites comment that a weak youth wants to strike down the giant and that they are about to hurry to report this to the king; meanwhile David repeatedly interjects, "Yes, I want to kill him," and David's brother Eliab expresses his shock, "What are you saying?" The other chorus that includes soloists, "Wir hoffen auf Goliaths muthige Stärcke," occurs just before the confrontation between David and Goliath. Like the first chorus of the oratorio, this one is a martial double chorus in da capo form and includes three trumpets and timpani; in this number the two choruses represent the Philistines and the Israelites. The former place their hope in Goliath, but the Israelites place theirs in God. The soloists are an unnamed Philistine (T) and Goliath, and both marvel that a weak boy thinks he can fell the giant. In addition to the two choruses with trumpets and timpani mentioned above, one more number including these instruments is "Kommt bei diesen Freudentagen," the chorus of Israelite Women who welcome Saul and David home from battle and who praise

David above Saul. (It is curious that Keiser did not restrict this number to women's voices but used SSSATB.) This is a majestic chorus in gavotte rhythmic style and with antiphony between the upper and lower vocal groupings. The chorus of the Christian Communion, which sings the third and sixth stanzas of the chorale "Wie schön leuchtet der Morgenstern," consists of the chorale tune stated in simple chordal style by voices and instruments—except for the first violin and continuo parts, which play sixteenth-note passage work throughout.

J. S. Bach's Oratorios

Although the oratorio was not generally cultivated in Leipzig, J. S. Bach designated three of his Leipzig works oratorios—the Easter Oratorio (*Oratorium festo paschali*, BWV 249),[33] the Christmas Oratorio (*Oratorium tempore nativitatis Christi*, BWV 248), and the Ascension Oratorio (*Oratorium festo ascensionis Christi*, BWV 11). These works as we now have them date from around 1735, although they depend heavily upon borrowings from Bach's earlier compositions. None of the three is an oratorio in the sense in which the term was normally used in the period. In its libretto the Easter Oratorio is the one closest to the most generally held conception of the genre, for the libretto is poetic throughout and has an essentially dramatic structure; yet the work is exceptional for its brevity. The other two oratorios do not have purely poetic librettos, as do most works called oratorios in the period, but their librettos include a story quoted from the Bible and reflective poetry interrupting that story.

The Easter Oratorio.[34] This is the earliest of Bach's three oratorios in the sense that it is based almost entirely on his secular cantata of 1725, with a pastoral text beginning "Entfliehet, verschwindet" (BWV 249a) by Friedrich Henrici (pseudonym, Picander); the performance materials of this cantata are lost, but the printed libretto survives.[35] Composed to celebrate the birthday (23 February 1725) of Duke Christian of Saxe-Weissenfels, the music of

33. The numbering of Bach's works is that of Schmieder, *BWV*.
34. Printed in Bach, *Werke*, vol. 21, pt. 3. To appear in Bach, *Neue Ausgabe*, ser. 2, vol. 7.
35. Dürr, "Chronologie," p. 79.

FIGURE V-3. Johann Sebastian Bach (1685–1750), from an oil painting by
Elias Gottlieb Haussmann, 1748.
      (Reproduced by permission of William H. Scheide, Princeton, N.J.)

this secular cantata has an interesting history of subsequent uses. Only a few weeks after the duke's birthday, the music was given a new libretto to form an Easter cantata—"Kommt, fliehet und eilet" (BWV 249, first version)—which was performed on 1 April 1725.[36] In the following year the music was supplied with yet another Henrici libretto—"Verjaget, zerstreuet" (BWV 249b), a mythological poem written to celebrate the birthday (25 August 1726) of Count Flemming; the performance materials of this version are lost, but a printed libretto survives.[37] Finally, a fourth known use of the music is for "Kommt, eilet und laufet" (BWV 249, second version), dating from around 1732–35. Only the materials of this latest version, the version known as the Easter Oratorio, are designated by the term *Oratorium*. Except for their recitatives the librettos of BWV 249, 249a, and 249b are similar in their meters, their affections, and at times even their vocabulary, which would account for the suitability of virtually the same music for them all.[38] Since the texts for the recitatives usually differ considerably from one another, however, they had to be set to new music for each new version of the work.

The text of the Easter Oratorio, by an unknown author, is in one structural part and is dramatic, with four personages: Mary the Mother of James (S), Mary Magdalene (A), Peter (T), and John (B). The dramatic development is extremely slight: Peter and John, and later the two Marys, are going to the tomb of Jesus on Easter morning; they arrive at the tomb and discover that Jesus has risen from the dead; and they express their joy at the Resurrection and their desire to see Jesus again. This slim dramatic structure is extended by reflective numbers: a duet for Peter and John at the beginning that is combined with a chorus (SATB); three arias for Mary the Mother of James, Mary Magdalene, and Peter; and a closing chorus of praise. The only instrumental number is the opening sinfonia. As indicated above, this work is like a normal oratorio of its time in its dramatic format, but it departs from the norm in its scant dramatic development and its relative brevity— about fifty minutes—in comparison with most eighteenth-century oratorios.

36. Ibid.; Dürr, *Weihnachts-Oratorium*, p. 46, n. 1.
37. Dürr, "Chronologie," p. 89.
38. For a comparison of the librettos of BWV 249 and 249b, see Smend, "Bach-Funde," pp. 4–8 (in reprint, pp. 139–44).

The opening and closing numbers of the Easter Oratorio provide a festive frame for the work as a whole. The three trumpets and timpani in the introductory sinfonia, in the duet and chorus that follow, and in the final chorus contribute much to the festive impression. Particularly noteworthy among the arias is Peter's "Sanfte soll mein Todeskummer nur ein Schlummer," with its gentle orchestral accompaniment, including two recorders and muted violins, and with extraordinarily long notes in the vocal line on the word "Schlummer" (slumber), as illustrated in Example V–11. Also of special interest are the ensemble recitatives—particularly that for all four personages, "O kalter Männer Sinn," in which they declaim not only separately, but also in pairs.

EXAMPLE V-11. Easter Oratorio (Bach, *Werke*, vol. 21, pt. 3, p. 45).

Gentle shall be my sorrow [at thy] death, only a sleep . . .

The Christmas Oratorio.[39] This is a monumental work in six parts. Just as the five-part oratorios for the Lübeck *Abendmusiken* of this period were intended to be performed in five separate concerts, the six parts of Bach's Christmas Oratorio were intended for church services on six feast days or Sundays during the Christmas season of 1734–35. Each part, which lasts from about twenty-five to thirty minutes, functioned as a cantata for the main service of the day. Parts 1–3 were performed on the three days of Christmas celebration (25–27 December), part 4 on New Year's Day, part 5 on the following Sunday, and part 6 on Epiphany.

Despite Bach's intention that the performance of the oratorio be distributed over a period of nearly two weeks, he clearly conceived it as a structural whole. The members of his congregation would readily have understood it as such, since the libretto for the entire oratorio was printed in advance: they could see the work as a whole from the outset and review the context of each part as they heard it. The printed libretto bears the title *Oratorium, welches die heilige Weyhnacht über in beyden Haupt-Kirchen zu Leipzig musiciret wurde* ("Oratorio Which Was Performed Musically During the Holy Christmas [Season] in Both Principal Churches of Leipzig").[40] The subjects of the six parts of the libretto are (1) the birth of Jesus, as told in Luke 2:1 and 3–7; (2) the Angel's announcement to the Shepherds, Luke 2:8–14; (3) the Shepherds' journey to Bethlehem to worship Jesus, Luke 2:15–20; (4) the circumcision and naming of Jesus, Luke 2:21; (5) the flight into Egypt, Matt. 2:1–6; and (6) the story of the Wise Men, Matt. 2:7–12. The oratorio is consistent throughout in that all six parts include both narrative passages, sung in recitative by the Evangelist (T), and reflective interpolations—recitatives, arias, chorales, and other choruses. The author of the reflective texts is unknown, but they may have been written by Henrici. The words of individual personages in the biblical story are given to soloists (an Angel, S; Herod, B), and those of groups are given to the chorus (the Angels, the Shepherds, and the Wise Men). The dramatic element in the work is minimal, however, since there are so few solo or ensemble passages for these personages.

39. Printed in Bach, *Neue Ausgabe*, ser. 2, vol. 6; Bach, *Werke*, vol. 5, pt. 2. For a historical and analytical study of the work, see Dürr, *Weihnachts-Oratorium*.

40. For a facsimile of the complete libretto, see Bach, *Neue Ausgabe, Kritischer Bericht*, ser. 2, vol. 6, pp. 147–58.

Because it includes strict quotations from a Gospel story, a solo setting of the Evangelist's part, some dramatic treatment of the roles of the personages, and reflective interpolations, this work may be understood historically as a descendant of the Lutheran *historia*, which originated in the sixteenth century. The Christmas Oratorio has much in common with the most prominent descendant of the *historia*, the oratorio Passion; yet this work differs from most examples of the oratorio Passion (including Bach's St. John and St. Matthew Passions) in its greater emphasis on reflection and lesser emphasis on narration and drama. As mentioned above, for this work and for the Ascension Oratorio Bach adopted a conception of the oratorio that was unusual in his time. Nevertheless, it was not long before Scheibe, in *Der critische Musicus* (26 November 1737), see above, pp. 106, 128), described a type of oratorio that uses a text combining prose and poetry; these two works by Bach are examples of this type. (Scheibe wrote his comments in Hamburg, but as a Leipziger who did not move to Hamburg until about 1736, he would probably have been familiar with the works that Bach called oratorios.)

The Christmas Oratorio as a whole is unified musically by tonality and instrumentation: parts 1, 3, and 6 are in D major and use trumpets; parts 2 and 5 are in the closely related keys of G and A major, respectively; and part 4 is in the more distant key of F major. The first three parts cohere as a large subunit: it begins and ends with D-major sections that include trumpets in the orchestra, it is unified textually by the events surrounding the birth of Jesus as told in Luke, and it was performed on three successive days, unlike parts 4–6. Another musical element contributing to the unity of the oratorio as a whole is the chorale tune "Herzlich tut mich verlangen," which appears in two prominent places: as the first chorale of part 1 (no. 5, with the text "Wie soll ich dich empfangen") and as the closing number of part 6 (no. 64, "Nun seid ihr wohl gerochen"). This tune, also sung in Bach's time with the Passion text "O Haupt voll Blut und Wunden," is important in Bach's St. Matthew Passion. The association of the tune with the Passion has led some scholars to conclude that Bach used it as a "premonition of Christ's death, immediately after his birth"[41] or for the purpose of making a theological point: "only through the

41. Spitta, *Bach*, 2:579.

ORATORIUM,
Welches
Die heilige Weyhnacht
über
In beyden
Haupt-Kirchen
zu Leipzig
musiciret wurde.

ANNO 1734.

FIGURE V-4. Title page of the libretto of J. S. Bach's Christmas Oratorio, printed for the performance in the Christmas season of 1734–35.
(Reproduced by permission of the Bach-Archiv, Leipzig.)

FIGURE V-5. First page of J. S. Bach's Christmas Oratorio, in
the composer's hand.
(Reproduced by permission of D-ddr/Bds.)

death of Jesus did the birth of the heavenly child result in the salvation of mankind."[42] Such conclusions have been questioned by Alfred Dürr, however, on the grounds that the tune in question was also sung with texts having nothing to do with the Passion, that Bach's congregation would thus not have been in a position to infer such a premonition or theological point from hearing the tune, and that other tunes were available to Bach to make this kind of meaning clear to his listeners had he wished to do so.[43]

Bach borrowed a large proportion of the musical numbers of the Christmas Oratorio from works that he had previously composed.[44] Although nearly all the twenty-seven recitatives are newly composed (the only exceptions being two accompanied recitatives), a large majority of the other numbers are borrowed: nine of the ten arias, five of the eight nonchorale choruses, the only duet, and the only trio. The works from which Bach borrowed most heavily for the Christmas Oratorio are three cantatas, two of which are secular and one sacred: he borrowed nearly all the music of "Lasst uns sorgen, lasst uns wachen," a birthday cantata of 1733 (BWV 213; Christmas Oratorio nos. 4, 19, 29, 36, 39, and 41); he also borrowed nearly all of another 1733 birthday cantata, "Tönet, ihr Pauken! Erschallet, Trompeten!" (BWV 214; Christmas Oratorio nos. 1, 8, 15, and 24); and he seemingly borrowed all the music of a sacred cantata, the date and text of which are unknown, that survives in only a few instrumental parts (BWV 248a; Christmas Oratorio nos. 54, 56, 57, and 61–64).[45] Works from which Bach borrowed one number each are a secular cantata of 1734, "Preise dein Glücke, gesegnetes Sachsen" (BWV 215; Christmas Oratorio, no. 47); the missing St. Mark Passion of 1731 (BWV 247; Christmas oratorio, no. 45); and presumably a missing cantata (Christmas Oratorio, no. 51).[46]

For most of the borrowed numbers, the librettist provided parodies of the original texts that use the same poetic meters and affections as do the originals; thus the composer would have the

42. Geiringer, Bach, p. 193.
43. Dürr, Weihnachts-Oratorium, pp. 42–43.
44. For details regarding the borrowing, see ibid., pp. 4–7, 9–12; and Bach, Neue Ausgabe, Kritischer Bericht, ser. 2, vol. 6, pp. 162–71, 199–219; Blankenburg, "Weihnachtsoratorium"; Möller, "Weihnachtsoratorium"; and Holst, "Weihnachts-Oratorium."
45. The number BWV 248a does not appear in Schmieder, BWV, but the number has been suggested by Alfred Dürr in Bach, Neue Ausgabe, Kritischer Bericht, ser. 2, vol. 6, p. 166, and in Dürr, Weihnachts-Oratorium, p. 5.
46. Dürr, Weihnachts-Oratorium, p. 5.

least possible need to revise the music. In the borrowed choruses, for instance, Bach set the new words to the borrowed music with virtually no changes. In setting the new aria texts, he often introduced small changes in the vocal line, and whenever the music of the original was transposed for use in the oratorio, he changed the orchestration as well. Occasionally the affection of a new aria text differs considerably from that of the original—as in no. 4 of the Christmas Oratorio, "Bereite dich, Zion, mit zärtlichen Trieben," based on BWV 213, no. 9, "Ich will dich nicht Hören, ich will dich nicht wissen." The original text conveys a harsh rejection of pleasure, but the new one is an exhortation to prepare for the coming of the Christ child: "Prepare thyself, Zion, with tender emotion, to welcome the fairest, the dearest one." By changing the orchestration and the manner of articulating the melodic line (cf. Examples V–12 a and b), Bach transformed the affection from harshness to tenderness. Much more extensive changes are found in the aria no. 47, "Erleucht auch meine finstre Sinnen," in which the metrical structure of the new text differs from that of the original.

EXAMPLE V-12.

Example a: Secular Cantata "Lasst uns sorgen, lasst uns wachen" (Bach, *Neue Ausgabe*, ser. 1, vol. 36, p. 52).

I will not hear you, I will not know . . .

(EXAMPLE V-12, continued)

Example b: Christmas Oratorio (Bach, *Neue Ausgabe*, ser. 2, vol. 6, p. 39).

Prepare thyself, Zion, with tender dispatch . . .

The musical styles of the Christmas Oratorio may be conveniently classified according to the types of texts used—biblical prose, chorale poetry, and free poetry.[47] By far the largest amount of biblical prose is that of the Evangelist, which is nearly always set in simple recitative, accompanied by continuo only. An interesting exception to this is the point in no. 50 at which the Evangelist quotes the Prophets: "Und du Bethlehem im jüdischen Lande." Here, to place in relief the prophetic words that had been fulfilled, Bach uses arioso style rather than simple recitative. The biblical words of individual personages are set either in simple recitative—as are those of Herod in no. 55, "Ziehet hin und forschet"—or in accompanied recitative—as is the Angel's announcement to the Shepherds in no. 13, "Fürchtet euch nicht." It is indicative of the essentially nondramatic nature of this oratorio, however, that after the reflective recitative and aria that interrupt the Angel, the angelic announcement is continued (no. 16, "Und das habt zum Zeichen"), not by the Angel in accompanied recitative, but by the Evangelist in simple recitative. Only three of the choruses in the oratorio represent groups of personages: the chorus of Angels (no. 21, "Ehre sei Gott in der Höhe"), of Shepherds (no. 26, "Lasset uns nun gehen gen Bethlehem"), and of Wise Men (no. 45, "Wo ist der neugeborne König"). All three of these, with biblical prose

47. This is the classification used in Dürr, *Weihnachts-Oratorium*, pp. 16–38, where Dürr presents detailed analyses of the styles and structures of selected numbers in each class.

texts, may be considered to derive from motet style: the texts are divided into sections, each represented by its own thematic material; the texture tends to be imitative; and the instruments tend to double the vocal lines.

Of the fifteen settings of chorales in the Christmas Oratorio, nine are in simple chordal style. More elaborate treatment is given to the chorales used as the final numbers of parts 1, 2, 4, and 6; all of these closing chorales include instrumental interludes between the chorale phrases. Of particular interest is the treatment of the chorale "Wir singen dir in deinem Heer" that closes part 2, for its instrumental parts quote the sinfonia, in *siciliano* style, with which part 2 begins. At two places in the oratorio, chorales—traditionally interpreted as expressions of the congregation's sentiments—are contrasted with individualistic reflections in accompanied recitative. In the first of these places—no. 7, "Er ist auf Erden kommen arm"—recitative passages sung by the bass are interpolated between chorale phrases sung by the soprano. In the second, no. 38, the bass begins in recitative, "Immanuel, o süsses Wort," after which the soprano joins him with a traditional chorale text, "Jesu du mein liebstes Leben," but apparently with Bach's own melody. This chorale is interrupted by an aria—no. 39, "Flösst, mein Heiland"—after which the recitative-chorale contrast continues in no. 40, "Wohlan, dein Name" (recitative) and "Jesu, meine Freud und Wonne" (the completion of the chorale begun in no. 38).

The musical settings of free poetry in the oratorio are recitatives, arias, ensembles, and choruses. Of the eleven poetic recitatives, only two are accompanied by continuo only; one of these (no. 63, "Was will der Höllen Schrecken nun") is for an ensemble (SATB) and is the only ensemble recitative in the oratorio. Of the nine orchestrally accompanied recitatives, seven use only wind instruments (oboes or flutes) in addition to the continuo; only one is accompanied by strings and continuo. Of the ten arias in the oratorio, four are in da capo form. The others are in various kinds of binary, ternary, or ritornello forms. The accompaniments of the arias, like those of the recitatives, emphasize wind instruments. Of special interest among the arias are no. 19, "Schlafe, mein Liebster," a delicate slumber song; no. 31, "Schliesse, mein Herze," the only aria of the oratorio that was not borrowed from another source and one that is noteworthy for its virtuosic solo violin part; no. 39, "Flösst, mein Heiland," a curious and effective echo aria for soprano, with echos by the oboe and the second soprano, the latter singing only the words "nein" and "ja" (Example V–13);[48]

EXAMPLE V-13. Christmas Oratorio (Bach, *Neue Ausgabe*, ser. 2, vol. 6, p. 180).

Nay, thou dost thyself say nay! Doth thy name wash away each tiniest seed of this terror?

48. For an interpretation of this aria as a folklike, symbolic expression, see Prautzsch, "Echo-Arie."

and no. 41, "Ich will nur dir zu Ehren leben," a masterful amalgamation of da capo structure and fugal procedure, with stretto passages and inversions of the subject (Example V–14). The duet and trio are structurally similar to the arias, with the former in da capo and the latter in ABA' form. The only choruses on free poetic texts are nos. 1, 24, 36, 43, and 54—which are those at the beginnings of parts 1, 3 (also repeated at the end of 3), 4, 5, and 6, respectively. These are structurally much like arias, in contrast to the choruses that use biblical words and relate structurally to the

EXAMPLE V-14. Christmas Oratorio (Bach, *Neue Ausgabe*, ser. 2, vol. 6, pp. 186–87).

I wish to live only to honor thee, my Savior, grant me strength and power . . .

motet. Two of the choruses have da capo forms (nos. 1 and 43), two have ABA′ forms (nos. 36 and 54), and one has a binary form (no. 24). The numbers that introduce parts 1, 4, and 6 of the oratorio are among Bach's most extended choruses.

The Ascension Oratorio.[49] First performed as a church cantata on the feast of the Ascension, 19 May 1735, this work is an oratorio in the same exceptional sense as is Bach's Christmas Oratorio. In duration and format it is much like a single part of the Christmas Oratorio: it lasts only about thirty minutes, and its libretto, by an anonymous poet, includes narrative passages from the New Testament sung by the Evangelist (T) and reflective poetic texts set as accompanied recitatives, arias, and choruses. The oratorio consists of eleven sections. At least three of the sections appear to have been borrowed from Bach's earlier works,[50] of which only the printed librettos are known to survive. The opening chorus, "Lobet Gott in seinen Reichen," may be based on the opening chorus of the festive cantata "Froher Tag, verlangte Stunden" (BWV Anh. 18), sung on 5 June 1732 for the dedication of the remodeled St. Thomas school, or perhaps on the chorus "Kommt, ihr angenehmen Blicke" from the secular cantata "Auf! zum Scherzen, Auf! zur Lust." The two arias of the oratorio, "Ach bleibe doch, mein liebstes Leben" and "Jesu, deine Gnadenblicke," appear to be borrowed. They are probably based on the arias "Entfernet euch, ihr kalten Herzen" and "Unschuld, Kleinod reiner Seelen," respectively, from a wedding serenade with a text by Gottsched that begins "Auf! süss entzückende Gewalt,"[51] which was performed on 27 November 1725.

The brief movements of simple recitative in which the Evangelist narrates the story of the farewell and Ascension of Jesus are no. 2, based on Luke 24:50–51; no. 5, Acts 1:9 and Mark 16:19; no. 7, Acts 1:10–11; and no. 9, Luke 24:52 and Acts 1:12. All other movements are reflective. The work is strongly unified by tonality: the three choral pillars at the beginning, in the middle (no. 6), and at the end are all in D major; of the two arias in the

49. Printed in Bach, *Werke*, vol. 2. To appear in Bach, *Neue Ausgabe*, ser. 2, vol. 7.
50. For differing opinions on this point, see Smend, "Himmelfahrts-Oratorium," and Dürr, "Himmelfahrts-Oratorium."
51. Cf. Smend, "Himmelfahrts-Oratorium." This serenade is not listed in Schmieder, *BWV*. For structural, historical, and bibliographical information about it, see Neumann, *Kantaten*, p. 251.

oratorio, the first, no. 4, is in A minor, and the second, no. 10, in G major. The first chorus, in ABA' form, is a jubilant expression, with an orchestra that includes three trumpets, timpani, and pairs of flutes and oboes; the central chorus is a simple chordal setting of a chorale tune, with *colla parte* orchestration; and the final chorus is an elaborate setting of another chorale, in which the sopranos sing the cantus firmus in long notes, the other vocal parts sing contrapuntal lines, and the same brilliant orchestra as used in the opening number frames and accompanies the chorale phrases. The first of the arias—no. 4, "Ach bleibe doch, mein liebsten Leben" (Example V–15)—sung by an alto, is a particularly moving expression of sorrow and anguish at the departure of Jesus. Bach later used this aria as the basis for the "Agnus Dei" of his Mass in B Minor.

EXAMPLE V-15. Ascension Oratorio (Bach, *Werke*, 2:28).

Ah but stay, my most beloved life, . . .

The Passions. Although the only works that Bach called *Oratorium* are those treated above, it would seem reasonable for him to have given his oratorio Passions the same genre designation, since the principles of organization of their text and music are so much like those of the Christmas and Ascension oratorios. Bach composed five Passions, according to the obituary written by his son Carl Philipp Emanuel and J. S. Bach's student Johann Friedrich Agricola. Of these five, only two are known to have survived in their entirety. The surviving works are the St. John Passion (BWV 245),[52] which was first performed on Good Friday of 1724, and the St. Matthew Passion (BWV 244),[53] first performed on Good

52. Printed in Bach, *Werke*, vol. 12, pt. 1. To appear in Bach, *Neue Ausgabe*, ser. 2, vol. 4.
53. Printed in Bach, *Werke*, vol. 4. To appear in Bach, *Neue Ausgabe*, ser. 2, vol. 5.

Friday of 1729. Known to survive only in its printed libretto is Bach's St. Mark Passion (BWV 247), first performed on Good Friday of 1731. In the extensive literature on the St. John and St. Matthew Passions,[54] they have long been recognized as among Bach's most important achievements and among the greatest monuments in the history of Passion music, with the St. Matthew Passion the more significant of the two. Since the existing literature about them is so extensive, the following comments on them are brief and confined to their relationship to oratorio history.

In their librettos Bach's Passions are characteristic of the oratorio Passion: the Gospel story is quoted verbatim, but it is interrupted from time to time by reflective, poetic interpolations. These express the reactions of either the congregation, by quoting chorale texts, or an individual, by free texts. In the St. John Passion the free texts, possibly provided by Bach, are modeled on the reflective portions of the Passion-oratorio libretto by B. H. Brockes, a work written more than a decade earlier and one that had already played an important role in the history of the German Protestant oratorio. Bach also incorporated into his St. John Passion some words from J. G. Postel's libretto for an oratorio Passion according to St. John, the same libretto that Handel is said to have set in 1704 as his St. John Passion and that Mattheson had set in 1723 as *Das Lied des Lammes* (cf. chap. 4, n. 27). For the libretto of Bach's St. Matthew Passion, the free texts were written by Henrici, but it is possible that Bach selected the chorales himself. An interesting relationship between the Passion oratorio of early in the century and Bach's St. Matthew Passion is Henrici's reference to the allegorical Daughter of Zion. This personage was introduced into the earliest-known work of Protestant Germany to be called an oratorio—Hunold's libretto of *Der blutige und sterbende Jesus* (1704), set to music by Keiser—and it is also found in the Brockes Passion. Henrici is also the author of the libretto of the St. Mark Passion. Bach's Passions follow an oratorio tradition of long standing in their division into two large structural parts.

In their basic musical procedures the St. John and St. Matthew Passions have much in common with the Christmas and Ascension oratorios. The part of the Evangelist (T in both Passions) is in

54. For a general treatment of Bach's Passions, together with references to some of the most important writings about them, see Geiringer, *Bach*, pp. 194–203.

simple recitative throughout, except for occasional arioso moments to place in relief certain passages of the text. The Gospel words of individual personages are also normally set in simple recitative; an important exception occurs in the St. Matthew Passion, however, in which the words of Jesus are distinguished by an accompaniment of strings. The Gospel words of a group, the chorales, and some of the free texts are given choral settings; most of the free texts, however, are set as accompanied recitatives or arias.

It is not clear why Bach chose to use the term *Oratorium* for certain works and not for others that follow the same principles of organization. It is worth noting, however, that his use of this term dates from about 1735 and his extant Passions are earlier. What influence might have stimulated his interest in *Oratorium* around 1735 remains an open question.

PART III

*Handel and
the English Oratorio*

CHAPTER VI *Antecedents and Origins*

ᔥ*Antecedents in Seventeenth-Century England*

On the continent oratorio arose as a sacred development within the musico-dramatic current of the early seventeenth century and tended to parallel the development of opera from the mid-century to the late Baroque. In seventeenth-century England, however, the musico-dramatic current was by no means as strong as on the continent; opera began late and with little vigor, and sacred dramatic music did not develop beyond the brief dialogue. English composers cultivated the dramatic dialogue with a secular text—particularly the pastoral genre—far more than that with a sacred text.[1] Among the earliest examples of English sacred dialogues are two works by John Hilton (1599–1657)—*The Dialogue of King Solomon and the Two Harlots* and *The Dialogue of Job, God, Satan, Job's Wife and the Messengers*—that were composed possibly as early as 1616.[2] Both compositions, accompanied by continuo only, include several exchanges among the characters and a concluding chorus. This type of English dialogue has been considered a dramatic development of the verse anthem; in fact, an extant text of a verse anthem by Richard Portman (d. ca. 1655), "How many hired servants" (1635), is a dialogue based on the story of the prodigal son.[3] In that text the dialogue among the

1. For surveys of the secular dialogue in early seventeenth-century England, see Spink, "Dialogues," pp. 159–62; Fogle, "Vocal Music."
2. The date 1616 for both works is suggested in Smallman, "Dialogues," p. 134. The MS sources of both are in GB/Lbm: Add. 11, 608. *The Dialogue of Job* is printed in Nagel, "Hilton," pp. 127–34; and both dialogues are edited in Fogle, "Vocal Music."
3. Spink, "Dialogues," p. 161, n. 17. The MS source of this text is in GB/Lbm: Harl. 6,346. For an outline comparison of this text with G. F. Anerio's dialogue from his *Teatro* (1619) on the same story, see Smallman, "Dialogues," pp. 139–40.

FIGURE VI-1. First page of John Hilton's *Dialogue of King Solomon,*
from the manuscript GB/Lbm: Add. 11, 608.
(Reproduced by permission of GB/Lbm.)

FIGURE VI-2. First page of Hilton's *Dialogue of Job*, from the same manuscript as Figure VI-1.

personages takes place in the verses, and the chorus sings the narrative passages. Two works from a somewhat later period, by John Wilson (1595–1674) and Henry Blowman, are dialogues among the devil, a dying man, and an angel.[4] The dialogue text "In guilty night," based on the story of Saul and the Witch of Endor (1 Sam. 28:8–20) and including three personages—Saul, the Witch, and Samuel—was set several times in the seventeenth century. The earliest-known setting is by Robert Ramsey (d. 1644?), whose work was revised, with a new continuo part, by Nicholas Lanier (1588–1666).[5] The only sacred dramatic dialogue by Henry Purcell (1659–95) is his intense setting of "In guilty night," mostly in arioso style, for three voices singing the roles of Saul (A), the Witch of Endor (S), and Samuel (B); the voices combine in introductory and concluding ensembles.[6] The same text was set in the late seventeenth or early eighteenth century by Benjamin Lamb, who became verger of St. George's Chapel, Windsor, in 1680 and served as organist of Eton College during the first quarter of the eighteenth century.[7]

The dialogues mentioned above indicate that English composers made a tentative beginning with the type of composition that might have led, perhaps by way of a dramatic verse anthem, to a fully developed English oratorio. They did not carry this development on to the oratorio, however, and when Handel arrived in England, he found audiences that were totally unfamiliar with the oratorio. The English oratorio is Handel's creation, his remarkable synthesis of elements derived from a variety of sources: the Italian *opera seria* and *oratorio volgare*, the choral style exhibited in his Latin psalms composed during his Italian period, the German oratorio, the French classical drama, the English masque, and English choral music. This synthesis resulted in a type of oratorio that differs remarkably from the genre as cultivated on the continent.

4. The MS sources are in GB/Lbm: Add. 29,396 and 30,382, respectively.
5. For MS sources of the Ramsey and Lanier versions, see GB/Lbm: Add. 11,608 and 22,100, respectively. For a discussion of the relationship between the two versions, with music examples, see Smallman, "Dialogues," p. 142. Ramsey's version is printed in *EECM*, 7:121–31; and Fogle, "Vocal Music."
6. Printed in Purcell, *Works*, 32:128–36.
7. The MS source is in GB/Lbm: Add. 31,453. For a brief discussion of the work, with a music example, see Smallman, "Dialogues," p. 144.

Handel the Opera Composer in England

George Frideric Handel[8] first arrived in London in the fall of 1710. A sojourn of only a few months at the court of Elector Georg Ludwig of Hanover, where Handel had accepted the position of Kapellmeister, separated his rich Italian experience from this London visit. During the season of 1710–11, Handel's sixth opera, *Rinaldo*, was composed and performed, and it was an overwhelming success. After a little more than a year back in Hanover, Handel received another leave of absence to return to London, and he never resumed his Hanover position. Thus in the fall of 1712 he was again in London, where he was to make his home for the rest of his life.

In London, as in Italy, Handel was successful in his relationship with the aristocracy. Early in this period he resided at the palace of the earl of Burlington, and from about 1717 to 1720 he apparently was in the service of James Brydges, the duke of Chandos, and possibly resided at Cannons, the duke's magnificent Middlesex residence.[9] It was also during this period that Queen Anne granted Handel an annual pension for his services, despite his being a foreigner, a fact that made this an illegal grant; soon after Elector Georg Ludwig of Hanover had become King George I of England (1714), he not only confirmed but doubled Queen Anne's pension for Handel.[10]

The year 1719 saw the formation of the Royal Academy of Music, an opera society for which King George I provided the

8. Among the many secondary sources on Handel's life and works, the following are particularly useful: Chrysander, *Händel*; Flower, *Handel*; Lang, *Handel*; Leichtentritt, *Händel*; Serauky, *Händel*; and Streatfeild, *Handel*. For an extensive Handel bibliography see Sasse, *Händel*; for more recent bibliographical information see Mann, "Handel Research" and Smither, "Baroque Oratorio." Of primary importance for Handel's English oratorios is Dean, *Oratorios*, an extremely thorough and extensive study; part 3 of the present volume, in its general structure and many of its details, relies heavily upon Dean's distinguished contribution. For a quite general treatment of Handel's oratorios, see Young, *Oratorios*. Among the most important sources of eighteenth-century commentary about Handel and his music are Burney, *Account*; Burney, *History*; Deutsch, *Handel* and Mainwaring, *Memoirs*.

9. It is uncertain whether Handel resided at Cannons or in London. According to Larsen, "*Esther*," p. 8, he probably resided in London. For the few known dates of Handel's activities in the period 1717–20, see Dean, *Oratorios*, p. 159.

10. There appears to be no evidence of strained relations between Handel and King George I, his former employer at Hanover, despite Handel's having ignored his agreement to return to the Hanover court; "the 'reconciliation' on the occasion of the famous barge party on the Thames when the *Water Music* was played is fictitious, and so, probably, are all the others." (Lang, *Handel*, p. 133.)

FIGURE VI-3. George Frideric Handel (1685–1759). From an oil painting by Thomas Hudson, 1748.
(Reproduced by permission of the Heather Professor of Music, Oxford University.)

chief financial backing. Among the numerous other backers were Handel's patrons, the earl of Burlington and the duke of Chandos. Known as an outstanding opera composer throughout his early London period, Handel was employed by the academy in the capacity of musical director, with the title Master of the Orchestra; in addition, Giovanni Bononcini (1670–1747) was brought from Rome in 1720 to compose operas for the academy and play in its orchestra.[11] Thus Handel began a ten-year period of intense operatic activity during which he composed thirteen operas; the period was marked by musical success, rivalry with Bononcini, and problems with singers—most notably and scandalously with the prima donnas Francesca Cuzzoni and Faustina Bordoni. The academy failed financially in 1728 after nine seasons in which 487 opera performances were given; about half of the performances were of Handel's operas.[12] Chiefly responsible for the academy's failure were its extravagant expenditures and the shift of public interest from Italian serious opera to popular entertainment, of which *The Beggar's Opera* (1728) is the prime example. Nevertheless, neither Handel's financial status nor his reputation as an artist seems to have been threatened by the academy's failure: he immediately joined with John Jacob Heidegger, long a successful theater manager, to establish a second academy for the performance of opera. Evidently not yet aware of the extent to which London audiences were losing sympathy for Italian opera, Handel and Heidegger continued to produce operas for several years. The failure of the second academy in 1734 was hastened by the formation in 1733 of a competing company, the Opera of the Nobility, under the musical direction of Nicola Porpora (1686–1766). Throughout the 1730s Handel continued to compose Italian operas, most of which were performed at the Theatre Royal in Covent Garden. His last two operas, *Imeneo* and *Deidamia*, were completed in 1740, but both were failures in the 1740–41 season at the Lincoln's Inn Fields Theatre, where they ran for two and three performances, respectively.

In his operas Handel worked generally within the confines of the *opera seria* conventions of his time. Essentially a dramatist, he would occasionally bend these conventions to suit the dynamics of

11. Deutsch, *Handel*, p. 97.
12. Chrysander, *Händel*, 2:188.

his dramatic conception, but he did not abandon them. The experience gained in his struggle to reconcile the highly stylized conventions of *opera seria* with his desire for dramatic action was undoubtedly of importance for the development of his less stylized and more dramatically continuous English oratorios, composed not for the theater but for "a theater of the imagination."[13]

Antecedents in Handel's English Music

Early Nondramatic Works in English

From the beginning of his London period, Handel set both English and Italian texts. The nondramatic works discussed here are antecedents of his English oratorios in the sense that they offered him the experience of setting English to music and of exercising his technique of choral composition, little used in opera but important in his English oratorios. For his oratorios Handel borrowed music, sometimes virtually unchanged, from most of his works mentioned here.

Handel's early English efforts led him, quite naturally, to a study of the music of Henry Purcell, the best and most popular English composer of the recent past. The *Utrecht Te Deum* and *Jubilate* (1713) depends for its general structure and some aspects of style on Purcell's *Te Deum* and *Jubilate* for St. Cecilia's Day of 1694,[14] and Handel's *Ode for the Birthday of Queen Anne* (1713) no doubt reflects the influence of Purcell's welcome and birthday odes.[15] The choruses of Handel's *Ode* are mostly brief, with the first and final choruses being the longest and most elaborate. All the choruses are preceded by solos or ensembles, which in several instances are continued without pause by the chorus; Handel had previously used this technique, common in the Baroque period, in the final choruses of both parts of his *La Resurrezione* and in his Latin psalms, all from his Italian period. In the *Te Deum* and

13. Dean, *Opera*, p. 19. Dean comments on Handel's attitude toward the conventions of *opera seria* in ibid., pp. 17–24.

14. For modern editions of these Handel and Purcell compositions, see Handel, *Werke*, vol. 31, and Purcell, *Works*, 23:90; for comments on the similarities, see Chrysander, *Händel*, 1:388, and Lang, *Handel*, p. 130.

15. For modern editions, see Handel, *Ausgabe*, ser. 1, vol. 1, and Purcell, *Works*, vols. 11, 15, 18, 23, and 24. For comments regarding Purcell's influence on this *Ode* by Handel, see Herbage, "Oratorios," pp. 74–75.

Jubilate the choruses are more numerous, extensive, and varied than in the *Ode*.

The Chandos Anthems,[16] twelve settings of English psalm texts composed from 1717 to 1720 for the duke of Chandos, are at times similar in style to the anthemlike choruses of the oratorios. The three choruses in the third anthem, *Have mercy upon me*,[17] foreshadow certain types of oratorio choruses in extent, contrapuntal technique, and manner of expressing the affections of lamentation and joy; uncharacteristic of the oratorio choruses, however, is the restriction of this anthem to three voices. Other choruses that are close in spirit and technique to many of those of the oratorios are the first and last choruses of the fifth Chandos anthem, *I will magnify Thee*,[18] in its *a 3* version, and the choruses "Glory and worship before Him" (*a 7*) and "Tell it out among the heathen" (*a 4*) in the larger version of the same work (anthem Vb).

The Coronation Anthems,[19] four works composed in 1727 for the coronation service of George II, anticipate some of Handel's oratorio choruses in their exploitation of sonority for massive effect. This is particularly true of the first two anthems, *Zadok the Priest* and *The King shall rejoice*, both of which employ large orchestras, including three trumpets and tympani, and emphasize chordal texture in the chorus. The third anthem, *My heart is inditing*, makes less use of massive effect than the first two, and the last one, *Let thy hand be strengthened*, generally the least imposing of the four, employs a reduced orchestration.

An Early Dramatic Work in English

An English composition that is particularly significant as an antecedent of Handel's English oratorios is *Acis and Galatea* (ca. 1718), composed for James Brydges, later the duke of Chandos.[20] Among Handel's earliest dramatic compositions in English, *Acis* was extremely popular throughout the eighteenth century and was revived more frequently during Handel's life than any of his other

16. Printed in Handel, *Werke*, vols. 34–36.
17. Printed ibid., vol. 34.
18. Printed ibid.
19. Printed ibid., vol. 14.
20. The present description of *Acis* is based on the two-act version printed in Handel, *Werke*, vol. 3. For an analysis of *Acis* and comments on its various versions, see Dean, *Oratorios*, pp. 153–90.

works.[21] Called a masque—but sung throughout in recitatives, arias (all but one in da capo form), ensembles, and choruses—*Acis* is essentially a short, pastoral opera, as are the several compositions called masques that were performed in London's public theaters from 1715 through 1718.[22] *Acis* differs from those works in a number of respects, however, among which are the absence of dancing, less emphasis upon spectacle, and more use of the chorus.

The libretto of *Acis*, mainly by John Gay but with contributions by Alexander Pope and John Hughes, is based on a Sicilian myth and is derived from Ovid's *Metamorphoses* (13. 750–897).[23] The conflict of the plot is between the lovers Acis (a shepherd, T) and Galatea (a sea nymph, S) on the one hand, and Polyphemus (a giant, B) on the other. Damon (T), the only remaining soloist and a minor character, advises Acis in act 1 and both Acis and Polyphemus in act 2. Act 1 is dominated by the lovers' pastoral bliss. In act 2 Polyphemus intrudes upon the joyful scene, declares his passion for Galatea, and kills Acis. After a scene of lamentation, Galatea uses her divine power to immortalize Acis by changing him into a fountain. In this form "through the plains he joys to rove,/Murm'ring still his gentle love."

Acis represents an important step toward the English oratorio, because of the function of the chorus of Nymphs and Shepherds (STTTB; in one instance TTB). The two choruses in act 1, which occur at the opening and closing of the act, contribute to the pastoral and joyful mood but are not essential to the dramatic action; they are relatively brief and primarily homophonic. The choruses in act 2, however, are involved in the dramatic action and are thus closer to most of those of the oratorios. The opening chorus of act 2, addressed to Acis and Galatea, communicates fate's harsh decree to the lovers; here the chorus generates the emotional conflict of the work and introduces the comical monster, Polyphemus, the agent of the tragic events to follow:

> CHORUS: Wretched lovers! fate has past
> This sad decree: no joy shall last.
> Wretched lovers, quit your dream!

21. For lists of performances of Handel's masques and dramatic oratorios during his life, see Dean, *Oratorios*, apps. C and D.
22. For a survey of the masques of those years, see ibid., pp. 155–59. According to Larsen, "*Esther*," p. 8, *Acis* may not have been staged at its first performance.
23. Handel's *Aci, Galatea, e Polifemo,* composed in Italy in 1708, treats the same subject but is a different work.

Behold the monster Polypheme!
See what ample strides he takes!
The mountain nods, the forest shakes:
The waves run frightened to the shores:
Hark, how the thund'ring giant roars!

The emotional intensity of the music of the first three lines, imitative and filled with suspension dissonances, is entirely worthy of the later Handel of the oratorios, who uses the chorus for similar affections in a comparable manner; and the setting of the monster's approach (Example VI-1)—with appropriate musical descriptions of the ample strides, the mountain's nodding, the forest's shaking, the frightened waves, and the roaring thunder—has much in common with the descriptive choruses of *Israel in Egypt*. In the subsequent choruses of act 2, the Nymphs and Shepherds continue to play a role in the drama by first consoling her ("Cease, Galatea, cease to grieve!") and later by continuing their consolation and reflecting on the conclusion of the story ("Galatea, dry thy tears").

EXAMPLE VI-1. *Acis and Galatea* (Handel, *Werke*, 3:54–62).

(EXAMPLE VI-1, continued)

(EXAMPLE VI-I, continued)

(EXAMPLE VI-1, continued)

The Beginning of the English Oratorio: 1718, 1732–33

It seems likely that Handel composed the early version of his first oratorio, *Esther*, in 1718. In the years 1732 and 1733 he revised and expanded *Esther* and composed two more oratorios, *Deborah* and *Athalia*—the latter is his first great work in this genre. With these three works the essentials of the Handelian oratorio were established. As an unstaged but normally dramatic genre, it was comparable to its counterpart on the continent; but it differed from the continental oratorio traditions in a number of respects, foremost among them the prominent role of the chorus.

Esther: *The First Version*

The first version of Handel's *Esther*[24] appears to have been composed in 1718 for James Brydges, later the duke of Chandos, thus

24. Printed in Handel, *Werke*, vol. 40. For a history and analysis of this work, see Dean, *Oratorios*, pp. 191–203.

at about the same time and for the same patron as *Acis and Galatea*. The story, mostly from Esther 2–8, had long been established in Italy as an oratorio subject, a fact of which Handel was probably aware.[25] Most of the manuscript sources of the work's first version call it simply *Esther*, without a genre designation; one of the sources calls it "The Oratorium Composed by George Frederick Handel Esquire in London, 1718";[26] and one source calls it a masque, and names it *Haman and Mordecai*.

Esther's anonymous libretto has been attributed to Alexander Pope and John Arbuthnot, among others; it appears to have been a collaborative effort, perhaps written chiefly by Arbuthnot with some assistance by Pope.[27] *Esther* is of particular importance for having first brought to the English oratorio, by way of French classical drama, the influence of ancient Greek tragedy; the libretto is indirectly indebted to Jean Racine's classical tragedy *Esther* (1688, first performed in 1689). Racine includes a chorus that both participates in and comments on the dramatic action. Most of the dialogue in Racine's work was spoken, but the songs and choruses were sung to musical settings composed by Jean-Baptiste Moreau (1656–1733).[28] Prior to Handel's work, Racine's tragedy had been the model for an English play—*Esther, or Faith Triumphant, a Sacred Tragedy*, by Thomas Brereton—published in 1717. Similarities of wording between the libretto that Handel set and Brereton's play indicate that the latter, rather than Racine's tragedy, was the librettist's source.[29]

The libretto of *Esther*'s first version is in one act of six scenes. The plot's conflict is between the Persians and the captive Jewish

25. The first Latin composition known to be called an oratorio is Della Valle's *Esther*, discussed in this study, vol. 1, chap. 4; Legrenzi and Stradella also composed oratorios on the subject of Esther; in 1703 Gregorio Cola's Latin oratorio on this subject was performed in Rome at Crocifisso (Alaleona, *Oratorio*, p. 357); and an oratorio on this story is included in Spagna, *Oratorii* (Rome, 1706—about the time that Handel arrived in that city).

26. I gratefully acknowledge the help of Professor Howard Serwer, who has advised me that in the course of research for his new editions of *Esther* in its shorter and longer versions, he has seen in private hands a MS dated 1718 that calls the work *Oratorium*. He considers both the date and the designation *Oratorium* to be authentic. It remains uncertain whether *Esther* was staged at its first performance. For an assumption that it was staged, see Dean, *Oratorios*, p. 191; for a contrary assumption, see Larsen, "Esther," p. 8.

27. Dean, *Oratorios*, p. 197.

28. For Racine's *Esther*, with commentary, see Racine, *Oeuvres*, 1:823–80. Concerning the background of Racine's *Esther*, see Dean, *Oratorios*, pp. 192–93, and Orcibal, *Esther*.

29. For comparisons between Brereton's play and the libretto, see Dean, *Oratorios*, pp. 194–95.

people. Haman (B) is a tyrannical Persian prince supported by a chorus of Persian Soldiers (SATTB). The representatives of the Jews, whom Hamon wishes to destroy, are Esther (S), the newly chosen queen of Persia; Mordecai (T), a priest for whom Haman has a particular hatred; and a chorus of Israelites (SATTB). Minor roles are those of the Persian Habdonah (T) and various Israelites (S, A, T). Esther intervenes on behalf of her people with her husband Ahasuerus (T), who is the king of the Persians. Because of her intervention Haman's plot against the Jews is defeated, he is put to death, and Mordecai is honored for having been instrumental in saving the king's life. Redundancy, poor motivation of the characters, and insufficient information conveyed to the audience make this libretto dramatically weak.[30] The work is significant, however, for having established several prominent characteristics of the English oratorio: the Old Testament story, a heroic attitude, and the prominence of the chorus, used in a manner similar to the chorus of ancient Greek tragedy.

The arias of *Esther*, like those of *Acis*, are nearly all in da capo form, and some are borrowed from the Brockes Passion, as are some of the other numbers.[31] The choruses appear mostly at the ends of scenes and tend to alternate between homophonic and polyphonic textures. The chorus of Persian Soldiers sings only once, at the end of the first scene; this chorus, "Shall we the God of Israel fear," is textually and musically related to Haman's aria, "Pluck root and branch," that precedes it. The chorus of Israelites makes its first appearance, "Shall we of servitude complain," in the second scene, one of rejoicing for Esther's having been made queen. In the choruses of subsequent scenes, the Israelites lament their captivity ("Ye sons of Israel, mourn"), call on God for help ("Save us, O Lord"), and reflect on Esther's virtue and God's help ("Virtue, truth, and innocence" and "He comes to end our woes"). In the finale, "The Lord our enemy has slain," the chorus of Israelites, Esther, and Mordecai rejoice and praise God for their victory. In its length, multisectional structure, and alternation of the chorus with solos and a duet, the finale is much like an anthem, and it is similar to the finales of some of the later oratorios. Particularly striking is the section, used as a ritornello throughout much of the finale, set to the text "For ever blessed be Thy

30. Cf. the analysis of the libretto ibid., pp. 196–97.
31. For a list of the borrowings in *Esther*, see ibid., p. 641.

Holy name" (Example VI–2). The combination of a theme in long notes with an eighth-note, repeated motive on the words "For ever" clearly foreshadows the similar treatment in the "Hallelujah" chorus of *Messiah*.

EXAMPLE VI-2. *Esther* (Handel, *Werke*, 40:114).

(EXAMPLE VI-2, continued)

The orchestra of *Esther*—oboe, trumpet, two French horns, two violins, harp, and basso continuo—is slightly larger than that of *Acis*. The overture is in three movements (andante, larghetto, and allegro), the last two of which are also found in Handel's trio sonata, op. 2, no. 4.

Esther: *The Second Version*[32]

For more than a decade after the composition of *Esther*'s first version Handel apparently did not return to the work, except perhaps for a performance of some numbers from it in Bristol in 1727. In 1732 Bernard Gates, the master of the children of the Chapel Royal, began a chain of events that led to the revision of

32. Printed in Handel, *Werke*, vol. 41.

FIGURE VI-4. The Crown and Anchor Tavern, where
Handel's *Esther* was staged on 23 February
1732. From a watercolor by J. Findlay,
1851.
(Reproduced by permission of GB/Lbm.)

Esther. On Handel's birthday, 23 February 1732, Gates presented
to the Philharmonic Society a staged performance of *Esther*, which
Handel reportedly attended, at the Crown and Anchor Tavern.
The title page of the printed libretto used two genre designations
for the work: "Esther: an Oratorio; or, Sacred Drama. The Musick

As it was Composed for the Most Noble James Duke of Chandos. By George Frederick Handel, in the Year 1720. And Perform'd by the Children of His Majesty's Chapel."[33] The word *oratorio* had been little used as a musical designation in England prior to this time—a fact that would account for its application in a broader manner there than in its native Italy. Staged performances of works called oratorios are virtually nonexistent on the continent during Handel's time;[34] thus to call a work such as *Esther*, when staged, an oratorio would be a highly exceptional use of the term on the continent. *Esther* was called an oratorio in London apparently because of its sacred subject. The genre classification of *Esther* was no doubt a stumbling block for many an Englishman of the time, as it was for Viscount Percival, a great admirer of Handel's music, who wrote in his diary on 23 February 1732: "From dinner I went to the Music Club [i.e., the Philharmonic Society], where the King's Chapel boys acted the *History of Hester*, writ by Pope, and composed by Hendel. This oratoria or religious opera is exceeding fine, and the company were highly pleased, some of the parts being well performed."[35] Thus the viscount employed three designations for the work, *history*, *opera*, and *oratoria*. (His spelling of the last term changed in subsequent entries in his diary during that year to *oratory* [2 May] and *oratorio* [6 May]).[36] The printed libretto for Gates's production of *Esther* mentions some aspects of the performance, including remarks of particular interest regarding the constitution and placement of the chorus: "Mr. Bernard Gates, Master of the Children of the Chapel-Royal, together with a Number of Voices from the Choirs of St. James's and Westminster, join'd in the Chorus's, after the Manner of the Ancients, being placed between the Stage and the Orchestra."[37] After the performance on Handel's birthday, Gates presented *Esther* twice more, on 1 and 3 March, for the Philharmonic Society and the Academy of Ancient Music, respectively.

33. Dean, *Oratorios*, p. 219. The date 1720 is probably that of a performance rather than of the work's origin.
34. This point, treated in the present study, vol. 1, chap. 6, is contrary to assumptions (in Dean, "Dramatic," p. 35, and Dean, *Oratorios*, pp. 7–8) that oratorios were staged on the continent.
35. Diary of Viscount Percival, 23 February 1732, in Deutsch, *Handel*, p. 286.
36. Diary of Viscount Percival, 2 and 6 May 1732, ibid., 290–91.
37. Dean, *Oratorios*, p. 204.

Although the above-mentioned performances of *Esther* were for private societies, in mid-April 1732 a forthcoming public performance was announced in a London newspaper, the *Daily Journal*: "*Never Perform'd in Publick before*, At the Great Room in Villars-street York Buildings . . . will be perform'd ESTHER an ORATORIO or, *Sacred Drama*."[38] It is not known who was responsible for this performance or whether it was staged; the score used was evidently pirated. The notice ran in the newspaper for several days prior to 20 April, the date of the performance. Handel appears to have acted quickly to counteract the pirates. On 19 April, just above the announcement in the *Daily Journal* of the unauthorized performance, Handel announced his own forthcoming presentation of the work:

By His MAJESTY's *Command*
At the King's Theatre in the Hay-Market, on Tuesday the 2d Day of May, will be performed, the *Sacred Story* of ESTHER: an *Oratorio* in *English*. Formerly compos'd by Mr. *Handel*, and now revised by him, with several Additions, and to be performed by the best Voices and Instruments.
N. B. There will be no Action on the Stage, but the House will be fitted up in a decent Manner, for the Audience. The Musick to be disposed after the Manner of the Coronation Service.[39]

Handel's announcement was clearly intended to make the pirated version of *Esther* obsolete and to promise an audience a better performance than the pirates could offer. Not only does he promise some new music, but also the "best Voices," implying the singers of the King's Theatre where *Esther* was to be performed. The announcement's reference to the coronation service evidently meant that the musicians would be seated as they had been at that service of 1727—that is, in an amphitheatrical arrangement[40]— and perhaps also that some of the music and the performing forces would be similar to those at that ceremonial occasion.

The note in Handel's announcement that "There will be no Action on the Stage, but the House will be fitted up in a decent Manner" reminds one of the normal Italian practice of presenting an oratorio: a concert performance, sometimes with a specially

38. *Daily Journal* (London) 19 April 1732, in Deutsch, *Handel*, p. 288.
39. Ibid.
40. Deutsch, *Handel*, p. 214.

FIGURE VI-5. The King's Theatre in the Haymarket, where Handel's
Esther was performed in an unstaged version in May
1732, and where many of his other oratorios were performed in subsequent years. From a watercolor by William Capon, 1783.
(Reproduced by permission of GB/Lbm.)

decorated stage and hall. In this manner, for instance, Handel's *La
Resurrezione* (1708) had been performed in Rome (cf. volume 1,
pp. 264–65). The composer's Italian experience and the oratoriolike subject matter of *Esther* would explain why Handel could have
accepted a performance of this work without action and with the
theater suitably decorated. Nevertheless, he may have originally
intended *Esther* to be staged—it had recently been successfully
performed as a staged work—and he would perhaps have preferred that it be staged at the King's Theatre. According to Charles
Burney, Handel did not stage *Esther* at the theater because he was
denied permission to do so by Bishop Edmund Gibson (1669–
1748):

Mr. Handel himself was present at one of these representations [of *Esther*, at the Crown and Anchor Tavern], and having mentioned it to the princess Royal, his illustrious scholar, her Royal Highness was pleased to express a desire to see it exhibited in action at the Opera-house in the Hay-market, by the same young performers; but Dr. Gibson, then bishop of London, would not grant permission for its being represented on that stage, even with books in the children's hands. Mr. Handel, however, the next year [actually in 1732], had it performed at the theatre, with additions to the Drama, by Humphreys; but in *still life*: that is, without action, in the same manner as Oratorios have been since constantly performed.[41]

Bishop Gibson, who was dean of the Chapel Royal, considered the opera house an immoral place, and his objections were apparently to a staged performance there of a work with a sacred subject and to the participation in that performance of the boys of the Chapel Royal.[42] Thus forced to compromise, Handel accepted for *Esther* the traditional continental manner of presenting oratorios. Except for the bishop's refusal to grant permission, English oratorio might well have become a staged genre. *Esther* was a great success in its new form and was performed six times between 2 and 20 May to full houses.[43] According to the *Daily Courant*, on 3, 6, 13, and 20 May "their Majesties, his Royal Highness the Prince of Wales, and the Three Eldest Princesses, went to the Opera-House in the Hay-Market, and saw an Entertainment of Musick call'd Esther, an Oratorio."[44] Significant in this report, and in others like it, is the word *entertainment*, for Handel's performances of *Esther* in the opera house established the English oratorio as a musico-dramatic entertainment without staging. Despite its sacred subject, the English oratorio was not intended primarily to be a vehicle of devotion; it was a concert genre more closely related to the theater than the church.

According to Burney, it was during the earliest performances of *Esther* and *Deborah*, in 1732 and 1733, "that Handel first

41. Burney, "Commemoration," pp. 100–101. Burney received this information "from Dr. Randall, the musical professor at Cambridge, and Mr. Barrow, who were among the original performers, when it [*Esther*] was dramatically represented." (Ibid., p. 100.)

42. Dean, *Oratorios*, pp. 205–6.

43. Deutsch, *Handel*, p. 292. According to Dean, *Oratorios*, p. 203, *Esther* was performed ten times between February and May.

44. Deutsch, *Handel*, pp. 290–92; quotation from *Daily Courant*, 22 May 1732, ibid., p. 292.

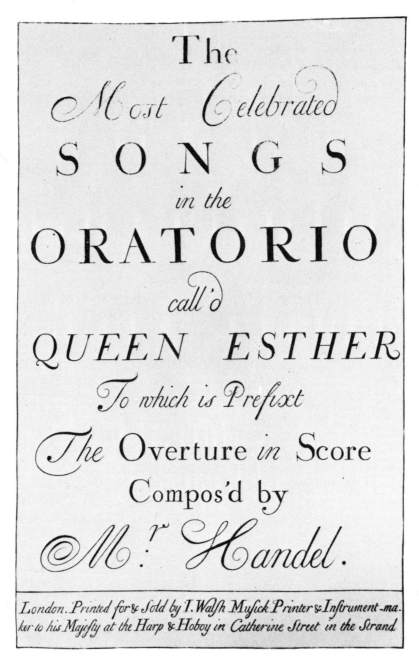

The
Most Celebrated
SONGS
in the
ORATORIO
call'd
QUEEN ESTHER
To which is Prefixt
The Overture in Score
Compos'd by
Mr. Handel.

London. Printed for & Sold by T. Walsh Musick Printer & Instrument-maker to his Majesty at the Harp & Hoboy in Catherine Street in the Strand

FIGURE VI-6. Title page of the first edition of the songs in Handel's
Esther (1732).
(Reproduced by permission of Gerald Coke, Esq.)

gratified the public by the performance of Concertos on the Organ, a species of music wholly of his own invention."[45] While Burney was probably correct in associating Handel's first organ concertos with performances of *Esther* and *Deborah*, he seems to have been wrong in his dates. Handel's earliest organ concertos were probably first performed between the acts of those oratorios when they were revived in 1735.[46] During the remainder of his career, Handel often performed organ concertos between the acts of his oratorios. Some of the concertos can be identified today as those introduced with certain oratorios.[47]

Handel's 1732 version of *Esther*[48] was divided into three acts with three scenes each. The additional text needed for the new version was supplied by Samuel Humphreys, the librettist of Handel's next two oratorios, *Deborah* and *Athalia*. In addition to the recitatives, the new music consists of six arias, one arioso, two duets, and three choruses; two of the choruses were borrowed from the Coronation Anthems (one from the massive *Zadok the Priest*) and one from the *Ode for the Birthday of Queen Anne*. A chorus and an aria were deleted from the 1720 version, and the B parts and da capos of three arias were also deleted—this revised work marks the beginning of Handel's diminishing interest in the da capo aria in the oratorios. The long finale of the first version was shortened to about one-third its former length, which created a more satisfactory balance, and the overture was expanded. Of special interest is the orchestration of the 1732 version. Not only did Handel borrow choruses from the Coronation Anthems, but he also called for the large orchestra of those works. He expanded the orchestra throughout the oratorio to include pairs of recorders, oboes, bassoons, and horns, three trumpets, tympani, strings, and continuo (including theorbo, harp, two harpsichords, and two organs).[49]

45. Burney, "Sketch," p. 23.
46. Gudger, "Concertos" (diss.), 1:95–99.
47. For a summary of "the best evidence of which concertos were introduced with which oratorios or odes," see the list in Gudger, "Concertos" (diss.), 1:324. For more information see ibid., chaps. 4–10 and vol. 2, app. 3. The principal conclusions of this dissertation are summarized in Gudger, "Concertos" (art.).
48. The edition of *Esther* in Handel, *Werke*, vol. 41, identified by the editor as the 1732 version, is a mixture of several versions; for detailed information on the various versions of *Esther*, see Dean, *Oratorios*, pp. 207–9, 214–19, and app. G.
49. Dean, *Oratorios*, pp. 209, 628.

Deborah[50]

After the highly successful performances of *Esther*, Handel evidently sought to profit by what appeared to be a trend in audience taste. The subject matter of *Deborah*, his new oratorio, may have been suggested by Maurice Greene's nondramatic composition (not called an oratorio) titled *Part of the Song of Deborah and Barak paraphrased from Judges 5*;[51] Greene's work was probably performed in October 1732. Handel completed his *Deborah* on 21 February 1733, and on 12 March the *Daily Journal* announced: "At the King's Theatre . . . on Saturday the 17th of March, will be performed, DEBORAH, an *Oratorio*, or *Sacred Drama*, in *English* Composed by Mr. Handel. And to be performed by a great Number of the best Voices and Instruments. N.B. This is the last Dramatick Performance that will be exhibited at the King's Theatre till after Easter. The House to be fitted up and illuminated in a new and particular Manner."[52] Thus Handel's second oratorio, like the first, was a substitute for opera and was first performed on a Saturday night (normally an opera night at the King's Theatre); it was advertised as an oratorio, a sacred drama, and a "Dramatick Performance." The "new and particular Manner" in which the theater was "fitted up and illuminated" was no doubt intended to substitute for the absence of the scenery one would normally expect in the theater. The *Daily Journal* was unclear about the genre of *Deborah*, for on 2 April the *Journal* reported: "On Saturday Night last [31 March] the King, Queen, Prince, and the three eldest Princesses were at the King's Theatre in the Haymarket, and saw the Opera called Deborah."[53] The lack of distinction between the terms *opera* and *oratorio* seems to have been common in London at this time.

Deborah's opening night was a box-office failure. Handel had doubled his usual prices and had designated the performance as being outside the regular subscription series. According to a contemporary letter by Lady A. Irwin, only 120 people bought tickets, although some subscribers, "insisting upon the right of their silver

50. Printed in Handel, *Werke*, vol. 29.

51. For a discussion of Greene's *Deborah*, see Dean, *Oratorios*, pp. 226–28; for a modern edition see Greene, *Deborah*. Handel's *Deborah* owes nothing of its libretto nor of its music to Greene's work.

52. *Daily Journal* (London), 12 March 1733, in Deutsch, *Handel*, p. 308.

53. *Daily Journal* (London), 2 April 1733, ibid., p. 310.

subscription tickets, forced into the House, and carried their point."[54] The initial failure of *Deborah* was publicized by an eight-line epigram, appearing in the weekly *Bee*, that compared the failure of Sir Robert Walpole's excise bill on tobacco (introduced in Parliament on 14 March) with that of Handel's oratorio; both men were satirized as having tried to fleece the public, and according to the final couplet, "*In half they succeeded, in half they were crost;/The* Tobacco *was sav'd, but poor* Deborah *lost.*"[55] *Deborah*'s five more performances at the King's Theatre (at lower prices) were received with mixed reactions, according to contemporary reports: Viscount Percival called it "very magnificent, near a hundred performers, among whom about twenty-five singers,"[56] but Lady Irwin wrote, "Tis excessive noisy, a vast number of instruments and voices, who all perform at a time, and is in music what I fancy a French ordinary in conversation."[57]

The three-act libretto of *Deborah*, by Samuel Humphreys, is based on Judges 4–5, which relates the story of a conflict between the Israelites and the Canaanites. This story, like that of Esther and most of the others that form the basis of Handel's oratorios, was one of those previously used as the subject of oratorio librettos in Italy.[58] In Humphreys's libretto the chief representatives of the Israelites are Deborah (S), Barak (A), Abinoam (B), and Jael (S); they are supported by three Israelite Women (S, S, S), the Chief Priest of the Israelites (B), and the chorus of Israelite Priests (SSAATTBB and smaller groupings). The Canaanites' chief representative is Sisara (A), and he is supported by the Chief Priest of Baal (B) and the chorus of Priests of Baal (SSATB and SATB). In act 1 Deborah, a prophetess and judge of Israel, calls on Barak to lead the Israelites in battle against the Canaanites, led by Sisara. Deborah prophesies that the Israelites will be victorious and that Sisara will perish by a woman's hand. A fruitless negotiation between the opposing sides takes place in act 2; the choruses of the Priests of Baal and of the Israelites call on their respective gods for help. At the beginning of act 3, the audience learns that the Canaanites were vanquished in the battle and Sisara has tried to

54. Irwin to Lord Carlisle, 31 March [1733], ibid., p. 310.
55. *Bee: or, Universal Weekly Pamphlet*, 24 March 1733, ibid., p. 309.
56. Diary of Viscount Percival, 27 March 1733, ibid., p. 309.
57. Irwin to Carlisle, 31 March [1733], ibid., p. 310.
58. For example, see Spagna's *La prudenza tra it perigli nell'historia di Debora*, in Spagna, *Oratorii*, 1:25–39.

escape. He was offered shelter by Jael, the wife of his ally, and while he slept in her tent, she fulfilled Deborah's prophesy:

> JAEL: The workman's hammer and a nail I seiz'd
> And, whilst his limbs in deep repose he eas'd,
> I through his bursting temples forc'd the wound,
> And riveted the tyrant to the ground.

The Israelites rejoice and praise Jael for her deed and Jehovah for his help.[59] Insufficient character development and human conflict make the libretto dramatically weak. Sisara, for example, is never made convincing as a tyrant; thus his cruel death seems insufficient cause for the rejoicing of the finale. The strength of the libretto, however, is in the dramatic role of the choruses, and particularly in the choral conflict between the priests of the opposing forces.

The music of *Deborah* seems to have occupied relatively little of Handel's time. Well over half of the numbers are borrowed from his earlier works (twenty-eight numbers from twelve sources), and over half of the borrowed numbers are used virtually without change.[60] The sources of the borrowings range from works of Handel's Italian period, through those of the Chandos period, to the more recent Coronation Anthems. Despite the uneven and somewhat disconnected quality of *Deborah*, this work clearly points the way to Handel's future oratorios in two respects: the dramatic use of the chorus and the tendency to minimize the use of the da capo form in arias. Over half of the arias are without the da capo (eleven out of nineteen); the result of the emphasis on the non–da capo aria is to allow less opportunity for vocal display and to hasten the dramatic action. Among the best arias, all highly effective in their contexts and all in non–da capo forms, are Deborah's "In Jehovah's awful sight," borrowed from the Brockes Passion; Abinoam's "Tears such as tender fathers shed," borrowed from the tenth Chandos anthem; and Barak's "Low at her feet," original in *Deborah*.

The chorus plays an extremely prominent role in *Deborah*, for there are nearly as many choruses as arias. All the choruses represent clearly identified groups, either the Priests of the Israelites or of Baal. The former, however, have most of the choruses; the

59. For a survey of the various interpretations of the character of Jael, see Dean, *Oratorios*, p. 229.
60 . For a discussion and list of the borrowings, see ibid., pp. 230, 642.

Priests of Baal participate in only three. All the acts are framed by large choruses, comparable in length to anthems, and long, anthemlike choruses are also used occasionally at other points. Most of the choruses are borrowed, in part or whole, from Handel's previous works. For instance, the finales of all three acts are borrowed from the Coronation Anthems: the pair of choruses, separated by a recitative, that closes act 1 ("Let my deeds be glorified" and "Despair all around") comprises the whole of the anthem *Let thy hand be strengthened*, with virtually no change but the text; the final chorus of act 2 ("The great King of Kings") is virtually the same as the first part of the anthem *The King shall rejoice*; and the last two sections in the finale of act 3 ("O celebrate" and "Alleluia") use the last two sections of *The King shall rejoice* ("Thou hast prevented" and "Alleluia").

The most dramatically effective use of the chorus is "All your boast will end in woe," which combines an ensemble (SAAB: Deborah, Sisera, Barak, and Baal's Priest, respectively) and a double chorus (SATB-SATB: the Priests of the Israelites and of Baal). The dramatic conflict develops throughout the ensemble, with Sisera and Baal's Priest in strong opposition to Deborah and Barak, and it reaches its climax with the entrance of the double chorus. Handel has underlined the dramatic conflict in the voices by providing two basso continuo parts—one for organs and basses and the other for harpsichord, violone, and contrabass; the organs are used only at the entrances of the Priests of the Israelites, to give them greater power than those of Baal. Three other choruses of special interest and effectiveness are "See the proud chief," "Plead thy just cause" (both of these borrowed from Handel's *Dixit Dominus* and adapted to the new text with great skill and insight), and "Doleful tidings," which is particularly beautiful for its affective use of the Neapolitan sixth chord during the chorus's final phrase, sung a capella, with the text "despair and death are in that sound."

The orchestra of *Deborah* is large: pairs of flutes, oboes, and bassoons; three horns; three trumpets; tympani; strings; harpsichord; and organs (probably two). The only instrumental number is the overture, in four movements—allegro, grave, poco allegro, and allegro. The overture is of special interest, for twice it uses material from the body of the oratorio: the second movement anticipates the point at which the Priests of the Israelites call on

Jehovah in "Lord of eternity," and the final movement anticipates the point at which the Priests of Baal call on their god in "O Baal! monarch of the skies!" Thus the overture draws attention to the opposing forces of the oratorio. Only once again, in *Judas Maccabaeus*, was Handel to foreshadow in the overture material to be used later in the oratorio.

Athalia[61]

The most mature of the early English oratorios, *Athalia* was composed and first performed during a troubled period in Handel's life. The work was finished on 7 June 1733, just two days before the closing of the opera season; immediately after the closing all of Handel's Italian singers but one resigned to join the newly formed competing company, the Opera of the Nobility. This blow marked the beginning of the end for Handel's and Heidegger's second academy, which lasted only one more season. With his company thus depleted, Handel nevertheless began to prepare for a series of performances at Oxford. On 23 June the *Bee* announced:

> Great Preparations are making for Mr. Handel's Journey to Oxford, in order to take his Degree of Music; a Favor that University intends to compliment him with, at the ensuing Publick Act. The Theatre there is fitting up for the Performance of his Musical Entertainments, the first [of] which begins on Friday Fortnight the 6th of July. We hear that the Oratorio's of Esther and Deborah, and also a new one never performed before, called Athaliah, are to be represented two Nights each; and the Serenate of Acis and Galatea as often. That Gentleman's Great *Te Deum*, *Jubilate*, and *Anthems*, are to be vocally and instrumentally performed by the celebrated Mr. Powell, and others, at a solemn Entertainment for the Sunday. The Musick [i.e., the musicians] from the Opera is to attend Mr. Handel.[62]

Thus *Athalia*'s first performance was part of a series of concerts celebrating Oxford's "Publick Act," the ceremony at which degrees were conferred. *Athalia* was no doubt composed specifically for the Oxford series, and according to the report of the author Antoine François Prévost, the work was "the expression of Mr. Handel's gratitude" for having been offered an honorary doctor-

61. Printed in Handel, *Werke*, vol. 5, and Handel, *Athalia*.
62. *Bee*, 23 June 1733, in Deutsch, *Handel*, pp.316–17.

ate.[63] It is puzzling, however, that Handel refused the doctorate; Prévost attributes the decision to Handel's modesty, but this conclusion seems inconsistent with the composer's character.[64]

An enormous crowd, with many visitors of distinction, attended both the act and *Athalia*. According to a report from Oxford in Read's *Weekly Journal* of 7 July (the week of the act): "Almost all our Houses not only within the City, but without the Gates, are taken up for Nobility, Gentry, and others . . . and we are so hurried about Lodging, that almost all the Villages within three or four Miles of this City made a good Hand of disposing of their little neat Tenements on this great Occasion."[65] The size of the audience at *Athalia*'s first performance, on 10 July in the Sheldonian Theatre, clearly reflects the large attendance at the act. According to the *Bee* of 14 July, Handel's *Athalia* "was performed with the utmost Applause, and is esteemed equal to the most celebrated of that Gentleman's Performances: there were 3700 Persons present."[66] Other reports agree with this one on the approximate size and great enthusiasm of the audience, although the *London Magazine* for July estimates the audience at "near 4,000."[67] Prévost mentions not only 3,700 persons and their applause and admiration but also their distinguished social position: "almost all ladies and gentlemen of the highest rank."[68] Amid the many glowing reports of Handel's success in Oxford, that of Dr. Thomas Hearne, who disapproved of both foreigners and theater people, is conspicuous for its expression of resentment of the presence of "Handel and (his lowsy Crew) a great number of foreign fidlers."[69]

The printed libretto of *Athalia* called the work "An Oratorio: or Sacred Drama,"[70] a combination of terms used previously for *Esther* (in its 1732 version) and *Deborah*. Like the libretto of *Esther*, that of *Athalia* is based on a tragedy by Racine; his

63. A. F. Prévost, *Le Pour et contre*, 20 vols. (Paris, 1733–40), 9:209, translated in Deutsch, *Handel*, p. 334.

64. For possible reasons for Handel's refusal of the doctorate, see Lang, *Handel*, pp. 246–47.

65. *Weekly Journal*, 7 July 1733, in Deutsch, *Handel*, p. 323.

66. *Bee*, 14 July 1733, ibid., p. 327.

67. Quoted in Deutsch, *Handel*, p. 329.

68. Prévost, *Le Pour*, 9:334, in Deutsch, *Handel*, p. 334.

69. Diary of Thomas Hearne, 5 July 1733, ibid., p. 319.

70. For the complete title page see Dean, *Oratorios*, p. 263.

FIGURE VI-7. Interior of the Sheldonian Theatre, Oxford, where Handel's
Athalia was first performed in 1733.
(Reproduced by permission of Gerald Coke, Esq.)

last play, *Athalie* (1690, first performed in 1691),[71] is based on
2 Kings 11. This biblical story had been previously used as the
subject of oratorios in Italy.[72] It has been said of Racine's *Athalie*
that "never, perhaps, was [Racine's] dramatic technique so sure
nor so able";[73] it may also be said that Handel's *Athalia* is
dramatically superior, in both libretto and music, to his previous
oratorios and that it ranks with his best works in this genre.

71. Printed in Racine, *Oeuvres*, 1:881–961.
72. For examples see the librettos by Luigi Bevilacque, *L'Attalia* (Ferrara, 1704; I/Rsc:
Carvalhaes 1521) and Francesco Laurentino, *Athalia* (Rome, 1705; I/Rli: 171.E.13[19]).
A. Zeno and P. Metastasio wrote Italian librettos on this subject.
73. Translated from Raymond Piccard in Racine, *Oeuvres*, 1:833.

Racine used the chorus in *Athalie* much as he had done in *Esther*, and again, as in *Esther*, Moreau set to music the choruses and songs. Racine's *Athalie* had been available in an English translation by William Duncombe for about ten years prior to the composition of the oratorio, but Handel's librettist, Samuel Humphreys, appears not to have depended upon the translation for his work.[74]

The protagonist of the oratorio, Queen Athalia (S), is a tragic figure whose lust for power leads to her ultimate destruction. Having usurped the throne of Israel, Athalia has turned away from Jehovah to worship Baal; she is supported by her Baalite attendant priest, Mathan (T). In conflict with Athalia are her people, the Israelites, whose rightful king is the young boy Joas (S). Other faithful Israelites are Joas's foster mother and father— Josabeth (S) and Joad (A), the latter of whom is also the high priest of the Israelites—and Abner (B), the commander of the army. According to the libretto printed for the first performance, the work includes three choruses: Israelitish Priests and Levites, Sidonian Priests (Baalites), and Young Virgins of the Tribe of Levi.[75] The edition in Handel, *Werke*, vol. 5, however, includes two more, the choruses of Attendants of Athalia and of Israelites. The numbers of voice parts required in the choruses varies: the Young Virgins are sung by S in unison and SSS, and the other choruses are variously represented by ATB, SATB, SSAATTBB, and SATB-SATB.

Act 1 opens with solos and choruses praising Jehovah and expressing determination to overthrow the tyrant. Athalia—"starting out of a slumber," according to Handel's notation in the autograph manuscript[76]—is horrified by her gory dreams; in one of these, she was killed by a boy dressed as a priest of Judah. She decides to visit the temple in search of such a boy. In the temple Joad and Josabeth plan to present Joas, the king of Judah, to his people. In act 2 Athalia visits the temple and sees that Joas is the boy of her dream; she leaves but is determined to return within the hour to take him away. In act 3 Joas is hailed as the king of Judah. Athalia enters and orders that he be seized, but Abner will no longer obey the tyrant. Athalia and Mathan realize that Jehovah is

74. Dean, *Oratorios*, p. 274.
75. Ibid., p. 263.
76. For Handel's "stage directions" in the autograph MS, see ibid., p. 264. Handel's indications of stage action in his MSS of a number of the oratorios reveal his visual, theatrical orientation in the act of composition even for works that he did not expect to be staged.

now victorious; yet in defiance Athalia proudly calls on the soul of her mother, Jezebel, for courage in her impending death:

Let Jezebel's great soul my bosom fill
And ev'n in death, proud priest, I'll triumph still.
   To darkness eternal
   And horrors infernal
   Undaunted I'll hasten away.

In the final scene Joad, Josabeth, Abner, and the chorus express their joy and thanksgiving. Although this libretto falls short of what a better author might have done with Racine's work,[77] it nevertheless offers much of value to which Handel was able to respond as a musical dramatist.

The music of *Athalia* is almost entirely new. Only the overture and five other numbers are known to use material borrowed from Handel's earlier works. Of special importance in *Athalia* is the close relationship between music and drama, made possible by greater flexibility of musical structure than is found in Handel's earlier oratorios and in most of his operas. An important factor contributing to dramatic continuity is the emphasis on non–da capo arias: about two-thirds of the arias are without the da capo. Thus the non–da capo aria is used more than in *Deborah*, and it is used even more in the next two dramatic oratorios, *Saul* and *Samson*. Handel's increasing interest in accompanied recitative in the oratorios is also shown in this work: five of the recitatives are accompanied by the orchestra, as opposed to only two in *Deborah*, and the number is increased to eight each in *Saul* and *Samson*.

A consideration of parts of the first and second acts will serve to illustrate the flexibility of musical structure and the close relationship of music and drama in *Athalia*. During the episode in the temple at the opening of act 1 (scenes 1 and 2 in the libretto as printed in Handel, *Werke*, vol. 5), the emotional tension gradually mounts: Josabeth's aria "Blooming virgins, spotless train" (one of only two da capo arias in act 1), in a dance style, establishes a relaxed attitude as she praises Jehovah. The following chorus ("The rising world Jehovah crown'd"), an equally relaxed expression of praise, is begun by the Young Virgins in unison over a free passacaglia bass and is continued by the Israelites ("Oh mortals, if

77. For a critique of the libretto, see ibid., pp. 248–49.

around us here"). The tension mounts in Josabeth's next aria with chorus, "Tyrants would in impious throngs." In this number the chorus, set almost entirely in chordal style, functions much as a *turba* in a Passion setting, with its interjections of "tyrants!" and "why?" as both Josabeth and the chorus, accompanied at times by agitated sixteenth notes in the strings, pour out their frustration and fury. The tension mounts further with Abner's ensuing aria, "When storms the proud to terrors doom," expressing the wrath of Jehovah in a manner characteristic of many an operatic rage aria (but non–da capo) with an agitated orchestral style and vocal coloraturas, especially on "roll" and "whirlwind." Abner's aria is incomplete (having modulated through several keys and clearly arrived at the subdominant) when the chorus, again functioning in the manner of a *turba*, bursts in with "Oh Judah, boast his matchless law." In a strongly rhythmic, homophonic style, accompanied by a continuation of the agitated orchestral figures, the Israelites express the awful power of Jehovah. The tension of the temple episode having reached its peak, it is allowed some release in Joad's two brief recitatives, the first simple and the next accompanied by sustained strings. The release in tension continues in Joad's following aria, "Oh Lord, whom we adore," a gentle prayer set in *siciliano* style; the A section of this aria concludes with a ritornello reaching a fermata on the tonic, and after a double bar the B section follows. One fully expects this aria to be in da capo form, but that expectation is unfulfilled; in place of the da capo, the chorus enters with the text of B set to musical material derived from A. The da capo convention is thus manipulated to express the same unanimity of feeling between soloist and chorus that was heard twice before.

Two other passages are of special interest with respect to the interdependence of music and drama: the episode in act 1 that takes place in Athalia's palace (scene 3)—she recounts her horrid, gory dreams in simple and accompanied recitatives while her Attendants and Mathan try to console her—and the episode in act 2 beginning with Athalia's vengeance aria, "My vengeance awakes me," and continuing through the reactions of Josabeth and Joas in their duet "My spirits fail" and the following duet of Josabeth and Joad, "Cease thy anguish." The emphasis upon relatively brief, non–da capo arias and upon choruses that are more like the dramatic crowd chorus than the anthem is characteristic of *Athalia* in general; equally characteristic is the tendency to subordinate musical means and conventional structures to the unfolding of the dramatic action and emotional tension.

Significant exceptions to the usually brief choruses in *Athalia* are the large choral sections, comparable to anthems, that frame act 2. The act begins with a three-part structure, ABC, in which A and C are powerful, chordal, choralelike sections *a 8* (the first time a chorus *a 8* has been heard in this oratorio) with active parts for large orchestra, and B is Joad's brief aria, "He bids the circling season shine"; the C section is also used as the oratorio's final chorus. Act 2 closes with a choral unit in three sections: the Young Virgins (SSS) begin with a commentary on the action, "The clouded scene begins to clear"; the Priests and Levites (ATB) continue with their moralizing lines, "When crimes aloud for vengeance call"; and the final section, "Rejoice, oh Judah, in thy God," reflects the joy of the Israelites.

The large orchestra of *Athalia*—two recorders and one transverse flute; pairs of oboes, bassoons, horns, trumpets, and tympani; strings, harpsichord, and organ—is comparable to that of *Deborah*. The largest orchestral combination used in the work is that accompanying the chorus *a 8* at the beginning of act 2 and at the end of act 3. Especially charming effects are achieved in the music of Athalia and those who attempt to console her during the palace scene of act 1. The opening sinfonia, which is an Italian overture (allegro, grave, allegro), includes in its two outer movements transcriptions of two of Handel's trio-sonata movements.

An Interlude: 1733–38

The five years that separated *Athalia* from *Saul* were primarily opera years for Handel. Despite the successes of his oratorios in 1732–33 and the declining popularity of Italian opera, Handel appears thus far to have had no intention of forsaking the genre to which he had devoted most of his life. In 1732 he had received a letter from the dramatist Aaron Hill, a friend since his early years in England, that appealed to him to compose English operas, to be "resolute enough to deliver us from our Italian bondage; and demonstrate, that English is soft enough for Opera, when compos'd by poets, who know how to distinguish the sweetness of our tongue, from the strength of it, where the last is less necessary."[78] Handel took no apparent heed of Hill's appeal, so interested was he in composing Italian opera, or perhaps in composing for the excellent Italian singers. Three years later, in 1735, Handel received an oratorio libretto from Charles Jennens—the librettist of *Saul*, *Messiah*, and *Belshazzar*—to whom he replied on 28 July: "I received your very agreeable Letter with the inclosed Oratorio. I am just going to Tunbridge, yet what I could read of it in haste, gave me great deal of Satisfaction. I shall have more leisure time there to read it with all the Attention it deserves. There is no certainty of any Scheme for next Season, but it is probable that some thing or other may be done, of which I shall take the Liberty to give you notice being extreamly obliged to you for the generous Concern you show upon this account."[79] Perhaps it was the libretto of *Saul* for which Handel thanked Jennens in this letter, but the composer was too busy with an Italian opera, *Alcina*, to devote much attention to an oratorio.

Alexander's Feast (1736), composed in the period between *Athalia* and *Saul*, is relevant to Handel's development as an oratorio composer. The libretto is an arrangement by Newburgh Hamilton (the future librettist of Handel's *Samson*) of John Dryden's second *Ode to St. Cecilia*. Hamilton divided Dryden's poem into units suitable for recitatives, arias, and choruses, and he added a brief conclusion of his own. In this work Handel continues the flexible approach to structure found in *Athalia*—an approach including emphasis on the non–da capo aria, the close relationship between solo and choral passages, and the frequent use of accompanied recitatives. Handel did not call the work an oratorio, nor would it be an oratorio according to the usual English meaning of the term in its time: according to Newburgh Hamilton (in 1743), an oratorio is "a musical Drama, whose Subject must be Scriptural, and in which the Solemnity of Church-Musick is agreeably united with the most pleasing Airs of the Stage."[80] Since the word *oratorio* was relatively new in England, however, it was vague enough in the public's mind that mistakes were made. For instance, in a letter written in 1739 to her sister, the devoted

78. Hill to Handel, 5 December 1732, in Deutsch, *Handel*, p. 299.
79. Handel to Jennens, 28 July 1735, ibid., p. 394.
80. Newburgh Hamilton, preface to the libretto of *Samson* (London, 1743), in Deutsch, *Handel*, p. 559.

Handelian Mrs. Pendarves says, "I go to-night to the oratorio—no I mean to Alexander's Feast—with Mrs. Carey."[81] Not all such mistakes were as carefully corrected as Mrs. Pendarves's, however, since *Alexander's Feast* was occasionally called an oratorio in printed announcements of performances in Dublin, Bath, and Worcester; in London the press seems to have distinguished it from the oratorios.[82]

Alexander's Feast was a great success, but this did not turn Handel aside from the composition and production of Italian opera. Throughout the season of 1736–37, he continued to produce operas as well as a revised version of his 1707 Italian oratorio, now called *Il trionfo del Tempo e della Verità* ("The Triumph of Time and Truth"). Handel's company lost money, as did the Opera of the Nobility, and at the end of the season both companies collapsed. An added blow to Handel was an apparent stroke in April 1737 that temporarily paralyzed his right arm and also affected his brain. In an effort to find a cure, Handel journeyed to the spa at Aachen; having amazingly recovered by November, he returned to London and began to compose a new opera.

On 20 November, shortly after Handel's return, Queen Caroline died. The opening of the theater season was postponed until the first of the year for a period of mourning; Handel began to work on the *Funeral Anthem for Queen Caroline*,[83] which was performed for the queen's burial on 17 December in Westminster Abbey. The *Funeral Anthem* is of significance for Handel's development as a choral composer and consequently as a composer of oratorios. In that work Handel faced the problem of writing a composition with neither recitatives nor arias that was as long as an act of an oratorio. The anthem consists of a remarkably varied series of SATB movements, two of which are for an ensemble of soloists. Thus Handel moved in the direction of his "choral oratorio" *Israel in Egypt* (1738), for the *Funeral Anthem* was to become its first act.

Despite his losses of the previous opera season, Handel produced his two newest operas, *Faramondo* and *Serse*, during the

81. Pendarves to Ann Granville, 17 February 1739, in Deutsch, *Handel*, p. 475.
82. Deutsch, *Handel*, pp. 566, 597 (Dublin); pp. 727, 764 (Bath); p. 806 (Worcester); p. 428 (among numerous other references, London).
83. Printed in Handel, *Werke*, vol. 11. For an analysis of this work, see Larsen, *Handel's "Messiah,"* pp. 68–75.

season that began in January 1738; both works were poorly attended. To regain some of his losses, he was induced to present a benefit concert on 28 March 1738; it was advertised as follows in the *London Daily Post*: "Hay-Market. For the Benefit of Mr. Handel, At the King's Theatre in the Hay-Market, this Day . . . will be performed An Oratorio. With a Concert on the Organ. . . . To begin at Six o'Clock. N. B. For the Better Conveniency there will be Benches upon the Stage."[84] Although this performance was announced both as "An Oratorio" and "Mr. Handel's Oratorio," it was by no means an oratorio according to the meaning that Handel had previously attached to the term. The concert included a Chandos anthem, items from *Esther* and *Deborah*, some Italian arias, one of the Coronation Anthems, and other works—with no unifying plan.[85] (This performance marks the earliest-known use of the word *oratorio* for a miscellaneous concert; in nineteenth-century America this use of the term became more common than its use to designate a genre.) The concert was extremely well attended: more than 1,300 persons were present. Handel's popularity was still great, despite his failure with the *opera seria*.

84. Deutsch, *Handel*, p. 455.
85. Ibid.; and Dean, *Oratorios*, pp. 212, 238, 261, 270.

CHAPTER VII

The First Mature Period of Handel's English Oratorio: 1738–1745

ᏏᎯHandel's return to oratorio after a period of five years began with *Saul*, which represents an intensification of the dramatic tendencies of *Athalia*. *Israel in Egypt* and *Messiah* constitute a digression to the nondramatic oratorio, but *Samson*, *Joseph and His Brethren*, and *Belshazzar* are again dramatic. During this period Handel finally abandoned opera for oratorio and created most of the oratorios for which he is best known.

The Oratorios of 1738

Saul[1]

Only when forced by economic pressure to abandon Italian opera did Handel turn again to oratorio. On 24 May 1738 the sale of subscription tickets for the 1738–39 opera season was announced,[2] but on 26 July plans for the season had to be canceled for lack of sufficient subscribers.[3] Three days prior to the cancellation, on 23 July, realizing that he must now change his course, Handel began the composition of *Saul*. An interruption during its composition reveals the composer's resistence to change; he had not yet decided to abandon Italian opera entirely, for he stopped working on *Saul*

---

1. Printed in Handel, *Werke*, vol. 13; Handel, *Ausgabe*, ser. 1, vol. 13.
2. *London Daily Post*, 24 May 1738, in Deutsch, *Handel*, p. 460.
3. *London Daily Post*, 26 July 1738, ibid., pp. 464–65.

early in September, after having completed the first two acts, and began the composition of a new opera, *Imeneo*. During this interruption of about two and one-half weeks, Handel sketched the entire opera, which he had no hope of staging in the immediate future: *Imeneo* was not to be finished until two years later. Between 20 and 27 September Handel finished *Saul*, and within three days he began the composition of *Israel in Egypt*; these were to be his two new works for the coming season, which also saw the revivals of *Alexander's Feast* and *Il trionfo del Tempo e della Verità*. *Saul* was favorably received at its first performance (16 January 1739), according to a newspaper report, and it was performed six times during the season.[4]

The libretto of *Saul*, given the usual designation "An Oratorio, or Sacred Drama" in its first printed version,[5] is by Charles Jennens, a wealthy amateur writer of considerable dramatic skill who had long admired Handel's music.[6] *Saul* has much in common with *Athalia*. It would be reasonable to assume that Jennens was stimulated to write *Saul* by hearing the 1735 revival of *Athalia* (five performances in April, the only London performances of the work until 1756) and that *Saul* is the libretto for which Handel thanked Jennens in a letter of 28 July 1735.[7] The subject of Saul and David had long been used for oratorios on the continent.[8] In England John Lockmann's nondramatic libretto *David's Lamentation over Saul and Jonathan* was set to music by William Boyce and called a "lyrical poem" when it was performed in London in 1736; in March 1738 a modified version of the same libretto was set by John Christopher Smith, Jr., and was called an oratorio for its first performance, which took place in London in 1740. Despite some similarity of subject matter, however, the oratorio of Jennens and Handel seems to be independent of these previous English works.[9] Jennens skillfully selected the most useful incidents for his

4. *London Daily Post*, 17 January 1739, ibid., p. 473; Dean, *Oratorios*, p. 297.

5. Dean, *Oratorios*, p. 303.

6. For a summary of a controversy regarding the authorship of this libretto, about which there is no longer any doubt, see Serauky, *Händel*, 3:54–55. For evaluations of Jennens's work, see Dean, *Oratorios*, pp. 276–77, and Lang, *Handel*, pp. 301–2.

7. Handel to Jennens, 28 July 1735, in Deutsch, *Handel*, p. 394. See above, p. 211, for a quotation from the letter.

8. Among the earlier oratorios on this subject are those attributed to Carissimi and Francesco Foggia, both mentioned in the present work, vol. 1, chap. 5; among those of the early eighteenth century is Reinhard Keiser's *Der siegende David*, discussed above, pp. 138–54.

9. Dean, *Oratorios*, p. 276.

Cha: Jennens Esq.
of Gopfal uncle to
Mrs Esther Curzon.

FIGURE VII-I. Charles Jennens (1700–1773), the librettist of Handel's *Saul*, *Messiah*, and *Belshazzar*. From an oil painting by Mason Chamberlin.
(Reproduced by permission of Gerald Coke, Esq.)

dramatic purpose from the long and complicated story of Saul in 1 Samuel; he also acknowledged, in the first printed libretto, that he derived from Abraham Cowley's *Davideis* (written ca. 1640, published in 1656) the behavior of the personage Merab.[10]

Like the central theme of *Athalia*, that of *Saul* concerns a leader of the Israelites whose tragic flaw alienates him from his people. Saul (B) is a noble figure whose unconquerable impulses of pride, fear, and envy ultimately drive him to his destruction. A simultaneous theme pervading the work is the struggle of the people of Israel against their enemies. From the moral flaw in Saul's nature stems his conflict with those around him: David (A, originally for a countertenor), who is the famous conqueror of the Philistines and of whom Saul becomes insanely jealous; Jonathan (T), Saul's son, whose close friendship with David results in his conflict with his father; Michal (S), Saul's younger daughter, whose love for and marriage to David place her in conflict with Saul; and Merab (S), Saul's older daughter, haughty and insensitive (characteristics derived from Cowley's treatment of her) yet a woman who comes to accept David as a brother-in-law and to recognize her father's cruelty. Lesser personages are Abner (T), the commander of the army; Doeg (B) Saul's messenger; the Witch of Endor (written first for T, modified for A); the Apparition of Samuel (B); an Amalekite (T); Abiathar (B), a Priest; and a High Priest (T, a part that Handel later deleted). As important in this tragedy as Saul himself is the chorus, the People of Israel (SATB throughout, except for one women's chorus, SSA); like the chorus in *Athalia*, this one voices its reactions to the events of the tragedy and deeply involves itself in the dramatic action.

At the beginning of act 1, David has already slain Goliath, and the People of Israel (chorus and soloists) sing what the libretto calls "An Epinicion, or Song of Triumph, for the victory over Goliath and the Philistines." Michal expresses her admiration for David; Saul praises him and offers him his daughter Merab in marriage; and a close friendship develops between Jonathan and David. After a lapse of time (indicated musically by a sinfonia), a chorus of Israelite women welcomes Saul and David home from a war and praise David above the king:

10. Ibid., pp. 279, 303.

Saul, who hast thy thousands slain,
Welcome to thy friends again!
David his ten thousands slew,
Ten thousand praises are his due.

This chorus generates the central theme of the work—Saul's jealousy, fear, and rage. His tragic decline begins as he says,

To him ten thousands, and to me but thousand!
What can they give him more? except the kingdom?
With rage I shall burst his praises to hear!
Oh, how I both hate the stripling, and fear!

Michal urges David to sooth Saul's "tortur'd soul with sounds divine," as he has done in the past, but David's attempt is vain. The infuriated Saul hurls his javelin at David, who escapes, and then Saul orders Jonathan to "destroy this bold, aspiring youth." Torn between "filial piety" and "sacred friendship," Jonathan chooses the latter.

In act 2 Jonathan warns David of Saul's intention to have him killed and tells him that Merab has been given to another in marriage. Jonathan tries to convince Saul to reverse his decision to kill David, and Saul appears to do so. After he offers David the hand of Michal to show his "good faith," the couple is married. Saul secretly hopes, however, that David will be killed in war with the Philistines. When David returns from the war, the enraged Saul makes another attempt on David's life. Michal helps David escape. At a religious feast Saul again plans to kill David, but the plan is again thwarted. Jonathan questions his father about David, and Saul becomes furious and attempts to murder his own son.

In act 3 Saul reaches the end of his tragic course. At the beginning of the act, he goes to see the Witch of Endor; he is disguised, for by his own law the penalty for witchcraft is death. Saul, no longer the madman, is at this point a sane and perceptive witness to his own destruction: he is aware of his responsibility for his wretched state ("Wretch that I am! of my own ruin author!"), for having driven away the "valiant youth" David, and for having been forsaken by God. Yet he cannot change; he is driven on by his pride and courage to ask the counsel of those he once abhorred: "Is Saul become a coward?—I'll not believe it!/If heav'n denies thee aid—seek it from Hell!" Saul asks the Witch to call Samuel back from death. When Samuel appears, Saul asks his advice for the coming battle, for he can turn to no one else. Samuel recounts Saul's previous disobedience in sparing the Amalekite, and he foretells that the kingdom will be given to David, that Saul and his sons will die, and that Israel will fall to the Philistines. His prophesy is fulfilled. After the battle (musically represented by a sinfonia) an Amalekite tells David of Israel's defeat and of the deaths of Saul and Jonathan. Saul had attempted suicide and had begged the Amalekite to "finish his imperfect work," which the Amalekite did. On learning the nationality of the Amalekite, David orders that he be killed. A "Dead March" and elegy for Saul follow, after which Abiathar addresses the Israelites:

> Ye men of Judah, weep no more!
> Let gladness reign in all our host;
> For pious David will restore
> What Saul by disobedience lost.

The Israelites conclude with a chorus of encouragement that exhorts David to "gird on thy sword," and to "pursue thy wonted fame."

Saul is a great music drama. The musical and dramatic elements are rarely as closely integrated in a Baroque oratorio or opera as in this work. Here Handel seems to be working out the dramatic-structural implications of *Athalia*, and these two compositions represent a breakthrough for the genre of oratorio. In *Saul* even more than in *Athalia*, Handel freely manipulates and at times disregards the conventions of *opera seria*, which oratorio had long ago adopted and from which he had already begun to free himself. The integration of music and drama may be seen in the large proportion of non–da capo arias (twenty-six out of thirty arias) and in the continuation of the dramatic action even during some of the arias and ensembles, a rare occurrence in the *opera seria* and oratorio of the time. For instance, Saul's rage aria "A serpent, in my bosom warm'd" is like a da capo aria throughout its A section (in B-flat major) and at the beginning of its B section (in G minor). After only four measures of the B section, however, the aria is abruptly and dramatically broken off (Example VII–1). The fifth measure of the B section closes the aria (still in G minor) with one measure of descending scale passages in thirty-second notes, depicting Saul throwing his javelin (according to the "stage" descrip-

EXAMPLE VII-1. *Saul* (Handel, *Ausgabe*, ser. 1, vol. 13, p. 119).

tion in the libretto) in his first attempt on David's life. The duet between Michal and David beginning "At persecution I can laugh" generates a feeling of urgency for immediate action as Michal virtually forces David to save his own life by escaping from Saul's "murd'rous band" as it approaches their dwelling. During David's aria "Impious wretch, of race accurst," he gives the order that the Amalekite be killed; information provided in the libretto indicates that the order is carried out while the aria is in progress.

More than any other character in the work, the tragic figure of Saul is masterfully drawn in the music, and this is done mostly in recitatives. Utterly unlike the protagonist of an *opera seria* or an *oratorio volgare*, who characteristically sings more arias than any other personage, Saul sings only three, as opposed to David's six and Jonathan's five. Of the eight accompanied recitatives, five are given to Saul; these are sometimes brief, as are the arias, but they are extremely effective, the more so because of their contexts. Saul's first two accompanied recitatives are brief expressions of his jealous reaction to the chorus's praise of David, and his anguish stands out in stark contrast to the joyful chorus, supported by the orchestra in which the carillon is prominent. Following his second response to the chorus, in accompanied recitative, is Saul's first aria, "With rage I shall burst." It is much like an operatic aria, with its motto beginning and *concitato* orchestral accompaniment to express Saul's rage, but it is brief. It has no introductory ritornello and is about as long as an A section of a da capo aria:

thus its length is sufficient for characterization, but the aria does not significantly delay the dramatic action. Saul is also enraged in his second aria, "A serpent, in my bosom warmed"—the aria, mentioned above, that is truncated by dramatic action, Saul's attempt to murder David. This aria's effectiveness is heightened by its placement, for it provides a harsh contrast after David's vain attempt to soothe the king with gentle music by the aria "Oh Lord, whose mercies numberless." Perhaps the greatest scene of the oratorio, both for its characterization of Saul and its purely theatrical effect, is that of Saul's visit to the Witch of Endor. The scene is placed at the opening of act 3, a location of special prominence—this is the only act that does not begin with a chorus. The scene unfolds largely in expressive recitative, both accompanied and simple; the only aria is the Witch's "Infernal spirits," eerie for its consistent four-beat figure accompanying a vocal line that proceeds in clear triple meter (Example VII-2). The simple musical means of this dramatically intense scene belie its supreme effectiveness in a performance that shows an awareness of the metrical conflict.

EXAMPLE VII-2. *Saul* (Handel, *Ausgabe*, ser. 1, vol. 13, pp. 246–47).

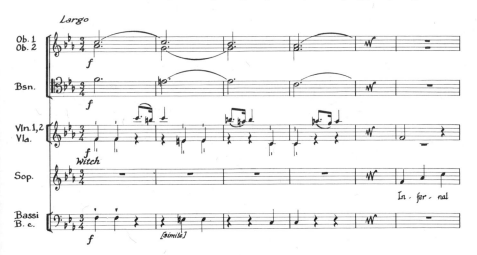

(EXAMPLE VII-2, continued)

Spi-rits, by whose Pow'r De-part-ed Ghosts in liv-ing forms ap-pear,

Saul is structurally balanced by the two large choral-solo complexes that frame the oratorio: at the beginning, the "Epinicion, or Song of Triumph," and at the end, the "Elegy on the Death of Saul and Jonathan," together with a concluding recitative and final, optimistic chorus. Both choral-solo complexes express the sentiments of the Israelites after battles: the first, their exultation after victory; the last, their lamentation over the deaths of their leader and his son and their encouragement of David and hope for the future. The tonality of C major-minor is common to both complexes and contributes to their framing and balancing function. The Epinicion opens and closes in C major, and the internal sections are in C minor and G major; this complex is further unified by a return of the opening chorus, "How excellent thy name, oh Lord," which is followed by a final "Hallelujah" chorus. The concluding complex of the oratorio begins with the famous "Dead March" in C major and closes with a chorus in C major; most of its other sections are in keys closely related to C major or minor. Other choruses functioning as frames for the acts and expressing the Israelites' concern for their king are at the end of act 1 and at the beginning and end of act 2. Perhaps the most effective chorus of the oratorio is the brief but powerful one that begins act 2, "Envy! eldest born of hell!" As illustrated in Example VII–3, the chorus at first unfolds in a sparse imitative texture over a one-measure basso ostinato (marked "organo tasto solo, e l'ottava, forte"), with a tense accompaniment of dotted patterns in the strings. At the words "Hide thee in the blackest night:/Virtue sickens at thy sight!" the ostinato, dotted patterns, and imitation are abandoned in favor of a thick, chordal texture; the harmony becomes increasingly chromatic. In the concluding section—at "Hence, eldest born of hell!"—the previous style and ostinato are resumed.

EXAMPLE VII-3. *Saul* (Handel, *Ausgabe*, ser. 1, vol. 13, pp. 149–50).

(EXAMPLE VII-3, continued)

The orchestra required for *Saul* is extremely large: pairs of flutes, oboes, bassoons, and trumpets; three trombones; timpani; harp; theorbo; carillon; strings; two organs; and harpsichord. The unusual carillon is used in two related choruses of act 1—"Welcome, welcome, mighty king!" and "David his ten thousands slew"—and in the sinfonia that precedes them. These are the choruses that provoke Saul's insane jealousy. According to a letter written by Jennens in September 1738, Handel was in possession of a carillon while composing *Saul*: "Mr. Handel's head is more full of maggots than ever. I found yesterday in his room a very queer instrument which he calls carillon (Anglice, a bell) and says some call it a Tubalcain, I suppose because it is both in the make and tone like a set of Hammers striking upon anvils. 'Tis played upon with keys like a Harpsichord and with this Cyclopean instrument he designs to make poor Saul stark mad."[11] It is of interest to note that the carillon is also used in Reinhard Keiser's oratorio *Der siegende David* (1728);[12] it is not known whether Handel knew Keiser's oratorio. The orchestration ranges from the grandiose effects of the Epinicion and final choral-solo complex to the more delicately colored aria accompaniments, such as Michal's "Fell rage and black despair" with its passages for unaccompanied flute. In the organ parts in *Saul*, Handel specified more fully than in his other oratorios when and how the organist is to play.[13] The opening sinfonia, mostly based on a previous trio sonata by Handel, is in four movements: allegro, larghetto, allegro, and andante. The other five sinfonie of the oratorio are used at points where a lapse of time is intended; each relates to a significant event in the drama: in act 1, the women welcoming Saul and David back from the war; in act 2, the marriage of David and Michal and the feast at which Saul plans to kill David; and in act 3, the battle and the funeral march.[14]

In *Saul*, for the first time in his oratorios, Handel borrowed material from the works of other composers. Six numbers are based on Francesco Antonio Urio's *Te Deum* and one on themes from keyboard sonatas by Johann Kuhnau. In every instance,

11. Jennens to Lord Guernsey, 19 September 1738, in Deutsch, *Handel*, pp. 465–66.
12. See above, Example V–10; Keiser, however, uses the instrument for a much different affection.
13. For details see Chrysander, "Orgelbegleitung."
14. Dean, *Oratorios*, pp. 282–83.

however, Handel borrowed only thematic material; the working out of the material was new.[15] A self-borrowing that Handel had planned was the use of much of the *Funeral Anthem for Queen Caroline* as the elegy on Saul's death; in the course of revisions, however, the plan was abandoned.[16]

Israel in Egypt[17]

As indicated above, Handel was composing intensely in the fall of 1738: having just completed *Saul* and a sketch of *Imeneo*, he turned immediately to *Israel*. He began with what is now part 2 of the oratorio, which he drafted between 1 and 11 October;[18] in its autograph manuscript this part is called *Moses' Song. Exodus. Chap. 15.* It is possible that this part (not called an act in the manuscript) was originally intended to stand alone as an anthem;[19] this would explain the procedure, unusual for Handel, of composing the movements in reverse order. Between 11 and 15 October Handel drafted what is today called part 1 but which he designated act 2 and entitled *Exodus*; he completed the entire work on 1 November. For act 1 he used the *Funeral Anthem*, which he had rejected about one month earlier for use as the elegy in *Saul*; for its new use he entitled the anthem *Lamentations of the Israelites for the Death of Joseph*, modified the text, and added an instrumental introduction.[20] Thus *Israel* grew from what may have been first conceived as a long anthem into a three-act oratorio, the form in which it was first performed. The *Funeral Anthem* was published in 1743 as an independent composition; for the 1756 revival of *Israel*, Handel compiled a new first act from portions of his *Occasional Oratorio* and *Solomon*.[21] *Israel* was first published in 1771 as a two-part oratorio without a first act,[22] and it has customarily been performed as such since that time.

The first performance of *Israel* took place on 4 April 1739,

15. Ibid., pp. 284–85, 643.

16. For a description of Handel's MS indications of his plan to use the *Funeral Anthem*, see ibid., p. 309.

17. Printed in Handel, *Werke*, vol. 16.

18. Concerning the origin of *Israel*, see Dean, *Oratorios*, pp. 311–12; and Serauky, *Händel*, 3:139–42.

19. Streatfeild, *Handel*, pp. 151–52; Dean, *Oratorios*, p. 312.

20. The original version of the *Funeral Anthem* in Handel, *Werke*, vol. 11, includes the added instrumental introduction.

21. Dean, *Oratorios*, p. 527.

22. On the early editions of Handel's music, see Smith, *Handel*.

"at the King's Theatre . . . with several Concertos on the Organ, and particularly a new one," according to the *London Daily Post*.[23] This performance was so poorly received that the second one, on 11 April, was announced in the *Post* as the last performance. The *Post* also stated that there would be "Alterations and Additions," by which *Israel* would be "shortned and Intermix'd with Songs," and that the performance would include "the two last new Concertos on the Organ.[24] Four songs were added: three Italian arias from earlier works and one in English—two of the arias were used in place of deleted choruses.[25] The changes made for the second performance were clearly intended to attract the opera enthusiasts, who would no doubt have been impatient with this preponderantly choral work. The second performance was not, in fact, the last one of *Israel* in 1739, for a third and final performance was given on 17 April.

If the choral emphasis in *Israel* was a stumbling block for an audience accustomed to opera and to Handel's previous oratorios, it was not the only reason for the work's poor reception. *Israel* is the first of Handel's oratorios in which the words are taken from the Bible with virtually no change. It apparently offended the religious sensitivities of many Londoners for sacred scripture to be sung by opera singers in the theater—a place of entertainment and, for the puritanical mind, a den of iniquity. On the day after the first performance of *Israel*, the *London Evening Post* registered its pleasant surprise that Handel had been granted permission from the Office of Licenser to perform *Israel* at the opera theater, despite its biblical nature, with "some Persons apprehending, with a good deal of Reason, that the Title of *Israel in Egypt* was, to the full, as obnoxious as that of *The Deliverer of his Country*: But as a Permit was granted for its Exhibition, we may conclude that Mr. *Handel* has work'd a greater Miracle than any of those ascrib'd to *Orpheus*, tho' the Poets give us their Words, that *Savages*, *Stocks* and *Stones*, were sensible of his Harmony."[26] To counteract objections to the use of scripture for the text of an oratorio performed in a theater, a long letter, signed only "R. W.," was published in the *London Daily Post* on 18 April, the day after *Israel*'s third

23. *London Daily Post*, 4 April 1739, in Deutsch, *Handel*, p. 478.
24. *London Daily Post*, 10 April 1739, ibid., p. 479.
25. For details see Deutsch, *Handel*, p. 479, and Chrysander, *Händel*, 3:91.
26. *London Evening-Post*, 5 April 1739, in Deutsch, *Handel*, p. 479.

performance. The letter supported *Israel* on the grounds that the work was a "truly-spiritual Entertainment" in which Handel had given to each of the "noble Thoughts" its "proper Expression in that most noble and angelic Science of Music." The letter defends the theater as a place of performance for such a work:

The Theatre, on this Occasion, ought to be enter'd with more Solemnity than a Church; inasmuch, as the Entertainment you go to is really in itself the noblest Adoration and Homage paid to the Deity that ever was in one. So sublime an Act of Devotion as this *Representation* carries in it, to a Heart and Ear duly tuned for it, would consecrate even Hell itself.— It is the Action that is done in it that hallows the Place, and not the Place the Action. . . . If this be going out of the way, on this Occasion, the stupid, senseless, Exceptions that have been taken to so truly religious Representations, as this, in particular, and the other *Oratorios* are, from the *Place* they are *exhibited* in, and to the attending, and assistance of them, by Persons of Piety and real Virtue, must be my *Apology*.[27]

This letter represents a new tendency, that of defending Handel's oratorios on spiritual grounds as works intended for edification and of playing down their theatrical and purely entertainment values. This tendency is responsible for the eventual development of Handel's popular image as primarily a sacred composer who reveals himself in his oratorios as a great moralist, a sublime preacher, rather than primarily a great musical dramatist who composed entertainments to sacred texts.[28]

The entire text of the present two-part *Israel* (and of the *Funeral Anthem* used as act 1 in the original three-part version) is drawn from the Bible. Part 1, "Exodus," uses verses selected from Exod. 1–14 and from Psalms 105, 78, and 106; part 2, "Moses' Song," is nearly verbatim from Exod. 15:1–21.[29] *Israel* is the first of Handel's two oratorios based on nondramatic biblical texts in prose, the second being *Messiah*. In neither libretto are there individual personages who carry on a dramatic action; rather, both librettos are narrative, descriptive, and reflective. In this respect they represent a significant departure from the norm, not only in Handel's oratorio production but in that of composers on

27. The entire letter is printed in Deutsch, *Handel*, pp. 481–83.
28. On the development from the eighteenth to the twentieth centuries of Handel's image as an essentially sacred composer whose works are intended primarily for edification, see Dean, *Oratorios*, pp. 134–49.
29. For the biblical sources of the individual numbers, see Handel, *Israel*-M, pp. i–iii.

the continent as well.[30] Part 1 of *Israel* narrates the oppression of the Israelites in Egypt, the series of plagues that assailed the Egyptians, and the Israelites' crossing of the Red Sea. Part 2 is the song of praise sung by Moses and the Israelites after their escape from Egypt; here the choruses, ensembles, and solos represent the people of Israel, but the biblical passage provides no individual roles for Moses or others. The compiler of *Israel*'s libretto is unknown, but it may have been the composer himself, as a contemporary observer conjectured.[31] Handel was evidently quite familiar with the Bible, for in 1727, according to Burney, in rejecting biblical texts sent to him by the bishops for the Coronation Anthems, he said, "I have read my Bible very well, and shall choose for myself."[32] *Israel*'s libretto is filled with images that lend themselves to musical description, images on which Handel capitalized in his musical settings.

The music of *Israel* departs as much from the norm of Handel's oratorios and of those composed on the continent as does its libretto. *Israel* may well be unique in its time as a work made up almost entirely of choruses and yet called an oratorio; it gives more the impression of being a large anthem, or group of anthems, than an oratorio. It is well to remember that Handel had used the term *oratorio* to describe a miscellaneous concert of his works in March 1738, about seven months before the completion of *Israel*. Although the latter, with its narrative element, is closer to the oratorio as a genre than is a concert of unrelated compositions, Handel did, nevertheless, stretch the meaning of the word *oratorio* in applying it to this work.

The *Funeral Anthem* consists of ten choruses and two quartets of soloists; and the two-part *Israel*, of about twenty choruses or choral complexes,[33] four arias, three duets, and four brief, simple recitatives. No independent instrumental numbers are used either in the *Funeral Anthem* or in the two-part *Israel*, except the brief introduction composed to precede the former. The introduction is in the key and mood of the *Funeral Anthem* and is conse-

30. The subject of *Israel* was often treated in dramatic oratorios on the Continent. For a dramatic oratorio that is part of a series of oratorios based on this subject, see Colonna's *Il Mosè*, discussed in this study, vol. 1, pp. 326–32.

31. Deutsch, *Handel*, p. 482.

32. Burney, *Account*, p. 34.

33. There are as many as twenty-eight choruses, counting separately the constituent sections of choral complexes.

quently inappropriate as an introduction to the two-part version. Thus rather than beginning with the usual overture, the two-part version begins with a recitative, which tends to convey the impression of a work already in progress. The choruses of the *Funeral Anthem* are all for SATB. Those of the two-part *Israel*, however, tend to create a more massive effect, since nearly half are double choruses, for SATB–SATB, the others being for SATB. The large orchestra of the two-part *Israel* (larger than that used in the *Funeral Anthem*) also contributes to its massive quality: two trumpets, three trombones, timpani, two flutes, two oboes, two bassoons, strings, harpsichord, and two organs (one for each chorus, as indicated in Handel's score of some of the double choruses).

The choruses of the two-part *Israel* are remarkable for their variety of texture and imagery, which probably accounts for much of the popularity that the work has achieved, despite its initial failure. The alternation and mixture of chordal and fugal textures is frequently in evidence, as are word painting and various illustrative devices. Textural variety, word painting, and more general textual illustration are well exemplified in the last two choral complexes of part I. These complexes are unified primarily by text: the first, consisting of three choruses, describes the passage through the Red Sea; the second, two choruses, relates the reaction of the Israelites. Each complex begins with a brief chorus in chordal homophony, after which fugal and chordal textures are mixed:

THE FINAL CHORAL COMPLEXES OF PART I

"He rebuked the Red Sea"—brief, chordal illustration of the text "and it was dried up," by an a cappella setting, producing a "secco" effect in comparison with the surrounding orchestrally accompanied passages.

"He led them through the deep"—fugal; word painting on "the deep" and illustration by increasing complexity of texture on "as through a wilderness."

"But the waters overwhelmed their enemies"—chordal texture in the chorus only; illustration of "waters" in the orchestra by undulating eighth-note runs.

"And Israel saw that great work"—brief, chordal.

"And he believed the Lord"—alternation of fugal and chordal textures.

A chorus of intimate charm with a variety of styles and textures is "But as for his people," which begins in a generally homophonic style and a pastoral mood (andante, in triple meter, with long pedal points) to suit the text "He led them forth like sheep" (Example VII–4a); at the words "He brought them out with silver and gold" (Example VII–4b) a fugue, which includes some chordal passages, begins; and at "there was not one, not one feeble person among their tribes" (Example VII–4c), the chorus closes with a homophonic section in dance style, much like a minuet, probably intended to illustrate the vitality of the people.

EXAMPLE VII-4. *Israel in Egypt* (Handel, *Werke*, 16:72, 74, 80–81).

Example a:

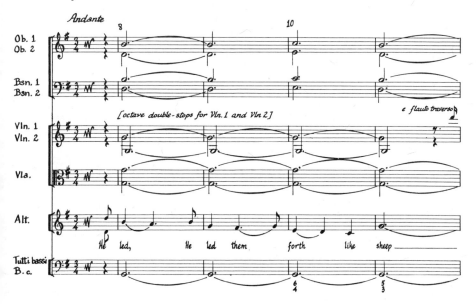

(EXAMPLE VII-4a, continued)

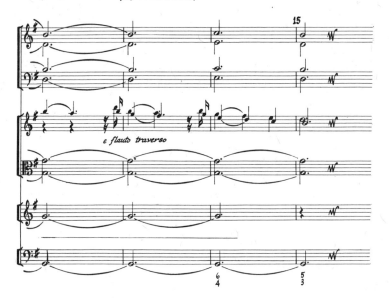

Example b:

(EXAMPLE VII-4b, continued)

he brought them out with sil - ver and gold, _____

out with sil - ver and gold, _____ with sil - ver and gold,

Example c:

Ob. 1
Ob. 2

Bsns.1,2

Vln. 1
Vln. 2

Vla.

Sop.
Alt.

there was not one, not one fee - ble per - son a - mong their tribes,

there was not one, not one fee - ble per - son a - mong their tribes,

Ten.
Bass

there was not one, not one fee - ble per - son a - mong their tribes,

Tutti Bassi
B. c.

Other choruses of special interest are the fugue "They loathed to drink of the river" (Example VII–5), with an angular and chromatic subject eminently suited to its text, although borrowed from one of Handel's keyboard fugues; the double fugue "He smote all the firstborn" (Example VII–6), with its strong "hammer-strokes," first in the orchestra and later in the chorus, to depict the text; "He spake the word" (Example VII–7), with its orchestral imitations of flies and lice; "He gave them hailstones" (Example VII–8), with its illustrative rhythmic regularity; "He sent a thick darkness" (Example VII–9), chromatic, with a generally low tessitura and some thick sonorities; and "The people shall hear, and be afraid" (Example VII–10), with its persistent, nervous rhythmic pattern. A particularly unusual feature of the first chorus in *Israel*, "And the children of Israel sighed by reason of the bondage," is its quotation of the first phrase of the chorale tune "Christ lag in Todesbanden" (Example VII–11). Handel rarely used chorale tunes in his music; here he probably intended a comparison of the bondage of the Israelites to Christ's "bonds of death," referred to in the chorale.[34]

EXAMPLE VII-5. *Israel in Egypt* (Handel, *Werke*, 16:17–18).

34. Schering, "Händel," pp. 34–36; Weismann, "Choralzitate," pp. 174–75.

(EXAMPLE VII-5, continued)

EXAMPLE VII-6. *Israel in Egypt* (Handel, *Werke*, 16:58).

EXAMPLE VII-7. *Israel in Egypt* (Handel, *Werke*, 16:27–28).

(EXAMPLE VII-7, continued)

EXAMPLE VII-8. *Israel in Egypt* (Handel, *Werke*, 16:41–42).

(EXAMPLE VII-8, continued)

EXAMPLE VII-9. *Israel in Egypt* (Handel, *Werke*, 16:55).

(EXAMPLE VII-9, continued)

EXAMPLE VII-10. *Israel in Egypt* (Handel, *Werke*, 16:226–28).

(EXAMPLE VII-IO, continued)

(EXAMPLE VII-10, continued)

(EXAMPLE VII-10, continued)

EXAMPLE VII-11. *Israel in Egypt* (Handel, *Werke*, 16:7–8).

The imposing solo-choral complex that concludes the oratorio seems to round off part 2 as if the part were an independent work, which it appears to have been in its original conception. This finale-complex includes repetitions, not only of its own material, but also of most of the second chorus (the first long chorus) of part 2:

FINALE OF PART 2
1. Chorus: "The Lord shall reign for ever and ever."
2. Recit. (T): "For the horse of Pharoah went in with his chariots."
3. Chorus: "The Lord shall reign for ever and ever"—repetition of item 1.
4. Recit. (T): "And Meriam the prophetess."
5. Solo (S) and chorus:
   "Sing ye to the Lord," brief solo passage;
   "The Lord shall reign for ever and ever," slightly modified repetition of item 1, mm. 6–11;
   "The horse and his rider," brief solo passage;
   "The Lord shall reign for ever and ever," repetition of item 1, mm. 12–17;
   "For he hath triumphed gloriously," repetition of most of second chorus of part 2 ("I will sing unto the Lord").

This complex forms a highly effective concluding unit—with its full orchestra and SATB-SATB choruses, its threefold statement of the predominantly homophonic chorus "The Lord shall reign," its mixture of solo and choral units, and its final repetition of the powerful fugal chorus that was heard early in part 2.

Israel is by no means balanced in its distribution of recitatives, arias, and duets. With the exception of one aria, all of these are in part 2. The da capo form, which Handel used with decreasing frequency in his previous oratorios, is absent from *Israel*. The nearest approximation of da capo form is the duet (BB) "The Lord is a man of war," which consists of a long introductory ritornello, an AB form in the vocal duet, and a repeat of the opening ritornello. The imagery so characteristic of the choruses in *Israel* is found in some of the arias and duets as well: particularly noteworthy are the aria (A) "Their land brought forth frogs," with its "hopping" melody and rhythm in the orchestral parts; the aria (S) "Thou didst blow with the wind; the sea covered them, they sank as lead," with undulating sixteenth-note passages in the orchestra and numerous instances of word painting in the vocal line; and the duet mentioned above (BB) with its fanfare-styled melodies.

In *Israel* more than in any other oratorio, Handel borrowed from the works of other composers. Nearly half of the numbers include borrowed material, mostly from a *Magnificat* by Dionigi Erba (fl. late 1600s–early 1700s), a *Te Deum* by Francesco Antonio Urio (fl. late 1600s–early 1700s), and the serenata "Qual prodigo" by Alessandro Stradella.[35] The use of previously composed works as a stimulus for further creativity was common, not only with Handel but with other composers in his time. Most of Handel's borrowings in his oratorios are from his own music, but the extent of his borrowings from other composers increases remarkably from 1736 to 1739. Although the reason for this increase is not entirely clear, it could be that Handel's mental illness of 1737, which might well have been coming on in the previous year, temporarily weakened his creative ability and forced him to make greater use of models.[36] Whatever the reason, Handel seldom failed to rework the borrowed material, at times extensively, to express the new text for which he used it. For example, in the double chorus "He spake the word" Handel modified a number with concerto grosso instrumentation from Stradella's serenata,[37]

---

35. Printed in Handel, *Werke*, supp. vols. 1, 2, and 3, respectively. For details of Handel's borrowing in *Israel*, including comparisons of Handel's versions with his sources, see Taylor, *Indebtedness*, pp. 47–163.

36. Dent, *Handel*, pp. 106–7; Dean, *Oratorios*, p. 56.

37. Printed in Handel, *Werke*, supp. vol. 3, p. 33; Taylor, *Indebtedness*, pp. 53–68.

and by adding the quick runs to depict the buzzing insects, he thus derived an illustrative choral number of tremendous energy from a simple, unassuming instrumental model. The following chorus, "He gave them hailstones," is likewise a remarkable transformation of the material from the same Stradella work.[38]

Israel includes much great music deserving of its considerable posthumous popularity; yet, as a whole it is a problematic work. It suffers from the lack of a convincing beginning, which Handel recognized and attempted to rectify, and it is unbalanced in its emphasis on the chorus and its placement of all the solos but one and all the duets in part 2. Furthermore, part 2 conveys more the impression of an independent work than of a unit within a larger whole, because of its greater variety than part 1 and because the repetition in its finale of material used near its beginning rounds it off as if it were a separate, closed structure.

An Interlude: 1739–1741

In the period 1739–41, after the first performances of *Saul* and *Israel* and before the composition of *Messiah*, Handel temporarily turned away from oratorio, probably in part because of *Israel*'s poor reception. Not only were no new oratorios composed in 1739 and 1740, but fewer were performed: 1738–39 saw nine performances of Handel's oratorios in London; 1739–40, three; and 1740–41, only one.[39] In this period Handel favored the secular ode rather than the oratorio. In 1739 he composed the *Ode for St. Cecilia's Day* to a text by John Dryden; and in 1740, *L'Allegro, il Penseroso ed il Moderato*, the first two parts to a text by John Milton, adapted by Charles Jennens, who wrote the third part, *Il Moderato*. Handel also turned briefly to opera in 1740 and 1741, when he completed and performed his final works in that genre, *Imeneo* and *Deidamia*.

38. Taylor, *Indebtedness*, pp. 68–72.
39. Dean, *Oratorios*, p. 314.

The Oratorios of 1741–1744

Messiah[40]

The earliest evidence of Handel's revival of interest in oratorio composition is the autograph manuscript of *Messiah*. This monumental work, the best known of his oratorios, was composed in twenty-four days, between 22 August and 14 September 1741.[41] The stimulus to return to oratorio was no doubt provided by an invitation from the duke of Devonshire, the lord lieutenant of Ireland, for Handel to give some concerts in Dublin for the benefit of the local hospitals and charities. Having completed *Messiah*, Handel began immediately to compose *Samson*, the first draft of which he finished on 29 October; less than a week later he set out on his journey to Dublin; he arrived there on 18 November and remained until 13 August 1742.

Handel's Dublin sojourn was a great success in every respect —musically, personally, and financially—for the composer and his music were received with great honor. From 23 December 1741 through 7 April 1742, Handel presented two concert series of vocal and instrumental music; the only oratorio included was *Esther*.[42] The new one, *Messiah*, was held back, for it had been composed for the Charitable Musical Society of Dublin, according to Faulkner's *Dublin Journal* of 10 April.[43] *Messiah* was to be the drawing card for the benefit concert of 13 April in support of three charities—"the Society for relieving Prisoners, the Charitable Infirmary, and Mercer's Hospital."[44] The formation of *Messiah*'s reputation began even before that performance, however, for the

40. Among the numerous modern editions are the following: Handel, *Werke*, vol. 45; Handel, *Ausgabe*, ser. 1, vol. 17; Handel, *Messiah*-C; Handel, *Messiah*-M; Handel, *Messiah*-S. Two facsimile editions are Handel, *Messiah*-A; Handel, *Messiah*-CS. More books and articles have been written about *Messiah* than about any of Handel's other oratorios. The following is a highly selective list of writings, which include further bibliography on this oratorio: Burrows, "Messiah"; Larsen, "Geschichte"; Larsen, *Handel's Messiah*; Larsen, "Tempoprobleme"; Mann, "Messiah"; Myers, *Handel's "Messiah"*; Shaw, *Handel's "Messiah"*; Siegmund-Schultze, "Arienwelt"; Siegmund-Schultze, "Gedankenwelt"; Tobin, *Handel's "Messiah."*

41. For detailed information on *Messiah*'s MS and printed sources, see Burrows, "Messiah"; Handel, *Ausgabe, Kritscher Bericht*, ser. 1, vol. 17; Larsen, *Handel's "Messiah"*; Shaw, *Handel's "Messiah"*; and Tobin, *Handel's "Messiah."*

42. For lists of works performed in Dublin, see Schoelcher, *Handel*, p. 246, and Serauky, *Händel*, 3:671.

43. Deutsch, *Handel*, p. 545.

44. *Dublin Journal* (Faulkner), 17 April 1742, ibid., p. 546.

Dublin News-Letter reported on 10 April: "Yesterday Morning, at the Musick Hall . . . there was a publick Rehearsal of the Messiah, Mr. Handel's new sacred Oratorio, which in the opinion of the best Judges, far surpasses anything of that Nature, which has been performed in this or any other Kingdom. The elegant Entertainment was conducted in the most regular Manner, and to the entire satisfaction of the most crowded and polite Assembly."[45] *Messiah* was to be performed at the Music Hall in Fishamble Street, and in order to make available the greatest possible amount of space, it was requested that "the Ladies who honour this Performance with their Presence would be pleased to come without Hoops, as it will greatly encrease the Charity, by making Room for more company."[46] A published report of the first performance of *Messiah* described it as "the most finished piece of music. Words are wanting to express the exquisite Delight it afforded to the admiring crouded Audience. The Sublime, the Grand, and the Tender, adapted to the most elevated, majestick and moving Words, conspired to transport and charm the ravished Heart and Ear. . . . There were about 700 People in the Room, and the Sum collected for that Noble and Pious Charity amounted to about 400*l*. out of which 127*l*. goes to each of the three great and pious Charities."[47]

Despite Handel's success with *Messiah* in Dublin, he was cautious about introducing it upon his return to London. During the season of 1742–43, he presented *Messiah* only after he had been successful with *Samson*, and even then he avoided advertising the work's title, no doubt to avoid offending those of puritanical views. On 19 March 1743 the *Daily Advertiser* announced *Messiah*'s first London performance:

> By Subscription
> *The Ninth Night*
> At the Theatre Royal in Covent-Garden, on Wednesday next March 23, will be perform'd A NEW SACRED ORATORIO. With a CONCERTO on the ORGAN. And a Solo on the Violin by Mr. DUBOURG.[48]

The polemics regarding the propriety of singing biblical words in a theater, which had begun with *Israel*, continued in the season of

45. Deutsch, *Handel*, p. 544–45.
46. *Dublin Journal* (Faulkner), 10 April 1742, ibid., p. 545.
47. *Dublin Journal* (Faulkner), 17 April 1742, ibid., p. 546.
48. Facsimile printed in Lang, *Handel*, pl. v.

FIGURE VII-2. Beginning and ending of Handel's composing score of *Messiah*, with indications of the first and last days of composition. At the bottom of the first page Handel wrote "♄ angefangen den 22 August 1741" (begun on Saturday, the 22d of August 1741), and at the bottom of the last page, "S. D. G. [Soli Deo Gloria] / Fine dell Oratorio. G. F. Handel. ♄ Septemb^r 12. / ausgefüllet den 14 dieses. 1741" (To God alone the glory. / End of the oratorio. G. F. Handel. Saturday September 12. / Filled out the 14th of this [month]. 1741). Handel designated the day of the week by the astronomical symbol for Saturn (Saturday).
(Reproduced by permission of GB/Lbm.)

The Music Hall in Fishamble St. Dublin, in which the first performance of the Messiah took place.

FIGURE VII-3. The Music Hall in Fishamble Street, Dublin, where *Messiah* was first performed. From a colored drawing by F. W. Fairholt, about 1840.
(Reproduced by permission of Gerald Coke, Esq.)

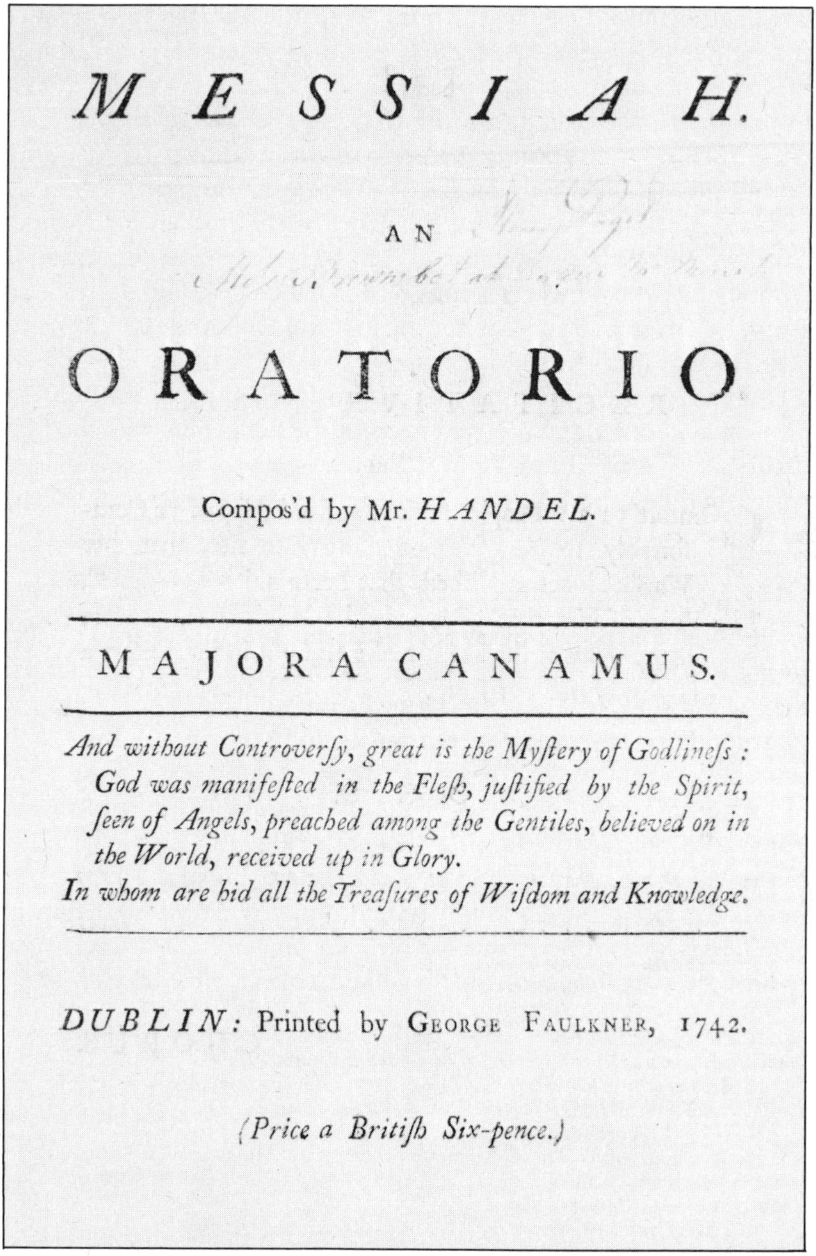

MESSIAH.

AN

ORATORIO

Compos'd by Mr. *HANDEL.*

MAJORA CANAMUS.

---

*And without Controverſy, great is the Myſtery of Godlineſs :
God was manifeſted in the Fleſh, juſtified by the Spirit,
ſeen of Angels, preached among the Gentiles, believed on in
the World, received up in Glory.*
In whom are hid all the Treaſures of Wiſdom and Knowledge.

DUBLIN: Printed by GEORGE FAULKNER, 1742.

(Price a Britiſh Six-pence.)

FIGURE VII-4. Title page of the libretto of *Messiah* as printed for the
first performance, in Dublin.
(Reproduced by permission of Gerald Coke, Esq.)

1742–43—indeed, such polemics were to continue throughout the eighteenth century.[49] *Messiah* was performed only three times in 1743—as opposed to *Samson*, eight times. At *Messiah*'s first London performance, according to a popular anecdote, the audience, including the king, introduced the tradition of standing during the "Hallelujah" chorus.[50] After a private performance of *Messiah* given in 1744 by the Academy of Ancient Music, Handel gave two public performances of it in 1745; he again advertised it without its title.[51] For the single performance that Handel gave in 1749, he advertised the title for the first time in London.[52] In 1750 *Messiah* was performed in the chapel of the Foundling Hospital at a concert for the benefit of that institution. All previous London performances of the work had been in theaters. This was the first time that one of Handel's oratorios was performed in a consecrated building, and *Messiah* was the only one of his oratorios to be performed in such a building during his life.[53] The concert was a great success, and it initiated an annual series of benefit performances of *Messiah* in the chapel of the Foundling Hospital.[54] Continuing for the rest of Handel's life and long thereafter, the performances in the Foundling Hospital's chapel served to strengthen the growing popular notion that *Messiah* and Handel's oratorios in general are essentially sacred music and appropriate for use in church.[55]

The libretto of *Messiah*, made up entirely of biblical quotations, was compiled by Charles Jennens.[56] He drew on the writings of the Prophets and on the Psalms, Gospels, Epistles of Paul and Revelation of John. Although Italian parallels prior to or during Handel's time can be found for most of his librettos, there seems to have been no Italian oratorio comparable to *Messiah*. Like that

49. For a particularly lively and revealing exchange during the period of *Messiah*'s first London performance, see the publications quoted in Deutsch, *Handel*, pp. 563–68.

50. This anecdote appears to have been written down for the first time in 1780. Cf. James Beattie to the Rev. Dr. Laing, 25 May 1780, in Deutsch, *Handel*, p. 854.

51. Deutsch, *Handel*, pp. 584, 611.

52. It is noteworthy that in the previous year, 1748, the puritanical Bishop Gibson (who had prevented Handel's staging of *Esther* in 1732) had been succeeded by Bishop Thomas Sherlock. (Ibid., pp. 660–61.)

53. Dean, *Oratorios*, pp. 41, 81.

54. For documents relating to this performance, see Deutsch, *Handel*, pp. 686–89. Regarding the great financial success of these benefit concerts, see Burney, *Account*, p. 28.

55. For a history of attitudes toward *Messiah*, see Myers, *Handel's "Messiah."*

56. In letters to Jennens, Handel spoke of "Your Oratorio Messiah" and "Your Messiah." Handel to Jennens, 29 December 1741 and 9 September 1742, in Deutsch, *Handel*, pp. 530, 554.

FIGURE VII-5. The interior of the Covent Garden Theatre, where *Messiah* was performed for the first time in London and where many of Handel's other oratorios were performed. The anonymous engraving shows a riot in 1763, during a performance of Thomas Arne's opera *Artaxerxes*.
(Reproduced by permission of Gerald Coke, Esq.)

of *Israel in Egypt*, the libretto of *Messiah* is nondramatic; it includes no personages and is essentially narrative and reflective, with the latter element far more important than the former. It is of interest that one of Handel's contemporaries, John Brown, refused to classify *Messiah* as an oratorio. In a writing of 1763, Brown states, "Though that grand Musical Entertainment [*Messiah*] is called an *Oratorio*, yet it is not dramatic; but properly a collection of *Hymns* or *Anthems* drawn from the sacred Scriptures: In strict Propriety, therefore, it falls under another Class of Composition."[57]

57. Brown, *Poetry*, p. 218, note d.

FIGURE VII-6. The London Foundling Hospital. At the time of this anonymous engraving (1748), only the wing to the left had been completed; the chapel, center, was under construction. Beginning in 1750, *Messiah* was performed annually in this chapel for the benefit of the hospital. (Reprinted from the *Gentleman's Magazine*, vol. 18, August 1748, opposite p. 397).

Messiah is in three parts, but these are not called acts, as are the large divisions of most of Handel's oratorios: part 1 includes the prophesy and the Incarnation; part 2, the Passion, the Resurrection, and the dissemination of the Gospel; and part 3 consists of reflections on Christian triumph over death—all of which, except the final chorus, are found in the Anglican service for the burial of the dead. The libretto of *Messiah* is a skillful compilation, not only for the logic and subtlety with which it reflects its theme but also for its inherent musical possibilities.

Although *Messiah* is similar to *Israel* in the nondramatic and biblical nature of its libretto, the music of the former is closer to that of Handel's normal English oratorio in its balance between solo and choral numbers; nevertheless, in *Messiah* the chorus is more prominent than in the dramatic oratorios. Each part of *Messiah* includes approximately as many choruses as arias; these numbers are often linked by simple or accompanied recitatives. Important to *Messiah*'s general structure are the subdivisions,

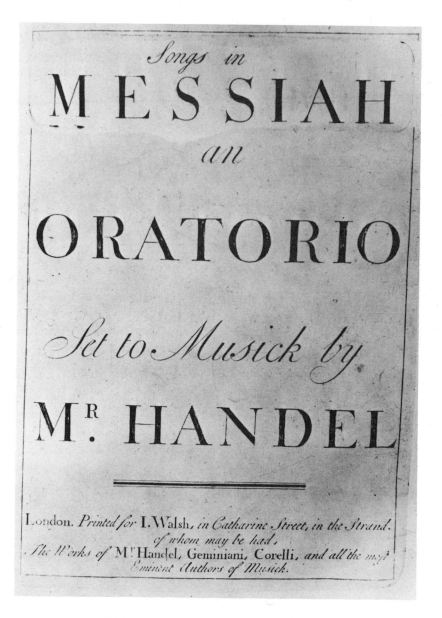

Songs in
MESSIAH
an
ORATORIO
Set to Musick by
Mr. HANDEL

London. *Printed for* I. Walsh, *in Catharine Street, in the Strand.
of whom may be had,
The Works of* Mr. Handel, Geminiani, Corelli, *and all the most
Eminent Authors of Musick.*

FIGURE VII-7. Title page of the first edition of the songs in *Messiah*,
published ca. 1749.
(Reproduced by permission of Gerald Coke, Esq.)

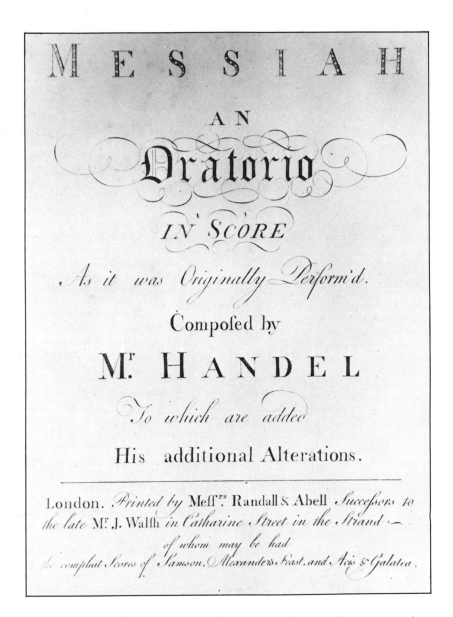

FIGURE VII-8. Title page of the first edition of *Messiah* in score, published in 1767.
(Reproduced by permission of Gerald Coke, Esq.)

FIGURE VII-9. Allegorical figures holding a sheet on which is a head of
Handel at the top of the first page of "Comfort ye, my
people." From an oil painting by Giovanni Battista
Cipriani that was probably commissioned by Charles
Jennens.
(Reproduced by permission of Gerald Coke, Esq.)

made clear both by text and by music, of each of the three parts. These subdivisions are often solo-choral complexes that rise in tension and elaboration from a recitative through an aria to a chorus. Part 1, for instance, begins with three such complexes:

COMPLEXES BEGINNING PART 1	TEXT	KEY
1. Accomp. recit. (T.), "Comfort ye, my people"	Isa. 40:1–3	E
Aria (T), "Every valley shall be exalted"	Isa. 40:4	E
Chorus (SATB), "And the glory of the Lord"	Isa. 40:5	A
2. Accomp. recit. (B), "Thus saith the Lord"	Hag. 2:6–7 Mal. 3:1	d
Aria (B; also versions for A and S), "But who may abide"	Mal. 3:2	d
Chorus (SATB), "And He shall purify"	Mal. 3:3	g
3. Simple recit. (A), "Behold, a virgin shall conceive" Aria (A) and chorus (SATB), "O thou that tellest good tidings"	Isa. 7:14 Isa. 40:9	D D

All three complexes employ the same sequence of recitative-aria-chorus, and all are more or less unified tonally—with the first in E major and A major, the second in D minor and G minor, and the third in D major. Each of the first two groups is further unified by its text, since each uses a continuous biblical passage. Not all the subdivisions of the oratorio's three parts are as clearly and simply organized as those just illustrated, but some kind of unification within small groups of numbers may be demonstrated throughout the work.[58]

The choruses of *Messiah*, since they are balanced by solo passages, tend to stand out more prominently from surrounding numbers than do those of *Israel*. Three choruses are musical continuations of solos or duets: "O thou that tellest" (solo-chorus), "How beautiful are the feet" (existing in a duet-chorus version, among others), and "O death, where is thy sting?" (duet-chorus).

58. Larsen, *Handel's "Messiah,"* pp. 97–102. According to Steglich, "Messias," pp. 23–78, Handel unified *Messiah* both musically and spiritually by the interval of an ascending perfect fourth, which Steglich terms the *Gewissheitsquarte* ("fourth of certitude") from its occurrence with the words "I know" in the aria "I know that my redeemer liveth"; although Steglich's analyses demonstrate the frequent occurrence of the interval of the perfect fourth, that this type of musical-spiritual *Leitmotiv* would have occurred to a composer of Handel's period seems questionable.

The chorus "Let us break their bonds asunder" is a logical continuation and completion of the aria "Why do the nations so furiously rage," although the two are not melodically related. Only twice in *Messiah* are there groups of successive choruses: near the beginning of part 2, "Surely He hath born our griefs," "And with his stripes," and "All we like sheep" are connected to form a choral trilogy; and for the finale of the oratorio, "Worthy is the Lamb" is followed by "Blessing and honor," and then by the "Amen" chorus.

Messiah is perhaps best known and most generally admired for its ceremonial, anthemlike choruses, of which the "Hallelujah" chorus, at the end of part 2, is the prime example. Among others of ceremonial character are "Glory to God in the highest" and the three-chorus complex forming the oratorio's finale. Of strikingly different character, however, are the first and second choruses of part 2, "Behold the Lamb of God" and "Surely, He hath borne our griefs," which contribute to the tragic mood of the oratorio's Passion section by their minor mode, slow tempo, and dotted rhythms. Other choruses, differing from both types just mentioned, are those lighter in character and in dance style, such as "And the glory of the Lord" and the choral continuation of the *siciliano* "How beautiful are the feet" (in the version for a duet [AA] and chorus).

Textural variety is remarkable in the choruses of *Messiah*, despite the virtual limitation to four voices: all the choruses are for SATB except one, "Lift up your heads," which uses SSATB in order to allow for effective antiphonal style, suggested by its text. The textures range between the extremes of a strictly chordal homophony, as in "Since by man came death," and a purely fugal style. Among the fugal choruses the strictest are the simple fugue "He trusted in God" and the double fugue "And with his stripes." Freer in their fugal treatment, and thus more characteristic of Handel's choral fugues, are "Let all the angels of God" (on two related fugue subjects), "Blessing and honor," and "Amen." By far the most prevalent type of chorus, however, is the type that includes a mixture of contrapuntal and homophonic textures. Some of these—such as "Glory to God in the highest," "Surely, He hath born our griefs," "Lift up your heads," and "The Lord gave the Word"—are largely chordal with occasional imitations. Others, such as the "Hallelujah" chorus and "For unto us a Child is born," employ a greater variety of textures—including imitative and nonimitative counterpoint, passages of thin "open-work" texture using one or two voice parts at a time, fugal texture in four parts, and tutti passages in chordal homophony. The "Hallelujah" chorus, probably the best known of all of Handel's choruses, well exemplifies the composer's interest in varied textures within one choral number. The chorus may be divided into six sections as follows (see Examples VII–12 a–e):

SECTIONS IN THE "HALLELUJAH" CHORUS

a   "Hallelujah" (mm. 1–16)
                Chordal; establishment of subject a, which provides material to be combined later with subjects b, d, and e. Tonal center, D.
b–a   "For the Lord God" (mm. 17–32)
                Unison, chordal, polyphonic; alternation and combination of new subject, b, with motive from subject a. Tonal centers, D, G, D.
c   "The kingdom of this world" (mm. 33–41)[59]
                Chordal, chorale style. Tonal center, D.
d–a   "And He shall reign" (mm. 41–51)
                Fugal, with subject d combined with motive from subject a, using the text "for ever." Tonal center, D.
e–a   "King of Kings" (mm. 51–69)
                Repeated-note subject e, combined with motive from a; climax of chorus. Tonal centers, D, G, A, B, D.
d–e–a   "And He shall reign" (mm. 69–94)
                Contrapuntal and chordal; alternations and combinations of material from subjects d, e, and a; functions as a coda and closes with a motive from subject a. Tonal center, D.

EXAMPLE VII-12. *Messiah* (Handel, *Ausgabe*, ser. 1, vol. 17, pp. 195–216).

Example a:

59. In Larsen, *Handel's "Messiah,"* pp. 152, 169–70, the melodies of this and the following section (subjects c and d), as well as the fugue subjects of the chorus "Let all the angels of God," are said to be derived from the chorale tune "Wachet auf, ruft uns die Stimme."

(EXAMPLE VII-12, continued)

Example b:

Example c:

Example d:

Example e:

The simplicity of the subjects, clarity of the structure, variety of textures and procedures, and overwhelming climax (in the "King of Kings" section) are among the reasons for the great popularity of this number.

Another chorus that capitalizes on textural variety and simple structure is "For unto us a Child is born." Constructed of three melodic ideas, the beginnings of which are illustrated in Example VII–13, this chorus consists of four distinct sections: in the first three sections a and b are presented successively in sparse "open-work" texture, usually for one or two voice parts, and c provides a powerful contrast with its chordal declamation; in the final section all three ideas are again successively presented but this time with more emphasis on chordal style to provide a climactic conclusion. The sections treating the a and b subjects of this chorus are derived from the first movement of Handel's Italian secular duet "Nò di voi non vo' fidarmi," which probably accounts for their quasi-chamber style. Other choruses in *Messiah* that Handel derived from his own Italian secular duets and that are sparse in texture, tending toward chamber style, are "All we like sheep have gone astray" (from the third movement of the duet just cited), "And He shall purify," and "His yoke is easy" (the last two from different parts of "Quel fior che all'alba ride").[60]

EXAMPLE VII-13. *Messiah* (Handel, *Ausgabe*, ser. 1, vol. 17, pp. 53–57).

Example a:

Example b:

Example c:

Handel's tendency to reject da capo form for the arias of his oratorios is clear in *Messiah*. Although the original score includes four da capo arias ("Rejoice greatly, O daughter," "He was despised," "How beautiful are the feet," and "The trumpet shall sound"), only two of these ("He was despised" and "The trumpet shall sound") retain their da capo forms in Handel's subsequent versions. The aria "Why do the nations so furiously rage" is

60. The duet "O death where is thy sting" and its concluding chorus are based in part on Handel's secular duet "Se tu non lasci amore." For comparisons of the numbers in *Messiah* derived from Italian duets with their models, see Taylor, *Indebtedness*, pp. 36–46. For the Italian duets see Handel, *Werke*, vol. 32.

constructed like the A and B sections of a da capo aria in its first version, but the original intention did not include a da capo (the following chorus, "Let us break," substitutes for the da capo). More characteristic is a large, subdivided binary form, as in "Ev'ry valley" or "The people that walked in darkness," or an ABA'B' form, as in "Thou art gone upon high" or "But who may abide" (in its revised version).

In their affections and styles the arias and duets of *Messiah* are similar to those of Handel's dramatic oratorios and operas, despite the popular conception of *Messiah* as church music. Approximately one-third of these numbers are in dance style (Example VII–14). The *siciliano* and styles closely related to it are prominent among the dance numbers, and they are used in the *siciliano*'s characteristic manner, to express either pastoral moods or gentle affections. Examples are "He shall feed his flock," "If God be for us," "How beautiful are the feet" (in all of its versions),

EXAMPLE VII-14. Dance Styles in Arias of *Messiah* (Handel, *Ausgabe*, ser. 1, vol. 17, pp. 81, 243, 170, 24, 217, 289).

Example a:

Example b:

Example c:

(EXAMPLE VII-14, continued)

Example d:

Example e:

Example f:

and "But who may abide" (the entire aria in its original version;
the A and A' sections in the Dublin revision). The aria "I know
that my redeemer liveth" is not quite a *siciliano*; yet it hints at that
style in its triple meter, larghetto tempo and its simplicity, and also
in some of its rhythmic patterns. A gigue is used to express joy in
the original version of the aria "Rejoice greatly, O daughter"; in
its Dublin revision, however, the aria is in duple meter and is
shortened. Characteristic of arias with similar texts in late Baroque
operas and dramatic oratorios is the martial rage aria "Why do
the nations so furiously rage" (Example VII–15), with its *concitato*
string parts, fanfare-styled melodic lines, and long melisma on the
word "rage"; "The trumpet shall sound" is an imposing example
of the trumpet aria. "Ev'ry valley" is an aria that uses a text with
numerous possibilities for word painting and expression: "shall
be exalted," "ev'ry mountain and hill made low," "the crooked
straight," and "the rough places plain" are all given special treatment. All the arias and duets are orchestrally accompanied, with
one exception: the duet "O death, where is thy sting" is accompanied by continuo only.

EXAMPLE VII-15. *Messiah* (Handel, *Ausgabe*, ser. 1, vol. 17, pp. 178–79).

Of the fifteen or sixteen recitatives in *Messiah* (the number depending on which version of "And lo, the Angel" is used), seven are simple and eight or nine are orchestrally accompanied. The first accompanied recitative, "Comfort ye," which is also the opening vocal number of the oratorio, is almost entirely in arioso style—with lyrical lines, melodic sequences, text repetitions, and unifying repetitions of material in the orchestra. The other accompanied recitatives, however, are more consistently declamatory, with careful attention paid to textual expression in both the vocal and the orchestral parts.

The orchestra used for *Messiah* is not large—by no means as large as that used for *Saul*. In his autograph manuscript, completed before leaving for Dublin, Handel scored the work for strings and continuo, plus two trumpets and timpani for the "Hallelujah" chorus and the finale (beginning with "Worthy is the Lamb"), two trumpets (marked "da lontano e un poco piano"— "from a distance and a little soft") for the chorus "Glory to God," and one trumpet for the aria "The trumpet shall sound." There are no indications of oboe, bassoon, horn, or organ parts, but these were all used in some of Handel's London performances of this oratorio.[61] The only two instrumental numbers in the oratorio are the opening French overture and the *Pifa* (also called the "Pastoral Symphony"), which is a *siciliano* for strings in the Nativity section of part 1.

Messiah is not only Handel's best-known oratorio, it is among his most significant works both in terms of its intrinsic musical value and its influence on subsequent history. Nevertheless, it has also been the source of much misunderstanding of Handel's oratorios: its frequent performance in churches has led to the popular misconception that Handel's oratorios are essentially narrative-reflective church works dominated by the chorus. Yet Handel never again returned to the type of oratorio represented by *Messiah*. In all his subsequent oratorios, and in all his previous oratorios but *Israel*, the role of the chorus is secondary to that of the soloists. *Messiah* represents the refinement of an idea that began with *Israel*—the narrative-reflective choral oratorio. These two

61. Regarding the orchestras used for Handel's performances at the Foundling Hospital, see Dean, *Oratorios*, p. 103; and Deutsch, *Handel*, pp. 751, 800. Regarding the significance of the extant Foundling Hospital orchestral parts for the performance practice of *Messiah*, see Shaw, *Handel's "Messiah,"* pp. 94–104.

works constitute a digression for Handel, after which he returned immediately to what had become the mainstream of his compositional activity, the dramatic oratorio. He digressed only once more, in the *Occasional Oratorio* (1746), which is neither narrative nor dramatic.

Samson[62]

Handel composed the first draft of *Samson* between 29 September and 29 October 1741, immediately after the completion of *Messiah* and before his departure for Ireland. He returned to London from his Irish sojourn in August 1742. Shortly thereafter, on 9 September, he indicated something of his plans, and uncertainties, in a letter to Jennens: "The report that the Direction of the Opera next winter is committed to my Care, is groundless. The gentlemen who have undertaken to meddle with Harmony cannot agree, and are quite in a Confusion. Whether I shall do some thing in the Oratorio way (as several of my friends desire) I can not determine as yet. Certain it is that this time 12 month I shall continue my Oratorio's in Ireland, where they are going to make a large Subscription allready for that Purpose."[63] Handel did not make the intended second journey to Ireland, but he soon decided to "do some thing in the Oratorio way"; he revised *Samson* for performance in the coming season and completed the finale of the new version on 12 October.[64]

Samson was first performed at the Theatre Royal in Covent Garden on 18 February 1743; it was an immediate success and was performed eight times, which surpassed all of Handel's other oratorios in the number of performances given during a first season. The success of *Samson* may be readily inferred from the numerous references to it in private correspondence and published accounts. Horace Walpole, an opera enthusiast who was not fond of oratorio, admitted in his letters to Horace Mann that "Handel has set up an Oratorio against the Operas, and succeeds" and that "the oratorios thrive abundantly."[65] A private letter printed in Faulkner's *Dublin Journal* on 15 March 1743 states that Handel "is

62. Printed in Handel, *Werke*, vol. 10.
63. Handel to Jennens, 9 September 1742, in Deutsch, *Handel*, p. 554.
64. For details of the 1741 draft and the 1742 revision, see Dean, *Oratorios*, pp. 346, 361–64.
65. Walpole to Mann, 24 February 1743, in Deutsch, *Handel*, pp. 560–61.

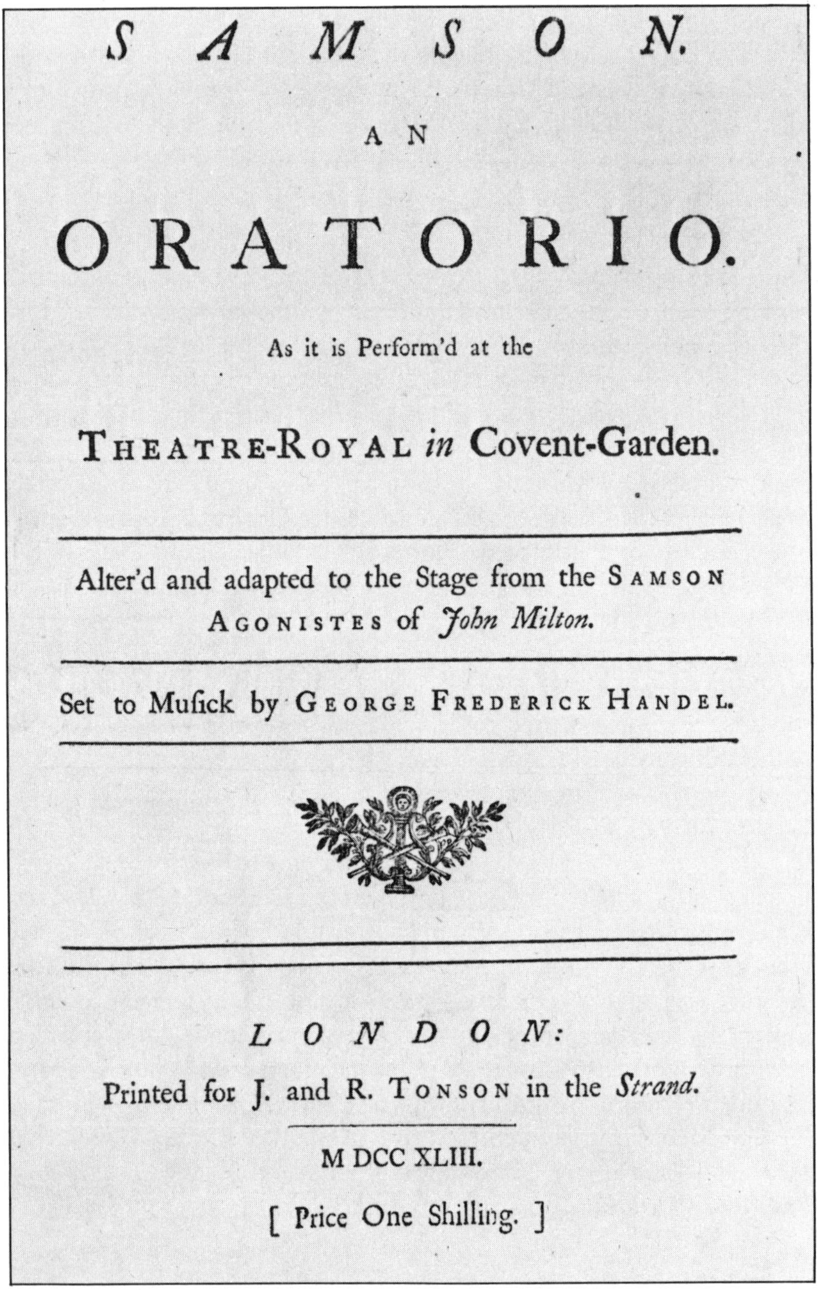

SAMSON.

AN

ORATORIO.

As it is Perform'd at the

THEATRE-ROYAL *in* Covent-Garden.

Alter'd and adapted to the Stage from the SAMSON
AGONISTES of *John Milton.*

Set to Musick by GEORGE FREDERICK HANDEL.

LONDON:

Printed for J. and R. TONSON in the *Strand.*

M DCC XLIII.

[Price One Shilling.]

FIGURE VII-10. Title page of the libretto to Handel's *Samson*, as
printed for the first performance, 1743.
(Reproduced by permission of Gerald Coke, Esq.)

more esteemed now than ever. The new Oratorio (called SAMSON) which he composed since he left Ireland, has been performed four Times to more crouded Audiences than were ever seen: more People being turned away for Want of Room each Night than hath been at the Italian Opera. Mr. Dubourg (lately arrived from Dublin) performed at the last, and played a Solo between the Acts, and met with universal and uncommon Applause from the Royal Family and the whole Audience."[66] *Samson*'s warm reception was repeated at its performances in subsequent London seasons and in the provinces. From its premiere to the present, this work has been the most consistently admired of all Handel's dramatic oratorios.[67]

The libretto of *Samson* was written by Newburgh Hamilton, who had arranged Dryden's second *Ode to St. Cecilia* as *Alexander's Feast*. Impressed by Handel's effective setting of Milton's *L'Allegro* and *Il Penseroso*, Hamilton decided to adapt the same author's *Samson Agonistes* for use as an oratorio libretto. His preface to the first printing of the libretto explains his general attitude toward Milton's work and his manner of adapting the poem for Handel's use:

Several Pieces of *Milton* having been lately brought on the Stage with Success, particularly his *Penseroso* and *Allegro*, I was of Opinion that nothing of that Divine Poet's wou'd appear in the Theatre with greater Propriety or Applause than his SAMSON AGONISTES. That Poem indeed never was divided by him into Acts or Scenes, nor design'd (as he hints in his Preface) for the Stage; but given only as the Plan of a Tragedy with Chorus's after the manner of the Ancients. But as Mr. *Handel* had so happily introduc'd here *Oratorios*, a musical Drama, whose Subject must be Scriptural, and in which the Solemnity of Church-Musick is agreeably united with the most pleasing Airs of the Stage: It would have been an irretrievable Loss to have neglected the Opportunity of that great Master's doing Justice to this Work; he having already added new Life and Spirit to some of the finest Things in the *English* Language, particularly that inimitable Ode of *Dryden's*, which no Age nor Nation ever excell'd. . . .

In adapting this POEM to the Stage, the Recitative is taken almost wholly from *Milton*, making use only of those Parts in his long Work most necessary to preserve the Spirit of the Subject, and justly connect it.

---

66. Deutsch, *Handel*, p. 562.
67. Dean, *Oratorios*, pp. 326, 351–55. For quotations from eighteenth- and nineteenth-century comments on *Samson*, see Myers, *Handel*, pp. 62–80.

In the Airs and Chorus's which I was oblig'd to add, I have interspers'd several Lines, Words, and Expressions borrowed from some of his smaller Poems, to make the whole as much of a piece as possible: Tho' I reduc'd the Original to so short an Entertainment, yet being thought too long for the proper Time of a Representation, some Recitative must be left out in the Performance, but printed in its Place, and mark'd to distinguish it.[68]

Hamilton clearly saw the relationship between the Handelian dramatic oratorio and ancient Greek tragedy. It is logical that he might view Milton's *Samson Agonistes*, acknowledged by its poet to have been modeled on "tragedy, as it was anciently composed,"[69] as suitable material for a libretto in the manner of *Athalia* and *Saul*. Yet Milton's work and Hamilton's adaptation are more strongly moralistic and didactic but less dramatic than either *Athalia* or *Saul*. In the process of adaptation, Hamilton preserved Milton's unities of time and place. He relied little on the biblical story (Judges 16) but primarily on the poetry of Milton. In addition to *Samson Agonistes*, he used paraphrases from at least fourteen of Milton's other poems.[70] To Milton's chorus of Israelites, Hamilton added an opposing chorus of Philistines, and he made Milton's Public Officer the Philistine giant, Harapha. Other departures from Milton are the opening festival of the Philistines and the character Micah, drawn from Judges 17.

The principal theme of the libretto is the spiritual development of Samson (T),[71] from his deep remorse for his past sins and resentment for his degradation as a blinded captive to his fulfillment as an instrument of divine will; yet his triumph is at once his tragedy, for he conquers the Philistines in a victory resulting in his own destruction. This spiritual development is symbolized by Hamilton as a progression from darkness to light, from the eclipsed to the rising sun, from Samson's aria "Total eclipse" of act 1 to his "Thus when the sun" of act 3; the symbolism is also suggested by the chorus "O first created beam" of act 1 and the final chorus of

68. Dean, *Oratorios*, pp. 328–29.
69. John Milton, *Samson Agonistes*, preface, line 1.
70. For a list of these poems, see Dean, *Oratorios*, p. 330.
71. This was Handel's first important role for a tenor, a vocal range rarely employed outside France for heroic parts, the castrato being preferred. Handel was probably prompted to compose the part of *Samson* for a tenor because of the growing prominence of John Beard, who first sang the part. (Ibid., p. 333.)

the oratorio, which calls for the seraphim and the cherubic host to praise Samson in "endless blaze of light."[72]

Samson's spiritual progression is revealed dramatically through his dialogues with those who come to visit him in his bondage. After an opening festival scene by the Philistines (SATB) that is reminiscent in mood and function of the Epinicion in *Saul*, Samson laments his tormented condition. He is then visited by his friend Micah (A), a chorus of Israelites (SATB), and his father, Manoah (B), who is negotiating for his ransom and release. In act 2 Samson's wife, Dalila (S), together with her chorus of Virgins (unison S), visits him. She wishes forgiveness and offers him voluptuous pleasure and domestic ease; he scorns her proposals and refuses her touch but forgives her from afar. The Philistine giant, Harapha (B), is the next visitor; he comes merely to observe the powerful enemy in captivity. Samson challenges him, but Harapha will not fight a blind slave. In act 3 Harapha comes again, this time to incite Samson to display his strength at a feast in honor of Dagon. Samson refuses, for he will not "abuse this consecrated gift of strength, again returning with my hair," by displaying it in honor of a false god. After another visit, however, Samson agrees, for "some inward motions do bid me go." After he leaves, Micah and Manoah discuss the latter's plans to free Samson while the Philistine festival is heard in the distance. Suddenly a "symphony of horror and confusion" interrupts the scene, and a messenger, an Israelite Officer (T), enters breathlessly to tell of Samson's death and triumph:

> Unwounded of his enemies he fell,
> At once did he destroy and was destroy'd;
> The edifice, (where all were met to see),
> Upon their heads, and on his own he pulled!

A lament and a Dead March follow, and the Israelites enter with the body of Samson; the end of the oratorio, like the beginning, is reminiscent of *Saul*. Manoah calls for lamentation to cease, however, for "Samson like Samson fell, both life and death heroic," and the work ends with a chorus of praise.

72. Although the symbolic progression from eclipse to sunrise was Hamilton's contribution, Milton suggests a progression from darkness to light in *Samson Agonistes*, lines 68ff. (darkness), 168ff. (light).

Musical characterization is of central importance in this oratorio. Samson's first two arias, "Torments, alas" and "Total eclipse" (Examples VII–16 and VII–17), show him in deep despair. They are in slow tempo and minor mode, and both introduce the voice without accompaniment after a brief orchestral introduction. This technique, which is not unusual in the late Baroque, here seems to emphasize the hero's loneliness in his blind and fettered state— "abandon'd, past all hope," as he is first described by Micah. In his next aria, "Why does the God of Israel sleep," he expresses his frustration by melismatic raging, particularly on the word "vengeance," and he calls on God to arise against the heathen. In the scene of Samson and Dalila, the latter is characterized as charming but superficial in her simile aria, "With plaintive notes and am'rous

EXAMPLE VII-16. *Samson* (Handel, *Werke*, 10:37).

EXAMPLE VII-17. *Samson* (Handel, *Werke*, 10:46).

moan" (Example VII–18), which includes both vocal and orchestral imitations of the turtledove's cooing; and she is equally superficial in "My faith and truth, oh Samson prove," her thoroughly
hedonistic, dancelike scene with her chorus of Virgins. Samson
recalls a bit wistfully his previous relationship with Dalila in his
tender *siciliano* "Your charms to ruin led the way"; yet the affection changes to that of harsh rejection in the duet of mutual
antagonism, "Traitor to love," which Samson and Dalila sing at
the close of this scene. In the episodes of Samson and Harapha, the
latter is characterized as a blustering braggart in his conventional
rage aria "Honor and arms" and as a harsh emissary of the enemy
in his threatening aria "Presuming slave," in which the vocal line is
reinforced throughout by the orchestra in unison and octaves.
Samson's calm assurance in the face of Harapha's rage is reflected
in his aria "My strength is from the living God," but he shows his
wrath in his duet with Harapha, "Go, baffled coward." In act 3,
when Samson makes his decision to attend the pagan festival and
"make Jehovah's glory known," he reveals his remarkable spiritual
change in the gentle, symbolic, and pictorial aria "Thus when the

EXAMPLE VII-18. *Samson* (Handel, *Werke*, 10:121–22).

sun from's wat'ry bed" (Example VII–19), the very antithesis of his "Total eclipse" in act 1. Although the characterizations of Samson, Dalila, and Harapha are the clearest and most convincing, that of Manoah as a loving father is conveyed particularly well in his aria "How willing my paternal love."

EXAMPLE VII-19. *Samson* (Handel, *Werke*, 10:219–20).

Only three of the arias in *Samson* use the da capo form. These arias are Micah's "It is not virtue," Harapha's "Honor and arms," and the aria version of the Philistine text "To song and dance we give the day."[73] Samson's "Why does the God of Israel sleep" uses an ABA' form, but most of the arias are in a large binary design. Of special interest among the binary arias is Manoah's "Thy

73. For the last-named number, see Handel, *Werke*, vol. 10, app. I.

glorious deeds," with its allegro first section in bravura style and its strongly contrasting second section, marked *largo e piano*, for the text "To sorrows now I tune my song." The various styles normally employed in opera and oratorio—including laments, bravura arias, and those with dance rhythms—are well represented.

The choruses of *Samson*, involved in the drama throughout, represent either the Israelite or the Philistine people; the latter tend to be portrayed in a more secular and dancelike style than the former. There are more choruses than in the previous dramatic oratorios,[74] but the choruses tend to be relatively brief and simple. Although fugal technique occasionally appears, only two of the choruses include fugues—"Then shall they know" and "O first created beam" (interesting for its augmented subject near the end, unusual in Handel's choral fugues). The latter chorus is particularly important for its influence on a later work: its prominent ascending fourth on the text "Let there be light" (Example VII–20) was probably the model for the similar treatment of these words in Haydn's *Creation*. The choruses in *Samson* often form parts of solo-choral complexes, and several times in the oratorio the chorus

EXAMPLE VII-20. *Samson* (Handel, *Werke*, 10:48).

74. For the numbers of choruses in the dramatic oratorios, see Dean, *Oratorios*, p. 627.

(EXAMPLE VII-20, continued)

completes a preceding aria. Perhaps the most musically effective solo-chorus complex is that beginning with Micah's beautiful "Return, return oh God of hosts," an aria that continues during the chorus "To dust his glory they would tread" in a kind of solo-choral relationship that is particularly prominent in *Athalia*.

Samson includes several instrumental numbers: the opening French overture, the following minuet, the "symphony of horror and confusion" to depict Samson's destruction of the Philistines' building, and the Dead March. It is possible that Handel never performed the Dead March composed for *Samson*, since that of *Saul* was substituted at an early date.[75] The orchestra of *Samson* consists of pairs of flutes, oboes, bassoons, horns, and trumpets plus tympani, strings, harpsichord, and organ. Two trombones would also be required for the original Dead March. Despite the fairly large orchestra most of the scoring is light, with sparing use made of the wind instruments.

Handel's borrowings in *Samson* include music from one of his own Italian cantatas and from works by Telemann, Muffat, Keiser,

75. Ibid., p. 345.

The First Mature Period of Handel's English Oratorio: 1738–1745   279

Legrenzi, Astorga, Porta, and Carissimi.[76] In most instances he borrowed only thematic material as a stimulus to his imagination and worked out the remainder of the number in his own manner and style. His borrowing from Carissimi, however, is unusual, for here he seems not to have assimilated Carissimi's material into a characteristically Handelian chorus: "Hear, Jacob's God"—clearly modeled on the final chorus of Carissimi's *Jephte*, "Plorate filiae Israel"—retains Carissimi's six-part setting (the only chorus in *Samson* that is consistently in six parts), essential melodic contours, and much of his mid-Baroque harmonic style.

Joseph and His Brethren[77]

Soon after the season of 1742–43 and before beginning the composition of *Joseph*, Handel set an English opera text, *Semele*,[78] originally written by William Congreve and arranged for Handel's use by an unknown poet. Although Handel had abandoned Italian opera by this time, his choice of *Semele* shows a continuing operatic interest. The work was composed between 3 June and 4 July 1743 and was first performed on 10 February 1744. *Semele* was not called an oratorio by its composer, no doubt because of its secular text. It was first advertised in the *London Daily Post*, 10 February 1744, as "SEMELE: After the Manner of an *Oratorio*,"[79]—that is, performed in an unstaged manner—and the earliest printed libretto bears the title *The Story of Semele*.[80] The work has been occasionally called an oratorio by commentators, both in Handel's time and later,[81] but its secular text places it clearly outside the generally accepted meaning of the word *oratorio* in Handel's time. Although it is among Handel's finest dramatic works, *Semele* was revived only once during his life and has seldom been performed since; the general lack of interest in *Semele* may be the result of its having been misunderstood as an "oratorio" falling short of its mark.[82]

76. For details of the borrowings, see ibid., pp. 334–36, 633–34; and Taylor, *Indebtedness*, p. 14.
77. Printed in Handel, *Werke*, vol. 42.
78. Printed ibid., vol. 7, and Handel, *Semele*.
79. Deutsch, *Handel*, p. 581.
80. Ibid., p. 582.
81. For a discussion of this point, see Dean, *Oratorios*, p. 365. In Schering, *Oratorium*, pp. 310–20, several works in addition to *Semele* are classified as "secular oratorios," a contradiction in terms for Handel's England.
82. For historical and analytical commentary on *Semele*, see Dean, *Oratorios*, pp. 365–97; Lang, *Handel*, pp. 408–19; and Serauky, *Händel*, 4:17–107.

Joseph was composed during August and September of 1743 and was first performed at the Theatre Royal in Covent Garden on 2 March 1744. The *London Daily Post* on 1 March advertised the performance as "a New *Oratorio*, call'd JOSEPH and his BRETHREN. With a *Concerto* on the *Organ*";[83] the first printing of the libretto carries the title *Joseph and his Brethren: A Sacred Drama.*[84] The oratorio appears to have been reasonably successful: the earl of Egmont called it "an inimitable composition,"[85] and Mrs. Mary Delany wrote, in her comments on Handel's oratorio series, "The oratorios fill very well, not withstanding the spite of the opera party: nine of the twelve are over. Joseph is to be performed (I hope) once more, then Saul, and the Messiah finishes."[86] *Joseph* was revived in four subsequent seasons (1745, 1747, 1755, and 1757), but it has been virtually ignored since the eighteenth century.

The libretto of *Joseph* was written by the Reverend James Miller of Wadham College, Oxford, who had previously written comedies, satires, and ballad operas as well as an English adaptation of Voltaire's tragedy *Mahomet*.[87] His only oratorio libretto, *Joseph* is based on the biblical story in Genesis 39–45. The libretto's theme, like that of the numerous Italian oratorios on this story that preceded it, is forgiveness—the powerful Joseph's magnanimous forgiveness of his brothers for having sold him into slavery.[88] The action of the drama takes place in Memphis. At the beginning of act 1, Joseph (A) is in prison for reasons that the libretto does not explain. (Miller evidently assumes that the listener will supply this and other missing background information from his knowledge of the biblical story.) During the course of act 1, Joseph is summoned from prison by Phanor (A), the chief butler to Pharaoh (B), in order to interpret Pharaoh's dreams. After Joseph's interpretation Pharoah, overwhelmed by Joseph's powers, appoints him to an administrative position second only to

83. Deutsch, *Handel*, p. 586.
84. Ibid., p. 585.
85. Diary of the earl of Egmont, 1 March 1744, ibid., p. 586.
86. Delany to Ann Granville Dewes, 10 March 1744, ibid., p. 587.
87. Dean, *Oratorios*, pp. 398–99.
88. Miller is said to have used Metastasio's *Giuseppe riconosciuto* ("Joseph Recognized") of 1733 as a model, in Leichtentritt, *Händel*, pp. 431–32, and Serauky, *Händel*, 4:145; aside from the biblical material, however, Miller's work has virtually nothing in common with Metastasio's until the recognition scene, which bears only a slight resemblance to that of Metastasio's libretto.

his own. Asenath (S)—daughter of Potiphera (A), the High Priest of On—falls in love with Joseph; they are married. Their marriage ceremony (described in the "stage" description of the libretto) forms the finale of the act. In act 2 (more than seven years later than act 1) Joseph's brother, Simeon (T), has been in prison for a year: he is being held a hostage until his brothers return to Egypt. Joseph summons Simeon and questions him about his father and brothers and particularly about the youngest brother, Benjamin. Phanor announces the arrival of the brothers; Benjamin (S) is among them, as are Ruben (B) and Judah (T). When Joseph questions them, he shows special interest in Benjamin. The act closes with a choral prayer for the protection of Israel. In act 3 the brothers have been arrested on the suspicion that one of them has stolen a silver cup. To Benjamin's surprise, the cup is found in his sack. Joseph orders him to prison, but Simeon offers to take his place, for Benjamin, the brothers say, is the only remaining son of Jacob and Rachel and is thus his father's dearest son. Upon hearing Simeon's self-sacrificing offer, Joseph is too touched to continue concealing his identity, which he reveals to his brothers. He asks them to "receive and give a kind embrace" and Benjamin to "forgive this harmless stratagem," by which he wished to test his brothers' loyalty to Benjamin. The oratorio closes with an anthem of rejoicing. Miller's work is weak dramatically for its omission of the incidents that motivate the action and poetically for its abundance of commonplace expressions and poverty of imagery.[89]

From the musical standpoint, too, *Joseph* is among Handel's least successful oratorios. The serious shortcomings of the libretto evidently inhibited his musical imagination, for this period was essentially a successful one for Handel: *Joseph* is preceded by *Samson* and *Semele* and followed by *Hercules* and *Belshazzar*—all great works with significantly better librettos. Together with its frequently routine settings of the text, however, *Joseph* includes some highly effective sections. Of special interest are the prison scenes of acts 1 and 2. At the opening of the oratorio, the imprisoned Joseph shows his resignation to the will of God in his aria "Be firm my soul," highly expressive for its stark introductory octaves in the strings and continuo, initial unaccompanied vocal

89. For a critique of this libretto, see Dean, *Oratorios*, pp. 399–402.

phrase, and accompanied recitative that functions as the B section of the written-out da capo aria. Simeon's prison scene in act 2, equally as effective as Joseph's in act 1, expresses his suppressed anxiety and frustration in the powerful accompanied recitative "Where are these Brethren"—with its orchestral introduction and accompaniment of dotted patterns, quick runs, wide skips, and trills on cadential notes. In his following aria—"Remorse, confusion, honor, fear, ye vultures"—Simeon bursts forth in a furious expression of his rage, with rushing scale passages in the orchestral and vocal lines and affective use of the rising augmented second as the vultures "gnaw" at his guilty breast. Other noteworthy passages of the oratorio are Joseph's *siciliano*, "The peasant tastes the sweets of life," with its long pedal points and folklike melody in which he recalls his former happiness as a shepherd; Phanor's aria "Our fruits, whilst yet in blossom die," expressing contrasting affections in the two halves of its binary form; the final chorus of act 2, "O God, who in thy heav'nly hand," with slow chordal opening and closing sections framing a triple fugue in quicker tempo; and the recognition scene, in simple recitative, with the basso continuo silent as Joseph reveals his identity: "Know, I am Joseph. Doth my father live? I am your brother, your long-lost brother, I am Joseph." After this totally unaccompanied recitative, the basso continuo again enters to accompany the brothers' exclamations.

Nearly half of the arias of *Joseph* are in da capo form; this is a larger proportion than in any of Handel's previous oratorios after *Deborah*. The oratorio includes only two duets, both for Asenath and Joseph. One of the duets, "What's sweeter than the newborn rose," also exists as a da capo aria for Asenath.

The chorus, which represents both the Egyptians and Joseph's brothers and is consistently for SATB, is used only ten times, which is less than in any of the previous oratorios except *Esther* and less than half as many times as in the immediately preceding oratorio, *Samson*. Several of the choruses, however, are developed at considerable length. The most extensive choruses or choral complexes, in addition to the final chorus of act 2 mentioned above, are the choral-solo complex that closes act 1 (beginning with the chorus "Immortal pleasures"), the opening chorus of act 2 ("Hail, thou youth," in two parts—both of which employ fugal treatment, with the second part consisting of a fugue with three subjects), the chorus "Blest be the man" (a combination of the French rondeau structure and the double fugue),[90] and the final number of the oratorio, "Alleluja! We will rejoice"—a fugal chorus borrowed entirely from the *Dettingen Anthem*, composed a few weeks earlier.[91]

The instrumental numbers in *Joseph* are the modified French overture at the beginning, the following minuet, the sinfonia that begins act 3 (a one-movement allegro), and "A grand March during the procession" in the wedding scene (based, curiously, on the Dead March composed for *Samson*). The orchestra of the oratorio includes pairs of transverse flutes and oboes, one bassoon, three trumpets, timpani, strings, harpsichord, and organ. The orchestration is not particularly noteworthy. All but one of the arias are accompanied by strings only; the exception is Pharaoh's "Since the race of time begun," which adds a trumpet and oboes. The full orchestra is used only for the final chorus of the oratorio, and the full orchestra minus one trumpet participates in the final chorus of act 1 and the acclamation chorus in act 2, "Blest be the man."

In addition to the borrowed numbers mentioned above (the wedding march and the oratorio's final chorus), Handel borrowed material from the overture to Stradella's *Serenata* "Qual prodigo" for the chorus "Joyful sounds."[92]

Belshazzar[93]

Just as *Joseph* had been preceded by *Semele*, *Belshazzar* was preceded by a secular dramatic work, *Hercules*, to be performed in the manner of an oratorio. Using a text by the Reverend Thomas Broughten, Handel composed *Hercules* between 19 July and about 21 August 1744; thus he finished it about two days before starting to work on *Belshazzar*. *Hercules* and *Semele* have in common the mythological origins of their texts, and it is significant for the understanding of the oratorio in this period that neither work was advertised as an oratorio during the season of its premiere. Handel seems to have carefully avoided using the term *oratorio* for *Her-*

90. For an analysis of this chorus, see Serauky, *Händel*, 4:172.
91. For this chorus as the finale of the *Dettingen Anthem*, see Handel, *Werke*, 36:143–53.
92. For the material that he borrowed, see Handel, *Werke*, supp. vol. 3, p. 5.
93. Handel, *Werke*, vol. 19.

cules in the advance publicity for his subscription series in which it was to be performed. His notice in the *Daily Advertiser* of 20 October 1744 states, "Mr. HANDEL proposes to perform by Subscription, Twenty-Four Times, during the Winter Season, at the King's Theatre in the Hay-Market, and engages to exhibit *two new Performances, and several of his former Oratorios*."[94] Handel thus grouped together the two new works, *Hercules* and *Belshazzar*, as "two new Performances," not oratorios. Nor was *Hercules* called an oratorio in subsequent notices, but "HERCULES, A new Musical Drama";[95] the designation "A Musical Drama" was also used on the title page of the printed libretto.[96] *Hercules* was revived three times during Handel's life: in 1749, in 1752, and in 1756. The first of these revivals was indeed advertised as "an ORATORIO call'd *Hercules*,"[97] but this exceptional use of the term *oratorio* did not recur: for the second revival he avoided any designation of a genre ("This Day will be performed HERCULES"),[98] and for the third revival a Salisbury newspaper clearly distinguished between "the Musical Drama of Hercules, and the Oratorio of Esther."[99] The earl of Shaftesbury's memoirs of Handel, written in the autumn of 1760, refer to "Performances in the Oratorio manner" of "the Drama of Hercules, and the Oratorio of Belshazzar."[100] Although *Hercules* has usually been counted among Handel's oratorios in nineteenth- and twentieth-century writings, it seems more appropriate to follow the prevailing terminology of Handel's time by viewing the work as its composer and his contemporaries generally did: as a secular musical drama, like *Semele*, performed in the manner of an oratorio.[101] Scarcely any dramatic work by Handel has received such high praise by twentieth-century

94. Deutsch, *Handel*, p. 596, italics added.

95. *General Advertiser*, 5 January 1745, and *Daily Advertiser*, 11 February 1745, ibid., pp. 601, 606.

96. Dean, *Oratorios*, p. 432. *Belshazzar*, on the other hand, was consistently called an oratorio in subsequent published advertisements and on the title page of its printed libretto.

97. *General Advertiser*, 24 February 1749, in Deutsch, *Handel*, p. 658.

98. *General Advertiser*, 21 February 1752, ibid., p. 719.

99. *Salisbury and Winchester Journal* (Salisbury), 11 October 1756, ibid., p. 778.

100. *Memoires of Handel*, by Anthony Ashley Cooper, fourth earl of Shaftsbury, ibid., p. 848.

101. Among the previous musicological writings on Handel's music, Dean, *Oratorios*, stands virtually alone in recognizing that "*Hercules* is not an oratorio but a 'musical drama'" (p. 414) and that "Handel was careful not to call *Hercules* an oratorio" in his published announcements of its premiere (p. 429).

commentators as *Hercules*;[102] yet it is rarely performed. As Lang points out, "the greatest of Baroque music dramas awaits the recognition it deserves."[103] *Hercules* has been neglected nearly as much as *Semele* and probably for much the same reason: it has been evaluated in terms of the oratorio rather than those of the secular music drama.[104]

Belshazzar was begun on 23 August 1744, about two days after the completion of *Hercules*. Handel started the work without seeing the entire libretto, as we know from his extant letters to Charles Jennens, *Belshazzar's* librettist. In a letter of 9 June, Handel had asked Jennens eagerly for act 1, and on 19 July (the day he began *Hercules*) he acknowledged its receipt and his satisfaction with it.[105] On 21 August Handel acknowledged the receipt of act 2 of *Belshazzar*, of which he wrote, "I am greatly pleased with it, and shall use my best endeavors to do it justice. I can only Say that I impatiently wait for the third Act."[106] Handel was indeed impatient, for he began the oratorio two days later, having seen only the first two acts of the libretto. On 10 September he completed the sketch of acts 1 and 2; three days later he wrote to Jennens a rare expression of his enthusiasm and anxiously requested act 3: "Your most excellent Oratorio has given me great Delight in setting it to Musick and still engages me warmly. It is indeed a Noble Piece, very grand and uncommon; it has furnished me with Opportunity to some very particular ideas, besides so many great Choru's. I intreat you heartily to favour me Soon with the last Act, which I expect with anxiety, that I may regulate my Self the better as to the Length of it. I profess my Self highly obliged to You, for so generous a Present."[107] Handel acknowledged the receipt of act 3 on 2 October and commented, "I think it a very fine and sublime Oratorio, only it is really too long, if I would extend the Musick, it would last 4 Hours and more." He further mentioned that he had done some cutting and would do even more.[108] The oratorio was probably completed by mid-October.

102. For a development of this point, with quotations from various writers on Handel's music, see Dean, *Oratorios*, p. 414.

103. Lang, *Handel*, p. 428.

104. For historical and analytical commentaries on *Hercules*, see Dean, *Oratorios*, pp. 414–33; Lang, *Handel*, pp. 421–29; and Serauky, *Händel*, 4:218–306.

105. Handel to Jennens, 9 June 1744 and 19 July 1744, in Deutsch, *Handel*, pp. 591–92.

106. Handel to Jennens, 21 August 1744, ibid., pp. 593–94.

107. Handel to Jennens, 13 September 1744, ibid., p. 595.

108. Handel to Jennens, 2 October 1744, ibid., pp. 595–96.

Belshazzar was first performed on 27 March 1745 and was repeated only twice during the extremely poor season. Financial difficulties had previously prompted him to propose, in the *Daily Advertiser* of 17 January, to "stop short" the series "before my Losses are too great to support" and to give refunds to his subscribers.[109] He was persuaded, however, to continue the series a bit longer. According to Burney, he "resumed the performance of his Oratorios of *Samson, Saul, Joseph, Belshazzar*, and the *Messiah*, in March; but I perfectly remember, that none were well attended, except Samson and the MESSIAH."[110] On 2 April a Mrs. Elizabeth Carter wrote to a friend that "Handel, once so crowded, plays to empty walls in that opera house."[111] Planned for twenty-four nights, the oratorio series was finally discontinued on 23 April after the sixteenth night. The quality of Handel's singers might well have been the reason for the failure of this oratorio season.[112] The state of the composer's health during the season is uncertain, but he suffered a physical collapse in the following summer and the mental illness from which he had suffered in 1737 appears to have returned.[113] Thus was *Belshazzar*'s premiere surrounded by the gloom of a difficult period. The work has received occasional performances since Handel's time, but it has never been among his most popular oratorios, despite its many dramatic and musical merits.

The theme of the libretto, the decline of a kingdom, is clearly set forth at the beginning of act 1 by Nitocris (S), the mother of the tyrannical king of Babylon, Belshazzar (T). In her opening speech, much like a prologue, Nitocris sketches the life cycle of an empire, from its infancy to its certain end. A follower of the captive Jewish prophet Daniel (A), she contrasts the "vain, fluctuating state of human empire" with the unchanging nature of God and his realm. The second scene of act 1 carries the following "stage" description in the printed libretto: *The Camp of Cyrus before Babylon. A view of the city with the River Euphrates running through it.* CYRUS, GOBRIAS; MEDES and PERSIANS. CHORUS of BABYLONIANS *upon the Walls, deriding Cyrus, as engaged in an impracticable*

109. Deutsch, *Handel*, p. 602.
110. Burney, *Account*, p. 29.
111. Carter to Catherine Talbot, 2 April 1745, in Deutsch, *Handel*, p. 610.
112. Lang, *Handel*, p. 438.
113. Ibid.; Dean, *Oratorios*, p. 455.

undertaking." Thus Cyrus (A), the prince of Persia, functioning as an instrument of God, is laying seige to Babylon; he is aided by Gobrias (B), an Assyrian nobleman who has abandoned Belshazzar's Babylon. Cyrus plans to divert the river Euphrates from its course and enter Babylon through the dried-up riverbed during the drunken celebration of the Babylonian feast of Sesach, the god of wine. Meanwhile, Daniel, in his house "with the *Prophesies of Isaiah, and Jeremiah open before him*" (according to the libretto's description), predicts that those prophesies are about to be fulfilled and the Israelites will soon be freed from their Babylonian captivity. Despite the opposition of his mother, Belshazzar proclaims the feast of Sesach and orders that the sacred vessels taken from the temple in Jerusalem be used in the revels honoring Sesach. Act 1 ends with a chorus of Jews predicting the wrath of God. At the beginning of act 2, Cyrus and his army are about to enter the city. The feast of Sesach is in progress and is described in the libretto as follows: "*A banquet room, adorned with the images of the Babylonian gods.* BELSHAZZAR, *his wives, concubines, and lords, drinking out of the Jewish temple-vessels, and singing the praises of their gods.*" Suddenly Belshazzar cries out, and the libretto again supplies a description: "*As he is going to drink, a hand appears writing upon the wall overagainst him; he sees it, turns pale with fear, drops the bowl of wine, falls back in his seat, trembling from head to foot, and his knees knocking against each other.*" The chorus calls for help for the king, and he points "*to the hand upon the wall, which, while they gaze at it with astonishment, finishes the writing, and vanishes.*" The wise men are called but cannot interpret the writing on the wall. Nitocris urges Belshazzar to call Daniel, and the latter interprets the ominous words, which foretell the end of Belshazzar's reign. By the end of act 2, Cyrus has entered the city. In act 3 a messenger reports that Cyrus is within the palace; a "Martial Symphony" is played during which, according to the libretto, "*a battle is supposed, in which* BELSHAZZAR *and his attendants are slain.*" The victorious Cyrus releases the captive Jews and professes their god as his. The Israelites conclude the oratorio with an anthem praising God.

Belshazzar is, of course, a biblical oratorio: its most significant scene, that of the feast and the writing on the wall, is based on Daniel 5;[114] the scene in Daniel's house draws on Jeremiah 29 and

---

114. The most widely known oratorio on this subject prior to Handel's, that by Carissimi, is confined to this biblical passage.

Isaiah 44–45; and two of the choruses of the Israelites, "Tell it out among the heathen" and "I will magnify thee," are borrowed from the Chandos Anthems (nos. 8 and 5, respectively), which are settings of Psalm texts. *Belshazzar* is also historical, however, and much of it is based on Herodotus's *History* and Xenophon's *Cyropaedia*. For the story of Gobrias, Jennens drew upon Xenophon (4. 6); for the account of the attack on Babylon, he used both Xenophon (7. 5. 13ff.) and Herodotus (1. 189); and for the character Nitocris he drew upon Herodotus (1. 185ff.). Jennens manipulated historical relationships for his poetic and dramatic purpose, but he fashioned one of the best dramatic librettos that Handel ever used, despite its verbosity. (Handel omitted setting more than two hundred lines of Jennens's libretto, although all these were printed in the libretto issued for the first performance.)[115]

The numerous "stage" descriptions that Jennens included, most of which are quoted above, seem to fulfill one of the functions of the *testo*, the role that would normally provide both narration and description in the seventeenth-century oratorio. There is some Italian precedent for including "stage" descriptions in the librettos of oratorios, and Handel, if not Jennens, would probably have known this. Some of Handel's previous oratorios included quite limited descriptions of scenes and action.[116] There is no doubt that "both Jennens and Handel had before their minds a full dramatic performance with scenery and action"[117] and that they wanted the audience to share this mental image. There is no evidence, however, that they either intended or expected the work to be staged.[118]

Particularly noteworthy in the music of *Belshazzar* is the characterization of the main personages. Even before the tyrannical, drunken Belshazzar appears, he is aptly described in Gobrias's aria "Behold the monstrous human beast, / Wallowing in excessive feast";[119] ponderous unisons and octaves in the orchestra frequently double the vocal line, which emphasizes "wallowing" by repetitions and long melismas. Two of Belshazzar's arias, "Let

115. The lines that Handel did not set are printed as footnotes in the libretto in Handel, *Werke*, vol. 19.

116. For examples of previous, limited descriptions of scenes or actions in the librettos or MSS of Handel's oratorios, see above, pp. 207, 219–20, 282.

117. Dean, *Oratorios*, p. 439.

118. Ibid., pp. 439–40.

119. Belshazzar is not named in this aria, but only he, as the symbol of the Babylonian worshipers of Sesach, could be the "human beast" of the aria.

festal joy triumphant reign" and "Let the deep bowl thy praise confess," are dancelike, in 3/8 and 6/8 time, and include long melismas in praise of wine. His last aria, "I thank thee, Sesach," sung just before his death, is martial and heroic in character, with bravura passages, but his is a wine-inspired heroism. Only during the terrifying, sobering scene of the handwriting on the wall does Belshazzar lose, momentarily, his image as a swaggering sot. His mother, Nitocris, is characterized as the wise and loving matriarch who tries in vain to temper her son's behavior. Her characterization is the most successful and her music the most attractive in the oratorio. She begins both acts 1 and 3 —the former with the long, philosophical, accompanied recitative "Vain, fluctuating state of human empire," followed by the aria reflecting on God's eternity, "Thou, God most high," a gentle largo in triple meter. Her opening aria of act 3, "Alternate hopes and fears," is a moving utterance, expressed in sarabande rhythm and a minor key, of her conflicting feelings toward her son and his misdeeds.[120] Of her other two numbers, one is an attractive simile aria, "The leafy honors," in which the description of the blowing leaves is melismatically presented as Nitocris tries to prevent her son's dissipation; the other is a *siciliano*—"Regard, oh my son, my flowing tears, / Proofs of maternal love"—that movingly reveals the pathos of her reaction to Daniel's ominous interpretation of the handwriting on the wall. Daniel's characterization is less successful, although his scene beginning "Oh sacred oracles of truth"—a mixture of accompanied and simple recitative, arioso, and aria styles—is a convincing portrait of the prophet poring over the sacred scriptures. Cyrus is effectively shown to be an instrument of God in his larghetto aria—"Great God! who, yet but darkly known," in which he prays for God's help—and in his pomposo aria "Oh God of truth! oh faithful guide," in which he praises God for assisting him in his military exploit; and he is clearly the magnanimous victor in the majestic, military aria with trumpets, "Destructive war, thy limits know." Gobrias, who appears in only two scenes, is characterized in his three arias as a person of deep emotions who, having deserted his Babylon because of its ruling tyrant, weeps for joy at its capture by the forces of Cyrus.

120. There are two settings of this text, both printed in Handel, *Werke*, 19:198–205, and both superb expressions of the same feelings.

The central dramatic action of the oratorio, the banquet scene, is of special interest, as it is treated in a strictly operatic manner. Drinking from the sacred Jewish vessels, Belshazzar has just finished singing his aria "Let the deep bowl thy praise confess" and is challenging the "God of Judah's boasted power" to "vindicate his injur'd honor," when a staccato, chromatic, unaccompanied string passage (Example VII–21) symbolizes the hand in

EXAMPLE VII-21. *Belshazzar* (Handel, *Werke*, 19:156–58).

(EXAMPLE VII-21, continued)

the act of writing on the wall. Only the "stage" descriptions reveal what is taking place; the music is a reaction to the events described, the events "on stage." Belshazzar cries out, and twice more the unaccompanied, staccato strings sound while he and the chorus exclaim at the mysterious event. This is among the most purely theatrical moments in all of Handel's oratorios. Effective as it is to a listener who reads the libretto's description carefully and can visualize the scene as Jennens and Handel intended him to do, this scene, nevertheless, strains the genre virtually to its breaking point. Here *Belshazzar* approaches the condition of an opera performed in the manner of an oratorio—as it does occasionally elsewhere, such as the scene of act 1 in which the Babylonians taunt the Persians from the walls of Babylon ("Behold, by Persia's hero made"), a scene that may be understood only from the "stage" description.

Five of the arias in *Belshazzar* are in da capo form and three are in ABA' form. The others are either binary, through-composed, or strophic. Cyrus's "Great God! who, yet but darkly known" is a strophic aria, rare in Handel's oratorios. *Belshazzar* includes eight accompanied recitatives, as many as do *Saul* and *Samson*. Like the accompanied recitatives in those works, some of these are of considerable length and importance for dramatic continuity and characterization. The oratorio includes two duets, the first between Nitocris and Belshazzar (in da capo form) and the second between Nitocris and Cyrus.

The chorus receives considerable emphasis in *Belshazzar*, for fourteen choruses represent three groups: Babylonians, Persians, and Jews. Most of the choruses are for SATB, although a few are for SAATB, SSAATTB, and SSAATB. Handel seems to have made some distinction among the musical styles of the choruses representing different nations,[121] but the distinctions are subtle and not entirely consistent. Although several of the choruses represent the brief exclamations of a crowd, more of them are like anthems in two or three sections, one or more of which is fugal. Among the latter type are the Jews' "By slow degrees," beginning with a slow, homophonic section and continuing with two fugal sections in contrasting tempos; and the Persians' "See, from his post Euphrates flies" and "O glorious prince," each of which consists of three contrasting sections. Two choruses are borrowed from the Chandos Anthems, as mentioned above; the placement of these borrowings was mentioned by Handel in his correspondence with Jennens.[122]

Belshazzar includes three instrumental numbers: the opening French overture; a sinfonia marked allegro postillions, with melodies imitating the post horn to indicate the summoning and arrival of the Wise Men to interpret the mysterious handwriting on the wall; and the "Martial Symphony," an allegro with trumpets and tympani to represent the battle in which Belshazzar is killed. The instruments employed in the oratorio are pairs of oboes and trumpets plus tympani, strings, harpsichord, and organ.

Six of the numbers in *Belshazzar* include material borrowed from other works, all but one from Handel's previous compositions; the exception is the allegro postillions, borrowed in part from Telemann.[123]

121. Dean, *Oratorios*, p. 441.
122. Deutsch, *Handel*, pp. 595–96.
123. For the details of the borrowings, see Dean, *Oratorios*, p. 644.

CHAPTER VIII *Handel's Later Oratorios*

§●*Four "Occasional" Oratorios: 1746–1748*

In 1745–46 the Hanoverian monarchy of England was engaged in a struggle with the forces of Prince Charles Edward, the "Young Pretender" who was intent on restoring the House of Stuart. Having sailed from France to Scotland in July 1745, Charles's forces gained Scottish support, took Edinburgh in September, and invaded England in November. By early December they had reached Derby, at which point, pursued by the army led by the duke of Cumberland, they were forced to retreat northward. The decisive battle, in which the duke of Cumberland defeated Prince Charles, was that of Culloden on 16 April 1746.

Clearly interested in demonstrating his support of the Hanoverian regime, Handel composed several patriotic works: the song "Stand round my brave boys," called *A Song Made for the Gentlemen Volunteers of the City of London* and published in the *London Magazine* of November 1745; the *Occasional Oratorio*, first performed on 14 February 1746; and the song "From scourging rebellion," called *A Song on the Victory Obtain'd over the Rebels by His Royal Highness the Duke of Cumberland*, published by J. Walsh, 26 May 1746. Thus the *Occasional Oratorio* was Handel's major effort of encouragement to the Loyalists during their struggle. Following the victory, Handel composed three other oratorios on themes of war, all of which were "occasional," in a sense, for they sought to find favor with a public still in a militaristic and nationalistic mood.

Occasional Oratorio[1]

No doubt because of Handel's illness in 1745, his musical productivity was held to a minimum during the summer and fall, his usual periods of composition. The *Occasional Oratorio* was composed early in 1746. Its first performance was announced simply as "a New Occasional Oratorio, which is design'd to be perform'd at the Theatre-Royal in Covent-Garden."[2] A letter written by a Reverend William Harris who attended a rehearsal of the work on 7 February, just one week before its premiere, praises it and points out its relationship to the duke of Cumberland's pursuit of Prince Charles: "Yesterday morning I was at Handel's house to hear the rehearsal of his new occasional Oratorio. It is extremely worthy of him, which you will allow to be saying all one can in praise of it. . . . The words of his Oratorio are scriptural, but taken from various parts, and are expressive of the rebels' flight and our pursuit of them. Had not the Duke carried his point triumphantly, this Oratorio could not have been brought on. It is to be performed in public next Friday."[3] The oratorio was performed four times in 1746 and was revived in one subsequent season, that of 1747.

The libretto of the *Occasional Oratorio* is anonymous, but evidence points to the authorship of the Reverend Thomas Morell,[4] who was to be Handel's next librettist. The libretto is largely scriptural, and like *Israel in Egypt* and *Messiah*, it is nondramatic. Parts 1 and 2 are mostly quoted from or based on Milton's verse translations of the Psalms, but part 3 includes borrowed numbers (text and music) from *Israel*, *Esther*, and the coronation anthem *Zadok the Priest* plus new texts written for the occasion. Unlike Handel's two previous nondramatic oratorios, this one has no story; in fact, it is more like an enormous anthem than an oratorio. This is the only composition with neither narrative nor dramatic elements that Handel termed an oratorio. In general, the text of part 1 deals with the misery of war, God's vengeance, and his protection of his people against the unjust; that of part 2, with the anticipation of peace; and that of part 3, with exultation and praise of God for victory.

1. Printed in Handel, *Werke*, vol. 43.
2. *General Advertiser*, 31 January 1746, in Deutsch, *Handel*, p. 629.
3. W. Harris to Mrs. Thomas Harris, 7 February 1746, ibid., pp. 629–30.
4. Dean, *Oratorios*, p. 461.

A

NEW OCCASIONAL

ORATORIO.

As it is Perform'd at the

THEATRE-ROYAL *in* Covent-Garden.

The Words taken from MILTON, SPENSER, &c.
And Set to Mufick by Mr. HANDEL.

LONDON:

Printed for J. and R. TONSON and S. DRAPER in the *Strand*.

M DCC XLVI.

1re reprelent 14 fevrier 1746

[Price One Shilling.]

unique avec le notre

FIGURE VIII-I. Title page of the libretto to Handel's *Occasional
Oratorio*, as printed for the first performance, 1746.
(Reproduced by permission of Gerald Coke, Esq.)

In keeping with its martial theme, grandiosity and pomp are the chief characteristics of the oratorio. This impression is conveyed by the large instrumental and vocal forces required as well as by the style. The orchestra consists of three trumpets, two horns, three trombones, timpani, two oboes, two bassoons, strings, harpsichord, and organ. Although no single number calls for the entire orchestra, the combination of trumpets, timpani, and oboes, plus strings and continuo, is used frequently enough to convey the martial effect. All the newly composed choruses are for SATB; the chorus borrowed in part from *Athalia*, "May God from whom all mercies spring," is for SSAATTBB; and the three borrowed from *Israel*—"I will sing unto the Lord," "Who is like unto Thee," and "He gave them hailstones"—are for double chorus, SATB-SATB.

Of the fourteen choruses (including two repetitions), seven are newly composed. Particularly noteworthy is the "Hallelujah" that closes part 2, a contrapuntal tour de force with five subjects or countersubjects in a variety of combinations. The first chorus of part 1, "Let us break off by strength of hand," functions as a ritornello in a choral-solo complex: an exciting allegro in 6/8 time, it is twice repeated in abbreviated forms after intervening tenor arias. Two of the new choruses, "Be wise at length" and "Prepare the hymn, prepare the song," are continuations of preceding arias; the latter of the two begins with a reminiscence of the second phrase of the Lutheran chorale "Ein feste Burg."[5] The choral finale of the oratorio pointedly praises the Hanoverian monarch by borrowing the powerful "God save the king" from *Zadok the Priest*.

The oratorio includes about twenty arias (fewer if the shorter ones are classified as ariosos), three accompanied recitatives, and one duet. Two of the arias—"Thou shalt bring them in" and "The enemy said: I will pursue"—are borrowed from *Israel*. Da capo form is used in only two arias, "Fly from threatening vengeance" and "Prophetic visions strike my eye," and in the duet; ABA' form is used in two arias, "His sceptre is the rod of righteousness" and "Jehovah is my shield, my glory." The remaining arias are either through-composed or binary in structure.

Because of the function of the oratorio and the nature of the libretto, considerable emphasis is placed in the arias on styles

5. Schering, "Händel," pp. 36–37.

expressing martial moods and those of heroism, vengeance, and patriotism. Noteworthy for their martial and heroic expressions are part 1's opening accompanied recitative (B), "Why do the gentiles tumult and the nations muse a vain thing," the text of which is Milton's translation of the same psalm as the *Messiah* aria (B) "Why do the nations so furiously rage"; the aria (S) "When warlike ensigns wave," with its fanfare-styled melodic lines, melismas on "wave," and contrasting folklike, pastoral section at the words "No pasture now the plain affords";[6] the aria (B) "The sword that's drawn in virtue's cause"; and the aria (T) "Tyrants, whom no cov'nants bind." Expressing the affection of vengeance are the arias "Fly from threatening vengeance" (S) with long coloratura passages and "His sceptre is the rod of righteousness, with which he bruiseth all his foes to death" (B), in F-sharp minor and marked *pomposo.* The aria (S) "Prophetic visions strike my eye" (Example VIII–1), includes a quotation from the beginning of Thomas Arne's famous patriotic song "Rule, Britannia" (Example VIII–2) from his *Masque of Alfred* (1740). Handel wanted the quotation to be clearly recognized, for it enters in the vocal line (to the words "war shall cease, welcome peace") unaccompanied after a strong cadence followed by a rest.[7] In addition to warlike and patriotic sentiments, those of peace and joy are also found in the oratorio—particularly in the aria (T) "Jehovah is my

EXAMPLE VIII-1. *Occasional Oratorio* (Handel, *Werke*, 43:100–101).

6. The use of ostinato and pedal point in this aria is interpreted as a Scottish bagpipe reference in Herbage, "Oratorios," p. 112; these techniques, however, are not exclusively Scottish but are common in Baroque expressions of pastoral texts.

7. For further comments on Handel's use of Arne's melody, see Serauky, *Händel*, 4:450.

(EXAMPLE VIII-1, continued)

EXAMPLE VIII-2. *Alfred* (Thomas Arne, *Alfred* [London: Harrison & Co.], 1785, p. 42).

shield," in a gentle, almost pastoral style; in the arias (S) "When Israel like the bounteous Nile" and "May balmy peace"; and in the duet (SS and ST) "After long storms and tempest overblown," in minuet style.

The only instrumental numbers are the overture that begins the oratorio and the sinfonia that introduces part 3. The former is in three movements: a French overture with trumpets, timpani, oboes, and strings; an adagio for oboe solo and strings; and a march with the instrumentation of the first movement. The sinfonia is in two movements, the first borrowed from the opening movement of Handel's concerto grosso op. 6, no. 1 and the second from the *Musette* of op. 6, no. 6.

Judas Maccabaeus[8]

Handel began to compose *Judas* on 8 or 9 July and completed it on 11 August 1746. The first performance, scheduled for March 1747, was postponed because of the sensational trial of Baron Lovat (Simon Fraser), a Scottish Jacobite who had openly espoused the Stuart cause during the rebellion led by Prince Charles Edward. On 1 April, however, the *General Advertiser* announced the work's premiere: "At the Theatre-Royal . . . this Day . . . will be perform'd a New Oratorio, call'd JUDAS MACCHABAEUS. *With a New* CONCERTO."[9] *Judas* was given five more times during this season and was thereafter among Handel's most frequently performed oratorios; he revived it every year but one (1749) for the rest of his life. Since Handel's time this work has consistently retained its position among the composer's most popular oratorios.

Judas is as much an occasional oratorio as its predecessor: the author of its libretto, the Reverend Thomas Morell, stated in a letter that "the plan of *Judas Maccabaeus* was designed as a compliment to the duke of Cumberland, upon his returning victorious from Scotland."[10] Handel had turned to Morell for the libretto upon the recommendation of the duke of Cumberland's brother, Frederick, the prince of Wales.[11] Morell had previously written poetry and various scholarly works; he was also the probable author of the libretto of the *Occasional Oratorio*, as mentioned above.[12]

Morell's libretto is based primarily on the story of Judas Maccabaeus as told in 1 Maccabees 2–8, with additions from Flavius Josephus's *Antiquities of the Jews* 12.6–10.[13] Although it is a dramatic oratorio, *Judas* includes only two named characters of significance: the Jewish hero Judas Maccabaeus (T), intended to represent England's hero of the moment; and Judas's brother, Simon (B). Anonymous characters are an Israelitish Woman (S), an Israelitish Man (Ms), a Messenger (A), and Eupolemus (B), the

8. Printed in Handel, *Werke*, vol. 22.
9. Deutsch, *Handel*, p. 638.
10. Morell to an unknown addressee, ca. 1764, ibid., p. 851.
11. Ibid.
12. For more information on Morell, see Dean, *Oratorios*, pp. 462–63.
13. Although stories from the Maccabees were seldom used for oratorios on the Continent, two examples are Latin oratorios performed at Crocifisso in Rome: Gregorio Cola, *Judas Machabaeus* (Rome, 1695), libretto in I/Rli:172.F.25(6); and Floriano Aresti, *Mater Machabaeorum* (Rome, 1704), libretto in I/Rli:171.E.13(14).

FIGURE VIII-2. Thomas Morell (1703–84), the librettist of Handel's
*Judas Maccabaeus, Alexander Balus, Joshua, Theo-
dora,* and *Jephtha.* After a drawing by William
Hogarth, engraved by James Basire.
(Reproduced by permission of GB/Lbm.)

Jewish Ambassador to Rome. The chorus represents the Israelitish Men and Women (SATB except twice, ATB and SSATB).

Act 1 begins with a scene of lamentation for the death of Mattathias, the father of Judas. The Israelites pray that God will grant them "a leader bold, and brave"; Simon, who feels "the Deity within," declares it God's will that Judas be Israel's leader. The people rally around Judas, who will lead them in their war for freedom. At the beginning of act 2, the Israelites are celebrating their victory over the forces of the Syrian generals Apollonius and Seron. The Messenger enters to warn of "new scenes of bloody war," for King Antiochus of Syria has sent another army, led by Gorgias, to "root out Israel's strength." The Israelites react despondently, but Judas issues a call to arms, and again the people prepare for war. Simon remains behind to purify the temple, desecrated by the enemy's sacrifices to heathen gods. Act 3 begins with the Israelites' celebration of the Feast of Lights. The Messenger enters with a report of Judas's new victories. Judas triumphantly enters and orders the Israelites to prepare obsequies "to those who bravely fell in war." Eupolemus arrives from Rome with an agreement between the Jews and the Roman Senate that will assure Judea's independence and security. The oratorio ends with a duet of peace and a final chorus of rejoicing. This libretto is weak both in plot and in characterization; it does little more than provide a framework for Handel to compose victory music to honor the duke of Cumberland and to satisfy the public's taste in a period after a victorious war.[14]

Some of the most effective music in *Judas*, that of the opening scene of lamentation, is stylistically some of the least characteristic of the work as a whole. The scene begins with a chorus, "Mourn, ye afflicted children," a largo in C minor in the style of a funeral march (particularly in the orchestra), with the word "mourn" frequently stressed by long notes. After a brief simple recitative there follows "From this dread scene," a duet in G minor by an Israelitish Woman and Man; it is a highly effective number with large skips in the melodic line (Example VIII–3) and predominantly imitative texture with some use of double counterpoint between the voices.[15] The following chorus, "For Sion lamentation

14. For surveys of conflicting evaluations of the libretto and music of *Judas*, see Dean, *Oratorios*, pp. 465–66; Lang, *Handel*, pp. 448–50.
15. For an analysis of this number, see Serauky, *Händel*, 4:484.

EXAMPLE VIII-3. *Judas Maccabaeus* (Handel, *Werke*, 22:14).

make" (Example VIII–4) is perhaps the finest number of the scene. Marked *larghetto, e un poco piano* and set in F minor and 12/8 time, the chorus successfully blends the style of the *siciliano*, usually reserved for gentler affections, with that of deep and anguished lamentation; this mood is conveyed by chromaticism and rhetorical repetitions of affective words and motives. Particularly striking are the descending chromatic continuo line and "sighing" bassoons at the beginning, the rhythmic ostinato in the continuo throughout most of the chorus, and the chromatic passage—over a B-flat pedal in the continuo—in the vocal and instrumental parts on the words "For Sion lamentation make, with words that weep, that weep, that weep" (mm. 17–19, not in the example). After another brief simple recitative the scene concludes with an aria by Simon (also existing in a transposed version

EXAMPLE VIII-4. *Judas Maccabaeus* (Handel, *Werke*, 22:18).

for an Israelitish Woman) with a most unfortunate text—"Pious orgies, pious airs, / Decent sorrow, decent prayers"—which, nevertheless, Handel set as a successful aria in E-flat major that is marked *largo e sostenuto*. Other than the opening scene, the only moment of depression in the oratorio is the number in act 2 that reflects the Israelites' despondency upon hearing that war will again be forced upon them: "Ah! wretched Israel," a solo and chorus that is among the most effective numbers of the work.

More characteristic of the prevailing style of *Judas* is the martial mood, which appears for the first time in Simon's aria "Arm, arm ye brave" and continues in the chorus "We come in bright array." This number occurs in act 1, just after Simon's assertion that Judas is God's choice as the Israelites' new leader. As is true of virtually all the martial music of the oratorio, fanfare-styled melodic lines characterize both the aria and chorus. Among the other numbers of this type are Judas's first aria, "Call forth thy powers, my soul"; the chorus "Lead on, Judah disdains the galling load of hostile chains"; the chorus "Fall'n is the foe," one of the best numbers of the oratorio; Judas's aria "Sound an alarm, your silver trumpets sound" and its attached chorus "We hear the pleasing, dreadful sound"; and Judas's final aria, "With honor let desert be crown'd." Unlike the *Occasional Oratorio*, which employs trumpets and timpani in the overture and all three acts, *Judas* introduces these instruments for the first time at a climactic point in act 2: Judas's aria "Sound an alarm," with its reference to "silver trumpets" in the text, is an ABA′ structure in which the A and B are accompanied by continuo only; A′ begins unaccompanied, but soon the full orchestra—three trumpets, timpani, two oboes, and strings—bursts forth with a fanfare that can produce an overwhelming effect in its context. The full orchestra is used in the remainder of the aria and the attached chorus.

Contrasting with the predominantly martial, bravura attitude of the oratorio, in addition to the sections of lamentation and despondency mentioned above, are the three "liberty" numbers, apparently intended to be sung in succession:[16] the arias "O liberty," "Come ever smiling liberty," and " 'Tis liberty, dear liberty alone" plus the duet version of the second aria, "Come ever smiling liberty." Other contrasts with the prevailing martial mood

16. Dean, *Oratorios*, p. 468.

are the expression of piety, in sarabande rhythm, of the aria "Wise men, flatt'ring may deceive us"; the prayerful and beautiful "Father of Heav'n," with which act 2 begins; the dancelike, joyful "So shall the lute and harp awake"; and the pastoral aria (also existing in a duet version) "Oh lovely peace."

For Handel's revivals of *Judas*, he often deleted and added numbers. As it was first performed, the work included seventeen arias, three of which use da capo form; three accompanied recitatives; five duets, more than in any of his other oratorios; and fifteen choruses, about half of which are continuations of either arias or duets.[17] The score of *Judas* generally accepted today includes four numbers originally composed for other oratorios: the aria "O liberty" (from the *Occasional Oratorio*); the duet and chorus "Sion now her head shall raise" (added to *Esther* in 1757 and to *Judas* probably in 1758); the aria "Wise men, flatt'ring" (added to *Belshazzar* in February 1758, and to *Judas* in March of that year); and the chorus "See, the conqu'ring hero comes" (originally composed for *Joshua* in 1747).[18]

In its original version *Judas* included only one instrumental number, the French overture with which it opens. (The march in act 3 was apparently introduced in 1747, but after the first performance.)[19] The subject of the overture's fugal allegro generally resembles the ritornello of the chorus "Disdainful of danger," although in this overture the foreshadowing of material to be used later is by no means as clear as that in the overture of *Deborah*.[20]

Alexander Balus[21]

Handel composed *Alexander* between 1 June and 4 July 1747; he finished it about two weeks before starting to work on *Joshua*. The premiere of *Alexander* took place at the Theatre Royal in Covent Garden on 23 March 1748, two weeks after that of *Joshua*. *Alexander* was intended to be a sequel to *Judas* but failed to achieve the popularity of its forerunner. Handel performed it

17. Regarding the numbers used in the first performance, see ibid., p. 627.
18. Some of these numbers include borrowings from the music of Handel and others; on the borrowings in *Judas*, see ibid., pp. 468–70, 645.
19. Ibid., p. 473.
20. For a discussion of the similarities and derivation of the melodic material common to the overture and the chorus, see Dean, *Oratorios*, pp. 466–67.
21. Printed in Handel, *Werke*, vol. 33.

three times in 1748 and twice in 1754, the year of its only revival. Performances since Handel's time have been rare.

The librettist of *Alexander*, Morell, freely based his work on the biblical story that follows that of Judas Maccabaeus in 1 Maccabees 10–11. He also borrowed fragments of verse from a variety of sources, including the works of Milton and Shakespeare and the earlier oratorios of Handel.[22] The story concerns the political relations among Alexander Balus (A), king of Syria and son of Antiochus Epiphanes; Johathan (T), chief of the Jews since the death of his brother, Judas Maccabaeus; and Ptolomee (Ptolemy, B), king of Egypt. Cleopatra (S) is Ptolomee's daughter and a pawn in his political maneuvers; in Morell's libretto (but not in the Bible) she is deeply in love with Alexander. Cleopatra is supported by her confidante, Aspasia (S). The chorus (SATB) represents the Israelites and the Asiates. Act 1 takes place in Ptolemais (according to the biblical story—Morell does not identify the location). At the beginning of the oratorio, the Asiates celebrate a victory that has made Alexander the king of Syria, and the new king concludes a treaty with Jonathan between the Syrians and the Jews. Ptolomee and Cleopatra congratulate Alexander for having ascended the throne. Alexander and Cleopatra fall in love. The act ends with the Israelites praising God for his gifts of "life, liberty, and fame." At the beginning of act 2, Alexander and Cleopatra are about to be married when shadows of gloom are cast over the scene, first by a false informer who claims that Jonathan plots against the throne—a notion Alexander rejects—and then by Ptolomee who reveals (to the audience) that he is planning to dethrone Alexander and gives him Cleopatra in marriage only to deceive him. In the final scene of the act, the mood of happiness returns, Alexander and Cleopatra are married, and the chorus of Asiates call for Hymen to "Show'r thy choicest blessings down/On the lovely, royal pair." Cleopatra is kidnapped by Ptolomee's ruffians at the beginning of act 3, for Ptolomee plans to force her to marry the young Demetrius, whom he expects to place on the Syrian throne. Alexander, furious, calls on his ally Jonathan to join him in his war against Ptolomee. In a highly dramatic scene Ptolomee tries in vain to turn his daughter against Alexander. During the war, messengers reveal its progress to Cleopatra: the

22. Dean, *Oratorios*, p. 484.

Jewish forces are victorious, but Alexander and Ptolomee have both been killed. Cleopatra prays that Isis will "Convey me to some peaceful shore / Where no tumultuous billows roar"; Jonathan meditates, "Mysterious are thy ways, O Providence! / But always true and just"; and the Israelites praise "th'eternal King."

Alexander is among the weakest oratorio librettos that Handel ever set: little of dramatic interest takes place until act 3; virtually no relationship is shown between the two themes, the love story and the glorification of the Israelites as the followers of the true God; and the protagonist, Alexander, is neither a tragic figure nor a well-characterized hero.[23] Nevertheless, act 3 had much to offer Handel in the character of Cleopatra, who emerges as the most significant figure of the drama.

Musically there is little of special interest in act 1 except the colorful orchestration in some of the numbers: the brass and woodwind scoring in the choruses of Asiates, "Flushed with conquest" and "Ye happy nations round"; and the two flutes, harp, mandolin, and pizzicato strings in Cleopatra's first aria, "Hark! hark! he strikes the golden lyre"—this aria is of added interest for its changes of tempo and meter. Act 2, likewise of little musical interest, nevertheless includes the striking chorus "O calumny," similar in expression to the chorus "Envy! eldest born of hell" in *Saul*. Constructed over an intermittently recurring melody in the bass, "O calumny" masterfully conveys the Israelites' revulsion to slander. The conclusion of this chorus is especially effective: the text "Go, with all thy base designing, / All thy forging, feigning, coyning, / And in darkness ever lie," is set, in its final statement, with "dark" sounds—successive dominant-seventh and diminished-seventh chords in a low register over a chromatically descending bass line (Example VIII–5).

The chief musical and dramatic interest of *Alexander* is concentrated in act 3, which may be divided into five scenes. In the opening scene Cleopatra, now Alexander's wife, is in the garden, where she sings her beautiful pastoral aria (larghetto, in 6/8 time), "Here amid the shady woods," which is attractively accompanied by muted violins and violas, and pizzicato violoncello; after what would appear to be the A section and beginning of the B section of

23. For similar evaluations of this libretto, see ibid., pp. 483–86; Lang, *Handel*, pp. 450–51. For a more positive evaluation, interpreting the libretto and its musical setting in symbolic, Germanic cultural terms, see Steglich, "Alexander."

EXAMPLE VIII-5. *Alexander Balus* (Handel, *Werke*, 33:118).

a da capo aria, she is suddenly interrupted by the ruffians (SATB) whom Ptolomee has sent to abduct her. In a purely theatrical and musically effective struggle, Cleopatra cries out, between the phrases of the ruffians' chorus, for help from the god Isis and from Alexander, but all in vain. The second scene, that of Alexander's, Jonathan's, and Aspasia's reaction to the abduction, is highlighted by Alexander's fury aria, "Fury, with red sparkling eyes" (Example VIII–6); the aria is cast in da capo form with a violent presto in C time for its A section but a strikingly contrasting larghetto in 3/4 time for the B, in which Alexander reflects that "cold death" may give "a kind release to the horrid pains I feel." Jonathan's aria "To god who made the radiant sun," and the Israelites' following chorus, "Sun, moon, and stars," provide effective contrasts to the tension of the preceding events. The third scene, also successful

EXAMPLE VIII-6. *Alexander Balus* (Handel, *Werke,* 33:174–75).

The Oratorio in the Baroque Era: Protestant Germany and England

both dramatically and musically, reveals the conflict between Cleopatra and her father. The latter, unable to dissuade his daughter from her love for Alexander, expresses his frustration and reliance upon force in his accompanied recitative "Ungrateful child," with strong orchestral punctuations, and in his violent da capo aria, "O sword, and thou, all daring hand/Thy aid alone I crave." Cleopatra, who by this time has the sympathy of the audience and is emerging as the tragic heroine, dominates the fourth scene with her two accompanied recitatives and two excellent arias. The first recitative, "Shall Cleopatra ever smile again," expresses her grief at her father's coercion. The aria "O take me from this hateful light"—which begins with four measures for unaccompanied voice, continues with eight measures of ritornello, then combines the two—is the expression of Cleopatra's death wish upon hearing that her husband is dead. Her last accompanied recitative, "Calm thou my soul," (Example VIII–7), and aria, "Convey me to some peaceful shore," (Example VIII–8), show her final reactions to the message that her father, too, has been killed; her reactions of resignation and withdrawal are convincing for the utter simplicity of their musical setting. The final scene—

EXAMPLE VIII-7. *Alexander Balus* (Handel, *Werke*, 33:203).

EXAMPLE VIII-8. *Alexander Balus* (Handel, *Werke*, 33:204).

that of Jonathan's "Ye servants of th'eternal train" and the Israel-ite's "Amen, hallelujah, amen"—is not the exuberant allegro finale one has come to expect from a "Hallelujah" chorus; Cleopatra's tragedy leaves its mark, and the finale is an andante in G minor.

In some respects *Alexander* is closer to the style of Handel's operas than his oratorios: more of the arias are in da capo form (ten out of twenty-five) than in most of the oratorios, and one-third, or five, of the non–da capo arias are in ABA' form; with only eight choruses the work minimizes the choral element—*Susanna* is the only other oratorio with so few choruses.[24] *Alex-ander* also includes three recitatives and two duets; its two instru-mental numbers are the French overture at the beginning and the brief, one-movement sinfonia preceding act 3. Ten of the numbers include borrowed material, all from Handel's own works.[25]

24. These figures are based on first-performance versions as given in Dean, *Oratorios*, p. 627.
25. Ibid., p. 645.

Joshua[26]

Composed between 19 July and 19 August 1747—immediately after *Alexander*—*Joshua* was first performed at the Theatre Royal in Covent Garden on 9 March 1748, together with "a new Concerto."[27] The oratorio was performed four times in the same month and at least fourteen times during Handel's life[28]—more than any of his oratorios since *Samson*, except for the extremely popular *Judas*. *Joshua* has continued to receive occasional performances down to our own time.

The libretto by Morell, based on events selected from the Book of Joshua, appears to be another attempt to recapture the spirit of militaristic nationalism to which audiences had responded so favorably in *Judas*.[29] Like the libretto of *Judas*, that of *Joshua* includes only God-fearing personages: Joshua (T), the leader of the Israelites; Caleb (B), Joshua's military commander; Othniel (A), a young warrior; Achsah (S), Caleb's daughter; an Angel (S); and the chorus of Israelites (SATB). Act 1 begins with the Israelites' thanksgiving to God and praise of Joshua for their miraculous passage through the Jordan river; Joshua orders that a monument of stones be made to commemorate the miracle. An angel appears to Othniel and Joshua with a message, "Leader of Israel, 'tis the Lord's decree,/That Jericho must fall, and fall by thee," after which Joshua calls the Israelites to arms. The act approaches its close with a pastoral love scene between Othniel and Achsah; the former then goes off to war but intends to return and ask Caleb for Achsah's hand in marriage. The chorus wishes him a safe return. At the opening of act 2, Joshua, whose troops have been at the walls of Jericho for six days, issues the order "Sound the shrill trumpets, shout, and blow the horns." The Israelites obey, and the "strong cemented walls,/The tott'ring tow'rs, the pond'rous ruin falls." Other events of this act are the celebration of the Passover, the lamentation of the Israelites defeated at the city of Ai, a love scene between Othniel and Achsah, and a victory of the Israelites and Gibeonites over the Canaanites. Act 3 consists primarily of thanksgiving for victories. One more city, Debir, remains to be

26. Printed in Handel, *Werke*, vol. 17.
27. *General Advertiser*, 9 March 1748, in Deutsch, *Handel*, p. 647.
28. Dean, *Oratorios*, p. 637.
29. The story of Joshua and the battle of Jericho had been occasionally used previously for oratorios, as in the anonymous *Jericho urbis casus* (Rome 1683), libretto in I/Rli: 170.F.22(24).

conquered. Caleb promises that his daughter will be the bride of the volunteer who will lead the forces in this final battle. Othniel volunteers, returns victorious to the famous strains of "See the conqu'ring hero comes," and accepts his prize, Achsah, by joining in a love duet with her. The final chorus states, "The great Jehovah is our awful theme,/Sublime in majesty, in pow'r supreme./Hallelujah." This libretto is little better than its predecessors by the same author; characterization and dramatic conflict remain at a minimum.

From the musical standpoint act 2 of *Joshua* is of greater importance than the others. The act opens with the conquering of Jericho. After a brief simple recitative in which Joshua commands his people to sound the trumpets and shout, a march is played. It is designated in the score as "A solemn March during the circumvention of the Ark of the Covenant." Trumpets, horns, and timpani are heard here for the first time in the oratorio. The following solo and chorus, "Glory to God," is of particular interest: it was extremely impressive to Haydn when he heard the oratorio in 1791.[30] Cast in an ABA' form, the allegro A section, in D major, begins with Joshua's solo passages on the text "Glory to God" and alternates with the chorus's declamatory, chordal "shouts" on the same text and its description of the falling of Jericho's walls; the andante B section, in B minor, effectively depicts its text—"The nations tremble at the sound/Heav'n thunders, tempests roar, and groans the ground"—with "trembling" sixteenth notes and "tempests" of thirty-second notes in the strings and continuo and with "thundering" trumpets and timpani; the final A' section returns to the material of A without Joshua's solo passages. The chorus "Almighty ruler of the skies," an imposing ceremonial number in which the Passover is celebrated, is built over a modulating basso ostinato; the number begins with solo passages by Joshua, continues with sections of the chorus entering individually, and achieves an effective climax near the end with the entrance of all four voices and full orchestra. This powerful affirmation of faith is followed, after some simple recitative, by a striking contrast: the chorus of defeated Israelites, "How soon our tow'ring hopes are cross'd"; set in E minor and beginning with a descending chromatic bass characteristic of lamentations, the chorus expresses the sorrow of

30. The composer William Shield quotes the enthusiastic comments that Haydn made to him about the middle section of this chorus in Shield, *Rudiments*, p. 69.

those defeated at Ai. Joshua's following rage aria, "With redoubled rage return," and the attached chorus begin to reestablish the martial mood. The return to battle is deferred, however, by a love scene between Othniel and Achsah: the former sings the gavotte "Heroes, when with glory burning," a pleasant tune used previously by Cesti, A. Scarlatti, Keiser, and Handel;[31] and Achsah replies with a *siciliano*, "As cheers the sun," a simile aria in which the orchestral description of "the tender flow'r,/That sinks beneath a falling show'r" first enters in the ninth measure and eventually dominates the texture. The return to battle against the Canaanites is represented by a "Flourish of warlike instruments," according to the autograph manuscript.[32]

The following solo and chorus, the finale of act 2, is the most remarkable number of the oratorio. Joshua begins with the solo "Oh! thou bright orb, great ruler of the day! / Stop thy swift course, and over Gibeon stay!" At the word "stop," a dominant pedal point begins in the high register—a sudden suspension of time, stopping the preceding sixteenth-note motion (Example VIII–9, m. 10). The pedal point continues with little interruption for twenty-five measures; thus Joshua's miracle of stopping the sun and the moon has evoked from Handel a truly marvelous representation of the situation's static quality. The dominant pedal

EXAMPLE VIII-9. *Joshua* (Handel, *Werke*, 17:146–47).

31. Dean, *Oratorios*, p. 646.

32. There are three flourishes for trumpets in the autograph MS that are not fully notated. In Handel, *Werke*, 17:142–45, the editor, Chrysander, has replaced two of these with an instrumental number from Handel's opera *Riccardo primo*. For details, see Dean, *Oratorios*, p. 508.

(EXAMPLE VIII-9, continued)

is soon joined by a low tonic pedal (m. 17, at "stand still," addressed to the moon) of shorter duration, and the chorus enters to comment, chordally, "Behold! the list'ning sun the voice obeys"; the Israelite victory is the result of the miraculously extended day.

Acts 1 and 3 include fewer numbers of interest, but the love scene in act 1 is particularly charming, with Othniel's accompanied recitative "In these blest scenes," followed first by a flexible series of recitatives and ariosos, then by a "bird call" aria for Achsah ("Hark, hark! the linnet and the thrush") with passages for solo flute and violin, and finally by the lovers' duet, "Our limpid streams with freedom flow." Noteworthy in act 3 are Caleb's largo aria "Shall I in Mamre's fertile plain" and its continuation by the chorus, "For all these mercies we will sing"; effective touches in the aria are the long continuo note at the word "remain" and the pedal point at "to have a place with Abrah'm in the grave," which symbolizes the aged Caleb's thoughts of retirement and final rest. Probably the most popular number in *Joshua* is the chorus "See, the conqu'ring hero comes" near the end of act 3; a simple, strophic march, first composed for *Joshua*, it has achieved popularity through its use in the more frequently performed *Judas*.

In *Joshua* the number of choruses, fourteen, is closer to the norm in Handel's oratorios than in the preceding *Alexander*. Like those of *Judas*, about half of the choruses are continuations of or attachments to solos. The structure of the arias, too, is closer than are those of *Alexander* to what had become the norm for Handel's oratorios: of the sixteen arias, only four use da capo form. Five accompanied recitatives and two duets constitute the remaining numbers. Seven numbers in *Joshua* include borrowings, mostly from Handel's previous works.[33]

Only two instrumental pieces—the opening one-movement "Introduzione," further marked "A tempo di Ouverture," which leads without pause into the first chorus, and the slow march at the beginning of act 2—were originally included. The instrumentation of the oratorio is approximately that of the previous "occasional" oratorios—two flutes, two oboes, bassoon, two horns, two trumpets, timpani, side drum, strings, harpsichord, and organ. The orchestration is varied and attractive, with special emphasis on the wind instruments, occasionally featured in solo passages.

The Last Four Oratorios: 1748–1752

With *Joshua* Handel brought to an end his series of martial "occasional" oratorios. The works of the late period differ notably from the four that preceded them, but they also differ from each other: *Solomon* reveals some continuing influence of the patriotism and pageantry of the "occasional" oratorios; *Susanna* and *Theodora* tend more toward the *oratorio volgare* (more specifically the *oratorio erotico* and the hagiographical oratorio, respectively) than do Handel's other English oratorios; and *Jephtha* is closer to ancient Greek drama, particularly in its treatment of the chorus, than are the other late works.

33. For the borrowings see Dean, *Oratorios*, p. 646; Taylor, *Indebtedness*, pp. 12–13.

Solomon[34]

Composed between 5 May and 13 June 1748, *Solomon* was first performed at the Theatre Royal in Covent Garden on 17 March 1749.[35] Nothing is known of the work's reception, but Handel repeated it only twice in 1749 and revived it once, in 1759 (six weeks before his death), in a drastically altered version.[36] The work has received occasional performances since Handel's time, but rarely is it presented in its original form.

The libretto of *Solomon* is anonymous. Although some commentators have attributed it to Morell,[37] this attribution is questionable, since numerous stylistic differences exist between *Solomon* and the librettos known to be by Morell.[38] Freely based on the descriptions of King Solomon's reign in 1 Kings, 2 Chronicles, and Josephus's *Antiquities of the Jews* 8.2–7, the libretto glorifies in turn several aspects of the great king and his realm: his religious dedication, marital happiness, and justice, and his kingdom's enormous wealth. At the beginning of act 1, the chorus of Priests (SATB-SATB), a Levite (B), Solomon (Ms), the high priest Zadok (T), and a chorus of Israelites (SATB-SATB), join in the ceremony of the dedication of the temple. Solomon's Queen (S) enters, and she and her husband extol the sexual pleasures of married love.[39] The text of the Queen's first aria shows how closely this scene is related to the *oratorio erotico* of Italy:

> Bless'd the day when first my eyes
> Saw the wisest of the wise!
> Bless'd the day when I was led
> To ascend the nuptial bed!
> > But completely bless'd the day,
> > On my bosom as he lay,
> > When he call'd my charms divine,
> > Vowing to be only mine.
> Bless'd the day: *Da Capo.*

34. Printed in Handel, *Werke*, vol. 26.
35. Deutsch, *Handel*, p. 659.
36. Dean, *Oratorios*, p. 527.
37. Among others, Chrysander in Handel, *Werke*, vol. 26, Foreword; Heuss, "Salomo," p. 339; and Leichtentritt, *Händel*, p. 491.
38. For a full discussion of this point, see Dean, *Oratorios*, p. 514.
39. This scene was heavily bowdlerized in editions of the work made in Victorian England. (Ibid., p. 529.)

After a love duet by the couple and an aria in which Zadok urges the King to "Indulge thy faith and wedded truth/With the fair partner of thy youth," Solomon says "My love admits of no delay," and the couple withdraws, as Solomon urges:

> Haste to the cedar grove
> Where fragrant spices bloom
> And am'rous turtles love,
> Beneath the pleasing gloom.

The final number of the love scene, and of act 1, is the chorus "May no rash intruder disturb their soft hours," usually called the Nightingale Chorus for its final line, orchestrally described, "While nightingales lull them to sleep with their song." Act 2 portrays Solomon's wisdom and justice and provides the chief dramatic episode of the oratorio.[40] After an opening religious ceremony two harlots, each claiming to be the mother of the same child, are brought before the king. Solomon hears their arguments and orders that the child be divided, "thus each her part shall bear." The Second Harlot (S) praises the decision, but the First Harlot (S) cries out in anguish and prefers to give up her child rather than see him killed. Solomon says, however, that his "stern decision" was merely "to trace with art/The secret dictates of the human heart," and he awards the child to the First Harlot, the true mother. The chorus of Israelites, Zadok, and the chorus of Priests praise Solomon's wisdom. In act 3 Solomon displays the pomp, splendor, and wealth of his kingdom to the visiting Nicaule, Queen of Sheba (S). He first shows her the temple and the new palace and then orders that she be entertained by a kind of masque in which the music rouses "each passion with th' alternate air": first a chorus of sweet music, then martial, then a lament, and finally the calm after a storm. The Queen praises the divine harmony and pays tribute to Solomon in gold, gems, and balsam; the Levite, Zadok, and the chorus praise her and her host. The king further displays the riches of his realm. The Queen, admiring his kingdom, graciously bids him farewell, and they sing a duet of mutual respect. The final chorus comments that the "fame of the just shall eternally last."

In two senses this oratorio could be considered a continuation

---

40. This judgment scene in the Bible was the basis for the oratorios entitled *Judicium Salomonis* by Carissimi and Charpentier, and for numerous other oratorios throughout the Baroque period.

of the "occasional" series: it would surely have been seen in its time as a glorification of King George II and his England, and like the "occasional" oratorios it emphasizes ceremony and pageantry more than drama. Yet this is not a martial work, and both its poetry and its music raise it to a much higher level of artistic achievement than the four works that preceded it. Most of *Solomon*'s characters seem more symbolic than human: Solomon represents the ideal monarch; his Queen, conjugal love; Zadok, orthodox religion; and the Queen of Sheba, foreign powers' respect for this great realm. Humanity is not lacking, however, for the love scene and the episode of the two harlots deal with human passions in a psychologically penetrating manner.

With pomp and circumstance playing such a prominent role in *Solomon*, the chorus is of major importance.[41] For the first time since *Israel in Egypt*, Handel composed double choruses for an oratorio.[42] Of the thirteen choruses in *Solomon*, seven are for SATB-SATB, five for SSATB, and one for SATB. Although this is a sacred work, for it is based on a biblical subject and most of its numbers have sacred or ethical texts, it also includes many secular passages. Only six of the choruses, all of which are double choruses, may be described as sacred or ethical: three occur in the opening scene of the dedication of the temple, another in the religious ceremony at the beginning of act 2, and two more ("Praise the Lord with harp and tongue" and the finale, "The name of the wicked shall quickly be past"), in act 3. These six choruses generally employ chordal-antiphonal style with some fugal texture. Most consistently fugal are the chorus "Throughout the land" and the middle section of the ABA' chorus "From the censer curling," that section being a double fugue. The chorus "From the censer curling" is also impressive for its grandiose effect of massed sound, representing the splendor of ceremonial religion; in this number the brass and timpani sound for the first time in the oratorio. The chorus "Praise the Lord with harp and tongue," in act 3, also uses brass and timpani, and it exploits the large forces for massive effect. The latter chorus includes two powerful statements in unison and octaves of the text "God alone is just, God alone is wise" on a melody that is nearly the same as the "Heilig" in the Sanctus

41. For a brief study of the choruses, see Heuss, "Salomo."
42. The *Occasional Oratorio*'s double choruses are borrowed from *Israel*.

of Luther's *Deutsche Messe*;[43] if this is a conscious quotation, it is a rare instance of a chorale quotation in Handel's music.

The seven choruses with essentially secular texts include the Nightingale Chorus at the end of act 1; the four entertainment or masque choruses of act 3; and two choruses in praise of Solomon —the gavotte "From the east unto the west" and the da capo finale of act 2, "Swell the full chorus to Solomon's praise." The Nightingale Chorus is perfectly suited to its function as a lullaby for lovers and is among the most delightful numbers in all of Handel's oratorios. The orchestra describes "ye zephirs, soft breathing" (slurred pairs of notes in thirds in the strings) and the call of the nightingale (flutes in canon, doubled by violins *senza ripieni* and unaccompanied) while the chorus sings its simple lullaby.

The masque in act 3 is a thoroughly entertaining suite of four choruses, each introduced by Solomon. It opens with the solo and chorus (SSATB) "Music, spread thy voice around,/Sweetly flow the lulling sound," a minuet in ABABA form. Next comes the solo and chorus (SATB-SATB) "Now a different measure try/Shake the dome, and pierce the sky"—a stirring, martial piece with dotted rhythms, fanfare melodic lines, chordal-antiphonal style, and full orchestra. Solomon, in a recitative, next asks for another change of affection:

> Then at once from rage remove;
> Draw a tear from hopeless love;
> Lengthen out the solemn air,
> Full of death and wild despair.

The last three lines constitute the text of the following choral lament (SSATB), which includes a melodically jagged line at "Draw the tear," a chromatic shift in the repeat of the words "from hopeless love," and affective chromaticism, cross relations, and dotted rhythms at "Full of death and wild despair." Following Solomon's final command in recitative, "Next the tortur'd soul release, / And the mind restore to peace," the solo and chorus (SSATB), in "Thus rolling surges rise," at first depict a tempest at

43. For Handel's passage see Handel, *Werke*, 26:287–89. For comments on this passage see Schering, "Händel," pp. 33–34; Serauky, *Händel* 5:185 (the latter quotes both the chorale and Handel's passage).

sea; the mood changes, however, at "But soon the tempest dies, / And all is calm again."

Although the dramatic element of *Solomon* as a whole is minimal, it is powerful in the judgment scene. After the two harlots have been introduced, the First Harlot tells her story in recitative; she then begins what appears to be an aria, "Words are weak to paint my fears," in which she pleads her cause with "heartfelt anguish, starting tears"; at the approach to a strong cadence, however, the number becomes a trio as the Second Harlot interrupts, in shorter note values, with "False is all her melting talk," after which Solomon enters with "Justice holds the lifted scale." The three personalities are represented here by contrasting melodic lines (Example VIII–10): the Second Harlot by declamatory style, predominantly in eighth notes; the First Harlot by continuing her lamentation; and Solomon by playing on the word

EXAMPLE VIII-10. *Solomon* (Handel, *Werke*, 26:154–55).

(EXAMPLE VIII-10, continued)

"scale" with continual repetition of a tranquil, scalewise melodic line. The First Harlot, who began the number but was interrupted, is eventually allowed to finish it. In simple recitative Solomon announces his first decision, to divide the child, to which the Second Harlot agrees in a fierce allegro aria full of syncopations, "Thy sentence, great king, is prudent and wise." The reaction of the First Harlot, the true mother, is poignantly expressed in her aria—*largo e piano* in F minor, "Can I see my infant gor'd"— with its dotted rhythms, suspension dissonances associated with the line "the purple tides gushing down his tender sides," and adagio measures for the words "but spare my child." Solomon's final judgment is announced in accompanied recitative and is followed by a joyful, dancelike duet, "Thrice bless'd be the king," for the First Harlot and Solomon and a festive chorus of praise, "From the east unto the west," providing a welcome release from the previous tensions.

Of the twenty-one arias in *Solomon*, five are in da capo and one in ABA' form. The texts of nearly half of the arias, as well as those of the secular choruses discussed above, use images derived from the sights and sounds of nature, which lend the oratorio a pantheistic quality and contribute to its pictorial tendencies. Especially interesting among the musical descriptions of natural scenery are Solomon's love song to his queen, "Haste, haste to the cedar grove," with its depiction of the turtledove's song and of the brook ("the little murmuring rill in whispers glides away"); Solomon's "How green our fertile pastures look," again with a description of a "gliding brook"; Zadok's "See the tall Palm that lifts the head," a simile aria that capitalizes on the words "tall" and "his tow'ring branches curling spread"; and the gentle pastoral aria of the First Harlot, "Beneath vine, or fig tree's shade," a simple *siciliano* in 6/8 time with solo flute, violin *senza ripieno*, and a drone bass accompaniment. Also inspired by visual images, although set with less word painting, are the arias glorifying the temple and the wealth of the kingdom: Zadok's "Golden columns, fair and bright," and the Queen of Sheba's "Ev'ry sight these eyes behold" and "Will the sun forget to streak." *Solomon* includes three accompanied recitatives, the first of which, "Almighty pow'r," is of special importance since it is Solomon's first number in the oratorio and is the most elaborately introduced and accompanied of the recitatives. In addition to the trio in the judgment scene, mentioned above, there are three other ensembles, all duets and all including Solomon: in act 1 with his Queen, in act 2 with the First Harlot, and in act 3 with the Queen of Sheba. All three duets celebrate joyful occasions.

The only two instrumental numbers in *Solomon* are the opening French overture followed by an allegro in binary form and the sinfonia—an allegro with two solo oboes alternating with the string orchestra—that introduces the Queen of Sheba at the beginning of act 3. Both of these use borrowed material, as do six other numbers.[44] The oratorio's instrumentation comprises pairs of flutes, oboes, bassoons, horns, and trumpets plus timpani, strings, harpsichord, and organ. *Solomon* is one of Handel's most elaborately and carefully orchestrated oratorios. Several of the numbers use concerto grosso style, with the concertino and ripieno parts specified in unusual detail.[45]

Susanna[46]

On 11 July 1748, about a month after the completion of *Solomon*, Handel began to compose *Susanna*, which he finished by the end of August. *Susanna*'s premiere took place at the Theatre Royal in Covent Garden on 10 February 1749, over a month prior to that of *Solomon*. After hearing the work's first performance, the count-

44. Most of the borrowings in *Solomon* are from Handel's works. For details see Dean, *Oratorios*, p. 646.
45. For details of the orchestration, see ibid., p. 525.
46. Printed in Handel, *Ausgabe*, ser. 1, vol. 28, and Handel, *Werke*, vol. 1.

ess of Shaftsbury commented in a letter: "I cannot pretend to give my poor judgement of it from once hearing, but believe it will insinuate itself so much into my approbation as most of Handel's performances do, as it is in the light *operatic* style . . . I think I never saw a fuller house. Rich [the manager of Covent Garden] told me that he believed he [Handel] would receive nearly 400 *l.*"[47] Despite this initial report of apparent success, however, *Susanna* did not become one of Handel's popular oratorios. The work was performed four times in its first season and was revived only once by Handel, in 1759. Since Handel's death it has been neglected.

Like the libretto of *Solomon*, that of *Susanna* is anonymous; so many parallels exist between these two librettos, however, that it seems certain the same author wrote both.[48] The source of the libretto is the apocryphal story of Susanna and the two elders (Daniel 13), which takes place during the Jews' Babylonian exile. The libretto begins with a chorus of Jews (SATB) lamenting their "slav'ry and pain." Joacim (A) and his wife Susanna (S) reflect on the joys of their married love, and Chelsias (B), Susanna's father, praises them as an ideal married couple. Joacim announces that he has been summoned out of the city for a week, and his wife sorrowfully replies. During Joacim's absence the First Elder (T) and Second Elder (B) reveal to each other their burning passion for the beautiful Susanna; they make plans to "rush upon the fair,/ Force her to bliss, and cure our wild despair." The final chorus of act 1 comments that the elders are observed by "righteous Heav'n" and that "his bolt shall quickly fly" for their punishment. Act 2 opens with Joacim's reminiscence of his home and wife. In the next scene Susanna and her Attendant (S) seek a cool garden retreat from the burning sun. Susanna sings of the beautiful surroundings in "Chrystal streams, in murmurs flowing," and the Attendant sings a song that Joacim had composed for Susanna; it is followed by another reflecting her own unhappy love. Susanna then sends her Attendant away for ointments while she bathes in a pool. Suddenly Susanna is startled as she sees the two elders approaching. The First Elder pleads, "With one smile dismiss my care," but the other is more demanding: "We long have languished

47. Countess of Shaftsbury to James Harris, 11 February 1749, in Deutsch, *Handel*, p. 657.
48. For a comparison of the two librettos, see Dean, *Oratorios*, pp. 537–38.

and now mean to prove/The Matchless sweets of long expected love." Susanna rejects them; so they call in the chorus of Jews and claim that they have just witnessed her in adultery with a youth who has escaped. She is then taken to be tried. When Joacim receives word of the accusation, he decides to hurry home to Babylon. Act 3 begins with the announcement by the chorus of Jews that Susanna is guilty and must die. As she is about to be led away, however, a young man in the crowd, Daniel (S), calls out that she is innocent and demands that the decree be reversed. A Judge (B) agrees that she may have a new trial and Daniel may act in her defense. Daniel separates the two elders and asks each under which tree the alleged crime was committed; their stories do not agree. Susanna is declared innocent; and the elders, guilty. Joacim and Chelsias enter, and they praise Susanna's faithfulness. The final chorus generalizes that "A virtuous wife shall soften fortune's frown,/She's far more precious than a golden crown."

In some respects *Susanna* approximates the *oratorio erotico* of Italy. Here sexuality is not confined to a single episode, as it was in *Solomon* (an essentially different type of work), but is the motivating force of the entire drama. The portrayal of the relationship between Susanna and Joacim is less erotic than that between Solomon and his Queen, but the lines of the elders are filled with expressions of their burning passion. Characteristic are the following lines in the First Elder's opening speech, set in accompanied recitative:

> Tyrannic love! I feel thy cruel dart,
> Nor age protects me from the burning smart.
> . . . .
> Shall I submit to the raging fires?
> Youth pleads a warrant for his hot desires;
> But when the blood should scarce attempt to flow,
> I feel the purple torrents fiercely glow.

And in the First Elder's soliloquy, as he sees Susanna in his fantasy, he pleads with her:

> Oh, sweetest of thy lovely race,
>   Unveil thy matchless charms;
> Let me adore that angel's face;
>   And die within thy arms:
> My ceaseless pangs thy bosom move
> To grant the just returns of love.

The Second Elder is equally passionate in such lines as "Love, frantick love does all this bosom rule,/To its hot rage, the burning dog-star's cool." The incongruity of youthful passion for a young and beautiful girl in dignified old men was considered inherently humorous (a situation often exploited in comic opera), and Handel underlined the humor in his musical setting, as Stradella had previously done in his oratorio *La Susanna*. The countess of Shaftsbury's perceptive remark, quoted above, that *Susanna* is in a "light *operatic* style," points to another link between *Susanna* and the Italian oratorio, which followed closely the structures and styles of opera. Like the *oratorio erotico*, *Susanna* has a dual purpose: entertainment of an erotic (and in this case, humorous) type, and edification. In the *oratorio erotico* the element of entertainment seems primary; in Handel's *Susanna* the two elements are evenly balanced, yet the edifying element, carried out especially by the chorus, seems out of place and unconvincing. The chorus, essential to the usual Handelian oratorio but virtually absent from the *oratorio volgare*, intrudes into what might otherwise have been a delightful English version of the *oratorio erotico*.[49]

Susanna's most prominent characteristic, its light operatic quality, is the result of several structural and stylistic aspects: the unusually large number of da capo arias (more characteristic of opera than of Handel's oratorios); the small number of choruses compared to the number of arias; the simple, *galant*, dancelike, pastoral, and comic tendencies in the arias and ensembles; and the generally light orchestration. Of the twenty-five arias in *Susanna*, sixteen are in da capo form—more than in any of Handel's other oratorios—and two are strophic. Only eight choruses—fewer than in any of Handel's oratorios except *Alexander Balus*—were included in the work's first performance. The remaining vocal numbers are three accompanied recitatives, two duets, and one trio.

The five numbers that most clearly reveal *galant* tendencies are those sung in act 1 by Susanna and Joacim during their love scene: the duet "When thou art nigh, my pulse beats high" and the arias "When first I saw my lovely maid" (Example VIII–11), "Would custom bid the melting fair," "Without the swain's assid-

---

49. Among the previous writings that relate *Susanna* to Italian antecedents are Schering, *Oratorium*, p. 303; Leichtentritt, *Händel*, p. 500; and Serauky, *Händel*, 5:192. In Dean, *Oratorios*, p. 192, *Susanna* is considered "an opera of English life, and a comic opera at that"; and Lang says, "It is useless to seek such antecedents in the old Italian oratorio; *Susanna* has no ancestors, it is a Handelian creation." (Lang, *Handel*, p. 473.)

EXAMPLE VIII-11. *Susanna* (Handel, *Ausgabe*, ser. 1, vol. 28, p. 34).

uous care" (Example VIII–12), and "The parent bird in search of food" (Example VIII–13).[50] These arias tend to begin with simple, regular phrase structure, although it is not retained throughout; they use dancelike rhythm, mostly in some species of triple meter (only one aria is in **C** time), and repeated rhythmic patterns; and all their accompaniments are for strings only. Another aria that could be grouped with these, although its folklike style makes it

EXAMPLE VIII-12. *Susanna* (Handel, *Ausgabe*, ser. 1, vol. 28, p. 42).

50. For brief analyses of the arias in this scene, see Heuss, "Susanna."

(EXAMPLE VIII-12, continued)

soon the sick-ly flow'r, de-priv'd of sun and cheer-ing air would with-er in her bow'r,

EXAMPLE VIII-13. *Susanna* (Handel, *Ausgabe*, ser. 1, vol. 28, p. 47).

even simpler, is the Attendant's "Ask if yon damask rose be sweet" in act 2.

The humorous numbers are those in which the two elders elaborate on their passionate feelings, plan their approach to Susanna, and attempt to carry out the plan; yet the humor is not so broad that it makes the characters absurd—these are not merely stock buffo personages. The First Elder's aria,

> When the trumpet sounds to arms,
> Will the ling'ring soldier stay?
> When the Nymph displays her charms,
> Who the call will disobey?

is a tongue-in-cheek version of the heroic fanfare aria. This is a "trumpet aria" without a trumpet (although trumpets are available and one is used later in Chelsias's "Raise your voice to sounds of joy"), and it is a mock-heroic piece with a minuet meter and tempo (3/8, andante) and a light string accompaniment (continuo and violins in unison, mostly *senza ripieni*). Expressing equally mock-serious attitudes are the Second Elder's two simile arias, "The oak that for a thousand years" and "The torrent that sweeps in its course." Particularly interesting from the standpoint of humorous characterization is the brief trio of Susanna and the two elders as they try to entice her; it begins with Susanna's cry, "Away, away! ye tempt me in vain" (Example VIII–14): the First Elder, always the more gentle of the two, expresses himself in plaintive chromatic pleading ("Yet stay, yet stay, and hear my lovesick strain!"), and the Second Elder, ever the aggressive one with basso buffo tendencies, threatens Susanna in a patter-song melodic line with a traditional *concitato*, dactylic rhythm of an eighth and two sixteenth notes ("I scorn to intreat when by force I may gain, / Relief to my sorrows and ease to my pain!").

The chorus in *Susanna*, always for SATB, represents the Jewish people in general, a crowd witnessing the accusation and trial of Susanna, and an anonymous, moralistic commentator; these different functions are not labeled, however, in either the libretto or the score. Although the choruses seem at times dramatically inappropriate, some of them are extremely effective as musical numbers. For example, the opening chorus, a powerful lament of the Jewish people, unfolds over a chromatic passacaglia bass that

EXAMPLE VIII-14. *Susanna* (Handel, *Ausgabe*, ser. 1, vol. 28, pp. 113–14).

is inverted in the chorus's middle section. The final chorus of act 1, "Righteous Heav'n beholds their guile," is a highly effective multi-sectional number with a double fugue, "Tremble guilt," as its final section.[51]

The only instrumental number of the oratorio is the opening French overture, which closes with a slow transition to the first chorus. The instrumentation of the oratorio is two oboes, bassoon, two trumpets, strings, and harpsichord (no organ is mentioned). The orchestration is generally light, as mentioned above, and is of little special interest.

Theodora[52]

Handel composed *Theodora* between 28 June and 31 July 1749. Its first performance was at the Theatre Royal in Covent Garden on 16 March 1750. Two more performances of the work were given in that season, and it was revived once, in 1755, for a single performance. *Theodora* was poorly received; its four performances make it the least-performed of Handel's oratorios during his life. Morell, the oratorio's librettist, reported that "the 2d night of *Theodora* was very thin, indeed, tho' the Princess Amelia was there. I guessed it a losing night."[53] His guess was probably accurate: Handel made a small bank deposit after the opening night and none after the second and third nights, although he made deposits following the performances of all his other oratorios that season (*Saul, Judas Maccabaeus, Samson,* and *Messiah*).[54] Perhaps concern about the earthquakes felt in the previous month, which probably accounts for Handel's having delayed until March the opening of the oratorio season,[55] made audiences smaller than usual. More likely reasons for *Theodora*'s failure, however, are its nonbiblical subject and the unusual subtlety of its music. Regardless of its failure with the public, *Theodora* is said to have been Handel's favorite among his oratorios. According to Morell, "Mr. Handel himself valued [*Theodora*] more than any Performances of the kind; and when I once ask'd him, whether he did not look

51. This chorus, which includes material from the "Sit locutus est" of Erba's *Magnificat*, is one of *Susanna*'s five numbers using borrowings, three from Handel's own music. For details, see Dean, *Oratorios*, p. 647.
52. Printed in Handel, *Werke*, vol. 8.
53. Morell to an unknown addressee, ca. 1764, in Deutsch, *Handel*, p. 852.
54. Dean, *Oratorios*, p. 572.
55. Deutsch, *Handel*, p. 684.

upon the Grand Chorus ["Hallelujah" chorus] in the Messiah as his Master Piece? 'No,' says he, '*I think the Chorus at the end of the 2d part in Theodora far beyond it.* He saw the lovely youth &c.' "[56] Despite its composer's opinion, *Theodora* has been among the least-performed of Handel's oratorios since his time.

Morell's libretto is based primarily on *The Martyrdom of Theodora and of Didymus*, a historical novel by Robert Boyle (1627–91) that was published in 1687; a few details seem to have been added from Corneille's drama *Thédore Vierge et Martyre*.[57] According to Boyle, Corneille, and Morell, Theodora was a virgin martyr who died in Antioch during the reign of Diocletian. Other sources, however, place the martyrdom of Saints Theodora and Didymus in Alexandria, rather than Antioch, about 304 A.D.[58] In the central conflict of the libretto, that of the Christians and the heathens, the unyielding representatives of each side are Theodora (S), a Christian of noble birth; and Valens (B), the tyrannical prefect of Antioch. More pliant representatives of the two sides are Irene (A), Theodora's Christian confidante, and Septimius (T), a Roman officer who takes pity upon the Christians. Didimus (A) stands between the two sides, for he is both a young Roman officer and secretly a Christian who is in love with Theodora.[59] The two sides are further represented by a chorus of Christians (SATB) and of Heathens (SATB except once, ATB). In act 1 Valens proclaims a celebration in honor of Diocletian's birthday. On this occasion all of Antioch must sacrifice to Jove or "feel our wrath in chastisement or death." Didimus pleads in vain with Valens to permit freedom of conscience to those who are loyal Romans but do not acknowledge the Roman gods. Didimus also appeals to Septimius, his superior officer and friend, who is sympathetic but cannot disobey Valens's command. The next scene introduces Theodora, Irene, and the chorus of Christians. Learning of Valens's proclamation, Theodora rejects the command to worship Jove, "though death be

<hr/>

56. Morell to an unknown addressee, ca. 1764, ibid., p. 852.

57. For a discussion of the relationship between the libretto and its sources, see Dean, *Oratorios*, pp. 558–59.

58. For comments on the Antioch-Alexandria confusion, see Corneille, *Oeuvres*, 5:103. The stories of Saints Theodora and Didymus as told in Simone Metaphraste's *Vitae sanctorum* and in St. Ambrose's *De Virginibus* (only the latter of which places the story in Antioch), are printed in Corneille, *Oeuvres*, 5:103–11. The legend of Saints Theodora and Didymus is generally regarded by scholars today as purely fictitious, according to *Butler*, 2:181.

59. Cf. the libretto analysis in Dean, *Oratorios*, p. 561.

our reward." Septimius informs her, however, that if she disobeys she will be sent to the temple of Venus to devote her charms to prostitution. She is taken to prison, but Didimus vows to rescue her. At the beginning of act 2, Valens and the chorus of Heathens are joyously sacrificing to Jove, Flora, and Venus and anticipating Venus's pleasures. Valens orders Septimius to give Theodora one last chance to sacrifice to Jove; otherwise, "the meanest of my guards *with lustful joy*/Shall triumph o'er her boasted chastity."[60] Next we find Theodora alone in prison; afraid, she is comforted by thoughts of heaven, saints, and angels. Didimus confesses to Septimius that he is a Christian and is in love with Theodora, and he successfully prevails upon Septimius to permit him to rescue her. Didimus enters the prison "at a distance, the visor of his helmet closed," according to the "stage" description. Theodora is at first startled, as she does not recognize him, but he reveals his identity to her; although she would prefer death by his hand, he convinces her to exchange clothes with him and escape. In act 3 Theodora returns to the Christian community and explains her escape; the Christians rejoice. A Messenger appears with the news that Didimus is being tried and faces the death penalty and that if Theodora is apprehended she will be executed. Theodora goes to the courtroom and offers her life to spare that of Didimus. The two compete for the death sentence, but Valens concludes that "If both plead guilty, 'tis but equity,/That both should suffer." They are led away to be executed. Irene and the chorus of Christians praise the strength of divine love and pray that they may be given zeal equal to that of the martyrs.

As with *Susanna*, Handel used a libretto for *Theodora* with strong Italian antecedents. Hagiography is by far the most important text source for the late Baroque *oratorio volgare*, and the subject of Theodora has antecedents in Italy (cf. Giovanni Paolo Colonna's *Santa Teodora*, to name only one of many examples). Not only is *Theodora* Handel's only hagiographical oratorio, it is his only dramatic oratorio in English based on a Christian subject. *Messiah*, his only other Christian oratorio in English, uses a nondramatic libretto drawn mostly from the Old Testament. *Theodora* represents a departure, not only in its libretto, but in its music as

60. The words in italics are omitted from Chrysander's edition in Handel, *Werke*, 8:103, and other editions. Like *Susanna*, but to a lesser degree, *Theodora* was bowdlerized in nineteenth-century editions. (Dean, *Oratorios*, p. 577.)

well. This oratorio is frequently grouped together with the following one, *Jephtha*, for both works have the reflective, detached quality often found in the last works of great composers. *Theodora* has been regarded as "more pensive, more personal, in some respects more emotional, than any of its predecessors."[61] In this work and in *Jephtha*, there may be felt "a spiritual serenity, a tranquility in facing a host of contradictions and assailing questions, and a preoccupation with the profundities of this life—and of that to come."[62] Defying analysis in concrete musical terms, these qualities, nevertheless, seem evident in Handel's last two oratorios.

The most convincing act of the oratorio, and one that well illustrates its musical and dramatic aspects, is act 2, which is in six contrasting scenes. The opening scene, that of Valens and the chorus of Heathens, musically reflects their joy on this occasion: the choruses "Queen of summer, queen of love" and "Venus laughing from the skies" are chordal and dancelike (the former is marked *menuetto*); they are separated by Valens's aria, "Wide spread his name," which praises the Roman emperor in a combination of dancelike gaiety, heroic fanfare motives, and long melismas emphasizing his "endless fame." Scene 2, Theodora's prison scene, forms a stark contrast with the revelries of the Heathens. Conceived as a whole, as if it were a solo cantata, this scene reveals Theodora's progression from the depths of human despair, from immersion in thoughts of darkness and death, to a state of joyous mysticism, of contemplation of heaven's "ever-singing, ever-loving choir / Of saints and angels in the courts above." Consisting of four numbers, all in the minor mode, with two short simple recitatives, the scene opens with a brief symphony —a largo effectively establishing the gloom of the prison by repeated chords in the strings alternating with single notes in the unison flutes, which appear here for the first time in the oratorio. Beginning after a short recitative, Theodora's first aria, "With darkness deep, as is my woe," is a strongly pathetic number of special interest at the melismas on the words "Your thickest veil around me throw,/Conceal'd from human sight!" and "embosm'd in the grave," where the orchestral accompaniment is suddenly "blackened" with a dense texture of sixteenth and thirty-second

61. Dean, *Oratorios*, p. 559.
62. Lang, *Handel*, p. 486.

notes. After an expanded repetition of the previous symphony and a brief recitative comes the final aria of the scene, "Oh that on wings I could rise" (Example VIII–15), which convincingly expresses Theodora's conquering of her previous despair.

EXAMPLE VIII-15. *Theodora* (Handel, *Werke*, 8:113–14).

Scenes 3 and 4 provide much-needed relief between scenes 2 and 5, both intense prison episodes. Scene 3, in which Didimus convinces Septimius to allow him to rescue Theodora, includes two arias, one by each of the two that successfully and subtly depict their attitudes; and scene 4 consists of a recitative and aria by Irene, who prays for the safety of Theodora. Scene 5, the prison scene of Theodora and Didimus, is the dramatic climax of the act. The scene consists of simple recitatives, two arias, an accompanied recitative, and a final duet. As Didimus first approaches the sleeping Theodora, he offers her his protection in the aria "Sweet rose and lily, flow'ry form"—a charming piece in triple meter, with violin *fioriture* furnishing instrumental similes. Theodora changes the affection with her plea for death by Didimus's sword in the aria "The pilgrim's home"—a gentle, poignant *siciliano*. Didimus immediately and forcefully rejects this notion in the accompanied recitative "Forbid it, Heaven!" In "To thee, thou glorious son of worth," the climactic farewell duet that closes the scene, the lovers part; they perhaps never again will see each other on earth but are convinced that they will meet in heaven. The duet is of interest for the unusual five-part orchestral texture, with the bassoons functioning independently of the continuo, and for the attractive variety created by the melodic modifications of the motive set to the words "but sure shall meet in heaven." In scene 6, the finale of the act, Irene is with the Christians; her brief recitative introduces a magnificent chorus (the one that Handel is said to have preferred over the "Hallelujah" chorus of *Messiah*) in which the Christians derive strength from recalling the story (Luke 7:11–15) in which Jesus, in Naim, sees the widow's son being taken to his burial and restores him to life. The opening section of the chorus, "He saw the lovely youth, Death's early prey," is a largo funeral march in B-flat minor, with chromatic inflections in the bass; the brief second section, beginning at the words "Rise, youth! he said," changes suddenly to B-flat major and *a tempo ordinario*; and the longer final section, "Lowly the matron bow'd," retains the B-flat major but changes to allegro and triple meter. This last section, with fugal texture and two subjects, creates a powerful conclusion for the act.

In addition to the relationship between *Theodora* and the *oratorio volgare* pointed out above, another is *Theodora*'s unusually large number of da capo arias. Of the twenty-five arias used in its first performance, thirteen have the da capo form;[63] only *Susanna* among Handel's English dramatic oratorios used more. *Theodora*'s eleven choruses, however, are both more numerous and more convincingly integrated into the drama than those of *Susanna*; thus in respect to the chorus, the former differs more from the *oratorio volgare* than the latter. The additional vocal numbers of *Theodora* are three duets and three accompanied recitatives.

The only instrumental number in *Theodora*, other than those in act 2 mentioned above, is the overture—consisting of a French overture followed by two dances, a minuet and a courante, both in binary form.[64] The instrumentation of *Theodora* comprises pairs of flutes and oboes, a bassoon, pairs of horns and trumpets, timpani, strings, harpsichord, and organ. The winds are used sparingly, and there is little of special interest in the orchestration.

Jephtha[65]

Handel's last musically new oratorio in the English tradition that he had established is *Jephtha*. Another work sometimes called Handel's last English oratorio, *The Triumph of Time and Truth*,[66] was first performed in 1757; but this work "contains no new music, with the possible exception of the overture and a few recitatives."[67] Its origin dates back to 1707; a revision was performed in Italian in 1737, with an English translation by George Oldmixton provided for the audience to read. The 1757 version uses a text by Morell based heavily on Oldmixton's translation; the music is based on the 1707 and 1737 scores with additions from Handel's English oratorios, operas, anthems, and cantatas from throughout his life.[68]

Handel began to compose *Jephtha* on 21 January 1751. By 13 February, having sketched all of act 1, he was working on the

63. Dean, *Oratorios*, p. 627.

64. All three movements of the overture are either borrowed, or include material borrowed, from other composers. Five additional numbers of *Theodora* include borrowings, only one of which is from Handel's music. For details of the borrowing in *Theodora*, see ibid., pp. 562–63, 647; Taylor, *Indebtedness*, pp. 10–12, 28–30.

65. Printed in Handel, *Werke*, vol. 44; for a facsimile of Handel's autograph MS, see Handel, *Jephtha*-A.

66. Handel, *Werke*, vol. 20.

67. Dean, *Oratorios*, p. 589.

68. For an analysis of the 1757 version that identifies most of the sources, see Serauky, *Händel*, 5:493–536.

final chorus of act 2, "How dark, O Lord, are thy decrees." At the end of the first section of the chorus, he noted on the score that he had reached that point on 13 February and was unable to continue because of trouble with his vision.[69] He began again on 23 February, his sixty-sixth birthday, and noted that he was feeling better.[70] He finished this final chorus of act 2 on 27 February but did not begin to work again on *Jephtha* for nearly four months, during which he lost the sight of one eye.[71] Nevertheless, he continued to be active during this period: he presented several oratorios and performances on the organ at the Theatre Royal in Covent Garden and the Foundling Hospital.[72] According to notices in the *Bath Journal* of 3 June and the *General Advertiser* of 15 June, Handel spent early June in Bath and Cheltenham Wells, "where he had been to make use of the Waters."[73] Having returned to London on 13 June, he began again on 18 June, to work on *Jephtha*, which he finished on 30 August. Because of Handel's visual handicap, he spent more time composing *Jephtha* than any of his other oratorios; the rough condition of the autograph manuscript makes clear the seriousness of his disability. *Jephtha* was first performed at the Theatre Royal in Covent Garden on 26 February 1752;[74] it was repeated twice that season and was revived in three subsequent years, for a total of seven performances during Handel's life. It is not known how well *Jephtha* was received, but it has been performed fairly frequently since Handel's time.[75]

The author of the libretto, Morell, considered *Jephtha* his favorite oratorio.[76] He based the libretto on the story in Judges 11, although he made some significant changes and introduced some new characters. Like Morell's libretto of *Alexander Balus*, that of *Jephtha* includes brief quotations from numerous other authors, among them Milton, Pope, Addison, and Burnet.[77] The last named is the librettist of Maurice Greene's oratorio *Jephtha*,

69. Handel, *Jephtha*-A, p. 182; see below, Figure VIII-3, p. 340, for a reproduction, transcription, and translation of Handel's comment.

70. Handel, *Jephtha*-A, p. 183. Transcriptions and translations of both notes are given in Deutsch, *Handel*, pp. 701–2.

71. Deutsch, *Handel*, pp. 703, 710, 713.

72. Ibid., pp. 702–9.

73. Ibid., p. 710. For documentation of Handel's presence in Bath on 3 June, see Hall, "Smith," p. 133.

74. Deutsch, *Handel*, p. 719.

75. Dean, *Oratorios*, p. 619.

76. Deutsch, *Handel*, p. 852.

77. For a list of Morell's quotations from other authors, see Dean, *Oratorios*, p. 593.

FIGURE VIII-3. The point in Handel's composing score of *Jephtha* at which he
stopped work for about ten days because of his failing
eyesight. At the bottom of the page he wrote the following
note in German, except for an English word, "relaxation,"
which he crossed out and then used as a German verb at the
end of the sentence: "biss hierher koṁen den 13 Febr. ♀
1751 / verhindert worden wegen ~~relaxation~~ / des gesichts
meines linken auges so relaxt" (got this far on Wednesday, 13
February 1751 / prevented [from continuing] because of the
weakening of the sight of my left eye). Handel designated the
day of the week by a variant of the astronomical symbol for
Mercury (Wednesday).

(Reproduced by permission of GB/Lbm.)

performed in 1737 at the King's Theatre in the Haymarket, a work that Handel may have known. The personages in Morell's libretto are Jephtha (T); Storgè (Ms), his wife; Iphis (S), their daughter; Hamor (A), a soldier in love with Iphis; Zebul (B), a soldier and half brother of Jephtha; an Angel (S, first sung by a boy soprano); and a chorus of Israelites (SATB except once, SS). Neither Storgè nor Hamor is in the biblical account; Zebul figures in Judges 9 but not in the story of Jephtha; and Jephtha's daughter is not named in the Bible. Morell presumably derived the name Iphis from Iphigenia of Greek mythology—whose fate, to be sacrificed by her father (Agamemnon) to appease the goddess Artemis, is parallel to that of Jephtha's daughter.

At the beginning of the oratorio, Zebul and his brothers recall their half brother Jephtha from his exile—an exile imposed because he is an illegitimate son by a harlot—and urge him to lead the Israelites in war against their oppressors, the Ammonites. Jephtha agrees, on the condition that he will remain their leader in time of peace. Storgè reflects on the painful separation from her husband during the approaching war, and Iphis and Hamor declare their mutual love before the latter departs. Jephtha vows to God that if he returns victorious, "What, or whoe're shall first salute mine eyes,/Shall be for ever thine, or shall fall a sacrifice." In "ghastly dreams" Storgè foresees that "some dire event hangs o'er our heads," but Iphis urges her, "Heed not these black illusions of the night." At the end of the act, Jephtha issues the call to arms, and the chorus comments figuratively on the powerful assistance the God of Israel will provide. Act 2 opens with Hamor's account to Iphis of the battle, in which the Israelites, assisted by "Thousands of armed Cherubim," have been victorious. Elated by the news, Iphis asks her attendant maidens to "Adorn me, like a stately bride, to meet/My father in triumphant pomp." Singing of their battle and victory, Zebul and Jephtha enter. After a joyful symphony Iphis and a semichorus of virgins enter to greet Jephtha; the latter, reminded of his vow, is horrified to see her and drives her away. Jephtha then explains his vow to Zebul, Storgè, and Hamor. Shocked that he would sacrifice his daughter, they urge him in vain to spare her. Iphis hears of the vow and accepts her fate nobly, because the vow was instrumental in Israel's triumph. Here Jephtha breaks down completely from the conflict between his honor, which makes the sacrifice inevitable, and his love for his only child. The concluding chorus comments on the uncertainties of bliss and peace on earth. At the beginning of act 3, the fulfillment of the vow is about to take place. Jephtha prays that angels may take his daughter to heaven, and Iphis sings her farewell. Yet the priests hesitate to sacrifice her, for to do so would contradict God's law; they pray that God may declare his will. In answer an Angel, functioning as a deus ex machina, appears and stops the sacrifice. The Angel explains that "No vow can disannul/The law of God;—nor such was its intent,/When rightly scann'd; yet still shall be fulfill'd." Iphis must dedicate herself to God "in pure and virgin-state for ever." The Angel tells Jephtha that "The Holy Spirit, that dictated thy vow,/Bade thus explain it, and approves thy faith." The remainder of the oratorio consists of joyous expressions culminating in a final chorus ending with "Amen. Hallelujah."

In Judges the story of Jephtha and his daughter has quite a different ending: after Jephtha's daughter learned of her father's vow, she asked only that she be allowed to go to the mountains for two months and bewail her virginity with her companions; at the end of that period, she returned, and her father "did with her according to his vow."[78] The Reverend Morell's change in the story was intended to make it compatible with a Christian point of view. In changing it, however, he effectively negated the libretto's tragic, dramatic impact. All the agony expressed by Jephtha, Storgè, and Hamor in act 2 seems to have been the result of a ridiculous misunderstanding when the Angel appears in act 3 and informs Jephtha that he had misinterpreted his own vow, that he had not "rightly scann'd" it. Furthermore, Jephtha is relieved of all responsibility for his trying to bribe God, since the Holy Spirit had dictated the vow. Morell's substitution of lifelong virginity for immediate sacrifice would have been, according to the traditions of the biblical story, a cause for lamentation; following the ideals of Christian asceticism, however, Morell makes it a cause for rejoicing. Regardless of the inconsistencies and dramatic weakness of its third act, this libretto provided Handel with the opportunity for writing some of his greatest music, particularly in act 2 and at the beginning of act 3.

78. Carissimi's *Jephte*, characteristic of the numerous other oratorios on this subject composed in Italy, follows this biblical account.

Of primary importance in this oratorio is Handel's masterful characterization—especially of the two central figures, Jephtha and Iphis. It seems likely that Handel's *Jephtha* is, in a sense, a self-portrait, that the composer "identified his own emotions with those of the character," presented as "an upright man" who is "the victim of an overwhelming and inevitable catastrophe that strikes at the root of his being";[79] it may well be that "it is not Jephtha who struggles here but Handel."[80] The first three numbers allotted to Jephtha, all in act 1, present him more as a type than an individual. His first aria, "Virtue my soul shall still embrace," is not an extraordinary number, although it is of interest for its particularly long melisma on the word "great" and its long pedal points in the basso continuo, which underpin the words "who builds on this steady base, dreads no event of fate." The second number is the accompanied recitative of Jephtha's vow, "If, Lord, sustained by thy almighty pow'r"—an unassuming, even understated, presentation of extremely significant lines. Jephtha continues to be more a type than a human being in his next aria, "His mighty arm," a warlike number with long vocal melismas and *concitato* orchestral passages. In act 2, however, when Jephtha returns victorious from the war, the tragic heroism of the individual begins to emerge in the aria "Open thy marble jaws, O tomb" (Example VIII–16), with its hollow octave ritornello, jagged melodic lines, and chromaticism over a continuo pedal point (mm. 13–16) on the words "open, O tomb,/And hide me, earth, in thy dark womb." Jephtha's role in the remarkable quartet "O spare

EXAMPLE VIII-16. *Jephtha* (Handel, *Werke*, 44:147).

79. Dean, *Oratorios*, p. 595.
80. Lang, *Handel*, p. 508.

(EXAMPLE VIII-16, continued)

your daughter" reveals his steadfast refusal to compromise, to
"recall the impious vow," as Storgè, Hamor, and Zebul—spiritually as well as musically aligned against him throughout the number—repeatedly insist. Jephtha's reaction to his daughter's nobility
in her willingness to die brings him to the climax of his emotional
conflict in a great accompanied recitative, "Deeper and deeper
still, thy goodness, child, / Pierceth a father's bleeding heart, and
checks / The cruel sentence on my falt'ring tongue"; fragmented
melody, wandering harmony, and skillfully changing patterns of
orchestral accompaniment combine to make this expression of
Jephtha's conflict between his love for Iphis and duty to God an
overwhelming experience. The opening of act 3, Jephtha's arioso
"Hide thou thy hated beams, O sun" (Example VIII–17) and its

EXAMPLE VIII-17. *Jephtha* (Handel, *Werke*, 44:188).

continuing accompanied recitative, show Jephtha still struggling, even at the moment of the sacrifice; but his following aria, "Waft her, angels, through the skies" (Example VIII–18) is a prayer of serene resignation to the inevitable. This is Jephtha's last statement of significance. His final number, "For ever blessed be thy holy name," a brief arioso after the Angel's clarification, is a simple expression of relief.

EXAMPLE VIII-18. *Jephtha* (Handel, *Werke*, 44:190).

(EXAMPLE VIII-18, continued)

Iphis is characterized as an uncomplicated and happy girl throughout act 1 and up to the point of her realization of her fate in act 2: every aria that she sings, and her duet with Hamor, is a lighthearted piece either in triple meter with a suggestion of dance rhythm or in duple meter with a dance label. The symphony that precedes her greeting to her father when he returns from war is a *siciliano*, and she and her semichorus of virgins greet him with a gavotte. She first achieves nobility after learning of her father's vow: in her brief accompanied recitative "For joys so vast, too little is the price/Of one poor life" and in the following aria, "Happy they! this vital breath/With content I shall resign." The latter is especially effective at its opening (Example VIII–19), in which the violins are in unison with the voice, and the continuo is

EXAMPLE VIII-19. *Jephtha* (Handel, *Werke*, 44:168).

(EXAMPLE VIII-19, continued)

silent; even in this number, despite the impending tragedy, Iphis's character is identified with a dancelike quality, for the aria occasionally suggests sarabande rhythm. Iphis's encouragement to the priests who are to perform the sacrifice is conveyed in an accompanied recitative, "Ye sacred priests," and in an aria, "Farewell, ye limpid springs and floods" (Example VIII–20) a *siciliano* in its first part; both numbers continue to reflect her heroism, selfless yet tinged with pain.

EXAMPLE VIII-20. *Jephtha* (Handel, *Werke*, 44:193).

(EXAMPLE VIII-20, continued)

well, fare-well, ye lim - pid springs and floods,

The chorus in *Jephtha* consistently plays the role of the Israelites. Except for the semichorus of virgins in act 2, the ten choruses
in this work are much like those of ancient Greek drama—they
are not dramatic crowd choruses, involved in the action, but are
highly emotional commentaries, detached from it. Of special interest in act 1 are the first and final choruses. The first, "Pour forth
no more," completes Zebul's opening aria in AB form—yet in a
surprising key, D major, rather than the aria's F major. Commenting on the Israelite's rejection of the worship of false gods, this
chorus effectively breaks into 12/8 time at the line (borrowed from
Milton) "In dismal dance around the furnace blue," and moves
into a fugal anthem style, a powerful section using trumpets for
the first time, at the line "Chemosh no more will we adore with
timbrell'd anthems to Jehovah due." The final chorus of act 1,
"When his loud voice in thunder spoke," is another powerful
number, this time demonstrating the incomparable strength of
Israel's God; particularly effective is the setting of the lines "They
now contract their boist'rous pride,/And lash with idle rage the
laughing strand," which constitutes the chorus's final section. The
most important chorus of the oratorio, and one of Handel's greatest choruses, is the finale of act 2, "How dark, O Lord, are thy
decrees!" It is in four sections with a balanced tonal structure and
contrasting tempos, time signatures, and textures.[81] As a whole,
this chorus expresses notions of darkness and uncertainty, yet

81. For detailed analyses of this chorus, see Dean, *Oratorios*, pp. 611–14; Serauky,
Händel, 5:440–43.

acceptance and resignation—particularly in the final section, a striking setting of the text "Yet on this maxim still obey:/Whatever is, is right," quoted from Pope's *Essay on Man*. Two of the choruses, "O God, behold our sore distress" and "Doubtful fear, and reverend awe," include double fugues.

Most of *Jephtha*'s choruses and several of its other numbers are based on the masses of the Bohemian composer Franz Johann Habermann (1706–83). In fact, *Jephtha* includes nineteen numbers with borrowed material, the majority of which come from Habermann and the remainder from Handel's earlier works.[82] Of the dramatic oratorios only *Deborah* includes more borrowed material than *Jephtha*. In nearly every instance, however, Handel borrowed only to stimulate his imagination; the development of the material is new, as is the emotional intensity derived from Handel's highly personal interpretation of the libretto of *Jephtha*.

Of the twenty-four arias in *Jephtha*, eleven are in da capo form. The work includes seven accompanied recitatives, more than any oratorio since *Belshazzar*. Two ensembles, the duet in act 1 and the quartet in act 2, were included in the first performance. The quintet in act 3 was inserted for the 1753 performance.

Jephtha includes three instrumental numbers: the overture, consisting of a French overture followed by a minuet; the brief *siciliano* in act 2 that introduces Iphis and her semichorus of virgins coming to greet Jephtha; and a sinfonia, an allegro in binary form, that introduces the Angel in act 3. Jephtha is scored for one flute, two oboes, one bassoon, two horns, two trumpets, strings, harpsichord, and organ. The orchestration is not particularly colorful but generally restrained and conservative.

The Chief Characteristics of Handel's Oratorios

For Handel in England the word *oratorio* normally designated a musical entertainment that used a three-act dramatic text based on a sacred subject; the musical setting employed the styles and forms of Italian opera and English sacred choral music, although at

82. For details of Handel's borrowing in *Jephtha*, see Seiffert, "Habermann"; Taylor, *Indebtedness*, pp. 15–27; and Dean, *Oratorios*, pp. 599–614 passim, p. 648. For an edition of Habermann's *Missa sancti Weneslai, martyris*, from which Handel borrowed extensively, see *ColM*, ser. 2, vol. 6.

times modified in their new context; the chorus was considered essential and was usually prominent; and the manner of performance was that of a concert, usually at a theater or concert hall, often with concertos performed between the acts. The greater prominence of the chorus and the division into three acts (Handel usually used *act*, rather than *part*, for an oratorio's structural divisions) are among the features that distinguish the Handelian English oratorio from the characteristic Italian oratorio. Among Handel's exceptions to his usual meaning of the word *oratorio* are its use for *Israel in Egypt*, *Messiah*, and the *Occasional Oratorio*, all of which have nondramatic librettos; another exception is his benefit concert in 1738, announced as "Mr. Handel's Oratorio," a miscellaneous program with no unifying plan. *The Triumph of Time and Truth* (1757), a revision of an Italian work, might also be considered an exception, since its text is more ethical and moral than religious, even though act 3 includes an anthem of petition to the Lord and closes with a "Hallelujah" chorus. Seven works by Handel are sometimes classified as "secular oratorios": *Acis and Galatea*, *Alexander's Feast*, *Ode for St. Cecilia's Day*, *L'Allegro*, *Semele*, *Hercules*, and *The Choice of Hercules*.[83] Nevertheless, none of these compositions was originally called an oratorio by its composer. In Handel's England the term *secular oratorio* was not used and would have seemed self-contradictory. Thus in a genre classification of Handel's works based on the terminology characteristic in England of his time, these seven compositions would be excluded from the oratorio category.

The Handelian oratorio functioned as an opera substitute, in a sense, since Handel eventually abandoned Italian opera for oratorio but continued to use opera theaters and, at least for a while, opera singers for oratorio performances. It was not an opera substitute for the same reason that the oratorio was in such cities as Rome and Venice, however, where opera was not performed during Lent, and oratorio took its place. Handel's oratorio seasons often coincided more or less with Lent because of the sacred subject matter of the oratorios, but during his life operas

83. Among the writings in which these works are classified as oratorios are: Herbage, "Secular," pp. 132–55; Larsen, *Handel's "Messiah,"* pp. 21–22; and Schering, *Oratorium*, pp. 310–20. In Lang, *Handel*, pp. 715–16, the works in this list are not classified as oratorios but as either "Cantatas and Serenades" or "English Pastorals, Odes, and Music Dramas"; for a discussion of classification questions, see Lang, *Handel*, p. 366.

were sometimes performed during Lent in London, and his oratorios were in competition with them.[84]

Handel never staged his oratorios, although in 1732 Bernard Gates gave a private performance of the first English oratorio, *Esther*, in a staged version. Handel planned to give another staged performance of the same work later in that year but was prevented from doing so by the bishop of London. Therefore Handel compromised by presenting *Esther* in a concert performance. This compromise established a precedent for all subsequent performances of Handel's English oratorios during the composer's lifetime. The compromise did not, however, force Handel to accept an abnormal manner of presenting his oratorios, but rather, it forced him to continue the normal manner practiced throughout Europe since the genre's inception. The dramatic nature of most of the oratorios and the "stage" directions found in some of the printed librettos and autograph manuscripts show that Handel continued to visualize the dramatic action in terms of staging, even after he had abandoned opera for oratorio and even though he neither intended nor expected his oratorios to be staged. In the twentieth century most of Handel's dramatic oratorios have been given staged performances, some of which are said to have been highly successful.[85] Regardless of the success or failure of such performances from a twentieth-century viewpoint, they have little to do with the practice of oratorio performance in the Baroque era.

The librettos of all Handel's oratorios, except *Messiah* and *Theodora*, are based on the Old Testament or the Apocrypha, and even *Messiah* contains more texts from the Old Testament than the New, despite its Christian theme. The Old Testament subject matter, which was considerably modified by the librettists, had a strong appeal to Handel's audiences. Not only were the audiences generally familiar with the stories, but they perceived a parallel between the Israelites and themselves: both intensely nationalistic, led by heroic figures, and given the special protection of God, who

---

84. Dean, *Oratorios*, pp. 81–82. For contemporary comments on the competition of opera and oratorio during Lent of 1743 (Lent began on 16 February that year), see Deutsch, *Handel*, pp. 560–62.

85. For a partial list of staged performances of Handel's oratorios from 1922 to 1970, and for some answers to the question "How Should Handel's Oratorios Be Staged?" see Dean, "How."

was worshiped with pomp and splendor.[86] Handel's librettists were influenced by classical drama more than by the contemporary masque, which in this period was a short English opera. The librettists sought to incorporate into their works much of the spirit and technique of ancient Greek drama—especially its use of the chorus. *Esther* and *Athalia* are particularly important for having established the classical tendencies of the Handelian oratorio; both are based on classical tragedies by Racine that include choruses in the ancient manner. Classical tendencies continued to be prominent in varying degrees in most of Handel's other dramatic oratorios—particularly in *Saul*, *Samson*, *Belshazzar*, and *Jephtha*. The classical emphasis, and with it the significant role of the chorus, makes the libretto of the Handelian oratorio decidedly different from that of the contemporary Italian oratorio; yet parallels exist between them: both are operatic entertainments, though unstaged (Handel's three-act structure is closer to opera, however, than the two-part oratorio common in Italy); both may include secular love scenes (*Solomon* and *Susanna* have elements in common with the *oratorio erotico*); and most of the subjects of Handel's oratorios had been used previously for oratorios in Italy. In their choral emphasis Handel's works are similar to the German Protestant oratorio; nevertheless, the German works, with their use of chorale tunes and their frequent performance in church, are more closely related to church music than are Handel's oratorios.

The chorus in Handel's dramatic oratorios functions at times within the action, in the manner of a Passion *turba* or an operatic crowd-chorus, and at other times outside the action, in the role of a commentator.[87] Among those functioning within the action are warlike choruses (*Judas Maccabaeus*, "Disdainful of danger we'll rush on the foe"), lamentations after defeat (*Joshua*, "How soon our tow'ring hopes are cross'd"), and victory choruses (*Joshua*,

86. For an elaboration of these aspects of the librettos in relation to English culture of the period, see Lang, *Handel*, pp. 383–90. For a study of Handel's oratorio texts in relation to the religious, philosophical, and social thought of the time, see Bredenförder, *Text*.

87. Regarding the types, functions, and musical styles of Handel's oratorio choruses, the most recent and extensive study is Meier, *Chorsätze*, which includes church and secular works as well as oratorios. Among the previous writings on the subject are Bukofzer, *Baroque*, pp. 38–40; Dean, *Oratorios*, pp. 40–41, 65–66; Lang, *Handel*, pp. 378, 603–12; Larsen, *Handel's "Messiah,"* pp. 40–95; and Leichtentritt, *Händel*, pp. 282–96. For studies of Handel's choral fugues, but not exclusively those in the oratorios, see Dietz, *Chorfuge*, and Wieber, *Chorfuge*.

"See, the conqu'ring hero comes"). Choruses with anthemlike texts—such as those of praise, thanksgiving, or petition to God—usually function either within the religious ceremonies depicted in the oratorios ("Your harps and cymbals sound" for the dedication of the temple in *Solomon*) or as the prayerful reactions of the people of Israel to the events of the drama (*I will magnify Thee*, a Chandos anthem for soloists and chorus used at the end of *Belshazzar*); such a chorus often forms the finale of an act. Fewer in number are the choruses functioning outside the action and commenting on it; among the best of these are "Envy! eldest born of hell," in *Saul*; "O calumny," in *Alexander Balus*; and "How dark, O Lord, are thy decrees," in *Jephtha*.

The most striking feature of Handel's choral style is its immense variety. The choruses may be generally classified according to a number of musical types—among which are those predominantly in a simple, homophonic style (*Saul*: "Welcome, mighty king"); those emphasizing massive chordal effect, at times in double-chorus antiphonal style (*Solomon*: "From the censer curling"); those in predominantly fugal texture, with one to three subjects (*Messiah*: "And with his stripes"); those using a basso ostinato, usually varied (*Joshua*: "Almighty ruler of the skies"); and those emphasizing freely imitative texture, in what might be called motet or madrigal style (*Samson*: "Then round about thy starry throne"). Nevertheless, it is difficult to find many choruses that are so consistent that they fit neatly into a single class, for there tends to be considerable variety within a chorus. This variety has much to do with the general popularity of Handel's chorus-dominated *Israel in Egypt* and *Messiah*. Handel's choruses often use changing combinations of fugal, freely imitative, openwork, "cantus-firmus," homophonic, antiphonal, unison, a cappella, and accompanied passages. Openwork texture (sometimes called *latticework*—that is, the texture in which only one or two vocal parts sound at a time, with melodic material passed from one part to another) gives a light, chamber-music quality to those choruses in which it predominates. Openwork, fugal, or freely imitative textures often alternate with passages in chordal homophony, used in a strongly rhythmic manner at climactic cadential points (*Messiah*: "And he shall purify," "For unto us a Child is born,"

"His yoke is easy").[88] "Cantus-firmus" passages (the term as used here does not necessarily imply the use of a *cantus prius factus*) are those in which one voice proceeds in long notes while the others weave counterpoints around it in shorter notes or accompany it with declamatory, chordal figures (*Deborah*: "Lord of eternity"). The use of a solo voice preceding and/or alternating with a chorus is fairly common. Most of the choruses are for SATB, but some are for five or six voices or for an eight-voice double chorus; in *Israel in Egypt* and *Solomon* the double chorus is particularly prominent. Handel seems always to have been acutely aware of the possibilities of the words of his choruses, and his settings abound in striking effects of word painting and symbolism. In no other oratorio, however, did he employ as much text description as in *Israel in Egypt*.

The arias and ensembles in Handel's oratorios generally resemble those of contemporary Italian opera in the expression of their affections but not in their structure.[89] Found in the oratorios are virtually all the aria types of opera—including rage and vengeance arias with long melismas in the vocal line and *concitato* orchestral accompaniments; heroic, martial arias with fanfares in the melodic lines and at times with a trumpet in the orchestra; lamentations, often using sarabande rhythmic style; pastoral or love texts, sometimes lamentations as well, using the *siciliano* style and often with long pedal points in the accompaniments of those with pastoral texts; joyful arias in minuet, gavotte, bourée, or gigue style; and various types of simile arias with vocal and orchestral imitations of bird calls and other phenomena of nature. The virtually invariable da capo structure of *opera seria* and *oratorio volgare*, however, is employed with generally decreasing frequency in Handel's oratorios from *Esther* through *Samson*. There is considerable fluctuation in the proportion of da capo to non–da capo arias after *Samson*, but only in *Susanna* and *Theodora* are there more of the former than the latter, and these works are both closer in several respects than Handel's other oratorios to the *oratorio volgare*. The non–da capo arias tend to be in binary, ABA', or occasionally strophic form. Most of the ensembles of the

88. These choruses are based on Italian duets; all such openwork choruses, with much one- and two-part writing, are termed "duet-choruses" and are considered to be derived from duet style in Larsen, *Handel's "Messiah,"* pp. 72–75, 82–83.

89. For a discussion of the arias and ensembles in Handel's dramatic oratorios, see Dean, *Oratorios*, pp. 67–70.

oratorios are duets, although there are a few trios and quartets. In most of the duets, the characters are in conflict either throughout the number or at the beginning; in the latter case they achieve a reconciliation as the duet proceeds. In other duets, as in most of those in *opera seria*, the characters are in love or otherwise in a state of emotional harmony. Unlike the duets of *opera seria* and *oratorio volgare*, those in Handel's oratorios are rarely in da capo form. Trios and quartets are few, and they are virtually all dramatic ensembles in which the characters retain their separate identities.

The French overture is the most prominent opening instrumental number of Handel's English oratorios; eleven of the seventeen oratorios considered above begin with a French overture, at times somewhat modified, and seven of these eleven include one or more additional instrumental numbers, mostly dances, after the French overture. Only *Athalia* begins with an Italian sinfonia (Allegro, Grave, Allegro). The overture of *Deborah* clearly uses material from the oratorio itself, and that of *Judas Maccabaeus* appears to foreshadow material of the oratorio, although less clearly than does that of *Deborah*. The instrumental numbers within the oratorios are usually intended to convey the impression of action (such as a battle or a procession) or of the passage of time (for instance, the instrumental numbers in *Saul*) or to establish a mood (as does the *Pifa* or "Pastoral Symphony" in *Messiah*). The orchestration of the oratorios represents virtually all the procedures of Handel's time, ranging from simple basso continuo support for arias and choruses through two-part accompaniments (continuo and unison violins) and richer accompaniments in four, five, six, or even more parts, to large concerto grosso accompaniments. In arias the vocal line is always of primary importance, and obbligato parts generally do not provide contrapuntal competition with it but complement it and fill in while the voice rests.[90]

Handel borrowed heavily from his own compositions and from those of others in his oratorios. This method of composition was common in his time, and his borrowing differed from that of his contemporaries only in degree.[91] His use of the music of other

90. For more details of the instrumental numbers and for the orchestration in the dramatic oratorios, see Dean, *Oratorios*, pp. 70–80.

91. For particularly perceptive treatments of Handel's borrowings in the oratorios, see ibid., pp. 50–57; Lang, *Handel*, pp. 559–69. For a list of all identified borrowings in the dramatic oratorios, see Dean, *Oratorios*, pp. 641–48. For useful comparisons, with music examples, of Handel's music and its models, see Taylor, *Indebtedness*.

composers was known by his contemporaries; despite his numerous opponents in London, however, he was never accused of plagiarism, for he did not borrow complete compositions of others and present them as his own.[92] In only a few instances did Handel include within one of his oratorios an unchanged movement from another composer's work; rather, he nearly always used the borrowed material to stimulate his imagination to develop the material in his own way, and he usually made significant improvements. For Handel, borrowing was a deliberate method of working. His manuscript collection of sketches of the music of other composers at the Fitzwilliam Museum in Cambridge served as a source book that he used to start the creative process; he incorporated as much or as little of the original as he chose into his own finished product. Although Handel composed with borrowed material throughout his life, his borrowing from the music of other composers increased remarkably from 1736 to 1739—the period of *Israel in Egypt*, which uses more borrowings than any other oratorio. It may be that his mental illness of 1737, which was perhaps beginning even in 1736, is the reason for his increased need for models to stimulate his creative powers. Yet even in *Israel* he transformed his borrowed material into an expression genuinely his own. In Handel's late oratorios more of his borrowings were for instrumental numbers than vocal and more for choral than solo pieces. *Jephtha*, his last oratorio, includes more borrowings than any of his oratorios except *Israel in Egypt*.

Handel's performing forces varied from time to time, but in his late oratorio period, depending upon the requirements of the oratorio being performed, he probably used an orchestra of about thirty-five to forty pieces, a chorus of about seventeen to twenty-four voices, and four to nine soloists.[93] For some of his performances the forces were larger, however, as *Deborah* was presented in 1733 with about seventy-five instrumentalists and twenty-five singers; and *Athalia*, in the same year, with about seventy performers. The tradition of performing Handel's oratorios with gigantic choruses may have begun in provincial festivals during Handel's later years but not under his direction.[94]

92. Handel's rival Giovanni Bononcini was so accused, in 1731 by the Academy of Ancient Music, for allegedly claiming authorship of a madrigal by Antonio Lotti.
93. For details of some of Handel's performances, see Dean, *Oratorios* p. 103.
94. Ibid., p. 105.

The soloists for Handel's earliest oratorio performances were mostly Italian opera stars, including castrati, and the performances were bilingual whenever any singer's English pronunciation was unacceptable. From *Saul* on, however, Handel tended not to select the stars of Italian opera as his soloists but either English singers or foreign singers with a good command of English. Handel virtually abandoned the castrato; yet he continued to consider the high voice appropriate for male personages (in the roles of Solomon and Alexander Balus, among others), and he assigned these roles to women. The practice of using less skilled soloists than Italian opera stars was significant for the development of the Handelian oratorio. Without the tyrannical opera stars less emphasis was placed on virtuoso singing, and the new singers were willing to subordinate themselves to the work being performed. Thus Handel was freer to develop his musical and dramatic ideas independently of singers' demands.[95] The singers for Handel's choruses were all male, including those for the high parts: the sopranos were boys selected mainly from the Chapel Royal but also from St. Paul's Cathedral and Westminster Abbey, and the altos were countertenors.[96] The soloists may have joined the chorus, however, when not occupied with their own parts.

Some Contemporaries of Handel

Handel was the undisputed master of the English oratorio in his time, and he clearly dominated the field. Nevertheless, some of his contemporaries occasionally composed English oratorios, about which little is known but which appear to have been influenced by his. The second oratorio performed in London, following the second version of Handel's *Esther* by about nine months, was Willem De Fesch's *Judith: An Oratorio or Sacred Drama*, performed at Lincoln's Inn Fields on 16 February 1733.[97] The music of this work is lost, but the libretto by William Huggins has survived.[98] The libretto, divided into three acts, includes some

95. For lists and discussions of Handel's soloists in the oratorios, see Larsen, *Handel's "Messiah,"* pp. 36–37; and Dean, *Oratorios,* pp. 107–8, 651–61.

96. Dean, *Oratorios,* p. 108.

97. Maurice Greene's *Deborah,* performed probably in October, 1732, is in no sense an oratorio, as pointed out above, in the discussion of Handel's *Deborah.*

98. For a brief description of the work, together with historical information, see Bremt, *De Fesch,* pp. 53–58, 108–110. Copies of the libretto are in GB/Lbm and US/Wc.

W. Hogarth Inv.   G. V. Gucht. Sc.

Per Vulnera Servor
Morte tuâ Vivens.

Virg. Æneid:

FIGURE VIII-4. Frontispiece of the printed libretto to Willem
De Fesch's oratorio *Judith* (1733). From a
drawing by William Hogarth, engraved by G.
Vandergucht.
(Reproduced by permission of GB/Lbm.)

FIGURE VIII-5. *A Chorus of Singers* (December, 1732), by William
Hogarth. This satirical etching shows a rehearsal of the
oratorio *Judith* by De Fesch.
(Reproduced by permission of Gerald Coke, Esq.)

"stage" descriptions comparable to those found in the printed librettos of some of Handel's subsequent oratorios. The chorus, which represents the Assyrian Officers and also the Bethulians, is used less than is normal in Handel's oratorios: three times each in the first two acts and only once in the third act, at the conclusion. It is of interest that Hogarth's engraving entitled "A Chorus of Singers," dating from 1732, is a caricature of a rehearsal of De Fesch's *Judith*. De Fesch's only other oratorio is *Joseph*, performed at Covent Garden in 1745, of which the music is also lost.

Maurice Greene's *Jephtha: An Oratorio in Two Parts* was performed at the King's Theatre in 1737.[99] The libretto follows the biblical story more closely than does that of Handel's *Jephtha*, particularly at the end of the work. In Greene's oratorio Jephtha's Daughter willingly accepts her sacrifice as inevitable and asks only,

> Let me awhile defer my Fate,
> and to the Mountains fly:
> There to bewail my Virgin state,
> And then return—and die.

Jephtha complies with her request, and the final chorus tells her that Israel's daughters will lament each year "in honor of thy fate." In Greene's *Jephtha* the chorus sings four times in part 1 and six times in part 2, and thus it is as prominent as it is in several of Handel's English oratorios. Greene's other oratorio is *The Force of Truth*, with a libretto by John Hoadly, performed in 1744.[100]

Other English oratorios known to have been performed during Handel's lifetime are Thomas Arne's *Abel* (performed in 1744 in Dublin and in 1755 in London) and John Stanley's *Jephtha* (1757). The only music known to survive from these works is the *Hymn of Eve* from Arne's *Abel*.

99. The printed libretto does not include the name of the librettist. The catalogue of GB/Lbm gives the name John Hoadly as the librettist, but Dean, *Oratorios*, p. 45, gives the name Burnet, as does Deutsch, *Handel*, p. 427.
100. A copy of the libretto is in US/NYp.

Bibliography

This bibliography lists all the sources referred to by short title in the main body of the book and also a few that are not referred to but may prove useful to the reader. Materials fully identified in the main body, mostly encyclopedia articles and primary sources, are omitted.

Abraham, "Passion" (I)
  Abraham, Gerald. "Passion Music in the Fifteenth and Sixteenth Centuries."
    Monthly Musical Record 83 (1953): 208–11, 235–41.
Abraham, "Passion" (II)
  ———. "Passion Music from Schütz to Bach." *Monthly Musical Record* 84
    (1954): 115–19, 152–56, 175–78.
Adrio, "Kühnhausen"
  Adrio, Adam. "Die Matthäus-Passion von J. G. Kühnhausen (Celle um 1700)."
    In *Festschrift für Arnold Schering zum sechzigsten Geburtstag*, edited by
    Helmuth Osthoff, Walter Serauky, and Adam Adrio, pp. 24–35. Berlin: A.
    Glas, 1937.
Alaleona, *Oratorio*
  Alaleona, Domenico. *Storia dell'oratorio musicale in Italia.* Milan: Fratelli
    Bocca, 1945. Reprint, with different pagination, of *Studi su la storia del-
    l'oratorio musicale in Italia.* 1908.
Ameln, *Kirchenmusik*
  Ameln, Konrad; Mahrenholz, Christhard; Thomas, William; et al., eds. *Hand-
    buch der deutschen evangelischen Kirchenmusik.* 4 vols. to date. Göttingen:
    Vandenhoeck & Ruprecht, 1932–.
Ameln, "Passionshistorie"
  Ameln, Konrad. "Die Anfänge der deutschen Passionshistorie." In *Interna-
    tional Musicological Society Fourth Congress, Basel, June 29–July 3, 1949:
    Report*, pp. 39–45. Edited by the Schweizerische Musikforschende
    Gesellschaft, Ortsgruppe Basel. Basel: Bärenreiter, [1951].
Baab, "Förster"
  Baab, Jerrold C. "The Sacred Latin Works of Kaspar Förster (1616–73)."
    Ph.D. dissertation, University of North Carolina at Chapel Hill, 1970.
Bach, *Neue Ausgabe*
  Bach, Johann Sebastian. *Die neue Bach-Ausgabe.* Edited by the Johann-
    Sebastian-Bach Institut, Göttingen, and by the Bach-Archiv, Leipzig. 7 series,
    43 vols. to date. Kassel: Bärenreiter, 1954–. *Kritischer Bericht.* Kassel:
    Bärenreiter, 1955–.

Bach, *Werke*
———. *Werke*. Edited by the Bach-Gesellschaft. 61 vols. in 47. Leipzig: Breitkopf & Härtel, 1851–1926.
Baltzer, *Judith*
Baltzer, Otto. *Judith in der deutschen Literatur*. Stoff- und Motivgeschichte der deutschen Literatur, vol. 7. Berlin: Walter de Gruyter, 1930.
Baselt, "Actus"
Baselt, Bernd. "Actus musicus und Historie um 1700 in Mitteldeutschland." *Wissenschaftliche Beiträge der Martin-Luther-Universität Halle-Wittenberg*: ser. G 1, *Hallesche Beiträge zur Musikwissenschaft* 8 (1968): 77–103. See also the shorter version, under the same title, in *Bericht über den Internationalen Musikwissenschaftlichen Kongress, Leipzig, 1966*, edited by Carl Dahlhaus, Reiner Kluge, Ernst H. Meyer, and Walter Wiora, pp. 230–37. Kassel: Bärenreiter; Leipzig: VEB Deutscher Verlag für Musik, 1970.
Becker, "Brockes"
Becker, Heinz. "The Brockes Passion by George Frederick Handel." Pp. 4–5 of booklet accompanying the recording of G. F. Händel, *Passion nach B. H. Brockes*, performed by the Regensburger Domchor and the Schola Cantorum Basiliensis, conducted by August Wenzinger. Archiv Produktion SAPM 198/418–20. 1967.
Becker, "Tagespresse"
———. "Die frühe Hamburgische Tagespresse als musikgeschichtliche Quelle." In *Beiträge zur Hamburgischen Musikgeschichte*, edited by Heinrich Husmann. Schriftenreihe des Musikwissenschaftlichen Instituts der Universität Hamburg, vol. 1, pp. 22–45. Hamburg: Selbstverlag des Musikwissenschaftlichen Instituts der Universität Hamburg, 1956.
Bircke, "Matthäuspassion"
Bircke, Joachim. "Eine unbekannte anonyme Matthäuspassion aus der zweiten Hälfte des 17. Jahrhunderts." *Archiv für Musikwissenschaft* 15 (1958): 162–86.
Bitter, *Oratorium*
Bitter, C[arl] H[ermann]. *Beiträge zur Geschichte des Oratoriums*. Berlin: R. Oppenheim, 1872.
Bittinger, *SWV*
Bittinger, Werner, ed. *Schütz-Werk-Verzeichnis (SWV)*. Short edition. Kassel: Bärenreiter, 1960.
Blankenburg, "Gotha"
Blankenburg, Walter. "Die Aufführungen von Passionen und Passionskantaten in der Schlosskirche auf dem Friedenstein zu Gotha zwischen 1699 und 1770." In *Festschrift Friedrich Blume zum 70. Geburtstag*, edited by Anna Amalie Abert and Wilhelm Pfannkuch, pp. 50–59. Kassel: Bärenreiter, 1963.
Blankenburg, "Weihnachtsoratorium"
———. "Das Parodieverfahren im Weihnachtsoratorium Johann Sebastian Bachs." *Musik und Kirche* 32 (1962): 245–54.
Blume, *Kirchenmusik*
Blume, Friedrich, et al. *Geschichte der Evangelischen Kirchenmusik*. 2d rev. ed. Kassel: Bärenreiter, 1965.
Blume, *Kirchenmusik*-Eng.
———, et al. *Protestant Church Music: A History*. New York: W. W. Norton, 1974.

Blume, *Monodische*

———. *Das monodische Prinzip in der protestantischen Kirchenmusik*. Leipzig: Breitkopf & Härtel, 1925.

Blume, *Syntagma*

———. *Syntagma musicologicum: Gesammelte Reden und Schriften*. Edited by Martin Ruhnke. Kassel: Bärenreiter, 1963.

Böhme, *Geschichte*

Böhme, Franz Magnus. *Die Geschichte des Oratoriums für Musikfreunde kurz und fasslich dargestellt*. 1887. Reprint. Walluf bei Wiesbaden: M. Sändig, 1973.

Böhme, *Oratorium*

———. *Das Oratorium: Eine historische Studie*. Leipzig: J. J. Weber, 1861.

Braun, *Choralpassion*

Braun, Werner. *Die mitteldeutsche Choralpassion im achtzehnten Jahrhundert*. Berlin: Evangelische Verlagsanstalt, 1960.

Braun, "Echtheit"

———. "Echtheits- und Datierungsfragen im vokalen Frühwerk Georg Friedrich Händels." In *Händel-Ehrung der Deutschen Demokratischen Republik, Halle 11.–19. April 1959, Konferenzbericht*, pp. 61–71. Edited by Walther Siegmund-Schultze. Leipzig: Deutscher Verlag für Musik, 1961.

Bredenförder, *Texte*

Bredenförder, Elisabeth. *Die Texte der Händel-Oratorien: Eine religionsgeschichtliche und literarsoziologische Studie*. Kölner anglistische Arbeiten, vol. 19. Leipzig: Bernhard Tauchnitz, 1934.

Bremt, *De Fesch*

Bremt, Fr. van den. *Willem De Fesch (1687–1757?), Nederlands Componist en Virtuoos: Leven en Werk*. Académie royal de Belgique, classe des beaux-arts, mémoires, collection en 8°, vol. 5, fasc. 4. Brussels: Palais des Académies, 1949.

Brown, *Poetry*

Brown, John. *A Dissertation on the Rise, Union, and Power, the Progressions, Separations, and Corruptions, of Poetry and Music*. London: L. Davis and C. Reymers, 1763.

Brucker, *Bilder-sal*

Brucker, Johann Jacob. *Bilder-sal heutiger Tages lebender u. -durch Gelarheit berümter Schrift-steller*. 10 pts. in 2 vols. Ausburg, 1746.

Bukofzer, *Baroque.*

Bukofzer, Manfred F. *Music in the Baroque Era*. New York: W. W. Norton, 1947.

Burney, *Account*

Burney, Charles. *An Account of the Musical Performances in Westminster-Abbey, and the Pantheon, May 26th, 27th, 29th; and June the 3rd, and 5th, 1784. In Commemoration of Handel*. 1785. Reprint. Amsterdam: Frits A. M. Knuf, 1964.

Burney, "Commemoration"

———. "Commemoration of Handel." In Burney, *Account*.

Burney, *History*

———. *A General History of Music*. 4 bks. 1789. Reprint (4 bks. in 2 vols.). London: G. T. Foulis, 1935.

Burney, "Sketch"

———. "Sketch of the Life of Handel." In Burney, *Account*.

Burrows, "Messiah"
    Burrows, Donald. "Handel's Performances of 'Messiah': The Evidence of the Conducting Score." *Music and Letters* 56 (1975): 319–34.
Butler
    [Butler, Alban.] *Butler's Lives of the Saints.* Edited by Herbert Thurston, S. J., and Donald Attwater. 4 vols. New York: P. J. Kennedy & Sons, 1962.
Buxtehude[?], *Jüngste*
    Buxtehude, Dietrich[?] *Das Jüngste Gericht: Abendmusik in fünf Vorstellungen.* Edited by Willy Maxton. Kassel: Bärenreiter, [1939].
Buxtehude, *Werke*
    ———. *Werke.* Edited by Willibald Gurlitt, Gottlieb Harms, Hilmar Trede, Dietrich Kilian, and Adam Adrio. 8 vols. to date. Hamburg: Ugrino, 1925–.
Cannon, *Mattheson*
    Cannon, Beekman C. *Johann Mattheson: Spectator in Music.* Yale Studies in the History of Music, vol. 1. New Haven: Yale University Press, 1947.
Carreras, *Oratorio*
    Carreras y Bulbena, Josè Rafael. *El oratorio musical desde su origen hasta nuestros dias.* Barcelona: Ronda de la Universidad, 1906.
Chrysander, *Händel*
    Chrysander, Friedrich. *G. F. Händel.* 3 vols. Leipzig: Breitkopf & Härtel, 1858–67.
Chrysander, "Oper"
    ———. "Die zweite Periode der Hamburger Oper von 1682 bis 1694, oder vom Theaterstreit bis zur Direction Kusser's." *Leipziger Allgemeine Musikalische Zeitung* 13 (1878): cols. 289–95, 304–12, 324–29, 340–46, 355–61, 371–76, 388–92, 405–10, 420–24, 439–42.
Chrysander, "Orgelbegleitung"
    ———. "Händel's Orgelbegleitung zu Saul, und die neueste englische Ausgabe dieses Oratoriums." *Jahrbücher für musikalische Wissenschaft* 1 (1863): 408–28.
Chw
    Blume, Friedrich, and Gudewill, Kurt, eds. *Das Chorwerk.* Berlin, Wolfenbüttel: Kallmeyer, Möseler Verlag, 1929–. Vol 26, *Passion nach dem Evangelisten Johannes, mit Intermedien,* by Thomas Selle, edited by Rudolf Gerber, 1933. Vol. 27, *Passion nach dem Evangelisten Johannes,* by Christoph Demantius, 1934. Vol. 50, *Passion nach dem Evangelisten Matthäus,* by Johannes Georg Kühnhausen, edited by Adam Adrio, 1937. Vols. 78–79, *Matthäuspassion,* by [Friedrich Funke], edited by Joachim Birke, 1961.
ColM
    Velimirović, Miloŝ, ed. *Collegium musicum: Yale University.* Series 2. Madison: A–R Editions, 1969–. Vol. 3, *Das Lied des Lammes,* by Johann Mattheson, edited by Beekman C. Cannon, 1971. Vol 6, *Missa sancti Weneslai, martyris,* by Franz Johann Habermann, edited by William O. Gudger, 1976.
Corneille, *Oeuvres*
    Corneille, P[ierre]. *Oeuvres.* New ed. Edited by Charles J. Marty-Laveaus. 12 vols. Paris: Hachette, 1862.
Culley, *German*
    Culley, Thomas. *A Study of the Musicians Connected with the German College in Rome during the 17th Century and of Their Activities in Northern Europe.* Sources and Studies for the History of the Jesuits, vol. 2, Jesuits and Music, vol. 1. St. Louis, Mo.: Jesuit Historical Institute, St. Louis University, 1970.

DDT

Liliencron, Rochus von; Kretzschmar, Hermann; Abert, Hermann; and Scher-
ing, Arnold, eds. *Denkmäler deutscher Tonkunst*. Series 1. 65 vols. 1892–
1931. Reprint (65 vols. and 2 supps.). Edited and critically revised by Hans
Joachim Moser. Wiesbaden: Breitkopf & Härtel; Graz: Akademische
Druck- und Verlagsanstalt, 1957–61. Vol. 5, *Ausgewählte Gesangswerke*, by
Johann Rudolf Ahle, edited by Johannes Wolf, 1957. Vol. 6, *Solokantaten
und Chorwerke mit Instrumentalbegleitung*, by Mattias Weckmann and
Christoph Bernhard, edited by Max Seiffert, 1957. Vol. 14, *Abendmusiken
und Kirchenkantaten*, by Dietrich Buxtehude, edited by Max Seiffert, 1957.
Vol. 17, *Passionmusiken*, by Johann Sebastiani and Johann Theile, edited by
Friedrich Zelle, 1958. Vol. 34, *Newe deutsche geistliche Gesenge für die
gemeinen Schulen, gedrückt zu Wittemburg, durch Georgen Rhau, 1544*,
edited by Johannes Wolf, 1958. Vols. 53–54, *21 Ausgewählte Kirchenkom-
positionen*, edited by Max Seiffert, 1958. (See also *DTB*.)

Dean, "Dramatic"

Dean, Winton. "The Dramatic Element in Handel's Oratorios." *Proceedings of
the Royal Musical Association* 79 (1952–53): 33–49.

Dean, "How"

———. "How Should Handel's Oratorios Be Staged?" *Musical Newsletter* 4
(1971): 11–15.

Dean, *Opera*

———. *Handel and the Opera Seria*. Berkeley and Los Angeles: University of
California Press, 1969.

Dean, *Oratorios*

———. *Handel's Dramatic Oratorios and Masques*. London: Oxford University Press, 1959.

Dent, *Handel*

Dent, Edward J. *Handel*. Great Lives. London: Duckworth, 1934.

Deutsch, *Handel*

Deutsch, Otto Erich. *Handel: A Documentary Biography*. New York: W. W.
Norton, [1955].

Dietz, *Chorfuge*

Dietz, Hanns-Bertold. *Die Chorfuge bei G. F. Händel: Ein Beitrag zur Kom-
positionstechnik des Barock*. Tutzing: Hans Schneider, 1961.

DLL

Kosch, Wilhelm; Berger, Bruno; and Rupp, Heinz, eds. *Deutsches Literatur-
Lexikon: Biographisch-bibliographisches Handbuch*. 4 vols. to date. 3d ed.
Bern: Francke, 1968–.

DMP

Engel, Hans, ed. *Denkmäler der Musik in Pommern: "Pommersche Meister des
16. bis 18. Jahrhunderts."* 5 vols. Kassel: Bärenreiter, 1930–36. Vol. 5,
*Vom reichen Manne und Lazaro: Actus musicus de Divite et Lazaro (Das
erste deutsche Oratorium), Stettin, 1649*, by Andreas Fromm, 1936.

DTB

Sandberger, Adolf, ed. *Denkmäler der Tonkunst in Bayern*. 38 vols. 1900–38.
(Series 2 of *DDT*.) Vol. 7/1, *Ausgewählte Werke*, by Johann Staden, edited
by Eugen Schmitz, Leipzig: Breitkopf & Härtel, 1906. Vol. 13, *Ausgewählte
Werke*, by Johannes Erasmus Kindermann, edited by Felix Schreiber, Leip-
zig: Breitkopf & Härtel, 1913. Vols. 29–30, *Cantiones sacrae*, by Andreas
Raselius, edited by Ludwig Roselius, Augsburg: Benno Filser, 1931.

DTÖ
  Schenk, Erich, ed. *Denkmäler der Tonkunst in Österreich*. 1894–. Vol. 16, *Dialogi oder Gespräche einer gläubigen Seele mit Gott*, by Andreas Hammerschmidt, edited by A. W. Schmidt, Graz: Akademische Druck- und Verlagsanstalt, 1959.

Dürr, "Chronologie"
  Dürr, Alfred. "Zur Chronologie der Leipziger Vokalwerke J. S. Bachs," *Bach-Jahrbuch* 44 (1957): 5–163.

Dürr, "Himmelfahrts-Oratorium"
  ———. "Der Eingangsatz zu Bachs Himmelfahrts-Oratorium und seine Vorlage." In *Hans Albrecht in memoriam: Gedenkschrift von Freunden und Schülern*, edited by Wilfried Brennecke and Hans Haase, pp. 121–26.

Dürr, *Weihnachts-Oratorium*
  ———. *Johann Sebastian Bach: Weihnachts-Oratorium BWV 248*. Meisterwerke der Musikgeschichte, vol. 8. Munich: Wilhelm Fink, 1967.

Edelhoff, "Abendmusiken"
  Edelhoff, Heinrich. "Die Abendmusiken in Lübeck." *Musik und Kirche* 8 (1936): 53–58, 122–27.

EDM
  Staatliches Institut für deutsche Musikforschung, ed. *Das Erbe deutscher Musik*. Series 1, Reichsdenkmale. Leipzig: Breitkopf & Härtel, 1935–42. Abteilung 9, Oratorium und Kantate, edited by the Musikgeschichtliche Kommission, Kassel: Bärenreiter, 1957–. Vol. 50 (Abteilung Oratorium und Kantate, vol. 4), *Geistliche Konzerte Nr. 1–11 aus dem Evangelien-Jahrgang*, by Augustin Pfleger, edited by Fritz Stein, 1961. Vol. 64 (Abteilung Oratorium und Kantate, vol. 5), *Geistliche Konzerte Nr. 12–23 aus dem Evangelien-Jahrgang*, by Augustin Pfleger, edited by Fritz Stein, 1964. Vol. 65 (Abteilung Oratorium und Kantate, vol. 6), *Geistliche Harmonien*, 1665, by Christoph Bernard, edited by Otto Drechsler and Martin Geck, 1972.

EECM
  Harrison, Frank L., and Doe, Paul, eds. *Early English Church Music*. London: Stainer and Bell, 1963–. Vol. 7, *English Sacred Music*, by Robert Ramsey, edited by Edward Thompson, 1967.

Eggebrecht, *Schütz*
  Eggebrecht, Hans Heinrich. *Heinrich Scuütz: Musicus poeticus*. Kleine Vandenhoeck-Reihe, vol. 84. Göttingen: Vandenhoeck & Ruprecht, 1959.

Eggert, *Weise*
  Eggert, Walther. *Christian Weise und seine Bühne*. Germanisch und Deutsch; Studien zur Sprache unk Kultur, vol. 9. Berlin: Walter de Gruyter, 1935.

Faber du Faur, *Literature*
  Faber du Faur, Curt von. *German Baroque Literature: A Catalogue of the Collection in the Yale University Library*. 2 vols. New Haven: Yale University Press, 1958–69.

Fischer, "Passionskomposition"
  Fischer, Kurt von. "Zur Geschichte der Passionskomposition des 16. Jahrhunderts in Italien." *Archiv für Musikwissenschaft* 11 (1954): 189–205.

Flemming, *Oper*
  Flemming, Willi, ed. *Die Oper*. Deutsche Literatur: Sammlung literarischer Kunst- und Kulturdenkmäler in Entwicklungsreihen. Reihe Barock, Barockdrama, vol. 5. Leipzig: Philipp Reclam jun., 1933.

Flemming, *Oratorium*

———. *Oratorium, Festspiel*. Deutsche Literatur: Sammlung literarischer Kunst- und Kulturdenkmäler in Entwicklungsreihen. Reihe Barock, Barockdrama, vol. 6. Leipzig: Philipp Reclam jun., 1933.

Flower, *Handel*

Flower, Newman. *George Frideric Handel: His Personality and His Times*. Rev. ed. London: Cassell, 1959.

Fogle, "Vocal Music"

Fogle, James C. B. "Vocal Music in Seventeenth-Century England as Reflected in British Museum MS Add. 11608." Ph.D. dissertation, University of North Carolina at Chapel Hill, in progress.

Franck, *Evangeliensprüche*

Franck, Melchior. *Deutsche Evangeliensprüche für das Kirchenjahr, 1623, für gemischten Chor*. Edited by Konrad Ameln. Kassel: Bärenreiter, [1937].

Franz, *Klaj*

Franz, Albin. *Johann Klaj: Ein Beitrag zur deutschen Literaturgeschichte des 17. Jahrhunderts*. Beiträge zur deutschen Literaturwissenschaft, vol. 6. 1908. Reprint. New York: Johnson Reprint, 1968.

Frederichs, *Brockespassionen*

Frederichs, Henning. *Das Verhältnis von Text und Musik in den Brockespassionen Keisers, Händels, Telemanns und Matthesons, mit einer Einführung in ihre Entstehungs- und Rezeptionsgeschichte sowie den Bestand ihrer literarischen und musikalischen Quellen*. Musikwissenschaftliche Schriften, vol. 9. Munich: Emil Katzbichler, 1975.

Geck, "Authentizität"

Geck, Martin. "Die Authentizität des Vokalwerks Dietrich Buxtehudes in quellenkritischer Sicht." *Die Musikforschung* 14 (1961): 393–415.

Geck, *Buxtehude*

———. *Die Vokalmusik Dietrich Buxtehudes und der frühe Pietismus*. Kieler Schriften zur Musikwissenschaft, vol. 15. Kassel: Bärenreiter, 1965.

Geck, "Nochmals"

———. "Nochmals: Die Authentizität des Vokalwerks Dietrich Buxtehudes in quellenkritischer Sicht." *Die Musikforschung* 16 (1963): 175–81.

Geiringer, *Bach*

Geiringer, Karl, and Geiringer, Irene. *Bach: The Culmination of an Era*. New York: Oxford University Press, 1966.

GK

Das geistliche Konzert. Stuttgart: Hänssler Verlag, [195–?]. No. 74, *Wer wälzet uns den Stein von des Grabes Tür*, by Andreas Hammerschmidt, edited by Herbert Hildebrandt, 1962. No. 80, *Oster-Dialog*, by Andreas Hammerschmidt, edited by Diethard Hellmann, [196–].

Göhler, "Messkataloge"

Göhler, Karl Albert. "Die Messkataloge im Dienst der musikalischen Geschichtsforschung." *Sammelbände der internationalin Musikgesellschaft* 3 (1901–4): 294–376.

Graupner, *Schelle*

Graupner, Friedrich. *Das Werk des Thomaskantors Johann Schelle (1648–1701)*. Wolfenbüttel and Berlin: Georg Kallmeyer, 1929.

Greene, *Deborah*

Greene, Maurice. *The Song of Deborah and Barak: An Oratorio*. Edited by Frank Dawes. German translation by Hilde Volhard. London: Schott, 1956.

Grout, *Opera*
    Grout, Donald J. *A Short History of Opera.* 2d ed. New York: Columbia University Press, 1965.
Grove-5
    Blom, Eric, ed. *Grove's Dictionary of Music and Musicians.* 9 vols. and 1 supp. 5th ed. London: Macmillan; New York: St. Martin's Press, 1954–61.
Gudger, "Concertos" (art.)
    Gudger, William O. "Handel's Organ Concertos: A Guide to Performance Based on the Primary Sources," *Diapason* 64 (1973): 3–7.
Gudger, "Concertos" (diss.)
    ———. "The Organ Concertos of G. F. Handel: A Study Based on the Primary Sources." 2 vols. Ph.D. dissertation, Yale University, 1973.
Günther, *Selle*
    Günther, Siegfried. *Die geistliche Konzertmusik von Thomas Selle nebst einer Biographie.* Giessen: Herm. Prinz [at] Bückeburg, 1935.
Haas, "Walther"
    Haas, Robert. "Zu Walther's Choralpassion nach Matthäus." *Archiv für Musikwissenschaft* 4 (1922): 24–47.
Haberlen, "Oratorio Passion"
    Haberlen, John Black. "A Critical Survey of the Oratorio Passion from 1650 to 1700." D.M.A. dissertation, University of Illinois, in progress.
Hall, "Smith"
    Hall, James S. "John Christopher Smith: Handel's Friend and Secretary." *The Musical Times* 96 (1955): 132–34.
Handel, *Athalia*
    Handel, George Frideric. *Athalia: An Oratorio or Sacred Drama.* Edited by Anthony Lewis. London: Oxford University Press, 1967.
Handel, *Ausgabe*
    ———. *Hallische Händel-Ausgabe (Kritische Gesamtausgabe).* Edited by the Georg-Friedrich-Händel-Gesellschaft. 4 series, 29 vols. to date. Kassel: Bärenreiter, 1955–. *Kritischer Bericht.* Kassel: Bärenreiter, 1958–. *Klavierauszüge.* Kassel: Bärenreiter, 1956–.
Handel, *Israel*-M
    ———. *Israel in Egypt: A Sacred Oratorio.* Edited and the pianoforte accompaniment arranged by Felix Mendelssohn-Bartholdy. London: Novello, Ewer, n. d.
Handel, *Jephtha*-A
    ———. *Das Autograph des Oratoriums "Jephtha" von G. F. Händel.* Fest-Ausgabe der deutschen Händel-Gesellschaft zur zweiten Säcularfeier am 23. Februar, 1885. Facsimile ed. Hamburg: Strumper, 1885.
Handel, *Messiah*-A
    ———. *Das Autograph des "Messias."* Edited by Friedrich Chrysander. 3 vols. Facsimile ed. Hamburg: Strumper, 1889–92.
Handel, *Messiah*-C
    ———. *Messiah: An Oratorio.* Edited by Jacob Maurice Coopersmith. New York: C. Fischer, 1947.
Handel, *Messiah*-CS
    ———. *Handel's Conducting Score of Messiah, Reproduced in Facsimile.* London: Novello, 1974.
Handel, *Messiah*-M
    ———. *Messiah: An Oratorio.* Edited by Alfred Mann. Documents of the Musical Past, no. 6. 3 vols. [New Brunswick, N. J.]: Rutgers University Press, 1959–65.

Handel, *Messiah*-S

⸻. *Messiah: A Sacred Oratorio*. Edited by [Harold] Watkins Shaw. London: Novello, [1965].

Handel, *Semele*

⸻. *Semele: An Opera*. Libretto by William Congreve. Edited by Anthony Lewis and Charles Mackerras. London: Oxford University Press, 1971.

Handel, *Werke*

⸻. *Werke*. Edited by Friedrich Chrysander. 96 vols. and 6 supps. Vol. 49 not published. Leipzig: Ausgabe der Deutschen Händel-Gesellschaft, 1858–1902.

Harsdörffer, *Frauenzimmer*

Harsdörffer, Georg Philipp. *Frauenzimmer Gesprächspiele*. Edited by Irmgard Böttcher. Deutsche Neudrucke, Reihe Barock, vols. 13–20. Facsimile ed. Tübingen: Max Niemeyer, 1968–69.

Herbage, "Oratorios"

Herbage, Julian. "The Oratorios." In *Händel: A Symposium*, edited by Gerald Abraham, pp. 66–131. 1954. Reprint. London: Oxford University Press, 1963.

Herbage, "Secular"

⸻. "The Secular Oratorios and Cantatas." In *Händel: A Symposium*, edited by Gerald Abraham, pp. 132–55. 1954. Reprint. London: Oxford University Press, 1963.

Heuss, "Salomo"

Heuss, Alfred. "Über Händels 'Salomo,' insbesondere die Chöre." *Zeitschrift für Musik* 92 (1925): 339–43.

Heuss, "Susanna"

⸻. "Die Braut- und Hochzeitsarie in Händel's 'Susanna.'" *Zeitschrift der internationalen Musikgesellschaft* 14 (1912–13): 207–14.

HMT

Eggebrecht, Hans Heinrich, ed. *Handwörterbuch der musikalischen Terminologie*. Wiesbaden: Franz Steiner, [1972–].

Hörner, *Telemann*

Hörner, Hans. *Gg. Ph. Telemanns Passionsmusiken: Ein Beitrag zur Geschichte der Passionsmusik in Hamburg*. Borna-Leipzig: Universitätsverlag von Robert Noske, 1933.

Hofmann, "Schütz" (I)

Hofmann, Klaus. "Zwei Abhandlungen zur Weihnachtshistorie von Heinrich Schütz. I: Die konzertierenden Instrumente im 4. Intermedium." *Musik und Kirche* 40 (1970): 325–30.

Hofmann, "Schütz" (II)

⸻. "Zwei Abhandlungen zur Weihnachtshistorie von Heinrich Schütz. II: Introduction und Beschluss—Zur Besetzung des Instrumentalchors." *Musik und Kirche* 41 (1971): 15–20.

Holst, "Weihnachts-Oratorium"

Holst, Ortwin von. "Turba-Chöre des Weihnachts-Oratoriums und der Markuspassion." *Musik und Kirche* 38 (1968): 229–33.

Horneffer, "Rosenmüller"

Horneffer, August. "Verzeichnis der Werke Johann Rosenmüller's." *Monatschefte für Musikgeschichte* 31 (1899): 45–47, 49–62, 65–69.

Huber, *Motivsymbolik*

Huber, Walter Simon. *Motivsymbolik bei Heinrich Schütz: Versuch einer morphologischen Systematik der Schützschen Melodik*. Basel: Bärenreiter, 1961.

Hudemann, *Dialogkomposition*
   Hudemann, Hans-Olaf. *Die protestantische Dialogkomposition im 17. Jahrhundert*. Freiburg im Breisgau: Rotaprint-Druck., 1941.
Ilgner, *Weckmann*
   Ilgner, Gerhard. *Matthias Weckmann, ca. 1619–1674: Sein Leben und seine Werke*. Kieler Beiträge zur Musikwissenschaft, vol. 6. Wolfenbüttel and Berlin: Georg Kallmeyer, 1939.
Israël, *Frankfurt*
   Israël, Carl., comp. *Frankfurter Concert-Cronik von 1713–1780*. Neujahrs-Blatt des Vereins für Geschichte und Altertumskunde zu Frankfurt am Main für das Jahr 1876. Frankfort on the Main: Verein für Geschichte und Altertumskunde, 1876.
Kade, *Passionskomposition*
   Kade, Otto, *Die ältere Passionskomposition bis zum Janre 1631*. 1893. Reprint. Hildesheim: Georg Olms, 1971.
Kaiser, *Mitternacht*
   Kaiser, Marianne. *Mitternacht—Zeidler—Weise: Das protestantische Schultheater nach 1648 im Kampf gegen höfische Kultur und absolutistisches Regiment*. Palestra: Untersuchungen aus der deutschen und englischen Philologie und Literaturgeschichte, vol. 259. Göttingen: Vandenhoeck & Ruprecht, 1972.
Kantate
   Grischkat, Hans, ed. *Die Kantate: Eine Sammlung geistlicher Musik für Chor und Instrumente*. Stuttgart-Hohenheim: Hänssler Verlag, [195–]. No. 155, *Es begab sich aber zu der Zeit (Weihnachtshistorie)*, by Thomas Selle, edited by Klaus Vetter, 1963.
Karstädt, *Abendmusiken*
   Karstädt, Georg. *Die "Extraordinairen" Abendmusiken Dietrich Buxtehudes*. Veröffentlichungen der Stadtbibliothek Lübeck, new series, vol. 5. Lübeck: Max Schmidt-Römhild, 1962.
Karstädt, "Buxtehude-Forschung"
   ———. "Neue Ergebnisse zur Buxtehude-Forschung." In *Bericht über den siebenten internationalen musikwissenschaftlichen Kongress Köln 1958*, by International Musicological Society, edited by Gerald Abraham, Suzanne Clercx-Lejeune, Hellmut Federhofer, and Wilhelm Pfannkuch, pp. 152–53. Kassel: Bärenreiter, 1959.
Karstädt, *Bux WV*
   ———, ed. *Thematisch- Systematisches Verzeichnis der Musikalischen Werke von Dietrich Buxtehude: Buxtehude-Werke-Verzeichnis (Bux WV)*. Wiesbaden: Breitkopf und Härtel, 1974.
Karstädt, "Textbuch"
   ———. "Das Textbuch zum 'Templum Honoris' von Buxtehude." *Die Musikforschung* 10 (1957): 506–8.
Keller, *Weihnachtsdichtung*
   Keller, Martin. *Johann Klajs Weihnachtsdichtung: Das 'Freudengedichte' von 1650, mit einer Einführung seinen Quellen gegenübergesetzt und kommentiert*. Philologische Studien und Quellen, vol. 53. Berlin: Erich Schmidt, 1971.
Kliewer, "Dialogues"
   Kliewer, Jonah C. "The German Sacred Dialogues of the Seventeenth Century." D.M.A. dissertation, University of Southern California, 1970.

Krickeberg, *Kantorat*
  Krickeberg, Dieter. *Das protestantische Kantorat im 17. Jahrhundert: Studien zum Amt des deutschen Kantors.* Berliner Studien zur Musikwissenschaft, vol. 6. Berlin: Merseburger, 1965.
Krüger, *Hamburg*
  Krüger, Liselotte. *Die Hamburgische Musikorganisation im XVII. Jahrhundert.* Sammlung Musikwissenschaftlicher Abhandlungen, vol. 12. Strassburg: Heitz, 1933.
Krummacher, *Choralbearbeitungen*
  Krummacher, Friedhelm. *Die Überlieferung der Choralbearbeitungen in der frühen evangelischen Kantate: Untersuchungen zum Handschriftenrepertoire evangelischer Figuralmusik im späten 17. und beginnenden 18. Jahrhundert.* Berliner Studien zur Musikwissenschaft: Veröffentlichungen des Musikwissenschaftlichen Instituts der Freien Universität Berlin, vol. 10. Berlin: Merseburger, 1965.
Krummacher, "Weckmann"
  ———. "Zur Quellenlage von Matthias Weckmanns geistliche Vokalwerken." In *Gemeinde Gottes in dieser Welt: Festgabe für Friedrich-Wilhelm Krummacher zum sechzigsten Geburtstag,* edited by Friedrich Bartsch and Werner Rautenberg, pp. 188–218. Berlin: Evangelische Verlagsanstalt, [1961].
Lang, *Handel*
  Lang, Paul Henry. *George Frideric Handel.* New York: W. W. Norton, 1966.
Lang, *Western*
  ———. *Music in Western Civilization.* New York: W. W. Norton, 1941.
Larsen, *"Esther"*
  Larsen, Jens Peter. "*Esther* and the Origin of the Handelian Oratorio Tradition." In Larsen, "Studies," pp. 7–14.
Larsen, "Geschichte"
  ———. "Zur Geschichte der 'Messias'-Aufführungstraditionen." *Händel-Jahrbuch* 13–14 (1967–68): 13–24.
Larsen, *Handel's "Messiah"*
  ———. *Handel's "Messiah": Origins, Composition, Sources.* London: Adam & Charles Black, 1957.
Larsen, "Studies"
  ———. "Handel Studies." *Journal of the American Choral Foundation,* vol. 15, no. 1 (Jan. 1972), pp. 1–48.
Larsen, "Tempoprobleme"
  ———. "Tempoprobleme bei Händel, dargestellt am Messias." In *Händel-Ehrung der Deutschen Demokratischen Republik, Halle 11.–19. April 1959, Konferenzbericht,* pp. 141–53. Edited by Walther Siegmund-Schultze. Leipzig: Deutscher Verlag für Musik, 1961.
Leichtentritt, *Händel*
  Leichtentritt, Hugo. *Händel.* Stuttgart: Deutsche Verlags-Anstalt, 1924.
Lott, "Passionskomposition"
  Lott, Walter. "Zur Geschichte der Passionskomposition von 1650–1800." *Archiv für Musikwissenschaft* 3 (1921): 285–320.
Lundgren, "Lorentz"
  Lundgren, Bo. "Johan Lorentz in Kopenhagen—organista nulli in Europa secundus." In *Bericht über den siebenten Internationalen Musicwissenschaftlichen Kongress Köln 1958,* edited by Gerald Abraham, Suzanne Clercx-Lejeune, Hellmut Federhofer, and Wilhelm Pfannkuch, pp. 183–85. Kassel: Bärenreiter, 1959.

Maertens, "Kapitänsmusiken"
  Maertens, Willi. "Georg Philipp Telemanns Hamburger 'Kapitänsmusiken,'"
  In *Festschrift für Walter Wiora zum 30. Dezember 1966*, edited by Ludwig
  Finscher and Christoph-Hellmut Mahling, pp. 335–41. Kassel: Bärenreiter,
  1967.
Mainwaring, *Memoirs*
  [Mainwaring, John.] *Memoirs of the Life of the Late George Frederic Handel*.
  London: R. & J. Dodsley, 1760.
Malinowski, "Oratorio Passion"
  Malinowsky, Stanley A., Jr. "The Baroque Oratorio Passion." Ph.D. disserta-
  tion, Cornell University, in progress.
MAM
  Federhofer, Hellmut, ed. *Musik alter Meister: Beiträge zur Musik- und Kul-
  tergeschichte Innerösterreichs*. Graz: Akademische Druck- und Verlags-
  anstalt, 1954–. Vol 4, *Historia des Leidens und Sterbens unsers Herrn und
  Heilands (Matthäuspassion)*, by Johannes Herold, edited by Hans Joachim
  Moser, 1955.
Mann, "Handel Research"
  Mann, Alfred, and Knapp, J. Merrill. "The Present State of Handel Research."
  Acta Musicologica 41 (1969): 4–26.
Mann, "Messiah"
  Mann, Alfred. "Messiah: The Verbal Text." In *Festkrift Jens Peter Larsen*,
  edited by Nils Schiørring, Henrik Glahn, and Carsten E. Hatting, pp. 181–
  88. Copenhagen: Wilhelm Hansen, 1972.
Marpurg, *Singcomposition*
  Marpurg, Friedrich Wilhelm. *Anleitung zur Singcomposition*. Berlin: Gottlieb
  August Lange, 1758.
Massenkeil, *Oratorium*
  Massenkeil, Günther. *Das Oratorium*. Das Musikwerk, no. 37. Cologne: Arno
  Volk Verlag Hans Gerig, 1970.
Massenkeil, *Oratorium*-Eng.
  ———. *The Oratorio*. Translated by A. C. Howie. Anthology of Music, no.
  37. Cologne: Arno Volk Verlag Hans Gerig, 1970.
Mathieu, *Dom*
  Mathieu, Kai. *Der Hamburger Dom*. Hamburg: Museum für Hamburgische
  Geschichte, 1973.
Matthäus, "Evangelienhistorie"
  Matthäus, Wolfgang. "Die Evangelienhistorie von Johann Walter bis Heinrich
  Schütz mit Ausschluss der Passion." Ph.D. dissertation, Johann Wolfgang
  Goethe-Universität, Frankfort on the Main, 1942.
Mattheson, *Capellmeister*
  Mattheson, [Johann]. *Der vollkommene Capellmeister*. 1739. Reprint. Edited
  by Margarete Riemann. Documenta musicologica, series 1, vol. 5. Kassel:
  Bärenreiter, 1954.
Mattheson, *"Capellmeister"*-Eng.
  Harriss, Ernest Charles. "Johann Mattheson's *Der vollkommene Capellmeis-
  ter*: A Translation and Commentary." 3 vols. Ph.D. dissertation, George
  Peabody College for Teachers, 1969.
Mattheson, *Critica*
  Mattheson, [Johann]. *Critica musica*. 2 vols. 1722–25. Reprint (2 vols in 1).
  Amsterdam: F. A. M. Knuf, 1964.

Mattheson, *Ehren-Pforte*

————. *Grundlage einer Ehren-Pforte, woran der tüchtigsten Capellmeister, Componisten, Musikgelehrten, Tonkünstler u. Leben, Werke, Verdienste u. erscheinen sollen.* Hamburg, 1740. Edited by Max Schneider. Berlin: Kommissionsverlag von Leo Liepmannssohn, 1910.

Mattheson, *Patriot*

————. *Der musikalische Patriot.* Hamburg: n. p., 1728.

Maxton, "Abendmusik"

Maxton, Willy, "Mitteilungen über eine vollständige Abendmusik Dietrich Buxtehudes." *Zeitschrift für Musikwissenschaft* 10 (1927–28): 387–95.

Maxton, "Authentizität"

————. "Die Authentizität des 'Jüngsten Gerichts' von Dietrich Buxtehude." *Die Musikforschung* 15 (1962): 382–94.

Maxton, "Denkmäler"

————. "Können die 'Denkmäler deutscher Tonkunst' uns heute noch als Quellen zweiter Ordnung dienen?" In *Bericht über den Internationalen Musikwissenschaftlichen Kongress Kassel 1962*, edited by Georg Reichert and Martin Just, pp. 295–98. Kassel: Bärenreiter, 1963.

MD

Akademie der Wissenschaften und der Literatur in Mainz; Veröffentlichungen der Kommission für Musikwissenschaft. *Musikalische Denkmäler.* 6 vols. to date. Mainz: B. Schott's Söhne, 1955–. Vol. 1, *Oberitalienische Figuralpassionen des 16. Jahrhunderts*, edited by Arnold Schmitz, 1955.

Meier, *Chorsätze*

Meier, Heinz. *Typus und Funktion der Chorsätze in Georg Friedrich Händels Oratorien.* Neue musikgeschichtliche Forschungen, vol. 5. Wiesbaden: Breitkopf & Härtel, 1971.

Menke, *Telemann*

Menke, Werner. *Das Vokalwerk Georg Philipp Telemann's: Überlieferung und Zeitfolge.* Erlanger Beiträge zur Musikwissenschaft, vol. 3. Kassel: Bärenreiter, 1942.

Mersmann, "Weihnachtsspiel"

Mersmann, Hans. "Ein Weihnachtsspiel des Görlitzer Gymnasiums von 1668." *Archiv für Musikwissenschaft* 1 (1918–19): 244–66.

MGG

Blume, Friedrich, ed. *Die Musik in Geschichte und Gegenwart.* 14 vols. and 1 supp. to date. Kassel: Bärenreiter, 1949–.

Miller, "Oratorios"

Miller, Kenneth Eugene. "A Study of Selected German Baroque Oratorios." Ph.D. dissertation, Northwestern University, 1963.

Mitjana, *Upsala*

Mitjana, Rafael, and Davidsson, Åke, eds. *Catalogue critique et descriptif des imprimés de musique des XVIᵉ et XVIIᵉ siècles conservés à la Bibliothèque de l'Université Royale d'Upsala.* 3 vols. Upsala: Almqvist and Wiksell, 1911–51.

Möller, "Weihnachtsoratorium"

Möller, Hans-Jürgen. "Das Wort-Ton-Verhältnis im Weihnachtsoratorium Johann Sebastian Bachs." *Neue Zeitschrift für Musik* 133 (1972): 686–91.

Moser, *Evangelium*

Moser, Hans Joachim. *Die Mehrstimmige Vertonung des Evangeliums.* 1 vol. Veröffentlichungen der Staatlichen Akademie für Kirchen- und Schulmusik Berlin, vol. 2. 2d ed. 1931. Reprint. Hildesheim: Georg Olms, 1968.

Moser, "Generalbasspassion"

———. "Aus der Frühgeschichte der deutschen Generalbasspassion." *Jahrbuch der Musikbibliothek Peters* 24 (1917): 18–30.

Moser, *Österreich*

———. *Die Musik im frühevangelischen Österreich*. Kassel: Johann Philipp Hinnenthal, 1954.

Moser, *Schütz*

———. *Heinrich Schütz: Sein Leben und Werk*. 2d ed. Kassel: Bärenreiter, 1954.

Moser, *Schütz*-Eng.

———. *Heinrich Schütz: His Life and Work*. Translated from the 2d ed. by Carl F. Pfatteicher. St. Louis: Concordia Publishing House, 1959.

Moser, "Unbekannte"

———. "Unbekannte Werke von Heinrich Schütz." *Zeitschrift für Musikwissenschaft* 17 (1935): 332–42.

Müller-Blattau, J., *Händel*

Müller-Blattau, Joseph. *Georg Friedrich Händel*. Die grossen Meister der Musik. Potsdam: Akademische Verlagsgesellschaft Athenaion, 1933.

Münnich, Review

Münnich, Richard. Review of Scheurleer, *Amsterdam*. *Zeitschrift der internationalen Musikgesellschaft* 5 (1904):387–94.

Myers, *Handel*

Myers, Robert Manson. *Handel, Dryden & Milton*. 1956. Reprint. Folcroft, Pa.: Folcroft Press, 1970.

Myers, *Handel*

———. *Handel, Dryden, & Milton. Being a Series of Observations on the Poems of Dryden and Milton, as Alter'd and Adapted by Various Hands, and Set to Music by Mr. Handel. To which are Added, Authentick Texts of Several of Mr. Handel's Oratorios*. London: Bowes & Bowes in Covent Garden, 1956.

Myers, *Handel's "Messiah"*

———. *Handel's "Messiah": A Touchstone of Taste*. New York: Macmillan, 1948.

Nagel, "Hilton"

Nagel, Wilibald. "Ein Dialog Joh Hilton's." *Monatshefte für Musikgeschichte* 29 (1897): 121–34.

Nausch, *Pfleger*

Nausch, Annmarie. *Augustin Pfleger: Leben und Werke. Ein Beitrag zur Entwicklungsgeschichte der Kantate im 17. Jahrhundert*. Schriften des Landesinstituts für Musikforschung Kiel, vol. 4. Kassel: Bärenreiter, 1954.

Neumann, *Kantaten*

Neumann, Werner. *Handbuch der Kantaten Johann Sebastian Bachs*. 4th rev. ed. Wiesbaden: Breitkopf & Härtel, 1971.

[Neumeister-Hunold], *Allerneueste*

[Neumeister, Erdmann.]. *Der allerneueste Art zur reinen und galanten Poesie zu gelangen . . . von Menantes*. Hamburg: Johann Wolfgang Fickweiler, 1712.

Noack, *Briegel*

Noack, Elisabeth. *Wolfgang Carl Briegel: Ein Barockkomponist in seiner Zeit*. Berlin: Merseburger, 1963.

Noack, *Darmstadt*

———. *Musikgeschichte Darmstadts vom Mittelalter bis zur Goethezeit*. Beiträge zur Mittelrheinischen Musikgeschichte, vol. 8. Mainz: B. Schott's Söhne, 1967.

Noack, "Erfurt"

———. "Die Bibliothek der Michaeliskirche zu Erfurt: Ein Beitrag zur Geschichte der musikalischen Formen und der Aufführungspraxis in der zweiten Hälfte des 17. Jahrhunderts." *Archiv für Musikwissenschaft* 7 (1925): 65–116.

Obrecht, *Werken*

Obrecht, Jacob. *Werken*. Edited by Johannes Wolf. 10 vols. Amsterdam: G. Alsbach, 1912–21.

Orcibal, *Esther*

Orcibal, Jean. *La genèse d'Esther & d'Athalie*. Autour de Racine, vol. 1. Paris: Librairie Philosophique J. Vrin, 1950.

Org

Seiffert, Max, ed. *Organum: Ausgewählte älterer vokale und instrumentale Meisterwerke*. Series 1, Geistliche Gesangmusik für Solo- oder Chorstimmen mit oder ohne Begleitung. Leipzig: F. Kistner & C. F. W. Siegel, [1924–]. Vol. 21, *Dialog von Tobias und Raguel*, by Johann Rosenmüller [*Sic*. Probably Matthias Weckmann], 1930.

Osthoff, "Michael"

Osthoff, Helmuth. "Die Historien Rogier Michaels (Dresden 1602): Ein Beitrag zur Geschichte der Historienkomposition." In *Festschrift für Arnold Schering zum sechzigsten Geburtstag*, edited by Helmuth Osthoff, Walter Serauky, and Adam Adrio, pp. 166–79. Berlin: A. Glas, 1937.

Oxford

Hartnoll, Phyllis, ed. *The Oxford Companion to the Theatre*. 3d ed. London: Oxford University Press, 1967.

Pirro, *Buxtehude*

Pirro, André. *Dietrich Buxtehude*. Paris: Fischbacher (Société Anonyme), 1913.

Prautzsch, "Echo-Arie"

Prautzsch, Ludwig. "Die Echo-Arie und andere symbolische und volkstümliche Züge in Bachs Weihnachtsoratorium." *Musik und Kirche* 38 (1968): 221–29.

PubAPTM

Eitner, Robert, ed. for the Gesellschaft für Musikforschung. *Publikationen älterer praktischer und theoretischer Musikwerke*. 29 vols. 1873–1905. Reprint. New York: Broude, [1966]. Vol. 22, *Zwanzig deutsche geistliche vierstimmige Lieder . . . , die Passion nach dem Evangelisten Johannes . . . und die Passion nach dem 22. Psalmen Davids*, edited by Anton Halm and Robert Eitner, 1898.

Purcell, *Works*

Purcell, Henry. *The Works of Henry Purcell*. Edited under the supervision of the Purcell Society. 32 vols. London: Novello, Ewer, 1878–1962.

Purdie, *Judith*

Purdie, Edna. *The Story of Judith in German and English Literature*. Bibliothèque de la revue de littérature comparée, vol. 39. Paris: Librarie Ancienne Honoré Champion, 1927.

Racine, *Oeuvres*

    Racine, [Jean-Baptiste]. *Oeuvres complètes*. Bibliothèque de la Pléiade, no. 5. 2 vols. Paris: Gallimard, 1951.

Raugel, *Oratorio*

    Raugel, Félix. *L'Oratorio: Forms, écoles et oeuvres musicales*. Paris: Larousse, 1948.

Rauschning, *Danzig*

    Rauschning, Hermann. *Geschichte der Musik und Musikpflege in Danzig, von den Angängen bis zur Auflösung der Kirchenkapellen*. Quellen und Darstellungen zur Geschichte Westpreussens, vol. 15. Danzig: Kommissionsverlag der Danziger-Verlags-Gesellschaft (Paul Rosenberg), 1931.

RDLg

    Kohlschmidt, Werner; Mohr, Wolfgang; and Kanzog, Klaus, eds. *Reallexikon der deutschen Literaturgeschichte*. 2 vols. to date. 2d ed. Berlin: Walter de Gruyter, 1955–.

Reese, *Renaissance*

    Reese, Gustave. *Music in the Renaissance*. Rev. ed. New York: W. W. Norton, 1959.

Reissmann, *Geschichte*

    Reissmann, August. *Allgemeine Geschichte der Musik*. 3 vols. Munich: Friedrich Bruckmann, 1863–64.

Riemann

    Riemann, Hugo. *Riemann Musik Lexikon*. Edited by Wilibald Gurlitt. 3 vols. 12th ed. Mainz: B. Schott's Söhne; New York: Schott Music Corp., 1959–67.

Sachs, *Berlin*

    Sachs, Curt. *Musikgeschichte der Stadt Berlin bis zum Jahre 1800*. Berlin: Gebrüder Paetel, 1908.

Sadie, *Handel*

    Sadie, Stanley. *Handel*. London: John Calder, 1962.

Sandberger, "Nürnberg"

    Sandberger, Adolf. "Zur Geschichte der Oper in Nürnberg in der zweiten Hälfte des 17. und zu Anfang des 18. Jahrhunderts." *Archiv für Musikwissenschaft* 1 (1918–19): 84–107.

Sasse, *Händel*

    Sasse, Konrad. *Händel Bibliographie*. 2d ed. Leipzig: VEB Deutscher Verlag für Musik, 1967.

Scheibe, *Compendium*

    Scheibe, Johann Adolph. "Compendium musices theoretico-practicum: Das ist kurzer Begriff derer nöthingsten Compositions-Regeln." Edited by Peter Benary. Appendix of *Die deutsche Kompositionslehre des 18. Jahrhunderts*, by Peter Benary. Jenaer Beiträge zur Musikforschung, vol. 3. Leipzig: Breitkopf & Härtel, [1961?].

Scheibe, *Critische*

    ————. *Der critische Musicus*. 2 vols. Hamburg: [vol. 1] Thomas von Wierings Erben, 1738; [vol. 2] Rudolph Beneke, 1740.

Scheidt, *Werke*

    Scheidt, Samuel. *Werke*. Edited by Gottlieb Harms and Christhard Mahrenholz. 14 vols. in 13. Hamburg: Ugrino, 1923–71. (Imprint varies.)

Schein, *Werke*

    Schein, Johann Hermann. *Sämtliche Werke*. Edited by Arthur Prüfer. 7 vols. Leipzig: Breitkopf & Härtel, 1901–23.

Schelle, *Himmel*
Schelle, Johann. *Vom Himmel hoch: Actus musicus auf Weih-Nachten.* Edited by Friedrich Wanek. Mainz: B. Schott's Söhne, 1969.

Schering, *Beispielen*
Schering, Arnold, ed. *Geschichte der Musik in Beispielen.* Leipzig: Brietkopf & Härtel, 1931.

Schering, "Entlehnungen"
————. "Zum Tema: Händel's Entlehnungen." *Zeitschrift der internationalen Musikgesellschaft* 9 (1907–8): 244–47.

Schering, "Händel"
————. "Händel und der protestantische Choral." *Händel-Jahrbuch* 1 (1928): 27–40.

Schering, *Leipzig*
————, and Wustmann, Rudolf. *Musikgeschichte Leipzigs.* 3 vols. Leipzig: Fr. Kistner & C. F. W. Siegel, 1926–41. Vol. 2, *Musikgeschichte Leipzigs . . . von 1650 bis 1723.*

Schering, *Oratorium*
————. *Geschichte des Oratoriums.* Kleine Handbücher der Musikgeschichte nach Gattungen, vol. 3. 1911. Reprint. Hildesheim: Georg Olms, 1966.

Scheurleer, *Amsterdam*
Scheurleer, D. F. *Het Musiekleven van Amsterdam in de zeventiende eeuw.* The Hague: Martinus Nijhoff; W. P. van Stockum & Zoon, 1900–1904.

Schmidt, "Passionshistorie"
Schmidt, Günter. "Grundsätzliche Bemerkungen zur Geschichte der Passionshistorie." *Archiv für Musikwissenschaft* 17 (1960): 100–125.

Schmidt, *Schürmann*
Schmidt, Gustav Friedrich. *Die frühdeutsche Oper und die musikalische Kunst Georg Caspar Schürmann's.* 2 vols. Regensburg: Gustav Bosse, 1933–34.

Schmieder, *BWV*
Schmieder, Wolfgang, ed. *Thematisch-Systematisches Verzeichnis der musikalischen Werke von Johann Sebastian Bach: Bach-Werke-Verzeichnis (BWV).* Wiesbaden: Breitkopf & Härtel, 1966.

Schoelcher, *Handel*
Schoelcher, Victor. *The Life of Handel.* London: Tübner, 1857.

Schöne, *Barock*
Schöne, Albrecht, ed. *Das Zeitalter des Barock.* Die deutsche Literatur: Texte und Zeugnisse. 2d ed. Munich: C. H. Beck'sche Verlagsbuchhandlung, 1968.

Schütz, *Christmas*
Schütz, Heinrich. *The Christmas Story.* Edited by Arthur Mendel. New York: G. Schirmer, 1949.

Schütz, *Dialogo*
————. *Dialogo per la Pascua,* SWV 443. Facsimile of the autograph, edited by Werner Bittinger. Kassel: Bärenreiter, 1965.

Schütz, *Neue Ausgabe*
————. *Neue Ausgabe sämtlicher Werke.* Edited on behalf of the Neue Schütz-Gesellschaft. 25 vols. to date. Kassel: Bärenreiter, 1955–.

Schütz, *Werke*
————. *Sämmtliche Werke.* Edited by Philipp Spitta, Arnold Schering, and Heinrich Spitta. 16 vols. and 2 supps. Leipzig: Breitkopf & Härtel, 1885–1927.

Schwartz, "Oratorium"
Schwartz, Rudolf. "Das erste deutsche Oratorium." *Jahrbuch der Musikbibliothek Peters* 5 (1898): 61–65.

Seiffert, "Habermann"
Seiffert, Max. "Franz Johann Habermann." *Kirchenmusikalsiches Jahrbuch* 18 (1903): 81–94.
Seiffert, "Schütziana"
———. "Anecdota Schütziana." *Sammelbände der internationalen Musikgesellschaft* 1 (1899–1900): 213–18.
Seiffert, "Weckmann"
———. "Matthias Weckmann und das Collegium Musicum in Hamburg: Ein Beitrag zur deutschen Musikgeschichte des 17. Jahrhunderts." *Sammelbände der internationalen Musikgesellschaft* 2 (1900–1901): 76–132.
Serauky, *Händel*
Serauky, Walter. *Georg Friedrich Händel: Sein Leben—sein Werk*. Only vols. 3–5 published. Kassel: Bärenreiter, 1956–58.
Serauky, *Halle*
———. *Musikgeschichte der Stadt Halle*. 2 vols. Halle: Buchhandlung des Waisenhauses, 1935–40.
Serwer, "Mühlhausen"
Serwer, Howard. "'Wiedrigkeit' and 'Verdriesslichkeit' in Mühlhausen." *The Musical Quarterly* 55 (1969): 20–30.
Shaw, *Handel's "Messiah"*
Shaw, [Harold] Watkins. *A Textual and Historical Companion to Handel's "Messiah."* London: Novello, 1965.
Shield, *Rudiments*
Shield, William. *Rudiments of Thorough Bass . . . Being an Appendix to an Introduction to Harmony*. London: J. Robinson, [1815].
Siegmund-Schultze, "Arienwelt"
Siegmund-Schultze, Walther. "Die Arienwelt des 'Messias'." In *Festkrift Jens Peter Larsen*, edited by Nils Schiørring, Henrik Glahn, and Carsten E. Hatting, pp. 181–88. Copenhagen: Wilhelm Hansen, 1972.
Siegmund-Schultze, "Gedankenwelt"
———. "Die musikalische Gedankenwelt des 'Messias'." *Händel-Jahrbuch* 13–14 (1967–68): 25–42.
Sittard, *Hamburg*
Sittard, Josef. *Geschichte des Musik- und Concertwesens in Hamburg vom 14. Jahrhundert bis auf die Gegenwart*. Altona and Leipzig: A. C. Reher, 1890.
Smallman, "Dialogues"
Smallman, Basil. "Endor Revisited: English Biblical Dialogues of the Seventeenth Century." *Music and Letters* 46 (1965): 137–45.
Smallman, "Forgotten"
———. "A Forgotten Oratorio Passion." *The Musical Times* 115 (1974): 118–21.
Smallman, *Passion*
———. *The Background of Passion Music: J. S. Bach and His Predecessors*. 2d rev. and enl. ed. New York: Dover, [1970].
Smend, "Bach-Funde"
Smend, Friedrich. "Neue Bach-Funde." *Archiv für Musikforschung* 7 (1942): 1–16. Reprinted in Smend, *Bach-Studien*, pp. 137–52.
Smend, *Bach-Studien*
———. *Bach-Studien: Gesammelte Reden und Aufsätze*, edited by Christoph Wolff. Kassel: Bärenreiter, 1969.

Smend, "Himmelfahrts-Oratorium"
    _____. "Bachs Himmelfahrts-Oratorium." In *Bach Gedenkschrift 1950*, edited by Karl Matthaei, pp. 42–65. Zürich: Atlantis, 1950. Reprinted in Smend, *Bach-Studien*, pp. 195–211.

Smith, *Handel*
    Smith, William C. *Handel: A Descriptive Catalogue of the Early Editions.* London: Cassell, 1960.

Smither, "Baroque Oratorio"
    Smither, Howard E. "The Baroque Oratorio: A Report on Research Since 1945." *Acta musicologica* 48 (1976): 50–76.

Söhngen, "Abendmusiken"
    Söhngen, Oskar. "Die Lübecker Abendmusiken als kirchengeschichtliches und theologisches Problem." *Musik und Kirche* 27 (1957): 181–91.

Spagna, *Oratorii*
    Spagna, Archangelo. *Oratorii overo melodrammi sacri.* 2 vols. Rome: Gio. Francesco Buagni, 1706.

Spink, "Dialogues"
    Spink, Ian. "English Seventeenth-Century Dialogues." *Music and Letters* 38 (1957): 155–63.

Spitta, *Bach*
    Spitta, Philipp. *Johann Sebastian Bach: His Work and Influence on the Music of Germany, 1685–1750.* Translated by Clara Bell and John Alexander Fuller-Maitland. 3 vols. 1889. Reprint. London: Novello; New York: Dover, 1951.

Staden, "Seelewig"
    Staden, Sigmund Gottlieb [Sigismund Theophil]. "Das älteste bekannte deutsche Singspiel, Seelewig [poetry by Georg Philipp Harsdörffer, music by Sigmund Gottlieb Staden; Nuremberg, 1644; new edition by Robert Eitner]." *Monatshefte für Musikgeschichte* 13 (1881): 53–147.

Stahl, "Abendmusiken"
    Stahl, Wilhelm. "Die Lübecker Abendmusiken im 17. und 18. Jahrhundert." *Zeitschrift des Vereins für Lübeckische Geschichte und Altertumskunde* 29 (1938): 1–64.

Stahl, "Ruetz"
    _____. "Kaspar Ruetz: Ein lübeckischer Zeit- und Amtsgenosse J. S. Bachs." In *Gedenkboek aangeboden aan Dr. D. F. Scheurleer op zijn 70sten Verjaardag,* [edited by Guido Adler et al.], pp. 327–38. The Hague: Martinus Nijhoff, 1925.

Stahl, "Tunder-Buxtehude"
    _____. "Franz Tunder und Dietrich Buxtehude: Ein biographischer Versuch." *Archiv für Musikwissenschaft* 8 (1926): 1–77.

Steglich, "Alexander"
    Steglich, Rudolf. "Über Händels 'Alexander Balus.'" *Zeitschrift für Musik* 95 (1928): 65–73.

Steglich, "Messias"
    _____. "Betrachtung des Händelschen 'Messias.'" *Händel-Jahrbuch* 4 (1931): 15–78.

Steude, "Markuspassion"
    Steude, Wolfram. "Die Markuspassion in der Leipziger Passionen-Handschrift des Johann Zacharias Grundig." *Deutsches Jahrbuch der Musikwissenschaft für 1969* 14 (1970; vol. 61 of *Jahrbuch der Musikbibliothek Peters*): 96–116.

Stiehl, *Organisten*
Stiehl, Carl Johann Christian. *Die Organisten an der Marienkirche und die Abendmusiken in Lübeck*. Leipzig: Breitkopf & Härtel, 1886.

Stollbrock, "Reuter jun."
Stollbrock, L. "Leben und Wirken des k.k. Hofkapellmeisters und Hofkompositors Johann Georg Reuter jun." *Vierteljahrsschrift für Musikwissenschaft* 8 (1892): 289–306.

Streatfeild, *Handel*
Streatfeild, Richard A. *Handel*. 2d rev. ed. 1910. Reprint. New York: Da Capo, 1964.

Szyrocki, *Barock*
Szyrocki, Marian. *Die deutsche Literatur des Barock: Eine Einführung*. Reinbeck bei Hamburg: Rowohlt, 1968.

Taylor, *Indebtedness*
Taylor, Sedley. *The Indebtedness of Handel to Works by Other Composers: A Presentation of Evidence*. Cambridge: Cambridge University Press, 1906.

Telemann, *Passionsoratorium*
Telemann, Georg Philipp. *Der für die Sünde der Welt gemarterte und sterbende Jesus: Passionsoratorium nach Barthold Heinrich Brockes*. Edited and arranged by Helmut Winschermann and Friedrich Buck. Hamburg: Hans Sikorski, 1964.

Tobin, *Handel's "Messiah"*
Tobin, John. *Handel's "Messiah": A Critical Account of the Manuscript Sources and Printed Editions*. London: Cassell, 1969.

UONNM
Vereniging voor Nederlandsche Muziekgeschiedenis, ed. *Uitgave van oudere Nord-Nederlandsche Meesteerwerken*. 47 vols. to date. Amsterdam: G. Alsbach & Co. 1869–1938, 1955–. Vol. 8, *Bloemlezing uit de 52 Sententia*, by Johannes Wanning, [edited by Robert Eitner,] 1878.

Valentin, *Frankfurt*
Valentin, Caroline. *Geschichte der Musik in Frankfurt am Main vom Anfange des XIV. bis zum Anfange des XVIII. Jahrhunderts*. Frankfort on the Main: K. Th. Völker, 1906.

Viles, "Rosenmüller"
Viles, Elza Ann. "Johann Rosenmüller: A Biography and Discussion of His Choral Music with Editions of Six Representative Cantatas." 2 vols. Master's thesis, University of Tennessee, 1970.

Vulpius, *Evangeliensprüche*
Vulpius, Melchior. *Sonntägliche Evangeliensprüche*. Edited by Hans Heinrich Eggebrecht. Kassel: Bärenreiter, 1950.

Wackernagel, *Kirchenlied*
Wackernagel, Philipp. *Das deutsche Kirchenlied von der ältesten Zeit bis zu Anfang des XVII. Jahrhunderts*. 5 vols. Leipzig: B. G. Teubner, 1864–77.

Walter, *Lüneburg*
Walter, Horst. *Musikgeschichte der Stadt Lüneburg vom Ende des 16. bis zum Anfang des 18. Jahrhunderts*. Tutzing: Hans Schneider, 1967.

Walter, *Werke*
Walter, Johann. *Sämtliche Werke*. Edited by Otto Schröder, et al. 6 vols. Kassel: Bärenreiter; St. Louis, Mo.: Concordia, 1953–70.

Wangemann, *Oratorium*
Wangemann, Otto. *Geschichte des Oratoriums von den ersten Anfängen bis zur Gegenwart*. 2d ed. Demmin: A Frantz, 1882.

Weismann, "Choralzitate"
   Weismann, Wilhelm. "Choralzitate in Händels Oratorien." In *Händel-Ehrung der Deutschen Demokratischen Republik, Halle 11.–19. April 1959, Konferenzbericht*, pp. 173–80. Edited by Walther Siegmund-Schultze. Leipzig: Deutscher Verlag für Musik, 1961.
Werner, "Dokument"
   Werner, Arno. "Ein Dokument über die Einführung der 'Concerten Musik' in Wittenburg." *Sammelbände der internationalen Musikgesellschaft* 9 (1907–8): 310–12.
Wieber, *Chorfuge*
   Wieber, Georg-Friedrich. *Die Chorfuge in Händels Werken*. Frankfort on the Main: n. p., 1958.
Wiedemann, *Klaj*
   Wiedemann, Johann. *Johann Klaj und seine Redeoratorien*. Erlanger Beiträge zur Sprach- und Kunstwissenschaft, vol. 26. Nuremberg: Hans Carl, 1966.
Winterfeld, *Kirchengesang*
   Winterfeld, Carl von. *Der evangelische Kirchengesang und sein Verhältnis zur Kunst des Tonsatzes*. 3 vols. 1843–47. Reprint. Hildesheim: Georg Olms, 1966.
Wolff, *Hamburg*
   Wolff, Hellmuth Christian. *Die Barockoper in Hamburg (1678–1783)*. 2 vols. Wolfenbüttel: Möseler, 1957.
Young, *Oratorios*
   Young, Percy M. *The Oratorios of Handel*. New York: Roy Publishers, 1950.

℘ Index

This index includes persons, places, institutions, terms, and works (musical, literary, architectural, and others in the visual arts). Page numbers in boldface type refer to pages that include music examples; numbers in italics refer to pages that include illustrations. After the titles of oratorios, operas, and works in related genres, the names of composers and librettists are placed in parentheses as follows: (composer/librettist), (composer and composer), (composer only), (—/librettist only). The name *Bach* without initials refers to Johann Sebastian Bach. Buildings and institutions are listed under their respective cities of location.

E
"Ecce quomodo moritur" (Handl), 32, 36
Egmont, John, Earl of. *See* Percival, Viscount
Elsbeth, Thomas, 44
Die Empfängnis unsers Herren Jesu Christi (Michael), 9
Engel, Hans, 33n
Engel- und Drachenstreit (Klaj), 73–74
England: politics in, mid-eighteenth century, 294, 300
"Entfliehet, verschwindet" (Bach/Henrici), 154, 156
Erba, Dionigi, 246, 332n
Erlebach, Philipp Heinrich, 29
Des Erlösers Christi und sündigen Menschens heylsames Gespräch (Kindermann), 55, 56–57
Der erschaffene, gefallene und aufgerichtete Mensch (Theile/Richter), 79
Erster Theil sontäglicher Evangelien fürnembsten Texte durchs gantze Jahr (Elsbeth), 44
"Es gingen zweene Menschen hinauf" (Schütz), 50, 53, 61
Essay on Man (Pope), 349
"Es sei denn" (Ahle), 60–61
Esther (Della Valle), 189n
Esther (Racine), 189, 207
Esther, 1718 (Handel), 188–90, **191–92**
Esther, 1732 (Handel), 188; music of, 138, *198*, 199, 283, 306, 352, 354; early performances of, 192–200, 204, 213, 248, 285, 351, 357; libretto of, 205, 352
Esther, or Faith Triumphant (Brereton), 189
"Et cum ingressus" (Förster), 59
Etliche geystliche, in der Schrift gegrünte (Sachs), 43
"Euch ist's gegeben zu wissen" (Bernhard), 53, 62
Evangelienjahrgang (Pfleger), 46, 55
Evangelischen Gespräch (Briegel), 46, 55
Evangelischer Blumengarten (Briegel), 46, 55
Evangelische Sprüche (Vulpius), 44
Evangelist, the: and Schütz, 13–14, 17–18, 22–24; and Klaj, 73; and oratorio terminology, 107, 128
Evangelium zum Heiligen Christtage (Selle), 20
exordium, 3, 8, 11, 14, 18, 21

F
Faber, Johann Ludwig, 79
Fairholt, F. W., 252
falsobordone, 5

Faramondo (Handel), 212
Fasch, Johann Friedrich, 111n
Festakt. *See* drama, sacred
Festspiel. *See* drama, sacred
Findlay, J., 193
Fleischberger, Johann Friedrich, 58
Flemming, Count, 156
Flemming, Willi, 74
Foggia, Francesco, 215n
The Force of Truth (Greene/Hoadly), 360
Förster, Kaspar, Jr., 45, 49, 59–60
Förtsch, Christian August, 121
Franck, Melchior, 44, 77
Frankfurt, 121–24; Barfüsserkirche, 121; Collegium musicum, 122, 124
Fraser, Simon (Baron Lovat), 300
Frauenzimmer Gesprächspiele (Harsdörffer), 78
Frederick (prince of Wales), 300
Freislich, Christian, 111n
Freudengedichte der seligmachenden Geburt Jesu Christi (Klaj), 73–75
"Froher Tag, verlangte Stunden" (Bach), 168
Fromm, Andreas, 28–29, 30, 31–33, 34–36, 37, 46, 62
Funcke, Christian Gabriel, 77
Funcke, Friedrich, 28, 41
Funeral Anthem for Queen Caroline (Handel), 212, 226, 229. See also *Israel in Egypt* (Handel)
Der für die Sünde der Welt gemarterte und sterbende Jesus: text by Brockes, 111, *113*, 127, 131–34, 170; setting by Handel, 111, 114, 125, 130–33, *134*–37, 138, 190, 202; setting by Keiser, 111, *113*, 114, 130n, 134n, 138–39; setting by Mattheson, 111, 113–14, 130n, 134n, 138; setting by Telemann, 111, 114, 121–22, 124–25, 130n, 131, 134n, 138

G
Gabrieli, Giovanni, 9
Gallus, 32, 36
Gates, Bernard, 192–94, 351
Gay, John, 181, 184
Die Geburt unsers Herren Jesu Christi (Michael), 9, 20
Geck, Martin, 96, 99n
Geistliches Oratorium (Bronner), 109–10
Gemmulae evangeliorum musicae (Franck), 44
George I (king of England), 179
George II (king of England), 183, 320
Georg Ludwig (elector of Hanover), 179
Gerlach, Elias, 9